高等学校规划教材·语言学

Consecutive Interpreting
交替传译

孙 荧 编著

西北工业大学出版社

西安

【内容简介】 本书主要讲解交替传译的基本知识及核心技能,并辅以专题性训练材料。本书分为三大模块,共十个章节,主要特点是结合口译的两种主要训练方式,即技能训练(skill-based training)和专题训练(theme-based training),充分考虑口译思维过程,循序渐进地引导学习者进行训练,逐步提升学习者的交替传译能力。

本书的适用对象为高等学校英语专业高年级本科生、研究生、翻译专业学位(MTI)研究生和口译方向研究者,同时也适用于有一定翻译理论基础、有较好的英语听辨能力和口头表达能力的口译爱好者,以及有一定口译实践工作经验并希望提升交替传译能力的自学者。

图书在版编目(CIP)数据

交替传译＝Consecutive Interpreting:英语/
孙荧编著.—西安:西北工业大学出版社,2020.8
高等学校规划教材.语言学
ISBN 978-7-5612-7048-6

Ⅰ.①交… Ⅱ.①孙… Ⅲ.①英语-口译-高等学校-教材 Ⅳ.①H315.9

中国版本图书馆 CIP 数据核字(2020)第 041199 号

JIAOTI CHUANYI
Consecutive Interpreting 交替传译

责任编辑:胡莉巾	策划编辑:何格夫
责任校对:万灵芝	装帧设计:李 飞

出版发行:西北工业大学出版社
通信地址:西安市友谊西路 127 号　　邮编:710072
电　　话:(029)88491757,88493844
网　　址:www.nwpup.com
印　刷　者:兴平市博闻印务有限公司
开　　本:787 mm×1 092 mm　　1/16
印　　张:26.5
字　　数:695 千字
版　　次:2020 年 8 月第 1 版　　2020 年 8 月第 1 次印刷
定　　价:88.00 元

如有印装问题请与出版社联系调换

前　言

随着经济全球化的进程及共建"一带一路"合作的进展，国家之间的政治、经济、文化交流日益密切，官方与非官方、商业与非商业国际交流日益增多，高素质的口译人才在对外开放的基本国策中显得越发重要，对口译人才的需求量也越来越大。本书主要讲解交替传译的基本知识和训练交替传译的核心技能，旨在结合口译的两种主要训练方式，即技能训练（skill-based training）和专题训练（theme-based training），逐步提升学习者的交替传译能力、临场应变能力及其他相关能力。

本书分为三大模块，即基础知识、技能训练和专题训练，共十个章节。

基础知识模块包括三个章节：第一章课程介绍，第二章口译、交替传译及译员介绍，及第三章译前准备。第一章主要介绍课程的基本内容、学习目标、课前准备及课程要求等；第二章主要介绍口译的定义、类型、质量标准，交替传译的特点、过程、学员素质等；第三章主要介绍交替传译中涉及的基本语言及交际技能、译前的场内及场外准备等。

技能训练模块包括六个章节：第四章信息加工能力，第五章代码转换能力，第六章数字口译，第七章记忆，第八章笔记，及第九章目的语表达。第四章主要介绍信息提取、分析、加工、储存等相关技能；第五章主要从句子层面及篇章层面介绍英汉、汉英转换技能；第六章主要介绍"点三杠四""缺位补零"等数字口译技能；第七章主要介绍记忆相关知识及记忆训练方法；第八章主要介绍笔记相关基本知识及笔记符号，并进行笔记句子及段落训练；第九章主要介绍目的语表达的原则及策略等。

专题训练模块包括一个章节，即第十章不同主题交替传译训练材料，主要向学习者提供六种常见交替传译主题的训练材料。

本书附录还提供了国际会议口译工作者协会（AIIC）关于职业道德准则的规定，常用口译词汇、表达方式，缩略语，以及推荐的学习网站等。

本书的特色是在内容安排上充分考虑口译思维过程，在训练上结合技能训练及专题训练两种主要训练方法，结合理论、实践与教学，为学习者提供较全面的交替传译知识及训练方法，并辅以大量练习及训练材料。

本书读者对象主要包括高等学校英语专业高年级本科生、研究生，翻译专业学位（MTI）研究生和口译方向研究者，同时也适用于有一定翻译理论基础、有较好的英语听辨能力和口头表达能力的口译爱好者，以及有一定口译实践工作经验并希望提升交替传译能力的自学者。

本书提供的训练资料及译文主要来自如新华社、中国日报、外交部网站等官方机构，文字内容主要来自国家政要的演讲致辞等。本书中的音频和视频资源可从西北工业大学出版社网站 www.nwpup.com 下载。

编写本书参考了诸多口译学者的研究及教学成果,同时本书受到西北工业大学中央高校基本科研业务费资助项目"基于威廉姆斯参数参照模式的口译质量及译员能力评估研究"(项目编号:3102016RW014)及西北工业大学学位与研究生教育研究基金项目"服务'一带一路'的创新型、复合型口译人才培养研究——以 MTI 口译专业为例"(项目编号:19GZ220102)的资助,在此一并表示衷心的感谢。

由于水平有限,书中难免存在欠妥之处,诚请广大读者批评指正。

孙 荧
2020 年 5 月

CONTENTS

MODULE I THE BASICS

Chapter I Course Introduction 3
   1.1 General Introduction to the Course 3
   1.2 Course Requirements 6
   1.3 Additional Information: Frequently Asked Questions 7
   Exercises and Practice 8
   Additional Materials 8

Chapter II Introduction to Interpreting, Consecutive Interpreting and Interpreters 14
   2.1 General Introduction to Interpreting and Consecutive Interpreting 14
        Exercises and Practice 31
   2.2 Introduction to Interpreters 32
        Exercises and Practice 41
   Additional Materials 41

Chapter III Preparation 48
   3.1 Basic Language and Communication Skills 48
        Exercises and Practice 62
   3.2 Preparation Before Interpreting 63
        Exercises and Practice 68
   Additional Materials 69

MODULE II SKILL-BASED CI TRAINING

Chapter IV Information Processing Skills 81
   4.1 Information Processing 81
        Exercises and Practice 100
   4.2 Information Storage 105
        Exercises and Practice 108
   Additional Materials 111

Chapter V Code-Switching Skills 117
   5.1 Code-Switching Skills—Sentence Level 117

	Exercises and Practice	125
5.2	Code-Switching Skills—Discourse Level	125
	Exercises and Practice	131
	Additional Materials	132

Chapter VI Interpreting Figures ······ 139

- 6.1 Basic Skills in Interpreting Figures ······ 139
  - Exercises and Practice ······ 145
- 6.2 Figure Interpreting Training ······ 145
  - Exercises and Practice ······ 151
- Additional Materials ······ 153

Chapter VII Memory ······ 161

- 7.1 Introduction to Memory ······ 161
  - Exercises and Practice ······ 168
- 7.2 Training Methods ······ 169
  - Exercises and Practice ······ 186
- Additional Materials ······ 192

Chapter VIII Note-taking ······ 202

- 8.1 Introduction to Note-taking ······ 202
  - Exercises and Practice ······ 206
- 8.2 Note-taking Method ······ 206
  - Exercises and Practice ······ 225
- 8.3 Note-taking Training ······ 225
  - Exercises and Practice ······ 268
- Additional Materials ······ 273

Chapter IX Reproduction ······ 280

- 9.1 Principles for Reproduction in the Target Language ······ 280
- 9.2 Strategies Used in Reproduction in the Target Language ······ 281
- Exercises and Practice ······ 286
- Additional Materials ······ 286

MODULE III THEME-BASED CI TRAINING

Chapter X Consecutive Interpreting Materials for Different Themes ······ 297

- 10.1 Politics and Diplomacy ······ 297
- 10.2 Economy and Trade ······ 309
- 10.3 Education and Cultural Exchange ······ 322

10.4	Science and Technology	333
10.5	Sports and Health	345
10.6	Environment and Terrorism	360

APPENDIX 374

    Appendix Ⅰ Interpreter's Code of Professional Ethics by International Association of Conference Interpreters (AIIC) 374

    Appendix Ⅱ Practical Phrases 376

    Appendix Ⅲ Names and Abbreviations 388

    Appendix Ⅳ Useful Websites 393

KEYS 395

BIBLIOGRAPHIES 415

MODULE I   THE BASICS

Chapter I Course Introduction

Learning questions:
✓ *What is the course "Consecutive Interpreting" about?*
✓ *What will we learn in this course?*
✓ *What are the prerequisites and course requirements?*

In this chapter, you will have a general understanding of what this course is about, what we will learn in this course, what we are hoping to achieve in this course, what the general prerequisites are for this course, and how we are going to arrange the teaching hours. You will also learn about the course requirements, and find the answers to some frequently asked questions.

1.1 General Introduction to the Course

1.1.1 Course introduction

"Consecutive Interpreting (CI)" is a course for students who have already obtained certain theoretical knowledge in translation and interpreting, and who have comparatively good listening and speaking abilities. Students range from junior and senior students of the English major and MTI (Master of Translation and Interpreting) students, to non-English major students who are skilled in English listening and speaking. Preferably, it is for students who have passed the CET-6 or the TEM-4 examinations. It would be optimal if students have already taken the following courses as foundation: intensive reading, extensive reading, listening and speaking, and translation theories. This course itself lays the foundation for the more advanced course, simultaneous interpreting.

There are three modules in this book (same as the course schedule): 1) The basics, 2) Skill-based training, 3) Theme-based training. The first aims at helping students get familiarized with the basic knowledge in interpreting and consecutive interpreting, and be well-prepared in related skills before learning the CI skills and doing actual CI training. The second module aims at teaching students the basic skills in CI, including verbal and non-verbal skills, noting and interpreting figures, memory training, note-taking skills and target language reproduction skills. The third module aims at training students to use the skills for different CI themes. The whole book/course covers the theoretical knowledge, skill training, and a range of CI training materials and exercises.

For this course, class contact hours, though limited, are required and are devoted to skill development, whereas knowledge acquisition should be part of students' daily routine outside their classes. Both Chinese-to-English (C - E) and English-to-Chinese (E - C) CI will be practiced, with a training focus on note-taking.

1.1.2 Learning Objectives

An independent professional interpreter is equipped with an array of skills in addition to superb language proficiency. To meet the challenge of producing interpreters who can adapt to the fast-changing world, traditional theme-based training has gradually given way to a more comprehensive approach.

This course is utilizing a comprehensive approach, and provides theoretical guidance, training methods and training materials for future interpreters, in the hope that through the skill-based training and a large amount of practices, students can improve their CI skills as well as their relevant communication and professional skills, increase their discourse analysis, visualization and message equivalence abilities, get familiar with words and expressions frequently used in different CI occasions, and eventually meet the required CI level set by relevant departments or the graduate school. Through this course, students will also acquire self-analysis and peer feedback skills.

1.1.3 General Prerequisites

1.1.3.1 Language Skills

Language allows human to communicate through the structured use of words. It is vital for a person to have proficiency in language in consecutive interpreting. When we learn a language, there are four basic skills that we need for communication: listening, speaking, reading and writing. Among them, listening is considered as the most basic skill while writing is considered as the most complex one. For learning this course, students need to have a relatively good command in all four aspects, and comparatively higher skills in listening comprehension and speaking.

Even though this course will focus more on improving your listening and speaking skills, as well as your language code-switching skills in an oral way, i.e., interpreting from one language to another, it is impossible to completely separate the four skills. For example, when you prepare for a conference CI, you may first of all need to read extensively about the conference theme and familiarize yourself with the theme-related vocabulary. If a speech note is provided for your CI work, you may also need to write the translation down before interpreting on scene. Therefore, it is important to combine the four aspects and improve the language proficiency as a whole.

1.1.3.2 Communication Skills

Communication includes not only being proficient in the language but also being able to listen to others and express themselves clearly. It involves being accurate and clear in communication with other. A student with excellent communication skills expresses himself/herself logically and confidently and uses the language to reach across to others. Communication skills usually encompass a wide variety of skills ranging from listening to speaking, from vocal aspects to non-vocal aspects. Mere proficiency in a language of a student does not guarantee that he or she has good communication skills. It also involves the ability the individual has in being effective and clear in his or her expressions, which is crucial in CI.

More detailed language and communication skills may include active listening skills, public speaking skills, cross-cultural communication skills and coping skills. These will be talked about in details in Chapter III.

1.1.4 Course Syllabus

Generally based on this textbook, the following syllabus is (see Table 1-1) is designed for a 40-hour training course. It can also be applied to a 32-hour training course, with some teaching contents combined or teaching hours reduced. Please note that this syllabus is subjected to changes according to actual teaching.

Table 1-1 Course Syllabus

Week	Course Content	Teaching Hours
1	Course introduction, introduction to interpreting and CI	2
2	Introduction to interpreters, skills to acquire before CI training	2
3	Off-spot preparation and on-spot preparation, information processing skills	2
4	Code-switching skills in CI	2
5	Interpreting figures	2
6	Introduction to memory, memory training (word repeating, story retelling, visualization)	2
7	Memory training (descriptive passages retelling), anti-distraction training	2
8	Interpreting sentences or short passages without note-taking	2
9	Introduction to note-taking, introduction to common symbols and abbreviations in note-taking	2
10	Note-taking through reading (creating symbols)	2
11	Note-taking—sentences or short passages (C-E)	2
12	Note-taking—sentences or short passages (E-C)	2
13	Note-taking—longer passages (C-E)	2
14	Note-taking—longer passages (E-C)	2

Continued Table

Week	Course Content	Teaching Hours
15	Reproduction in the target language	2
16	Theme-based CI training—politics and diplomacy	2
17	Theme-based CI training—business, trade and economy	2
18	Theme-based CI training—cultural exchange and education	2
19	Theme-based CI training—science and technology	2
20	Theme-based CI training—sports and tourism	2

1.2 Course Requirements

For this course, both in-class performance and out-class practices are required. Students are asked to be fully committed. We encourage each student to find a partner to practice with. Home assignments are quite often done in student pairs. For final assessment, in-class performance, home assignments, tape hours and the final examination will all be considered.

1.2.1 In-Class Performance

Though limited, the 40 hours/32 hours of in-class learning is the minimum requirement for all students. It is the best place for students to acquire the theoretical knowledge and polish their skills in CI. Students will be asked to answer questions, participate in pair or group works, and accomplish in-class activities and assignments. Students may also be asked to do self-assessment or peer-assessment in class or after class. Class attendance and in-class concentration are crucial.

1.2.2 Tape Hour

To be proficient in interpreting, 40 hours of classroom learning is far from enough. Besides the home assignments, tape hour is also one of the course requirements. Tape hour refers NOT to the time learners or interpreters spend on training, but to the length of the training materials in audio format (sometimes video), no matter which source language it is in. For example, if a speech is 30 minutes in length, no matter how much time a student has spent on practice, it is considered 0.5 tape hour. It is quite common for beginners to spend a whole day just to accomplish the training of 1 tape hour. Zhu Tong, a professional interpreter from the Ministry of Foreign Affairs, once said, "To be a qualified interpreter, one needs to accomplish at least 1,200 tape hours' intensive listening and interpreting training." For professional training institutions for interpreters, the required tape hour is at least 300 hours. For this course, at least 80 tape hours should be accomplished besides home assignments. That means, if the course lasts for 20 weeks, for each week's in-class learning, you are required to accomplish 4 tape hours' intensive training outside of classroom. This is truly the minimum requirement for someone who aspires to become an interpreter.

1.3 Additional Information: Frequently Asked Questions

(1) Q: I'm a non-English major student. Can I take this course?

A: It depends. Consecutive Interpreting is a course that is usually provided for junior or senior students of English major or MTI student. In universities abroad, it is often only provided in graduate school. It requires students to have a good language foundation in both English and Chinese, especially in listening comprehension and speaking. Therefore, this course can be taken by students who have passed the CET-6 or TEM-4 examinations, or students with equivalent language competence. It is also suitable for students with good English listening and speaking abilities, strong logical analysis ability and good memory.

(2) Q: What if I do not have a training partner?

A: For in-class and after-class training, it would be best to work with a partner. Many times the training materials are in written form, and it would be best if it can be read by your partner. If you cannot find a partner because the class student number is an odd number, you can work in a group of three. If you cannot find a partner from this class, it is also a good idea to find someone who are also interested in interpreting to train with you, even though they may not be from our class. If a partner cannot be found, it is best if you can find someone to read and record the training materials for you.

(3) Q: What if I cannot meet with my partner regularly to accomplish the home assignments?

A: If you cannot meet with your training partner regularly, you can ask your partner to read and record the training materials for you and vice versa, you can record the training materials for your partner.

(4) Q: Where can I find the listening materials?

A: There are many places to find the listening materials. Books on CI would be a good source. These books are often accompanied with CDs where you can find the audio or video materials from the books. Beside this book, you can find some recommended books in the "Bibliographies" section of this book. The Internet is another good source of information. Many websites provide high-quality audio or video materials. Some websites also provide listening materials in slower or standard speed. Please refer to the Appendix section of this book for more useful websites.

(5) Q: What will happen if I miss a class or not hand in my homework.

A: Class attendance is required. A missed class without proper explanation may lead to deduction in your final score. Home assignments also need to be handed in on time. A late hand-in will result in a deduction in the grading of that assignment. Missed homework will result in a deduction in the final score.

(6) Q: Can I take the CATTI (China Accreditation Test for Translators and Interpreters) examination after taking this course?

A: It depends on how much time you spend on this course. If you hope to pass the exam only with 40 hours of in-class training, it is not very likely, unless you are highly-skilled in English abilities. If you have accomplished the required tape hours along with all our home assignments, then you can try CATTI level three as a start.

Exercises and Practice

1-1 Study the course syllabus carefully and familiarize yourself with this book and with the contents of this course.

1-2 Explain to your partner what a tape hour is.

1-3 Talk with your partner about the requirements for this course. Discuss how to ace the class.

Additional Materials

习近平在第二届"一带一路"国际合作高峰论坛记者会上的讲话
Remarks by H. E. Xi Jinping, President of the People's Republic of China at the Press Conference of The Second Belt and Road Forum for International Cooperation
2019年4月27日,北京　Beijing, 27 April 2019
中文来源:新华网
http://www.xinhuanet.com/politics/leaders/2019-04/27/c_1124425067.htm
译文来源:外交部英文网站
https://www.fmprc.gov.cn/mfa_eng/wjdt_665385/zyjh_665391/t1659452.shtml

女士们,先生们,

记者朋友们:

Ladies and Gentlemen,

Friends from the Media,

下午好!

Good afternoon!

欢迎大家参加第二届"一带一路"国际合作高峰论坛记者会。共建"一带一路"倡议提出5年多来,一直受到媒体朋友们广泛关注。本届高峰论坛开幕以来,记者朋友们持续关注和报道高峰论坛,记录下各个精彩瞬间,传播了各种好声音,展现了共建"一带一路"合作的丰硕成果。我谨代表中国政府和各国与会代表,对记者朋友们的支持和辛勤工作表示感谢!

Welcome to the press conference of the Second Belt and Road Forum for International

Cooperation (BRF). Since it was put forth over five years ago, the Belt and Road Initiative (BRI) has caught much media attention. All of you have been following and covering the second BRF since its opening, recording memorable moments, spreading key messages, and reporting on the fruitful outcomes of Belt and Road cooperation. On behalf of the Chinese government and delegates from all participating countries, I wish to express our appreciation to all of you for your support and hard work!

这是中国第二次举办"一带一路"国际合作高峰论坛。同首届论坛相比,本届论坛规模更大、内容更丰富、参与国家更多、成果更丰硕。高峰论坛期间,我们举行了开幕式,召开了高级别会议,举办了12场分论坛和一场企业家大会,来自150多个国家的各界代表参加。今天,来自38个国家的领导人和联合国、国际货币基金组织负责人在这里举行了领导人圆桌峰会。

This year's BRF, the second China has hosted, is larger and more substantive than the first one, attracting more countries and producing more results. This year, delegates and business representatives from over 150 countries have participated in the opening ceremony, the high-level meeting, 12 thematic forums and a CEO conference. The Leaders' Roundtable held today was attended by leaders from 38 countries as well as the United Nations (UN) and the International Monetary Fund.

这次高峰论坛的主题是"共建'一带一路'、开创美好未来"。圆桌峰会上,与会领导人和国际组织负责人围绕"推进互联互通,挖掘增长新动力""加强政策对接,打造更紧密伙伴关系""推动绿色和可持续发展,落实联合国2030年议程"等议题进行深入讨论,完善了合作理念,明确了合作重点,强化了合作机制,就高质量共建"一带一路"达成了广泛共识。这些共识反映在圆桌峰会一致通过的联合公报中,将成为今后共建"一带一路"国际合作的行动指南。

The theme of this year's Forum is "Belt and Road Cooperation: Shaping a Brighter Shared Future". Earlier today, leaders of participating countries and international organizations held in-depth discussions on "Boosting Connectivity to Explore New Sources of Growth""Strengthening Policy Synergy and Building Closer Partnerships" and "Promoting Green and Sustainable Development to Implement UN 2030 Agenda". We reached extensive consensus on promoting high-quality Belt and Road cooperation with refined principles, clear priorities and stronger mechanisms. The leaders' common views are reflected in the Joint Communiqué adopted by consensus at the Leaders' Roundtable and will guide our efforts as we advance Belt and Road cooperation in years to come.

——我们积极评价共建"一带一路"合作取得的进展和意义。我们都认为,共建"一带一路"是通向共同繁荣的机遇之路。共建"一带一路"5年多来,特别是首届高峰论坛以来,在各方共同努力下,政策沟通范围不断拓展,设施联通水平日益提升,经贸和投资合作又上新台阶,资金融通能力持续增强,人文交流往来更加密切。共建"一带一路"合作取得的早期收获,为各国和世界经济增长开辟了更多空间,为加强国际合作打造了平台,为构建人类命运共同体作出了新贡献。

—We spoke positively of the progress and value of Belt and Road cooperation. We shared the view that Belt and Road cooperation has created opportunities for common prosperity. Since the BRI was proposed over five years ago, and especially after the first BRF, countries concerned have made concerted efforts to expand policy communication, upgrade infrastructure connectivity, advance economic, trade and investment cooperation, enhance financial cooperation, and facilitate people-to-people exchange. The "early harvests" of Belt and Road cooperation achieved so far have opened up greater space for national and global economic growth, provided a platform for enhancing international cooperation, and made a fresh contribution to building a community with a shared future for mankind.

——我们丰富了共建"一带一路"合作理念,一致重申致力于高质量共建"一带一路"。我们将坚持共商共建共享原则,由各方平等协商、责任共担、共同受益,欢迎所有感兴趣的国家都参与进来。我们一致支持开放、廉洁、绿色发展,反对保护主义,努力建设风清气正、环境友好的新时代丝绸之路。我们同意践行高标准、惠民生、可持续理念,积极对接普遍接受的国际规则标准,坚持以人民为中心的发展思想,走经济、社会、环境协调发展之路。这些共识为共建"一带一路"合作的发展指明了方向,我们的共同目标是,携手努力让各国互联互通更加有效,经济增长更加强劲,国际合作更加密切,人民生活更加美好。

—We enriched the concept of Belt and Road cooperation and jointly reaffirmed our commitment to its high-quality development. Guided by the principle of extensive consultation, joint contribution and shared benefits, the parties have conducted consultation as equals, jointly shouldered responsibilities and enjoyed the benefits together. All interested countries are welcome to join us. We are committed to supporting open, clean and green development and rejecting protectionism, and are working hard to develop a clean and green Silk Road for the new era. We have agreed to act on the principles of high standard, people-centered and sustainable development, align our cooperation with universally accepted international rules and standards, follow the philosophy of people-centered development, and pursue coordinated progress in economic, social and environmental dimensions. These common views have pointed the way for Belt and Road cooperation toward our common goal, that is, to realize more effective connectivity between countries, promote stronger economic growth and closer international cooperation, and deliver better lives to our peoples.

——我们明确了未来共建"一带一路"合作的重点,决定加强全方位、多领域合作。我们将继续推进陆上、海上、空中、网上互联互通,建设高质量、可持续、抗风险、价格合理、包容可及的基础设施。我们将推进建设经济走廊,发展经贸产业合作园区,继续加强市场、规制、标准等方面软联通,以及数字基础设施建设。有关合作项目将坚持政府引导、企业主体、市场运作,确保可持续性,并为各国投资者营造公平和非歧视的营商环境。我们将继续拓宽融资渠道,降低融资成本,欢迎多边和各国金融机构参与投融资合作。我们还同意广泛开展内容丰富、形式多样的人文交流,实施更多民生合作项目。我们都支持共建"一带一路"合作坚持发展导向,支持全球发展事业特别是落实联合国2030年可持续发展议程,努力实现清洁低碳可持续发展,同时帮助发展中国家打破发展瓶颈,更好融入全球价值链、产业链、供应链并从中受益。

——We set clear priorities for Belt and Road cooperation and decided to strengthen all-round and multi-tiered cooperation. We will continue to promote land, sea, air and cyber connectivity and develop high-quality, sustainable, resilient, affordable, inclusive and accessible infrastructure. We will advance the development of economic corridors and economic and trade cooperation zones, enhance the alignment between markets, regulations and standards, and encourage the development of digital infrastructure. In all Belt and Road cooperation projects, the government will provide guidance, enterprises will act as the main players and market principles will apply. This will make the projects more sustainable and create a fair and non-discriminatory environment for foreign investors. We will continue to diversify financing channels, reduce financing costs, and welcome the participation of multilateral and foreign financial institutions in investment and financing cooperation. We have also agreed to conduct extensive and multi-faceted people-to-people and cultural exchanges, and launch more cooperation projects for the benefit of our peoples. We all want to make Belt and Road cooperation development-oriented, and all support global development, particularly the implementation of the UN 2030 Agenda for Sustainable Development, and will strive for clean, low-carbon and sustainable development. It is also necessary to help developing countries break bottlenecks to development and better partake in and benefit from global value, industrial and supply chains.

——我们一致支持着力构建全球互联互通伙伴关系,加强合作机制。为此,我们将深入对接各国和国际组织经济发展倡议和规划,加强双边和第三方市场合作,建设中欧班列、陆海新通道等国际物流和贸易大通道,帮助更多国家提升互联互通水平。我们参阅了高峰论坛咨询委员会政策建议报告,期待咨询委员会为共建"一带一路"合作和高峰论坛发展提供更多智力支持。我们将坚持多边主义,推动形成以高峰论坛为引领、各领域多双边合作为支撑的架构,使我们的合作既有理念引领、行动跟进,也有机制保障。大家普遍认为,"一带一路"国际合作高峰论坛是重要多边合作平台,支持高峰论坛常态化举办。

——We all supported the idea of building a global partnership on connectivity and agreed to strengthen mechanisms for Belt and Road cooperation. To this end, we will find greater complementarity between the economic development initiatives and plans of interested countries and international organizations, step up bilateral cooperation and cooperation in third markets, and continue to develop the China-Europe Railway Express, the New International Land-Sea Trade Corridor and other international transportation and trade links, in order to help more countries improve connectivity. We reviewed the report of the BRF Advisory Council, and look forward to more intellectual support from the Advisory Council for Belt and Road cooperation and the BRF. We will uphold multilateralism, and work to foster a framework led by the BRF and underpinned by multilateral and bilateral cooperation in various areas. The goal is to see that our cooperation is guided by an overall vision, followed up by actions and supported by concrete institutions. The leaders share the view that the BRF is an important platform for multilateral cooperation and support holding the Forum on a regular basis.

——我们都支持加强务实合作,取得更多实实在在的成果。在这次论坛筹备进程中和举办期间,各方达成了283项务实成果,包括签署政府间合作协议,开展务实项目合作,发起成立专业领域多边对话合作平台,发布共建"一带一路"进展报告、高峰论坛咨询委员会政策建议报告等。中方作为主席国,将汇总发布一份成果清单。论坛期间举行的企业家大会吸引了众多工商界人士参与,签署了总额640多亿美元的项目合作协议。这些成果充分说明,共建"一带一路"应潮流、得民心、惠民生、利天下。

—We all supported more results-oriented cooperation and more concrete outcomes. In the run-up to and during the course of this Forum, the parties reached 283 deliverables, including inter-governmental cooperation agreements, practical cooperation projects, the initiation of multilateral dialogue and cooperation platforms in specific areas, and the release of a Belt and Road cooperation progress report as well as the report of the BRF Advisory Council. As the host of the Forum, China will release a deliverables list. A great many business representatives participated in the CEO conference and signed project cooperation agreements worth over US $ 64 billion. All of this shows that Belt and Road cooperation is in sync with the times, widely supported, people-centered and beneficial to all.

昨天,我宣布了中国将采取的一系列重大改革开放措施。大家普遍认为,这对中国和世界都是好消息,将为共建"一带一路"和世界经济发展提供重要机遇。

Yesterday, I announced a series of major reform and opening-up steps that China will take. They are seen by all sides as good news for both China and the world at large and important opportunities for Belt and Road cooperation and development of the world economy.

这届论坛对外传递了一个明确信号:共建"一带一路"的朋友圈越来越大,好伙伴越来越多,合作质量越来越高,发展前景越来越好。我多次说过,共建"一带一路"倡议源于中国,机会和成果属于世界。共建"一带一路"是一项长期工程,是合作伙伴们共同的事业。中国愿同各方一道,落实好本届高峰论坛各项共识,以绘制"工笔画"的精神,共同推动共建"一带一路"合作走深走实、行稳致远、高质量发展,开创更加美好的未来。希望媒体记者朋友们继续积极支持共建"一带一路"合作。

This year's Forum sends a clear message: more and more friends and partners will join in Belt and Road cooperation, and the cooperation will enjoy higher quality and brighter prospects. I have noted on many occasions that while the BRI was launched by China, its opportunities and outcomes are shared by the world. Belt and Road cooperation is a long-term endeavor and a common cause of all its cooperation partners. China will work with all parties to implement the consensus reached at this year's Forum, advance results-oriented

Chapter I Course Introduction

implementation of projects in the spirit of an architect refining the blueprint, ensure substantive, steady, sustained and high-quality development and usher in a brighter future of Belt and Road cooperation. I hope our friends from the media will continue to actively support Belt and Road cooperation.

谢谢大家。
Thank you.

Chapter Ⅱ Introduction to Interpreting, Consecutive Interpreting and Interpreters

Learning questions:
- ✓ What are interpreting and consecutive interpreting?
- ✓ What are the differences between interpreting and translation?
- ✓ What are the criteria for good interpreting and good interpreters?

After speaking so much about the course, let's now focus on the term "consecutive interpreting?" What exactly is consecutive interpreting? In this section, we will learn about the history and definition of interpreting and consecutive interpreting, different types of interpreting (including consecutive interpreting), the differences between interpreting and translation, the working process of interpreting, and the criteria for good interpreting and qualified interpreters. We will also learn about the training programs and the career development of an interpreter, and ways of self-assessment and improvement.

2.1 General Introduction to Interpreting and Consecutive Interpreting

2.1.1 Definition of Interpreting

Interpreting, also called interpretation or oral translation, is an extempore oral reproduction, in one language, of what is said in another language. It is an activity that consists of establishing, simultaneously or consecutively, oral or gesture communication between two or more speakers not speaking the same language. Though sometimes also called "interpretation," because the word "interpretation" is also used in English to refer to the act of mediation, the word "interpreting" is more commonly used instead in translation studies in order to distinguish the two aspects.

Necessary elements of interpreting include "one occasion, two languages and three identities". "One occasion" means interpreting is a kind of inter-communicative activity that happens in a specific occasion for a specific purpose. "Two languages" refers to the two languages involved in the communicative activities. "Three identities" means the three identities of an interpreter, namely, the listener, speaker and interpreter.

In interpreting, the meaning, or the message of the source language is listened and retrieved and immediately switched to linguistic symbols of the target language, so as to deliver the message in the target language. "Message" here refers to the thinking of a speaker, the ideas or content which the interpreter has to convey to the audience (or listeners in conversations). For the audience, "message" is the content which they have understood, with the help of the interpreter. That's why we say message in discourse is the object of interpreting. In other words, it is the message rather than words that are being transferred. Therefore, in listening, the interpreter should try to understand the message of the speaker, or the meaning the words the linguistic structure conveys. In most cases, Interpreting should not be done word-for-word, especially from Chinese to English.

2.1.2 History of Interpreting

Interpreting plays a crucial role in diplomatic, political and economic exchanges, and in fields of military, tourism, sports, education and cultural exchanges.

Historically speaking, interpreting can be traced back to the early ages of human society. Throughout the history, the economic, cultural and all other kinds of communication between different nations, to a degree, are all accomplished with the help of a "middleman". It is said that in history, these "middlemen" were also called "the tongue people". In a sense, the history of interpreting is even longer than that of translation.

In the historical development of human society, interpreting has become a lubricant to propel the wheel of human society to roll. Human interpreting activities have faithfully recorded the communication activities among people of all nations in the world for thousands of years. In ancient society, there were the exchange of the achievements of the Eastern and Western civilization, the outward spread of Buddhism, Christianity, Confucianism and Islam, the marriage of Princess Wencheng to the Western Regions, Marco and Polo's travel to China, Columbus' discovery of the New World, Zheng He's trip to the Western Ocean, and Jianzhen's journey east to Japan; in modern society, there were the ups and downs between the Western world and China in politics, military, economy, and culture, the outbreak of two World Wars in modern society, the establishment of the United Nations and the formation of the WTO, the all-round opening up of China in the contemporary society and the sustained and rapid economic development, the development of "global village" in today's information age, the establishment of the Euro zone and APEC, and the convening of the Eurasian Summit. All these events in human history have been marked by the activity of interpreting. It is apparent that interpreting plays a role of catalyzer in human intercultural and cross-ethnic communication.

Interpreting as a profession, has over 2,000 years of history in China. In Western countries, for hundreds of years, there had been people who specialized in interpreting, but most of them were temporary part-time staff. Interpreting, as a formal profession in the world, was a product of the early 20th century. In 1919, after the end of the World War I, the Paris Peace Conference recruited a large number of interpreters to do consecutive interpreting for the conference as a formal profession. Ever since then, the profession of interpreting was recognized, and the training methods were studied. After the World War II, in the Nuremberg Trials of Nazi war criminals, the new form of simultaneous interpreting was used. People started to value highly of the profession of interpreting.

With the establishment of the United Nations and the emergence of various global and regional organizations, international exchanges have become increasingly frequent. On the multilateral and bilateral stages of the world, a series of vivid modern plays have been performed. Interpreters play a unique role in these plays. The status of professional international conference interpreters is getting higher and higher. The United Nations has established a special translation agency and a senior translator organization. The interpreting principles and methods have also been studied in higher education institutions. The first interpreting school was set up in 1950 in Geneva, Switzerland. AIIC, the International Association of Conference Interpreters, was founded on Nov. 11, 1953 with its Secretariat located in Geneva. Founded in Paris in 1953, FIT is an international federation of translators' associations which are located in nearly 50 countries throughout the world. These are all symbols of the formal establishment of interpreting as a profession.

For half a century, senior interpreters have been favored by various international institutions, governments, and cross-cultural institutions and organizations. Professional interpreting has become a highly respected profession. Especially for senior international conference interpreters, they are respected for being both intelligent linguists and knowledgeable international diplomats.

Since the founding of New China, China has become increasingly active in the international arena. China is playing an increasingly important role in the fields of world politics, economy, trade, culture and sports, which makes excellent interpreters in higher need. Since China returned to the United Nations in the early 1970s, its international status has risen rapidly. After entering the 1980s marked by reform and opening up, China's economy began to take off, and the door to the outside world was opening even wider. In the 1990s when many countries and regions in the East and West were in recession, China's economic train continued to run at high speed with strong vitality. China, having chosen a socialist market economy without hesitation and made tremendous success, has become the preferred target of many overseas investors and tourists. With increasing needs for foreign exchanges, the demand for all kinds of interpreters is increasing on a daily basis, and the contradiction between supply and demand of senior interpreters is becoming more and more prominent.

Today, the wheel of history has brought us into a new century. With extensive exchanges and common prosperity between Chinese culture and the cultures of all ethnic groups in the world, this is the golden age of interpreting profession. As an indispensable intermediary force in Sino-foreign exchanges, interpreters shoulder an important historical task. Today, more than ever before, China needs a large number of qualified full-time or part-time interpreters to jointly build and strengthen the bridge in foreign exchanges.

2.1.3 Characteristics of Interpreting

When speaking of the nature of interpreting, theorist Seleskovitch said, "Interpreting is in essence communication." Interpreting is to accurately and smoothly express the meaning of the speaker in an oral way. This nature and way of expression determine that interpreting has the following basic characteristics:

1. Instantaneity (即时性)

Interpreting is a kind of inter-communicative activity. In order to ensure the continuous and smooth expression and reception of information, interpreters must complete the task of information transmission smoothly and quickly in a short time.

2. Diversity of the source language (原语多样性)

In interpreting, the information of the source language is quite often diversified. First, the themes of interpreting are varied, involving various fields of Sino-foreign exchanges. Second, even in a single-themed conference, speakers may speak about other fields. Third, speakers may come from diverse backgrounds, speak of various contents and use different styles of speech. And fourth, coming from different countries or regions, the speaker often has different local accents. To deal with the above diversified situations calmly, interpreters need to be knowledgeable and adaptable.

3. Colloquial in nature (口语性)

The colloquial nature of interpreting is mainly embodied in two aspects. On the one hand, the speakers' source language is conveyed in the form of spoken language. On the other hand, the interpreters' target language is also conveyed in the form of spoken language.

In this sense, interpreters must have excellent bilingual listening and speaking abilities, especially those in the foreign language. In addition, interpreters must also have good oral expression ability, which means they not only need to speak with good pronunciation and enunciation, but also in an organized and logical way. It means that they should "speak clearly" so that the listeners can "understand clearly".

Besides the above three basic characteristics, interpreting may also have the following features:

4. Unpredictability (不可预测性)

Interpreters often work with limited preparation. Sometimes they are asked to immediately get into the state of code-switching without given any background information. With various interpreting themes, the content is highly unpredictable. Even with ample preparation, or even with the speech note at hand, the speakers may still improvise and change the speech content. It can be said no matter how much preparation interpreters have done—it is never enough.

5. Highly-pressured work environment (高压工作环境)

The on-site highly-pressured work environment is another characteristic of the work of interpreting. Some interpreting occasions are very serious, such as international conferences and diplomatic negotiations. The solemn atmosphere in these formal occasions will cause great psychological pressure on inexperienced interpreters, and it in turn will affect their self-confidence. Stage fright can make interpreters frequently make mistakes. The ever-changing work environment can make the interpreters slow in response.

6. Work of independence (独立性)

Another characteristic of interpreting lies in its independent work and heavy responsibility. The interpreters' work is highly independent. In most cases, they are isolated and helpless in the whole process of interpreting. They must deal with any problems that they may encounter independently at all times. Some problems belong to the linguistic category, which is related to the interpreters' bilingual knowledge; some belong to the cultural category, which is related to their common knowledge; some belong to natural science category, which is related to their disciplinary knowledge; and more belong to social science category, which is related to their basic knowledge of the society, culture, national conditions and current affairs.

In the process of interpreting, the interpreters cannot inquire for reference books or related reference materials, nor can they interrupt the speakers frequently and ask the other party to repeat what they have said or explain the contents. Occasionally, errors in interpreting can be corrected in the drafting of the written agreements in the future. However, many interpreters, such as the ones for international conference, do not have remedial opportunities in the subsequent process.

7. Comprehensiveness (综合性)

Interpreting is a process that integrates visual, listening, speaking, writing and reading skills. "Visual" refers to the interpreters' ability to observe and capture the speaker's facial expressions, gestures, emotional changes and other non-verbal factors. "Listening" refers to the ability of the interpreters to understand different kinds of words with local accents and different speech speeds. "Speaking" refers to the ability of the interpreters to express themselves fluently in their mother tongue and foreign language. "Writing" refers to the ability of the interpreters to take notes quickly in the process of interpreting. "Reading" refers to the interpreters' ability to read and understand quickly in sight interpreting.

Interpreting is a multi-dimensional mode of information dissemination. Multi-level information sources and communication channels, on the one hand, bring difficulties to interpreting work, such as the difficulties brought by the speakers' strong local accent and too-fast speech speed; but on the other hand, they also create favorable conditions for interpreting work. For example, the speakers' voice, intuitive body language, vivid intonation, and scenery related to interpreting content, are all favorable conditions for assisting interpreting.

2.1.4 Interpreting vs. Translation

Interpreting and translation are closely connected, yet vastly different. Though having some commonalities, they have their own characteristics and requirements, and therefore respective assessing criteria.

Interpreting and translation have the same working process: understanding the source language, analyzing the information, and reconstructing in the target language. They both require the interpreters or translators to have a comparatively high level ability in Chinese and the foreign language, extensive knowledge and a strong sense of responsibility.

However, interpreting and translation are still largely different due to their unique features, and their differences can be seen in the following aspects:

1. Time constraints and work pressure

As we have mentioned, interpreting is instantaneous. It needs to be done on the spot and in real time. What interpreters usually hear are words that are spoken only once and are no longer repeated. With correct understanding, they must interpret independently and immediately in one try. Time is strictly controlled. Generally speaking, it is impossible for interpreters to turn to others, consult dictionaries or other materials on the spot. If mistakes are made, it is not very likely for interpreters to have the chance to correct them. So interpreters often work under tremendous pressure.

As for translation, even though there is often a deadline to meet, translators have comparatively more freedom in time control. With the original text at hand, they have more time to brew on the translation of one expression, or consult a dictionary or someone for reference. Comparatively speaking, they are working under less pressure.

Compared with translation, interpreting may present more difficulties. However, interpreting also has some advantages. For example: the speakers' voice, intonation, gesture and facial expression can help the interpreters understand the content of the speech. In informal occasions or in the presence of a small number of people, interpreters can also ask the speakers to explain or clarify certain points, which is not possible for translators.

2. Working methods

The different working methods of interpreting and translation are mainly caused by the different nature of oral and written languages and the different forms they adopt respectively. Compared with translation, interpreting has strong oral characteristics and requires high instantaneity.

Translation is to understand the source text by "reading" and get information. Interpreting relies on "listening" to understand the source text. After listening to the speakers' words, the interpreters immediately express them in the target language. This requires interpreters to have a good listening comprehension of the source language. In addition, translators hold the whole text in hand, and they can understand the original text according to the internal connection of the context. When they encounter expressions that they can't understand at first, it's possible that they can find the answers when they read the following part or after reading the full text. Interpreters, on the other hand, do not have the chance to take a panoramic view of the whole conversation. They can only judge the meaning of the speech according to the "unit of meaning" that they hear.

3. Relationship between the interpreters and the speakers, and between the translators and the authors

Translators work in an environment separate from the authors and the readers. They only work with the original texts, which are the only basis for the translators' work. However, interpreters work in a communicative environment with the speakers and the listeners. Therefore, besides the speakers' speech, they also have the "non-verbal information", such as the body language, facial expressions, gestures, intonation and so on.

4. Literal translation or free translation

There has long been a debate between literal translation and free translation in the translation circles. The essence and focus of this debate is how to deal with the differences between the two languages. The so-called "literal translation" is to maintain the content of the original text as well as the form corresponding to the language of the original text. The so-called "free translation" is to maintain the content of the original text only. When the content of the original text contradicts with the language form of the translated text, the content is maintained while the language form is not.

However, such disputes may only exist in the field of translation. Interpreting is very different. Interpreters do not have time to deliberate on the translation of specific words or sentences. They must capture the content and spirit expressed by these words and sentences, and immediately reproduce the content of the source language with the words and sentences of the target language he masters.

2.1.5 *Types of Interpreting*

Interpreting can be categorized according to the interpreting methods, direction, general communication purposes and specific purposes.

a. According to the interpreting methods

Consecutive interpreting (交替传译), simultaneous interpreting (同声传译), whispering interpreting (耳语传译), sight interpreting (视译), liaison interpreting (联络口译), relay interpreting (接力口译), etc.

b. According to direction of interpreting

One-way interpreting (单向口译), two-way interpreting (双向口译).

c. According to general communication purposes

Conference interpreting (会议口译), community interpreting (社区口译), interpreting for special purposes (特殊目的口译), etc.

d. According to specific purposes

Ceremonial interpreting (礼仪口译), escort interpreting (陪同口译), guide interpreting

(导游口译), diplomatic interpreting (外交口译), court interpreting (法庭口译), military interpreting (军事口译), business interpreting (商务口译), medical interpreting (医学口译), technical interpreting (技术口译), exhibit interpreting (展览口译), performance interpreting (演出口译), media interpreting (媒体口译), etc.

Here we will introduce two basic types of interpreting:

1. Consecutive interpreting

Consecutive Interpreting (CI) (交替传译、即席口译、连续传译、接续传译、接续口译、逐步传译、逐步口译), refers to the translation practice in which the interpreters listen while the speakers speak, and when the speakers finish part or all of the speech in the source language, interpreters reproduce the information expressed by the speakers in the target language to the audience orally. It is a versatile form of verbal translation between languages. With or without taking notes, interpreters begin to deliver messages in the target language when speakers pause their speech or conversation. It was the default interpreting service in the United Nations before technology became available to enable simultaneous interpreting in 1927.

There are three types of CI, CI with translated text, CI with source text but without translated text, and CI without either.

Consecutive Interpreting is the title of this textbook, and will be our main focus.

2. Simultaneous interpreting

Simultaneous Interpreting (SI) (同声传译、同声翻译、同声口译、同步口译), refers to the translation practice in which the information expressed by the speakers is reproduced orally in the target language at almost the same speed as that of the speakers. In SI, interpreters often sit in a booth and listen to the speakers through earphones, and speak into a microphone in the target language. It is most frequently used in international conferences.

Although SI has the advantages of not taking-up conference time, and it is possible to interpret simultaneously in different languages, CI also has its advantages.

Before interpreting, interpreters receive a large amount of information from the source language with rich contexts and relatively complete utterances, which is conducive to the interpreters' listening comprehension at the information level rather than at the linguistic level.

With a thorough and more comprehensive understanding, CI is easier for interpreters to reproduce in a way that facilitate communication, rather than mechanical interpreting.

The interpreters, speakers and the listeners are in closer distance. It is more convenient for real-time communication between the three parties. Interpreters can timely understand the on-site situation and intervene if needed.

Although CI has become less central in conferences and meetings of larger scale, it still is in demand elsewhere, mainly due to its lower technological requirements than SI. It is practiced by professional as well as non-professional interpreters, some only with limited training and proficiency, such as interpreters in conflict zones.

2.1.6 *Process of Interpreting*

2.1.6.1 The Process

To many people, interpreting is considered only a simple code-switching process, while in fact, it is much more complicated than that. The interpreting process, for whichever type of interpreting, can be divided into the following four basic steps: listening comprehension (听辨理解), memorizing (记忆), code-switching (转换) and delivering (表达), as is shown in Fig. 2-1.

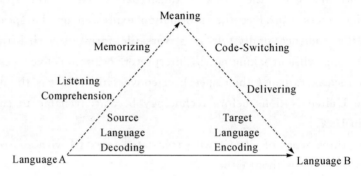

Fig. 2-1 The Interpreting Process

If the interpreters only stay on the level of code-switching, they cannot interpret well, and it is difficult for both sides to achieve effective communication. To successfully accomplish the task of interpreting, interpreters must always keep in mind that they are engaged in a communicative activity. To achieve both cross-linguistic and cross-cultural communication, interpreters should fully understand the meaning of the source language while listening to the speech and store it in memory. This process is called "source language decoding". At the same time, they should quickly find the corresponding expression in the target language, and then deliver the meaning of the source language in the target language. This process is called "target language encoding".

In practice, interpreting is an activity that is highly instantaneous. In fact, the four basic steps of interpreting are completed in a very short time. It can be vividly described as a "four-in-one" process, that is, the four basic steps must be completed simultaneously. In consecutive interpreting, when the speakers stop speaking, interpreters must begin to interpret, while in simultaneous interpretation, the target language must be kept in close synchronization with the source language. A careful study of the interpreting process reveals that the four basic steps of interpreting are not accomplished step by step in a linear order, but are carried out at the same time. In this sense, the thinking mode of interpreting is a coordinated multi-tasking working mode centered on the skills of listening comprehension, short-term memory, code-switching and delivering, as shown in Fig. 2-2.

Chapter Ⅱ Introduction to Interpreting, Consecutive Interpreting and Interpreters

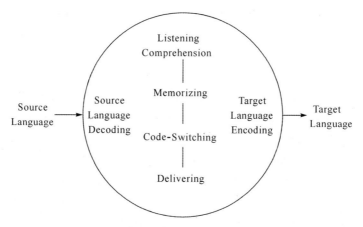

Fig. 2-2 The thinking mode of interpreting

2.1.6.2 The Four Basic Steps

1. Listening comprehension (听辨理解)

Listening Comprehension is the first step in interpreting. Listening Comprehension itself can be further divided into two parts: listening + comprehension. Of course, the two are interrelated and are closely tied together.

⊙ **Listening** (听辨)

Listening refers to the hearing and distinguishing of different sounds, vocabulary, intonation and syntax. It is the first step of source language decoding.

Interpreting begins with the input of linguistic information. In most cases, interpreters receive linguistic information from the speakers in an auditory way. Therefore, the interpreters' hearing and understanding of the auditory information are the first barriers to break in interpreting. For Chinese interpreters, this is especially true when interpreting from English to Chinese, because our mastery of English is far less proficient than that of our mother tongue. Listening comprehension is always our weakness in English-Chinese interpreting. If the interpreters do not fully understand or misunderstand the speaker, they will not be able to accurately and completely convey the original intention of the speaker, or even cause misunderstanding, leading to the failure of communication between the two sides or even more serious consequences. Therefore, interpreters must have a keen sense of hearing, a good language sense and the ability to distinguish different sounds, intonations, vocabulary and syntax.

Competent interpreters can understand not only the standard English spoken by British and American people, but also various English varieties spoken by native speakers, such as Irish English, Scottish English, Canadian English, Australian English, New Zealand English and South African English. They must also understand the English spoken by people who use English as a second or official language, such as Indian English, Singapore English, Philippine English, and English spoken by people from West African countries, as well as the English spoken by non-English speaking countries. Compared with standard English, English spoken by people in the above regions may be inaccurate in pronunciation, wording and even grammar.

For Chinese interpreters, it is very important to understand English of different countries and regions. China is now open to the outside world in an all-round way. We are not only dealing with English-speaking countries, but also developing exchanges and cooperation with people from all over the world. Interpreters should consciously train and cultivate their ability to adapt to and distinguish different English varieties in phonetics, intonation, vocabulary and syntax, and strive to improve their English listening comprehension ability, which is a crucial step in improving the quality of interpreting.

Chinese-English interpreting is different. Except for strong local accents, dialects, idioms, slang or professional terms, it is generally not a problem for Chinese interpreters to understand Chinese. Code-switching and English expression are then the main training focuses.

⊙**Comprehension**(**Understanding**)(理解)

Comprehension is a process in which interpreters analyze, interpret and synthesize the received linguistic information and then make correct judgments and understandings. The message conveyed by the speakers is composed of many factors, both linguistic and non-linguistic. The interpreters' understanding of the received information includes the following aspects.

a. Language

Language is the main carrier of information. The transmission of information mainly depends on the interpreters' understanding of the source language, including the speakers' pronunciation, intonation, grammar, vocabulary, meaning and text, which are based on the first step—listening. Therefore, interpreters must have a solid knowledge of the source language and a rich vocabulary. They should not only master the common expressions, idioms, slangs and proverbs of the two languages, but also be good at capturing the "illocutionary meanings", i.e., the true meaning of the speakers' captured from their mood, intonation, hidden language and context. Thus, the understanding at the linguistic level is based on the interpreters' proficiency in both languages, especially in the foreign languages.

In addition, language is closely tied to culture. Since the two languages used by both parties have their own social and cultural connotations, it is difficult to understand and master a language without understanding its social and cultural backgrounds. Therefore, interpreters should have good bilingual cultural awareness. The more thoroughly the interpreters understand the two cultures, the better they can understand the speakers' original intention.

b. Topical knowledge

Interpreting involves a wide range of contents. In addition to exchanges in politics, diplomacy, trade, culture and sports, various professional and academic meetings are happening more and more frequently. If the interpreters have enough relevant professional knowledge, they can analyze and understand the content of the conversation from a professional point of view. On the contrary, if the interpreters lack the professional knowledge of the topic of the conversation, it is impossible to fully understand the content even if they are highly competent in the foreign languages. Thus, knowledge is closely tied to understanding. The more knowledgeable the interpreters are, the deeper their understanding of the conversation will be and the smoother their interpreting will be.

Successful interpreters should be versatile. Of course, this does not mean the interpreters should know everything, but they must have a minimum of international common sense, and basic knowledge of politics, economy, commerce, law, humanities, science and technology. They need to have a general idea of the political, economic, historical, and social background of the country of origin, and be familiar with China's national conditions, foreign policies and position, and views and attitudes on major international issues. If conditions permit, interpreters should be fully prepared beforehand and be as familiar as possible with the topics to be discussed and the knowledge involved.

The interpreters' knowledge acquisition mainly depends on their unremitting efforts in everyday accumulation. Interpreters should seize every practical opportunity, constantly accumulate and expand knowledge, and improving their level of interpreting.

c. **Logical connection**

In addition to the language information and the topical knowledge of the conversation, interpreters can also improve their understanding by analyzing the content of the conversation and its logical reasoning. In communication, both sides participate in the conversation with different identities and positions. Both sides have their own ideas, ways and purposes when talking, and the content of the conversation is usually logically connected. Interpreters should recognize the speakers' identity, status and occupation, understand the intention of the conversation, grasp the inner connection of the conversation, and understand the real meaning of the speakers accurately through analyzing the logical reasoning of the conversation. In this way, they can still understand even if they occasionally miss a piece of the conversation. Even when the speakers make a slip of the tongue or switch the order of the conversation, interpreters can still correctly deduce their meaning and interpret correctly.

⊙ **The core of understanding—meaning**

As we have mentioned earlier, and as is shown in Fig. 2-1 and 2-2, the core of understanding is to capture the meaning (or the message or the key information) of the source language. "Meaning" refers to the thinking of a speaker, the ideas or content which the interpreter has to convey to the audience. It is more than just the meaning of words or sentences. In a sense, it is more of contextual meaning.

In the process of interpreting, interpreters mainly retell the main points of the source content, interpret the meaning of the key words, numbers and terminology, and convey the internal logical connection. This characteristics of interpreting is mainly caused by the contradiction between the instantaneity of the spoken language and the limitation of the amount of information that can be processed by the interpreters. It is impossible for interpreters to perceive and remember all the words in source language. What the interpreters' brain can retain is only the "essential points" extracted from the source language, as well as the key words and their internal connections. If the interpreters attempt to interpret the information of all the words in the source language, they will inevitably be limited by the amount of information that can be processed by the human brain, and may very likely fail.

⊙ **Factors affecting understanding**

From the above illustration about listening comprehension, we can summarize some of the factors that may affect the interpreters' understanding.

a. **Bilingual abilities**

Interpreters should be proficient in both languages, which means they should have the basic linguistic knowledge of phonetics, intonation, words, syntax, structure, semantics, and etc., on the basis of which, they need to have the ability to use the language, as in listening, speaking, reading, writing and translating. In addition, interpreters need to be proficient in dealing with information from gestures, intonation, topics, context and communication environment.

b. **Background knowledge**

Background knowledge includes encyclopedic knowledge, professional knowledge and contextual knowledge. Background knowledge must be integrated with linguistic information to create meaning.

c. **Analytical abilities**

Interpreting is an analytical process. It includes analysis in phonetics, grammatical structures, semantics, discourse, rhetoric, culture, and sociopsychology, and deduction in meaning.

d. **Other objective factors**

Many objective factors may affect interpreting. They may include: time pressure, multitasking, the speed of the speakers' utterance, accents or dialects, stress, noise, the interpreters' health status, interpreting environment, etc.

The above are some factors that may affect understanding. Interpreters must actively cope with these factors, lay a solid foundation in both languages, expand knowledge, form a habit of active analysis while listening, get used to the pressure and other external factors in interpreting, get familiar with different accents, and form a habit of knowledge accumulation.

2. **Memorizing（记忆）**

In processing the received linguistic information, interpreters need to keep the acquired information in memory temporarily in order to prevent information loss, omission or

Chapter II Introduction to Interpreting, Consecutive Interpreting and Interpreters

mistranslation in the process of code-switching and expression. Therefore, it is particularly important for interpreters to have a strong memory, especially when interpreting consecutively, because the speaker usually speaks for 2 - 3 minutes or even 4 - 5 minutes before stopping. Interpreters should not add or subtract the speakers' content at will, nor can they fabricate it against the speakers' original intention. They must express the speakers' original intention faithfully, completely and timely.

Therefore, interpreters must mobilize their memory as much as possible at the moment of understanding, memorize the meaning of the conversation, and then choose the appropriate words and sentences to express it. Memory and understanding are interrelated, complementary and almost happening simultaneous. What is understood can be easily remembered, and memory can influence understanding and expression. In fact, interpreters listen, memorize and understand at the same time while interpreting.

Memory has two forms: memorizing by heart and memorizing by note-taking. In simultaneous interpreting, speaking and interpreting are almost simultaneous, so there is basically no time to take notes, because notes can distract attention and affect the listening and interpreting of the next sentence. Thus, interpreters in SI mainly memorize by heart. Consecutive interpreting is different. Interpreters have to wait until the speakers finish a whole paragraph before interpreting, so they rely on notes to help them remember. But they cannot rely too much on notes, otherwise their understanding will be affected. Whether SI or CI, it requires interpreters to have excellent memory. Therefore, interpreters should strengthen their memory through practical exercises. Memory and note-taking are specialized interpreting skills, which will be discussed in Chapter VII and Chapter VIII of this book.

3. Code-switching (转换)

Code-switching is a process where the language code is switched from the source language to the target language. It is a process that start with listening and continues throughout the entire interpreting process. In code-switching between Chinese and English, we need to pay special attention to the following differences.

⊙ **Parataxis (意合) vs. hypotaxis (形合)**

Parataxis and hypotaxis are two ways languages are organized. Parataxis refers to the realization of the connection of the words or phrases without the help of the language form but the logical meaning of the words or phrases. Hypotaxis refers to the realization of the connection of the words or phrases, with the help of language forms (including vocabulary and forms). The former one (Chinese) focuses on the coherence of meaning, while the latter (English) focuses on the language cohesion in form.

Chinese sentences are formed on the basis of meaning rather than structure. Very often, Chinese sentences may have no clear subject or no subject at all. The sentence structure can be quite complicated and there seems to be no rules to follow. English sentences, however, are formed on the basis of forms. There are specific grammatical rules to follow. It emphasizes on the completeness of sentence structure and compliance to rules. In most cases, each English sentence needs to have a subject and a predicate.

Therefore, based on the hypotaxis feature of English, in Chinese-English code-switching, one of the strategies is to add connectives in English sentences, which includes relative pronouns (who, whom, which, that, what), relative adverbs (when, where, why, how), coordinators (and, or, but, both... and..., either... or..., neither... nor..., not only... but also..., so that, as well as, rather than, etc.), and subordinators (when, as, while, every time, as soon as, because of, as a result of, for fear that, seeing that, considering, though, although, even if, no matter, in spite of, despite, so that, in order to, so as to, etc.)

⊙**Sentence structure**

Comparing Chinese and English sentences, we can tell the following main differences:

a. Chinese's "topic-prominent"（主题突出）vs. English's "subject-prominent"（主语突出）

In Chinese, the part in front of predicate is not necessarily subject. Many Chinese sentences have no subject at all, while in English, a complete sentence (except imperatives) must have a subject. So in Chinese-English code-switching, one of the first priorities is to find the subject or implied subject in Chinese sentences.

b. Chinese: words of different part of speech used as predicate vs. English: verb-based predicate

In Chinese, the predicate is not necessary verbs. Adjectives, adverb and even nouns can also work as predicate. For example, "这朵花很美。", the adverb "很" works as the predicate. Because of this special feature, many learners of Chinese may make the mistake and translate it as "这朵花是很美". In English, the predicate must be verbs. In Chinese-English code-switching, it's important to determine the subject and verb in English expression.

c. Chinese's "modifier + center word" vs. English's "center word + modifier"

In Chinese, modifiers are always put in front of the center word, while in English, modifiers often appear after the center word, and they often appear in the forms of prepositional phrases, non-predicate verb phrases, attributive clauses, appositional clauses, and adverbial clauses.

d. Chinese: "analytical language"（分析型语言）vs. English: "comprehensive language"（综合型语言）

Chinese is an analytical language while English is a comprehensive language. "Analytical language" means the meaning is shown not through the change of forms of the words themselves, but through the use of function words or the change of word order. "Comprehensive language" means that the meaning is expressed through the change of the forms of words.

⊙**General vs. specific**

Chinese expressions tend to be more general and vague while English expressions tend to be more specific and accurate. Chinese pays special attention to discourse structure and the use of four-word structures or parallel structures. English emphasizes on the strict compliance to rules in word forms and sentence structures.

As we have mentioned, the core of understanding is to capture the meaning. In code-switching, information is also the key. Interpreters should focus on the message delivered rather than specific words or phrases. That means, in CI code-switching, free translation is very often used. It is more flexible and can better help interpreters explain the underlying meaning or cultural elements. It doesn't mean we cannot use literal translation. Literal translation is mainly used in interpreting simple sentence structures or sentences that have same or similar sentence structures in both Chinese and English.

Detailed code-switching strategies will be talked about in Chapter V of this book.

4. Delivering (表达)

Delivering, also called expression or reproduction, is the process in which the interpreters express the speakers' original intention in the target language on the basis of a full understanding of the source language. The ultimate purpose of listening, understanding, memorizing and code-switching is to express. In the process of expression, interpreters should decode the information and concepts they understand, recode them, synthesize and generalize them, select the appropriate words, and finally interpret them timely and accurately. Interpreters should have clear pronunciation, accurate intonation, appropriate wording, smooth and effective sentences and naturalness and fluency. These are not only the basic requirements of expression, but also the important indicators reflecting the quality of interpreting.

Successful expression can not only convey the speakers' information completely, accurately and fluently, but also maintain the speakers' style and characteristics. Excellent interpreters can make the conversation between the two sides go on as if there is no language barrier. In some international conferences, it is common to see this phenomenon: when the speakers make an impassioned speech, the interpreters in the interpreting room are speaking with the same passion while interpreting, even waving their arms like the speakers. The interpreters' effective expression depends on their linguistic skills and public speaking ability. That means, interpreters should not only have pure mother tongue and skilled foreign language, but also have certain public speaking skills. They should be able to express themselves with a clear speech, a loud voice, a beautiful timbre and a suitable rhythm.

Delivering (reproduction) will also be discussed fully in Chapter IX of this book.

2.1.7 Criteria of Interpreting

The three basic features of interpreting determine that the evaluation criteria for interpreting should be different from those of translation. Even for consecutive interpreting and simultaneous interpreting, the criteria are different. For SI, interpreting happens simultaneously with the speaking of the speakers, and the information interpreters get is often partial at the moment of interpreting, so interpreters may have no time to reorganize their language. They may even need to omit some less important information in interpreting or make some generalization. So some of the criteria for CI may not apply to SI. Here, we are mainly talking about the evaluation criteria for CI. Evaluating from different perspective, we have the following criteria.

In terms of the content of the source language, accuracy and completeness are the main criteria.

(1) Accuracy: For interpreting, accuracy is the most basic requirement. Inaccurate interpreting such as made-up interpreting, interpreting that violates the original meaning, or misinterpretation are all intolerable. Accuracy is the soul and lifeline of interpreting. It requires the interpreters to convey the content of the source language to the target language in a complete and correct manner. Specifically speaking, the accuracy of interpreting involves the accuracy of theme, spirit, arguments, style, words, figures, expressions, speed of utterance and the way of speaking. Ultimately, an accurate interpreting should keep the meaning and style of the source language. Accuracy is not only the guarantee of the success of bilingual communication, but also the embodiment of interpreters' professional ethics and level. It reflects not only the respect and responsibility of the interpreters for the communicative activities.

(2) Completeness: To be accurate in interpreting, completeness is a must. It means whether the interpreters express the whole content of the source language. To achieve completeness, interpreters need to have a powerful memory and a good note-taking ability. For CI, interpreters are usually required to achieve at least 90%-95% of completeness of the source language. For SI, this requirement is lowered to about 75%-80%, which means interpreters can omit some unimportant information, or make generalization.

In terms of delivery, logicality, professionalism, fluency and speed, clarity, conciseness and pronunciation and intonation are the main evaluation criteria to be considered.

(1) Logicality: Logicality is mainly reflected in the cohesion and coherence of sentences and discourse. Sentences must be logically connected throughout the entire interpreting process, so that the audience can easily understand.

(2) Professionalism: Professionalism is mainly embodied in the accurate use of words, sentence structure, terminologies and so on.

(3) Fluency and speed: Fluency means to interpret in a smooth and timely fashion. The characteristics of instantaneity of interpreting require that the interpreting process should be shorter than longer, and the rhythm tighter than looser. Interpreting is a tool of communication, and its value lies in its utility and efficiency. So how to measure the fluency of interpreting? The fluency of interpreting includes the speed at which the interpreters perceive and interpret the source language, and the speed at which he encodes and expresses it in the target language. Generally speaking, we can judge whether an interpreter is fluent

or not according to whether the interpreting time used by the interpreter is roughly equal to the speaking time of the speaker. Interpreting at twice the speaking time of the speaker cannot be regarded as fluent.

(4) Clarity: Clarity means to be able to express in a clear way. It means the audience will have a clear understanding of the topic, the content and the speakers' intention.

(5) Conciseness: Conciseness is on the basis of completeness. Only when the content is complete, can conciseness be considered. It means to be able to express the speakers' key information in a short and simple way.

(6) Pronunciation and intonation: Pronunciation and intonation are the basic abilities of the interpreters. Especially when the target language is a foreign language, pronunciation and intonation should be accurate. Interpreters' accent must not affect understanding.

In terms of audience perception, expressiveness, acceptability and understandability are the main criteria.

(1) Expressiveness: Expressiveness refers to whether the interpreters can express accurately to the audience the speakers' speech information, intention and communication purposes.

(2) Acceptability: Acceptability refers to how much the target language can be accepted by the audience. It includes correct pronunciation, intonation, collocation, grammar, style and terminologies.

(3) Understandability: Understandability refers to how easily the target language can be understood by the audience. Interpreters should fully express the speakers' intended meaning, organize language in a way that meets the language habit of the audience, add explanations if needed, speak in a coherent and logical way, and meet the cross-cultural communication purposes.

Exercises and Practice

2-1-1 Work in a group and answer the following questions.
1. What are the different types of interpreting?
2. What is the definition of consecutive interpreting?
3. What are the differences between interpreting and translation?
4. What are the main factors affecting understanding in interpreting?
5. What are the main criteria for consecutive interpreting?

2-1-2 List out the advantages and disadvantages of consecutive interpreting and simultaneous interpreting.

2-1-3 Fill in the blanks.
1. The four basic steps in the interpreting process are: _____, _____, _____, and _____.

2.

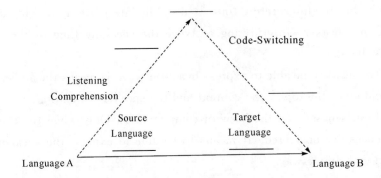

2-1-4　Interpret the following sentences into English. Pay attention to the hypotaxis feature of English and add subject or connectives if necessary.

1. 我们应该相互尊重,相互学习,取长补短,共同进步。

2. 我们应该牢牢把握中美关系的大局,妥善解决分歧,不断朝着增进了解、扩大共识、发展合作、共创未来的目标前进。

3. 加大投入力度,建立稳定的医疗保障体系。

4. 真正发挥人才的引领作用,给他们提供能够发挥作用的舞台,充分信任、放手使用。

5. 原打算五月份访华,后不得不推迟,深感失望。由于贵公司的努力,访问这么快得以重新安排,非常高兴。

2.2　Introduction to Interpreters

2.2.1　Role of Interpreters

Traditional interpreting theory holds that interpreting activities are only the communication and interaction between the two sides through the interpreters' language conversion. Qualified interpreters should be "transparent" or "invisible" in the process of interpreting. This view may be too idealistic, but it also shows that the traditional interpreters only play a passive role of word-passing. However, the purpose of interpreting activities is to communicate with people from different cultural backgrounds through oral translation. The understanding of interpreting should not be limited to the simple conversion of language, but also be regarded as a communicative behavior. Therefore, it is necessary for interpreters to have a profound understanding of the cultural background of the two languages and their special roles in the process of communication so as to eliminate the communication barriers in different languages and ensure smooth communication. Under the background of globalization, interpreters should constantly develop themselves and play versatile roles.

1. Interpreter

As interpreters, the most basic and important task is to do well in interpreting. This includes not only the work of interpreting, but also translation, not only Chinese to English,

Chapter II Introduction to Interpreting, Consecutive Interpreting and Interpreters

but also English to Chinese interpreting, and not only consecutive interpreting, but also simultaneous and other forms of interpreting. In order to become qualified interpreters, learners should make good use of all possible time and resources to enhance their language ability, increase their accumulation of abundant knowledge and constantly improve their English and Chinese level and interpreting skills.

2. Service provider and middleman

The first job of interpreters is to provide service. That means, interpreters should not become the focus, but provide service to people who are the focus. They play a similar role as logistic workers. They should be properly dressed for the occasion and stay low-profiled. In interpreting, they should not steal the thunder of the speakers.

Interpreters work as the middlemen. They should not raise new topics, guide topics, express personal views or comment or even criticize certain point of views. Their position is always neutral. They should not put their personal feelings into interpreting, and add, delete or distort original content based on their interests or preferences.

3. Liaison and coordinator

Interpreters often work as liaison or coordinator between the parties involved. Sometimes they may work with multiple parties, such as speakers, audience (listeners), organizers, sponsors, equipment providers, and more. They may need to help each party contact the others, coordinate time and place, book hotels, arrange and print files, work out itineraries, resolve issues and do other relevant works. This requires the interpreters to work efficiently, and have a strong sense of time.

Interpreters sometimes also work as mediators or language filters. When speakers are speaking in an illogical way, they have to change it to more logical expressions. When speakers are speaking in a round-about way (Chinese), they have to change it to a more direct way (English), or vice versa. When speakers are using insulting languages, they may need to filter those parts to keep the conversation going.

4. Receptionist and guide

In the foreign reception activities, interpreters sometimes work not only as just interpreters, but also receptionists or guides. They may need to deal with all kinds of reception works such as picking up or seeing off guests at the airport or train station, arranging hotels, restaurants and transportations, the writing, printing and translating of documents, and coordinating media, meetings, visits, banquets, gift exchanges and other activities.

Interpreters also need to have extensive knowledge in food, lodging, transportation, entertainment, shopping and tourism. Many times, they may need to work as a tour guide. This requires the interpreters to have encyclopedic knowledge in history, geography, literature, arts and local customs.

5. Cultural promotor

Many times, foreign guests may have very limited knowledge about China, especially about the modern China. It's important for interpreters to be familiar with China's national conditions, foreign policies and position, views and attitudes on major international issues, and to promote the culture of the Chinese nation to the outside world. This requires the interpreters to be familiar with the China's history, geography, climate, natural resources, social and political status, economy, demography, ethnic groups and so on.

6. Public speaker

Interpreters often need to stand next to the speakers and speak in front of an audience. Stage-fright can greatly affect interpreters' work and the audience's understanding. This requires the interpreters to have good public speaking skills, both verbally and non-verbally.

7. Errand runner

Interpreters very often have to run all kinds of errands for both parties. They sometimes work almost as secretaries and deal with all kinds of relevant or irrelevant issues.

To sum up, interpreters play a crucial role in foreign affairs. They sometimes determine the success or failure of the communication activities. Therefore, interpreters must have a strong sense of responsibility, constantly improve themselves and expand their knowledge so as to excel in this profession. Next, we'll talk in details about the qualities of qualified interpreters based on these versatile roles of the interpreters.

2.2.2 Qualities of Qualified Interpreters

Interpreting is a profession with high professional requirements. Although people who have a good command of both languages can do some simple interpreting work, they cannot undertake the formal tasks of interpreting. In order to become excellent professional interpreters, besides meeting some necessary physiological and psychological requirements, it is usually necessary for learners to train and refine the qualities that professional interpreters must possess through specialized study and intensive training. So what are the basic requirements for professional interpreters?

1. Professional ethics and patriotism

Interpreters must have good professional ethics and patriotism. Interpreting belongs to activities of foreign affairs. Interpreters' actions, words and deeds are directly related to the image of the country and the interests of the institutions. Interpreters should abide by the disciplines in foreign affairs and financial activities, strictly keep state secrets and comply to the operational procedures of interpreting. Interpreters must be faithful to their duties, responsible to both sides of the conversation, and strictly keep the confidentiality of their clients. They should do nothing that is detrimental to the national interest and individual character.

2. Bilingual abilities

Interpreters must have a solid knowledge of two or more languages. Their bilingual competence refers not only to their knowledge of basic language, such as pronunciation, intonation, syntactic structure, lexical and semantic knowledge, but also to their ability to use the linguistic knowledge (such as listening, speaking, reading, writing and translation). In addition, interpreters should also understand various styles and pragmatic functions of different languages, and master the interpreting methods of idioms, slangs, terminologies, proverbs, euphemisms, abbreviations, poems, etc.

3. Ability of clear expression

Interpreters must have the ability to express clearly, fluently and expressively. Speed should also be considered in interpreting. No hurrying, no delaying, no intonation that is too high or too low, interpreters must have a clear and natural articulation, a clean expression, an accurate and appropriate choice of words, a concise use of sentences that are easy to understand, and a vivid language use.

4. Encyclopedic knowledge

Interpreters must have extensive knowledge. They should have a general knowledge in current affairs, politics and economy, humanities, science and technology, business, law, history and geography, international relations, customs, common sense of life and so on.

5. Comprehensive abilities

Interpreters must have an acute mind, a fast reaction, an outstanding memory, and strong judging, analytical, logical thinking and improvising abilities.

6. Personal manners

Interpreters must have good personal manners, and be well-mannered, properly dressed, polite, humble, and graceful in interpreting works.

7. The "Interpreter Quotient"

Besides all of the above requirements, interpreters also need to have strong abilities in communicating, thinking, concentrating and learning, to have the awareness to serve and to be psychologically prepared for high pressure. Altogether these are referred to as the "Interpreter Quotient".

2.2.3 *Professional Training and Career Development*

2.2.3.1 Professional Training

1. MTI programs

MTI (Master of Translation and Interpreting) is a master's degree in translation and interpreting. In order to meet the needs of high-level talents in the socialist market economy, the Academic Degree Committee of the State Council approved the establishment of the MTI program. MTI is one of the 20 professional degrees in China. In 2007, the first batch of MTI pilot teaching institutions approved by the Academic Degree Committee of the State Council totaled 15, including Peking University, Beijing Foreign Studies University, Fudan University, Guangdong University of Foreign Studies, PLA College of Foreign Languages, Hunan Normal University, Nanjing University, Shanghai Jiaotong University, Nankai University, Shanghai University of Foreign Studies, Tongji University, Xiamen University, Southwest University, Central South University and Sun Yat-sen University. In

2019, the number of MTI programs have exceeded 150 throughout the country.

MTI has been divided into full-time and on-the-job classes. Some schools are called autumn classes and spring classes. For on-the-job MTI programs, students need to take part in the GCT unified examination as preliminary examination. The second examination is generally a translation or interpreting practical ability test, but it may vary for each school.

2. BA, MA, PhD, and other professional training programs domestic and overseas

The first interpreting school was set up in 1950 in Geneva, Switzerland. AIIC, the International Association of Conference Interpreters, was founded on Nov. 11, 1953 with its secretariat located in Geneva. It has since become one of the most recognized interpreters' association worldwide. All over the world, 38 interpreting schools are recognized by AIIC (e. g. University of Leeds, University of Westminster). Programs of MA in C – E translation are also offered at Bath University, Middlesex University (London) & The University of New Castle in Britain, Monterey Institute of International Studies in USA (AIIC), The University of Griffith in Australia and The University of Auckland in New Zealand, etc.

In Chinese mainland, there are interpreting programs at BA and MA level at Beijing Foreign Studies University, Sino-EU Interpreter Training Centre, UIBE (the sole program in China that has formal cooperation with SCIC: the Directorate-General for Interpreting of the Commission of the European Communities), Xiamen University, Guangdong University of Foreign Studies and Shanghai International Studies University (recognized by AIIC).

In Hong Kong, BA, MPhil and PhD in Translation are offered at the Chinese University of Hong Kong, Hong Kong Baptist University, City University of Hong Kong, The Hong Kong Polytechnic University, and Lingnan University of Hong Kong. In Taiwan, two famous programs in Fu Jen Catholic University and Taiwan Normal University are recognized by AIIC. The Graduate Institute of Translation and Interpretation Studies (GITIS), College of Foreign Languages, Fu Jen Catholic University currently offers three courses, each lasting a minimum of two years. The MA in Translation and MA in Conference Interpreting share some common courses in translation and special topics, and are full-time programs requiring class attendance and practice during the working week. The "On-the-Job" MA in Translation is a "night and summer school" program designed for students in fulltime employment.

3. Self-training

Another important way to improve interpreting skills is self-training. After all, not everyone has the opportunity to get specialized vocational training. Some interpreters have been working on the front line for a long time and have good linguistic and psychological qualities. If they know the content and main methods of interpreting training, they can carry out self-training. But the training of interpreting is a hard process. Learners must have perseverance, patience and determination, and formulate practical learning plans to gradually improve their interpreting level. Of course, not everyone can learn interpreting. It requires learners to have the afore-mentioned qualities, and understand the basic steps and common methods in professional training in interpreting. Some of the common training methods such as retelling and shadowing exercise in memory training and sight note-taking will be discussed later in this book.

2.2.3.2 Career Development

With the unprecedented scale of foreign exchange and cooperation among governments, enterprises, institutions, social organizations and even individuals, there is an ever-increasing demand for interpreters. The number of full-time interpreters is far from meeting the market demand, and a team of freelance, semi-freelance and part-time interpreters has gradually formed in the market.

Freelance interpreters do not have formal or full-time employers. They participate in the market by contract. Semi-freelance interpreters may give priority to providing interpreting services to a certain employer on a regular basis, but they also participate in the interpreting market. There are also some part-time interpreters who work in universities, training institutions, embassies and consulates, governmental or public institutions. Freelance interpreters and semi-freelance interpreters are the main bodies of the interpreters' market.

Whichever type of career path one is taking, learners must acquire the afore-mentioned qualities of qualified interpreters, understand clearly the different roles of interpreters, and abide by professional ethics. Learning ability is an important part of interpreters' professional development. After leaving school and entering the market, whether learners can rapidly grow into professional interpreters depends on their learning ability. New interpreters should constantly improve their language proficiency, enrich their knowledge system, accumulate work experience and improve their communication level through learning. Every interpreting job is an important learning opportunity to learn about new fields, broaden their knowledge, expand their vocabulary, and learn from senior interpreters.

In the process of interpreters' growth, the focus of learning should gradually shift from language and interpreting skills to knowledge learning and accumulation, and then to the promotion of their professional brand and reputation, as well as the construction and maintenance of their professional network.

2.2.3.3 Self-Assessment and Learning Journal

No matter professional training or self-training, it's a good idea for learners to keep track of the learning progress. Two simple ways are doing constant or periodical self-assessments and writing learning journals.

1. Assessment after each practice

After a day's practice, it's a good idea to review and note down the places for improvement. There is no fix form of assessment. It can be answering some prepared questions, or filling an assessment form. There is no fix assessment form. Here are two sample assessment forms (Table 2-1 and Table 2-2) for reference only.

Table 2-1 Self-Assessment Form Sample 1

Part Ⅰ **Vocabulary**
1. Words or expressions missed (漏译):
2. Words or expressions misused (误译):
3. Incorrect words or expressions (错译):
4. Incorrect pronunciation:
5. Unnecessary sounds made:
6. New words or expressions learned:

Part Ⅱ **Sentences**
1. Grammatical mistakes:
2. Coherence and cohesion problems:
3. Logical problems:

Part Ⅲ **Culture and Knowledge**
1. Common sense mistakes:
2. Topical knowledge mistakes:
3. Cultural knowledge mistakes:
4. New knowledge acquired:

Part Ⅳ **Delivery**
1. Pause for too long:
2. Repetition:
3. Intonation problem:

Part Ⅴ **Note-taking**
1. To be improved:
2. Symbols learned or created:

Part Ⅵ **Other issues**

Table 2-2 Self-Assessment Form Sample 2

Speech Title	
Type of Interpreting	
Length	
Source of the Material	
1. Preparation—What Have You Prepared for This Task?	
Objectives of this practice	
What have you prepared?	
2. Self-Reflection	

Chapter Ⅱ Introduction to Interpreting, Consecutive Interpreting and Interpreters

Continued Table

Quality Overview
Major Problems and Reasons
3. Suggestions for Further Improvements

2. Periodical assessment

Learners can also periodically assess their progress by answering some prepared questions. The following (Table 2 – 3) are some sample questions based on *China's Standards of English Language Ability*.

Table 2 – 3 Self-Assessment Questions Based on China's Standards of English Language Ability

1. Can I recognize and properly deal with the major mistakes made by the speakers in interpreting?
2. When encountering difficulties, can I interpret with the help of pre-interpreting preparation or accumulated experience?
3. Can I collect relevant background information about the speakers and the interpreting assignments through organizers or the Internet?
4. In the process of consecutive interpreting, can I use the skills and strategies of CI comprehensively and make sure the language is flexible and appropriate, the expression conforms to the habits of the target language, the manner is natural and the articulation is clear?
5. Before interpreting, can I familiarize myself with the speakers' speaking habits, such as pronunciation, intonation, speaking speed and word preference?
6. Can I reflect on the interpreting process and the reasons for the difficulties in time afterwards?
7. In the long consecutive interpreting, can I ensure the accuracy, completeness and fluency of the output of the target language by adding, omitting, adjusting word order or explicitation (显化)?
8. Can I avoid obvious grammatical errors, express fluently and use non-linguistic methods to ensure effective communication in long consecutive interpreting?
9. Can I understand, analyze and memorize (by heart or by note-taking) the speakers' information, and express the source language information in target language fluently?

Continued Table

10. Can I understand the speakers' main intention, memorize the key information of the speech, and interpret the source language information in the target language accurately?

11. Can I recognize the obvious mistakes in my interpreting and correct them in time?

12. Can I turn to the speakers or the audience for help in interpreting?

13. In simultaneous interpreting, can I use the skills and strategies of simultaneous interpreting comprehensively and make sure the language is flexible and appropriate, the expression conforms to the habits of the target language, and the pronunciation is clear?

14. Can I interpret simple communication scenarios, such as airport pick-up, escort shopping, etc., and interpret important information with my understanding of the theme and related background?

15. Before interpreting, can I prepare accordingly, such as understanding the schedule, theme and content of the activities?

16. With the help of notes, can I interpret speeches in activities such as business visits, science lectures, tourist visits with moderate information density, normal speech speed, and short paragraphs?

17. Can I accomplish the interpreting of familiar topics with short paragraphs without notes in activities such as business reception, tourist visits, etc.?

18. In simultaneous interpreting, can I use strategies such as prediction, omission and generalization to distribute my attention, analyze and segment the source sentences according to proper meaning groups while listening, and interpret the speech information accurately, completely and fluently?

19. In simultaneous interpretation of political speeches, live events and expert arguments, can I interpret speeches with low information density, normal speech speed and no obvious accent?

20. In the long consecutive interpreting, can I use context and relevant background knowledge to analyze the speakers' logic?

21. In the long consecutive interpreting of press conferences, academic reports and business negotiations, can I use notes to interpret speeches with normal speed, high information density, more specialized and a certain degree of accent?

22. In simultaneous interpretation of government press conferences and major emergencies, can I accurately, completely and smoothly interpret the source language information?

23. In difficult and professional consecutive interpreting such as meetings of heads of government and trial of major cases, can I interpret the source language information accurately, completely and fluently, and the register and style of the translated language are identical with those of the speakers?

24. In interpreting, can I monitor the accuracy, fluency and coherence of the translated language in real time and correct errors in time?

25. Before interpreting, can I learn relevant knowledge, make vocabulary and proactively predict interpreting information according to the theme and the speakers' background?

3. Learning journals

It is also a good idea for learners to keep a learning journal. Every day, note down some of the improvements or mistakes you have made, what you have learned from each interpreting job, or anything you would like to note down in your interpreting learning process. The writing of the learning journals is totally up to each individual learner, and there is no set format for it.

Exercises and Practice

2-2-1 List out all the possible roles of an interpreter.

2-2-2 What are the main qualities of a qualified interpreter?

2-2-3 Discuss with your partner your career development plans.

2-2-4 Watch the video "Role of an Interpreter" (Video 2-2-4) from the European Union's interpreters' training course, and discuss with your partner what led to the communication failure in the short drama.

2-2-5 Watch the video "Professionalism" (Video 2-2-5) from the European Union's interpreters' training course, and discuss with your partner what the interpreter did violated interpreters' code of conduct in the short drama.

Additional Materials

1. 2015年土耳其G20峰会开幕习近平讲话要点
来源：中国新闻网
http://www.chinanews.com/m/gn/2015/11-16/7625649.shtml
主题：共同行动以实现包容和稳健增长
Theme: Collective Action for Inclusive and Robust Growth

二十国集团既要治标以求眼下稳增长，又要治本以谋长远添动力。
G20 should work to maintain a stable economic growth in the short term, while seeking to inject new impetus into the world economy in the long run.

这次国际金融危机复杂程度远超以往，解决起来绝非一日之功。
The current financial crisis is far more complex than any of the previous crises, and it cannot be fixed overnight.

第一，加强宏观经济政策沟通和协调，形成政策和行动合力。
Strengthen communication and coordination on macroeconomic policies.

第二，推动改革创新，增强世界经济中长期增长潜力。
Promote reform and innovation to enhance growth potential.

第三，构建开放型世界经济，激发国际贸易和投资活力。
Build an open world economy to bring out vigor in international trade and investment.

第四，落实2030年可持续发展议程，为公平包容发展注入强劲动力。
Implement the 2030 Agenda for Sustainable Development to inject strong impetus into

equitable and inclusive development.

中国有信心、有能力保持经济中高速增长,继续为各国发展创造机遇。
China, as the world's second largest economy, has the confidence and ability to sustain a medium-high growth rate and continue to create development opportunities for other countries.

中国在世界经济最困难的时刻,承担了拉动增长的重任。2009年到2011年间,中国对世界经济增长的贡献率达到50%以上。
China shouldered the responsibility of driving economic growth in times of the world economic hardship. China had contributed up to 50% of world economic growth from 2009 to 2011.

目前,中国经济增速虽有所放缓,对世界经济增长的贡献率仍在30%以上,仍是世界经济重要动力源。
Despite a recent slowdown, China still contributes 30% to world economic growth, which means that China still acts as a major world economic powerhouse.

未来5年,中国将按照创新、协调、绿色、开放、共享的发展理念,着力实施创新驱动发展战略,坚持新型工业化、信息化、城镇化、农业现代化同步发展。
In the next five years, China will adhere to a path of innovative, coordinated, green, open and shared development, and will encourage a system that nurtures innovation. The country will try to realize the synchronous development of the new type of industrialization, IT application, urbanization and agricultural modernization.

坚持绿色低碳发展,改善环境质量;坚持深度融入全球经济,落实"一带一路"倡议。
In the coming years, China will highlight green and low-carbon development, improve its environmental quality, become heavily involved in global economy, and carry out the Belt and Road Initiative.

坚持全面保障和改善民生,使发展成果更多更公平惠及全体人民。
The world's second largest economy will continue to vigorously improve its people's well-being and ensure that the benefits of development are shared by all.

2. 中华人民共和国主席习近平在金砖国家工商论坛开幕式上的讲话(上)(2017年9月3日,厦门) President Xi's speech at the opening ceremony of BRICS Business Forum (Part Ⅰ)
中文来源:新华网 http://www.xinhuanet.com/politics/2017-09/03/c_1121596338.htm
译文来源:新华网 http://www.xinhuanet.com//english/2017-09/03/c_129695215.htm

Chapter II Introduction to Interpreting, Consecutive Interpreting and Interpreters

共同开创金砖合作第二个"金色十年"
Working Together to Usher in the Second "Golden Decade" of BRICS Cooperation

尊敬的特梅尔总统、尊敬的祖马总统,
Your Excellency President Michel Temer, Your Excellency President Jacob Zuma,

各位工商界代表,
Representatives of the Business Community,

女士们,先生们,朋友们:
Ladies and Gentlemen, Dear Friends,

下午好!很高兴同大家相聚在风景怡人的"鹭岛"厦门。明天,金砖国家领导人会晤就要拉开帷幕。我谨代表中国政府和中国人民、代表厦门市民,并以我个人的名义,向参加会议的各位嘉宾表示热烈的欢迎!

Good afternoon! It is my great pleasure to have all of you with us in the beautiful city of Xiamen, renowned as the "Egret Island". The BRICS Summit will be held tomorrow. On behalf of the Chinese government and people and the people of Xiamen, and also in my own name, I warmly welcome all of you to the Business Forum.

厦门自古就是通商裕国的口岸,也是开放合作的门户,正所谓"厦庇五洲客,门纳万顷涛"。1985年我来到福建工作,厦门是第一站。当时的厦门身处中国改革开放前沿,是先行先试的经济特区,也是一片发展的热土。30多载春风化雨,今天的厦门已经发展成一座高素质的创新创业之城,新经济新产业快速发展,贸易投资并驾齐驱,海运、陆运、空运通达五洲。今天的厦门也是一座高颜值的生态花园之城,人与自然和谐共生。

Xiamen has been a trading port since ancient times as well as a gateway of China's opening up and external cooperation. Embracing the vast ocean, the city has hosted visitors from around the world. On a personal note, Xiamen is where I started off when I came to Fujian Province to take up a new post in 1985. Back then, being one of the earliest special economic zones in China, the city was at the forefront of China's reform and opening up endeavor and was brimming with development opportunities. Three decades later, Xiamen has become well known for its innovation and entrepreneurship, with burgeoning new economic forms and new industries, robust trade and investment and easy access to the world with air, land and sea links. Today, Xiamen is a beautiful garden city with perfect harmony between man and nature.

闽南民众常说,"爱拼才会赢"。这其中蕴含着一种锐意进取的精神。厦门这座城市的成功实践,折射着13亿多中国人民自强不息的奋斗史。改革开放近40年来,在中国共产党领导下,中国人民凭着一股逢山开路、遇水架桥的闯劲,凭着一股滴水穿石的韧劲,成功走出一条中国特色社会主义道路。我们遇到过困难,我们遇到过挑战,但我们不懈奋斗、与时俱进,用勤劳、勇敢、智慧书写着当代中国发展进步的故事。

There is a popular saying here in southern Fujian, "Dedicate yourself and you will win," which embodies an enterprising spirit. Xiamen's success is a good example demonstrating the perseverance of the 1.3 billion-plus Chinese people. In close to 40 years of reform and opening up, under the leadership of the Communist Party of China, we Chinese have forged ahead, fearless and determined, and we have successfully embarked on a path of socialism with distinctive Chinese features. We have encountered difficulties and challenges on the way forward. But we have persevered and kept pace with the times. With dedication, courage and ingenuity, we are making great progress in pursuing development in today's China.

女士们、先生们、朋友们!

Ladies and Gentlemen, Dear Friends,

金砖合作正处在承前启后的关键节点上。观察金砖合作发展,有两个维度十分重要。一是要把金砖合作放在世界发展和国际格局演变的历史进程中来看。二是要把金砖合作放在五国各自和共同发展的历史进程中来看。

BRICS cooperation has now reached a crucial stage of development. In assessing its performance, it is important to bear two things in mind: the historical course of global development and evolving international landscape and the historical process of development of the BRICS countries, both individually and collectively, in the context of which BRICS cooperation is pursued.

现在,我们正处在一个大发展大变革大调整的时代。虽然全球范围内冲突和贫困尚未根除,但和平与发展的时代潮流愈发强劲。世界多极化、经济全球化、文化多样化、社会信息化深入发展,弱肉强食的丛林法则、你输我赢的零和游戏不再符合时代逻辑,和平、发展、合作、共赢成为各国人民共同呼声。

We are in a great era of development, transformation and adjustment. Although conflict and poverty are yet to be eliminated globally, the trend toward peace and development has grown ever stronger. Our world today is becoming increasingly multipolar; the economy has become globalized; there is growing cultural diversity; and the society has become digitized. The law of the jungle where the strong prey on the weak and the zero-sum game are rejected, and peace, development and win-win cooperation have become the shared aspiration of all peoples.

在这样的大背景下,一大批新兴市场国家和发展中国家异军突起,在国际事务中发挥着日益重要的作用。金砖合作也应运而生,我们五国怀着追求和平与发展的共同愿望走到一起。在过去10年中,金砖国家携手同行,成长为世界经济的新亮点。

Against such a backdrop, a large number of emerging market and developing countries have come to the fore, playing an ever greater role in international affairs. BRICS cooperation is a natural choice made by our five countries, as we all share a desire for peace and development. In the past decade, we BRICS countries have surged ahead and become a bright spot in the global economy.

——10年中,金砖国家探索进取,谋求共同发展。2008年爆发的国际金融危机突如其来,直接导致世界经济急刹车,至今未能重回正轨。面对外部环境突然变化,我们五国立足国内,集中精力发展经济、改善民生。10年间,五国经济总量增长179%,贸易总额增长94%,城镇化人口增长28%,为世界经济企稳复苏作出突出贡献,也让30多亿人民有了实实在在的获得感。

—The past decade has seen the BRICS countries making headway in pursuing common development. The sudden outbreak of the 2008 global financial crisis left the world economy reeling, which is yet to fully recover. Facing the external shock, our five countries have held the ground by strengthening the domestic economy, boosting growth and improving people's livelihood. In the past ten years, our combined GDP has grown by 179%, trade by 94% and urban population by 28%. All this has contributed significantly to stabilizing the global economy and returning it to growth, and it has delivered tangible benefits to three billion and more people.

——10年中,金砖国家务实为先,推进互利合作。我们五国发挥互补优势,拉紧利益纽带,建立起领导人引领的全方位、多层次合作架构,涌现出一批契合五国发展战略、符合五国人民利益的合作项目。特别是新开发银行和应急储备安排的建立,为金砖国家基础设施建设和可持续发展提供了融资支持,为完善全球经济治理、构建国际金融安全网作出了有益探索。

—The past decade has seen the BRICS countries advancing results-oriented and mutually beneficial cooperation. Leveraging our respective strengths and converging interests, we have put in place a leaders-driven cooperation framework that covers wide-ranging areas and multiple levels. A number of cooperation projects have been launched that are in keeping with our five countries' development strategies and meet the interests of our peoples. In particular, the New Development Bank and the Contingent Reserve Arrangement have provided financing support for infrastructure building and sustainable development of the BRICS countries, contributing to enhanced global economic governance and the building of an international financial safety net.

——10年中,金砖国家敢于担当,力求在国际舞台上有所作为。我们五国秉持多边主义,倡导公平正义,就国际和地区重大问题发出声音、提出方案。我们五国积极推动全球经济治理改革,提升新兴市场国家和发展中国家代表性和发言权。我们五国高举发展旗帜,带头落实千年发展目标和可持续发展目标,加强同广大发展中国家对话合作,谋求联合自强。

—The past decade has seen the BRICS countries endeavoring to fulfill their international responsibility. Committed to multilateralism, fairness and justice, our five countries have staked out our positions on major regional and international issues and made our proposals to address them. We have promoted reform of global economic governance to increase the representation and say of emerging market and developing countries. As a champion of development, we have taken the lead in implementing the Millennium Development Goals and Sustainable Development Goals, and engaged in close dialogue and cooperation with other developing countries to pursue development through unity.

万丈高楼平地起。如今,金砖合作基础已经打下,整体架构轮廓初现。回望来时路,我认为有3条启示十分重要,应该在今后的合作中发扬光大。

As an old saying goes, the construction of a tall building starts with its foundation. We have laid the foundation and put in place the framework of BRICS cooperation. In reviewing the past progress of BRICS cooperation, I believe there are three important practices that should be carried forward.

一是平等相待、求同存异。金砖国家不搞一言堂,凡事大家商量着来。我们五国尊重彼此发展道路和模式,相互照顾关切,致力于增进战略沟通和政治互信。我们五国在国情、历史、文化等方面存在差异,合作中难免遇到一些分歧,但只要坚定合作信念、坚持增信释疑,就能在合作道路上越走越稳。

First, treating each other as equals and seeking common ground while shelving differences. In terms of BRICS cooperation, decisions are made through consultation among us all, not by one country alone. We respect each other's path and model of development, accommodate each other's concerns and work to enhance strategic communication and political mutual trust. Given differences in national conditions, history and culture, it is only natural that we may have some differences in pursuing our cooperation. However, with strong faith in cooperation and commitment to enhancing trust, we can achieve steady progress in our cooperation.

二是务实创新、合作共赢。金砖国家不是碌碌无为的清谈馆,而是知行合一的行动队。我们五国以贸易投资大市场、货币金融大流通、基础设施大联通、人文大交流为目标,推进各领域务实合作,目前已经涵盖经贸、财金、科教、文卫等数十个领域,对合作共赢的新型国际关系作出生动诠释。

Second, taking a results-oriented, innovative approach to make our cooperation benefit all. BRICS is not a talking shop, but a task force that gets things done. Our goal is to build a big market of trade and investment, promote smooth flow of currency and finance, improve connectivity of infrastructure and build close bond between the people. In pursuing this goal, our five countries are engaged in practical cooperation across the board, covering several dozen areas, including economy, trade, finance, science, technology, education, culture and health, thus giving concrete expression to the endeavor of building a new type of international relations featuring win-win cooperation.

三是胸怀天下、立己达人。金砖国家都是在发展道路上一步一步走过来的,对那些身处战乱和贫困的百姓,我们感同身受。我们五国从发起之初便以"对话而不对抗,结伴而不结盟"为准则,倡导遵循联合国宪章宗旨和原则以及国际法和国际关系基本准则处理国家间关系,愿在实现自身发展的同时同其他国家共享发展机遇。如今,金砖合作理念得到越来越多理解和认同,成为国际社会的一股正能量。

Third, developing ourselves to help others with the well-being of the world in our mind. Having gone through an arduous course of development, we BRICS countries share the agony of those people who are still caught in chaos and poverty. Since the very beginning, our five countries have been guided by the principle of dialogue without confrontation, partnership without alliance. We are committed to observing the purposes and principles of the UN Charter, international law and basic norms governing international relations in conducting state-to-state relations. When developing ourselves, we are ready to share development opportunities with other countries. The philosophy of BRICS cooperation has gained growing appreciation and endorsement, and it has become a positive energy in the international community.

这些都是金砖精神的具体体现,是我们五国历经 10 年合作凝聚的共同价值追求。这种精神在实践中不断升华,为五国人民带来福祉,也让世界因金砖合作而有所不同。

All this is what the BRICS spirit is about. It is the shared value that has bound us in the past decade's cooperation. This spirit, constantly enriched over the years, has not only benefited our peoples but also enabled us to make a difference in the world.

Chapter III Preparation

Learning questions:
- ✓ What are the basic language and communication skills? Why are they important for CI?
- ✓ What do we need to prepare off and on-spot for an interpreting task?

In this chapter, we will study some of the basic language and communication skills in consecutive interpreting. They include: active listening skills, public speaking skills, cross-cultural communication skills and coping skills. These skills are the prerequisites for learning this course. They lay the foundation for further CI training. We will also learn about the preparation we need to make off-spot and on-spot for an interpreting task.

3.1 Basic Language and Communication Skills

3.1.1 Active Listening Skills

3.1.1.1 Active Listening vs. Passive Listening

Learning to interpret begins with learning how to listen effectively. It's important for learners of CI to be aware of the difference between passive listening and active listening.

Passive listening is what happens when one is busy doing something while some type of sound is going on around him/her—like a radio, or the television, or music. Active listening is paying full attention to the speaker and making an effort to understand the message. It is an intent to "listen for meaning". Although there are language learning systems based on passive learning that encourage people to listen and learn while doing housework, sleeping, or any other activities, it isn't all that effective for listening comprehension training, especially for the purpose of CI. Active listening should gradually become learners' default listening mode.

Listening is an active process. It involves the listeners' conscious desire to determine the meaning of what is heard. One is not just catching words or sentences, but getting the meaning and reorganize the sentences in mind. Many times, pre-listening preparation, background, common sense and prediction all play important roles in active listening. Active listening can be divided into three stages: pre-listening, during listening, after listening.

3.1.1.2 Three Stages of Listening

1. Pre-listening

At this stage, some preparation work needs to be done. They include:

(1) Memorize some relevant words, phrases, or terminologies.

(2) Predict from title or other hints what the speech or listening material you are going to listen may be about.

(3) Try to answer the following five "Wh-" questions:

Who is the speaker?

What is the subject?

What is the occasion?

Who is the audience?

What type of speech is it? Informative? Persuasive? Commemorative?

(4) Prepare yourself for the listening activity, both physically and psychologically. That means, you need to adjust to the environment and understand the complexities of listening.

(5) Tell yourself that you are going to focus on main ideas or key information

2. During listening

During listening, you need to stay fully focused on the listening assignment.

(1) Get yourself adjusted to the accent and speaking style as quick as possible.

(2) Identify the level of formality and the style of speech.

(3) Concentrate on understanding what the person is saying. (Is the person trying to make a point or to describe an event? What is the ultimate purpose?...)

(4) Utilize your topical knowledge, common sense or other background information to understand.

(5) Identify the central theme, main ideas and supporting details.

(6) Focus on ideas or key points. Pay more attention to the message flow rather than single words or phrases. Find the logic in and between sentences.

(7) Notice but do not pay too much attention to the way words are spoken (pause, intonation, body language, etc.).

(8) Take notes properly when necessary.

(9) Deduce incomplete information.

(10) Deduce unfamiliar vocabulary.

3. After listening

(1) Learn from the listening experience.

(2) If possible, listen as many times as possible until you digest every word, phrase and sentence. It's a good idea to listen for the main idea when listening for the first time. Then listen with the text at hand for the second time. And then listen again without the text for the third time and try to distinguish and understand each word without the text.

(3) Review, memorize useful words, phrases, and relevant terminologies.

(4) Read the listening texts out loud.

3.1.1.3 Listening Strategies

1. Seizing key words

The key words in listening comprehension refer to those words that contain a lot of information, which often constitute the key to the whole sentence or even the whole text. When interpreters grasp these words, they can often have a better understanding of the whole text. These key words which carry a lot of information are more often the content words (实词) in the text, namely nouns, verbs, adjectives and adverbs. When these words are spoken, they are more often stressed and spoken with a slower speed.

2. Paying special attention to discourse markers—signal words and logical connectors

A speech is not just composed of a series of independent sentences; on the contrary, there are logical relations between sentences which cannot be separated. They are interrelated and mutually corroborated, thus determining the meaning of the whole speech. When interpreters understand a discourse, they must first identify various viewpoints, and then analyze the logical connection between them. It is these discourse markers (signal phrases or logical connectors) that are the words or sentences that express all kinds of logical connections and enable the interpreters to analyze the discourse. The following (Table 3 – 1) are some frequently used discourse markers.

Table 3 – 1 Signal Words and Logical Connectors

Purpose of the speaker	Signal phrases or logical connectors
To introduce a topic	Today, I'd like to talk about..., What I am going to discuss is...
To develop an idea	If we examine the situation..., The most significant point is...
To emphasize a point	I am sure you will agree with me..., I'd like to emphasize..., The point you must remember is..., As we all know..., As you know...
To show transition of ideas	My next point is..., Now let me move on to the next point..., First..., Second..., Finally...
To add a point	moreover, in addition, furthermore, what's more
To show segmentation	right, OK, and, now, that will be all for this part
To conclude	finally, I'd like to summarize, to conclude
To indicate time	eventually, for the time being, on (date), not long after, now, as, before, after, when, during, until, in the first place, next, previously, after that
To explain	because, cause, since, therefore, consequently, as a result, this led to, so, so that, nevertheless, accordingly, if... then, thus...
To compare and contrast	in contrast, however, however, but, as well as, on the other hand, not only... but also, either... or..., while, although, similarly, yet, unless, meanwhile, likewise, nevertheless, otherwise, compared to, despite...
To exemplify	in other words, for example, for instance

3. Making prediction

Prediction competence in listening comprehension in CI refers to the interpreters' ability to judge and infer the speakers' meaning before listening to all the speakers' utterances, relying on certain communicative occasions and background, and on relevant grammatical and topical knowledge. Prediction is not a purely subjective assumption, but a logical reasoning. Correct application of prediction strategies can greatly reduce the auditory burden of interpreters.

In CI, active prediction is quite necessary. It can be used in the following situations: the early recognition of a set collocation, a logical sequence of ideas, discursive arguments or logical sequences. Prediction can be used in two aspects: linguistic prediction and non-linguistic prediction. The former refers to semantics, while the latter refers to ideas and information to be expressed by the speakers.

Linguistic prediction refers to the interpreters' prediction of what the speakers will express next according to linguistic rules, such as word collocation, sentence structure, conjunctions between sentences, communication context, etc. For example, in English, the probability of a preposition followed by pronouns or nouns is very high, while by another preposition or verb is very low. The sentence following the connective word "however" often carries the opposite information as the one preceding the word. In a conference, when the expression "I'd like to extend..." is spoken, the following part is likely to be "my warmest welcome" or "my gratitude". It is these kinds of rules that can help interpreters predict the meaning of words or what's to come in specific contexts.

Non-linguistic prediction refers to the interpreters' prediction of the speakers' purpose, content and conclusion based on non-linguistic knowledge such as encyclopedic, professional or situational knowledge. Speakers' identities or backgrounds often determine their purpose of speech and point of view. With ample preparation, interpreters' correct prediction can help interpreters better understand the content.

3.1.1.4 Basic Training Methods

In CI, there are three main reasons for difficulties in listening comprehension. They are: being too nervous and fear that they would miss even one word; improper note-taking, not knowing what to note down or noting down too much; and insufficient professional vocabulary or knowledge. Listening comprehension is the first step in CI; therefore, training in listening comprehension is crucial. The following are some training methods:

(1) Extensive listening: listen extensively, both actively and passively, and accumulate extensively the vocabulary and knowledge. Exercises that can be used are retelling stories or summarizing main points.

(2) Intensive listening: listen intensively for details. This usually requires learners to

listen to each piece of training material multiple times, with and without text. Exercises that can be used are cloze and dictation.

(3) Shadowing exercise: it is also called source language retelling exercise. It is to imitate the pronunciation, intonation and pauses of the speakers' speech, pre-recorded news recordings or conference materials in almost the same manner as if the imitator is a shadow of the speaker. It is a training exercise that is more often used in SI training, but it can also be used in the training of listening comprehension and memory expansion. This exercise will be introduced in more details in Chapter Ⅶ.

In addition, learners should formulate a habit of information extracting and note-taking while listening.

3.1.2 Public-Speaking Skills

Public speaking is another key skill at the initial stage of CI training. A good interpreter must be a trained public speaker. Very often, interpreters need to stand in front of an audience and speak. The benefit of public speaking training is predominantly associated with better verbal and non-verbal presentation. Because speakers give talks to make a point, any point made, the way the points are connected or sign-posted, together with their supporting information, should reach the listeners who rely on the interpreting service. By practicing active listening (to get the point) and delivering semi-prepared speeches (to make a point), students can better capture the keywords, connectives and phrases in a speech, which lays the foundation for further note-taking training. Public speaking itself is a course that can be taught for an entire semester. Here, we will only briefly talk about some non-verbal skills of it.

3.1.2.1 Dealing with Public Speaking Anxiety

Public speaking anxiety, also called stage fright, stage nervousness or fear of public speaking, is commonly seen among people. Everyone gets nervous when speaking in front of an audience, even just the thought of it could be nerve-wrecking.

The symptoms of anxiety range from physical to cognitive, varying from individual to individual. Common physical symptoms may include:

(1) Flushed face;
(2) Profuse sweat;
(3) A pumping heart;
(4) Hyperventilation;
(5) Dizziness;
(6) Shaking;
(7) Vomiting;

(8) Memory loss.

Cognitive anxiety may include negative thoughts such as "I don't think I can do it" or "people are going to laugh at me".

Know that public speaking anxiety is physically normal. These symptoms are caused by a chemical released by our body called adrenalin when we are in a fight-or-flight situation. And remember that you are not alone. Public speaking is one of the biggest fears for many people. So how do we deal with public speaking anxiety in CI? Here are some tips:

(1) Prepare well: background information, vocabulary, topical knowledge, etc. ;

(2) Utilize your notes: Note-taking can help ease the burden of memory;

(3) Give full concentration in listening;

(4) Mirror practice at home;

(5) Practice in front of family or friends;

(6) Visualize your success;

(7) Do breathing exercise to help you with physical symptoms;

(8) Do relaxing things such as listening to music or taking a walk.

Remember that in most cases, people cannot see your nervousness even though your heart may be pumping hard. Don't start with an apology saying that you are nervous. First impression is crucial. Know that most of the time, people will understand your nervousness. No one is perfect. Everyone makes mistakes. If you make a mistake, don't panic. Sometimes a simple "excuse me" would suffice. One of the biggest fear for interpreters is the fear that they could not understand the source language or forget what is said. So full concentration on the information expressed by the speakers and note-taking may help. Even if you forget, it's not the end of the day. You can simply ask the speaker to repeat what is said.

3.1.2.2 Non-verbal Skills

Non-verbal communication skills also determine the success of your interpreting job. Interpreters with good language skills and topical knowledge may fail because they cannot effectively get their message to the audience.

Non-verbal skills in public speaking include: eye contact, gestures, stance, platform movements, facial expression, personal image, voice elements and performance elements. In CI, some of the non-verbal skills may not apply.

1. Eye contact

Eye contact is crucial in communication. In many cultures, it shows respect. Good eye contact shows confidence and your willingness to exchange ideas with the audience. With good eye contact, the audience will accept you as a person, and find it easier to believe what you are saying. While evading eye contact shows lack of confidence, staring at one person may cause discomfort. Good interpreters can balance note-taking with eye contact.

2. Gestures

Gestures can be used to emphasize a point, to express emotion, to release tension and to engage your audience. Good use of gestures are effective ways to show your emotions and enthusiasm, while unwanted gestures such as some unconscious repetitive movements can become distractions. However, in interpreting, it is not encouraged to use too many gestures, especially exaggerated ones. Interpreters should not be too enthusiastic and become the focus, but provide service to people who are the focus. Do not make funny faces, stick out your tongue or frown when making mistakes.

3. Stance

Stance is an issue that inexperienced interpreters may feel uncomfortable with. How you stand in front of the audience actually says a lot about you, such as are you confident or are you feeling uncomfortable. When you stand in front of your audience, putting even weight on your feet and leaning slightly forward show your willingness to engage with the audience. But do not lean to one side of your body. And it's best not to lean on the wall, or lean with one arm on something. When you are standing still and talking to your audience, stand still and quietly. Do not stomp your feet, and do not sway your body.

4. Personal image

To leave a good first impression on the audience, your personal image plays an important role. Your personal image is the first thing that comes to their eyes before you speak. Experienced interpreters always dress properly and accordingly. Most of the time, formal dress is required. If you are not sure, better go with formal than casual. For male, suit, shirt and tie would do. But be aware of color combination. Usually dark colored suit is more suitable for formal occasions, which means a lighter color shirt and a dark color tie can go with it. If you are wearing striped shirt, avoid wearing striped tie. For female, pant suit or skirt suit are both fine. Long evening dresses are only suitable for some occasion. Avoid wearing too much perfume and too many accessories. No matter what you wear, keep them neat and clean.

5. Voice elements

Voice elements, though having something to do with your voice, are an important set of non-verbal skills. In interpreting, it's not just what you say (verbal skills) that matters, but also how you say it. The voice elements in CI include: volume, pitch, rate and pronunciation and enunciation.

Volume is how loud or soft you speak to your audience. Good control of volume shows your confidence and capability. Volume that is too low is seen as lack of confidence or preparation, even though it is simply caused by your nervousness. Low volume also draws distance between you and your audience, and they will quickly lose interest in you. On the other hand, volume that is too high may be seen as too aggressive, making the audience feeling uncomfortable. When a microphone is provided, check if it works well and how it works before you start, and leave it alone when you speak. Do not speak too close into the microphone.

Pitch is the highness or lowness of the speaker's voice. Pitch which is too high can be irritating to the audience while too low can be hard to be heard. There should be changes in pitch which is known as inflections. Speaking without changing in pitch is flat and boring, and can easily make the audience fall asleep. So it is important to vary your pitch. But do it naturally. Pitch change that is too dramatic can also cause uncomfortable feelings in the audience.

Rate, or pace, is how fast or how slow you speak. Speaking too fast or too slow can both cause uncomfortable feelings. Some people, when nervous, tend to speak faster than their normal speed. It's ok to pause a bit when the audience is applauding or laughing.

Pronunciation is the way a word is pronounced according to the dictionary. Enunciation means you pronounce a word clearly. In simple words, pronunciation is to speak the word correctly while enunciation is to speak the word clearly. Together, they determine whether the audience will be able to understand you. For Chinese learners, when speaking English, many may make some pronunciation errors or speak with certain degree of accent, but if not too serious, they are, most of the time, understandable and are accepted by the audience. But enunciation problems can cause the audience great difficulty in understanding. So it is always important to speak clearly, which means not only pronounce the words clearly, but also completely.

To sum up, in using the voice elements, always adjust them to the occasion and the audience, and always do it naturally. Avoid speaking in too low a voice, too fast, too flat or too unclear.

3.1.3 *Cross-Cultural Communication Skills*

With the deepening of globalization, we are living in a time when cross-cultural communication happens more and more frequently, and everyone can be a part of the cross-cultural communication activities. We may encounter cultures which are entirely different from our own at any time. Getting in contact with different cultures and communicating with people of different cultural backgrounds has become an inevitable part of our lives.

Communication is a process of encoding and decoding. Encoding is a process of changing thoughts, feelings and ideas into language codes, while decoding is a process of giving meaning and explanation to symbols and information received from the outside world.

Effective communication can only be achieved when both the sender and the receiver of information share a unified or similar code system. That is to say, the communicators speak in the same language. If they do not use the same language and have different cultural backgrounds, then the communication between them becomes cross-cultural communication. In cross-cultural communication, the different languages of the two communicating parties and the different cultures with languages as the carriers will inevitably become obstacles to communication. At this time, interpreters become particularly important and a bridge for successful cultural communication between the two communicating parties.

Interpreting is a complex process of receiving, decoding and encoding information, which is very often in the form of conversation. The topics of conversation, such as weather, greetings, age, income, personal privacy, have different social meanings in different cultures. How to discuss a topic is also influenced by different linguistic and cultural psychology, historical background and traditions. As Lyons, a famous British linguist, said, every language corresponds to a particular culture. When different cultures are involved, communication becomes more complex. What you see is only the tip of an iceberg, the cultural iceberg (see Fig. 3-1). The language structure, communication mode, speakers' thinking and psychology are largely influenced or even restricted by cultural concepts. In cross-cultural communication, the task of decoding the original information falls on the interpreters. In interpreting, decoding includes not only the decoding of non-cultural information, but also that of linguistic and non-linguistic cultural factors directly affecting the accurate interpreting. When cross-cultural communication is conducted through interpreters, inappropriate interpreting can lead to misunderstanding or even conflict, thus failing to achieve the desired purpose.

One of the cross-cultural mistakes in CI is called pragmatic transfer（语用迁移）. It refers to the phenomenon where interpreters are influenced by their mother tongue and their own culture in interpreting. Due to the lack of understanding of the differences in cultural background, value orientation and social norms between the two sides in communication, the original expressions are often interpreted literally into the target language, resulting in pragmatic transfer and pragmatic failure in interpreting.

Eg. 这是老弱病残专座。

* This is a seat for the old, weak, sick or disabled[①].

This is a typical example of pragmatic transfer. China is a country that pays attention to collectivity. Helping the old, the weak and the disabled is the fine traditional virtue of the Chinese nation. Under its influence, people are used to helping the weaker and take pride in

---

① * : Incorrect or inappropriate use of English.

it. In English, "the old" and "the weak" are almost taboo words. Take the U. S. as an example. Americans emphasize on independence and individuality. They would consider "the old" or "the weak" as discriminative expressions. "Courtesy seat" would be a better choice.

Other mistakes may include incorrect or incomplete transfer of cultural information. For example, "You can't compare them. They are apples and oranges." If translated literally as "你无法比较它们,它们是苹果和橘子。", though partly understandable, it would be unidiomatic. It would be better to say "你无法比较它们,它们天差地别。"。

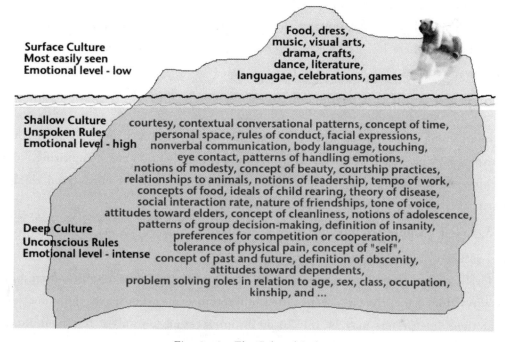

Fig. 3 - 1 The Cultural Iceberg

(http://twassistant.com/uncategorized/how-to-develop-your-cultural-intelligence/)

There are many reasons for pragmatic failure in interpreting. It is mainly determined by the characteristics of interpreting itself. Interpreting is a special communicative activity with the characteristics of instantaneity, complexity and high intensity which requires the interpreters to have a high level of bilingual ability, a powerful memory and a rapid response. If the interpreters' English and Chinese language proficiency has not reached the corresponding level, they may be busy with note-taking and code-switching, and have no time or energy to think more about the cultural factors in interpreting.

This instantaneity of interpreting results in literal translation in interpreting. Indeed, in order to gain time, literal translation of the semantic meaning of the target language becomes the best strategy for many interpreters. However, literal translation of cultural factors has its inevitable defects. It often leads to misunderstanding due to cultural differences.

Therefore, free translation is considered the best strategy for interpreting cultural factors.

In Interpreting, we need to minimize the loss or misinterpreting of information. Misinterpreting of cultural factors violates the basic criterion of interpreting, the accurate and complete reproduction of the meaning of the source language. Therefore, it is necessary to strengthen the self-cultivation of cross-cultural communication awareness and cultural sensitivity. However, this is not achieved overnight. It is a gradual process of constant training and accumulation. Only through this can we gradually eliminate errors and succeed in cross-cultural communication.

Cross-cultural communication is a discipline on its own, and we can only make a brief introduction of it here in this book. We encourage students to read more related books or take relevant courses.

3.1.4 Coping Skills

Interpreting is a complex process full of challenges. It almost never happens the way you expect it to be. From preparation, to listening comprehension and memorizing, to code-switching and delivering, each link is full of variables, and many unexpected things can happen. It is how we cope with them that matters.

3.1.4.1 Coping Strategies

1. Insufficient preparation

Ideally, interpreters can fully prepare off-spot or on-spot for each interpreting job; but in reality, for many reasons, very often interpreters may not have the time for full preparation. Interpreters may be told to do an interpreting job only a few hours ahead of time, or without given any information about the content.

In these cases, interpreters should go to the interpreting location and get in contact with the main participants as soon as possible so as to have a holistic understanding of situation. Without interfering with the normal work of the organizers and participants, interpreters can try to obtain the theme, purpose, procedure and content of the event, and the nationality, professional and educational background of the speakers and audience. For prepared speakers, interpreters may ask them for their speech manuscript; for those who speak without prepared text, interpreters can ask about the general framework of the speech. If on-spot preparation is not possible, interpreters can make use of the a few minutes before the beginning of interpreting to communicate with the speakers briefly, and politely ask them to speak slower or pause for interpreters more frequently. Other information can be obtained from observing the promotional slogans, videos, brochures and billboards at the location.

In short, interpreters should seize any possible opportunity to learn as much as possible about the event without interfering with the work of all parties concerned. More detailed off

Chapter III Preparation

and on-spot preparation will be talked about in the next section of this chapter.

2. Failure to understand the speakers

In the process of interpreting, it is only ideal for interpreters to understand all of the speech information. Even for experienced interpreters who have made adequate preparation, there is still the possibility of difficulties or mistakes in listening comprehension and code-switching. There are three main reasons as follows:

a. Accents

A major difference between interpreting and translation is that interpreters deal directly with the speakers of the original text. Speakers may come from any country, region or culture in the world. Even though they try to speak the same language, most of the time, English, their pronunciation may vary greatly due to accents. In addition, different people have different educational and professional background, personal accomplishment and speaking habits. No matter for professional interpreters or interpreting learners, accents can be said to be a huge obstacle in interpreting.

However, many accents have their own regional characteristics. For example, people from France or Quebec, Canada, usually have a strong French accent:/p/ is often pronounced as /b/, /t/ as /d/, /k/ as /g/, i. e., making voiceless sounds voiced; and /r/ is often pronounced as /h/, which is similar to the pronunciation rules of French. So "two good reasons why US companies should invest in Quebec..." may sound like "Doo good heasons why US combanies should invest in Geibec..." Many other countries tend to pronounce /r/ as /l/, such as Japan and Spanish-speaking countries.

Besides regional accents, every speaker has his or her own idiolect. If possible, interpreters can communicate briefly with the speakers in advance. Many times, the speakers' particular way of speaking can be told after listening just a few sentences. In this way, interpreters can be psychologically prepared. It is also necessary to summarize the speakers' way of pronunciation while interpreting, and get used to it as soon as possible.

If accents truly affect interpreters' understanding, interpreters can only adjust their mentality and try their best to make full use of the contextual information, such as the theme of the activity, the purpose, the topic of the speech and the participants, and make full use of the skills of association, prediction and guessing. Grasping the main framework of the speech and the main viewpoints and positions, interpreters should pay attention to key points and figures and employ the translation strategies such as omission, generalization or abbreviation.

b. Language, culture and topical knowledge

Speakers and interpreters may be vastly different in cultural and educational background, resulting in various barriers in the understanding of the language, culture or topic knowledge. Language barriers refer to the difficulties in the construction of the meaning of the two languages; cultural barriers refer to the difficulties in understanding the cultural factors in languages, such as idioms, proverbs, slangs, poems, etc. ; knowledge barriers refer to the difficulties caused by the lack of encyclopedic knowledge, topical knowledge and the way to express the knowledge.

When these barriers arise, interpreters can adopt strategies such as inquiry, imitation, generalization, ellipsis, etc. Inquiry means that the interpreters can ask the speakers, the audience, other interpreters or personnel on the spot to obtain information about the parts that are not comprehensible or ambiguous.

Imitation refers to the phonetic imitation of some professional words, proper nouns, or abbreviations, because the audience may understand these words in the source language. For example, in a conference about micro-electro-mechanical system (MEMS), the abbreviation of MEMS is understood by everyone in this field, so the interpreter chose to use it directly instead of interpreting the full term. For some names and proper nouns, if there is no established translation, sometimes imitation can also be used.

Generalization refers to the strategy of interpreting information vaguely on the premise that the interpreters can understand the general direction of the speech and the general content of the information. It is applicable to the situation where there is too much redundant information in the source language, and it does not affect the communicative function of the speech. It is achieved by using more general expressions. For example, in a press conference, the speaker listed many kinds of weapons. The interpreter chose to generalize it and interpreted as "all kinds of weapons". For some long numbers, if interpreters do not have the time to note them down and specific numbers are not required, they can generalize it to round numbers. For example,"今年一季度我省的贸易额达到了三百五十一亿三千四百六十万美元" can be translated as "In the first season of this year, the total trade volume in our province reached about 35 billion US Dollars". Of Course, more accurate translation is preferable.

Ellipsis refers to the act where interpreters omit some information that is not fully understood or redundant, and it does not seem to affect the effective communication in interpreting. For example,"欢迎来自世界五大洲的学子" can be translated as "Welcome students from all over the world". "五大洲" can be omitted.

Whichever strategy is used, it must not affect the original meaning and communicative purpose of the speakers.

c. Way of speaking

Speaking too fast and incessantly: for reasons of the occasion or personal habits, some speakers speak at a high speed without stopping, forgetting the presence of the interpreters.

Interpreters should be prepared for these speakers. Depending on the situation, they can give the speakers a gentle reminder in a polite and modest manner. Of course, these reminders often fail to work. In this case, interpreters can only resort to the strategies above mentioned.

Speaking illogically: many speakers like to stray away from their speech topic and speak about all kinds of things. Some speakers don't even know what they are talking about and speak in an illogical way. In these cases, interpreters must process the source language, reorganize the information, and speak in a simple, clear and proper way.

3. Unexpected events

a. Physical discomfort

Due to heavy work load and high pressure, it's possible that interpreters may suddenly fall ill. If that happens and if not too serious, the interpreters should try their best to overcome it, reduce the workload through various strategies, and ensure that the communicative effect is not greatly affected. If the interpreters are no longer physically well enough to interpret, then they can explain the reasons and politely ask to be replaced if possible. Of course, interpreters should have a good understanding of their physical condition when they accept the task.

b. Equipment failure

On the interpreting site, various devices, including microphones, may suddenly fail to function due to power failure, battery exhaustion or other reasons. In these cases, interpreters should remain calm, if possible, continue to interpret through raising their voice, or wait for the equipment to be restored. If the speakers' equipment fails and the interpreters' hearing is affected, interpreters should promptly signal the speakers or the field staff to replace or repair the equipment. In the case of simultaneous interpreting, if the equipment fails and cannot be restored, interpreters may ask to switch to consecutive interpreting so as not to affect the activity.

c. Noises

Noises in interpreting mainly refer to all kinds of interference that may affect the interpreters' listening comprehension of the source language. They include sound interference from the audience (people talking, coughing, phone ringing, etc.), equipment noise, noise from the outside and other kinds of interference. Noise on spot can greatly affect the interpreters' work, especially when interpreting from a foreign language to mother tongue. So in such cases, interpreters should ask the relevant parties to intervene or coordinate. If the problem cannot be eliminated, interpreters can only try their best to adapt.

d. Disputes

In cross-cultural communication, disputes or even conflicts may happen on scene due to cultural differences, different interests, misunderstanding or misinterpreting. When disputes arise, interpreters should stay neutral and shoulder the responsibility of resolving contradictions and promoting communication. They need to remember that they are the bridge of the cross-cultural communication and the objective and impartial third party. At the beginning of the dispute, interpreters should try their best to filter some rude comments of the conversation, so as to continue interpreting without escalating the dispute. If the situation worsens, interpreter need to communicate with all parties patiently, and make all efforts to keep the communication going in a direction that is conducive to achieving the communicative purposes. Interpreters themselves should avoid becoming part of the dispute.

e. Mistakes by interpreters

Everyone makes mistakes. Even experienced interpreters do. In case of misinterpreting, interpreters should remain calm and quickly decide whether corrections need to be made. If mistakes are tiny and do not affect audience' understanding, then no correction is needed. But if mistakes (especially with numbers) may affect audience's understanding, cause misunderstanding, or even cause failure to achieve the desired purpose, then interpreters should acknowledge their mistakes, apologize and make correction as soon as possible.

Exercises and Practice

3-1-1 Read the following statements and decide whether they are true or false. Write T for true and F for false.

1. Active listening is what happens when one is busy doing something while some type of sound is going on around him/her—like a radio, or the television, or music.

2. During listening, one should focus on the main ideas or key points rather than single words or phrases.

3. Discourse markers are the words or sentences that express different kinds of logical connections.

4. In consecutive interpreting, there is no way for interpreters to predict what the speakers may say.

5. Extensive listening means to listen intensively for details. It usually requires learners to listen to each piece of training material multiple times, with and without text.

3-1-2 Listen to a piece of English news on current affairs and retell it in your own words. Afterwards, do more research into the topic and make it into a speech. Pay attention to the non-verbal elements in delivery. Visual aids such as PowerPoint can be used.

3-1-3 Interpret the following sentences. Pay special attention to the cultural factors in

them. If needed, free translation can be used.

1. A: It's too hot today.
   B: Why not go swimming?
   A: Good idea!
2. Thieves love crowds. Watch your wallet.
3. 这个产品老少皆宜。
4. 今天照顾不周,请多多包涵。
5. 远道而来,辛苦了,辛苦了。
6. 她是我们这儿的活雷锋。

3-1-4 Watch the Video "Cultural Awareness" (Video 3-1-4) from the European Union's interpreters' training course, and discuss with your partner what led to the embarrassing situation in the short drama.

3.2 Preparation Before Interpreting

Preparation is crucial for interpreters. Good preparation can help interpreters be more confident and less nervous. Even experienced interpreters are always well-prepared if condition allows. Preparation before interpreting can be divided into two stages: off-spot preparation and on-spot preparation. Off-spot preparation is the work done from the moment interpreters accept the tasks to arriving at the interpreting location. On-spot preparation is the work done after arriving at the location and before actually doing interpreting. Both are crucial for the success of an interpreting task.

3.2.1 Off-spot Preparation

3.2.1.1 Accepting Interpreting Tasks

Before accepting an interpreting task, interpreters should ask for the basic information of the interpreting activity and judge whether the interpreting arrangement is reasonable, whether it conforms to their own desires, habits and abilities, whether it can fit into their current itinerary, and avoid some possible problems ahead of time.

1. Types of interpreting

If it is consecutive interpreting, interpreters need to acquire the following information: is it half a day, all day or multiple days? Is it one person working all day or two people working together? How to divide the work load, according to the source languages or speakers or other ways?

If it is simultaneous interpreting, interpreters should acquire the following information: is it simple SI, or SI interlaced with CI? Has another interpreter been arranged (some clients do not understand that simultaneous interpreting requires two people)? Is the SI equipment ready for use (some clients do not know that SI requires standard equipment)? Is it half a day, all day or multiple days? Is it paid by hour or by day?

2. Interpreting topics

Interpreters work for different occasions. Many of them, especially academic conferences, involve professional knowledge that the interpreters may not be familiar with. Thus, it is necessary for interpreters to find out the specific theme and general content of the interpreting activities before taking the job, and they should not draw conclusion based on the name of the meeting alone. Interpreters should assess their competence and cautiously decide whether to take the job or not. If they do, they need to make adequate preparation based on the specific topics.

3. Interpreting time, place, itinerary, etc.

Before interpreters accept an interpreting job, they should ask for the time and location of the interpreting activity. If possible, they should ask for the itinerary so as to ensure that the work does not affect other interpreting jobs they have accepted, and they have ample time for preparation. The location should be given in details, because there is often more than one hotel of the same brand in one city. Interpreters are also advised to set aside sufficient time for changes such as flight or activity delays to make sure arriving at the location on time and the interpreting job does not affect the next task accepted.

3.2.1.2 Requesting for Relevant Information

After accepting the task, interpreters, if possible, should request for the following information from the client:

(1) Activity schedule and general information: name of the meeting, time, location, purpose, theme, detailed itinerary, etc.

(2) Speakers' brief introduction: nationality, title, working language, education and work background, honors received, etc.

(3) Audience information: educational background, occupation, field of work, purpose of participation, etc.

(4) Other information: invitation letter for this event, various announcements for this event, past similar activities, audio, video or other information of previous activities, etc.

(5) Speakers' PPT, speeches, or summaries of speeches.

(6) For academic conferences: a collection of academic papers and abstracts.

(7) For training seminars: training materials, video or audio teaching materials, student exercise, answers to exercise and other training materials.

(8) For major events or governmental events: a list of guests, presenters, etc.

(9) It should be noted that the specific itinerary of the meeting, the list of speakers and the topics of speeches often change, so they should be updated in a timely manner.

3.2.1.3 Vocabulary and Topical Knowledge Preparation

After acquiring all the information needed, interpreters need to start their preparation on related vocabulary and topical knowledge. It can be done through the following resources.

Chapter Ⅲ Preparation

1. Websites of relevant conferences or institutions

Interpreters can acquire the information about the theme, holders, sponsors, contractors, co-sponsors, keynote speakers, or other related information from the official website of the conference or websites of the institutions involved. They can familiarize themselves with the English and Chinese expressions of the organization names and titles from the website. They can also learn about the product or service to be discussed in the interpreting activity. Other information that can be downloaded from the websites of relevant institutions includes product or technology introduction, user manuals, introduction videos, etc.

2. Online encyclopedias

Interpreters can use online encyclopedias such as Wikipedia or Baidu Encyclopedia (百度百科 https://baike.baidu.com) to search for some theoretical knowledge such as definitions, concepts, origin, history, theoretical framework, research progress, future trends, phenomena, mechanisms, principles, systems, etc. It's a good idea for interpreters to search the same term in both the English version (http://www.wikipedia.org) and Chinese version (http://zh.wikipedia.org/zh-cn/) of Wikipedia, compare the two, and learn the expression of various terminology while acquiring various knowledge.

3. Digital libraries and periodical databases

Sometimes, it is necessary for interpreters to have a systematic understanding of the topical knowledge through reading journals or books related, the full text of which can often be found in some online libraries or periodical databases. One of the most well-known ones in China is CNKI (http://www.cnki.net/). Interpreters can search by theme, keywords or author to read relevant academic papers. However, these databases often charge a certain amount of money for downloading the full text. If possible, interpreters can gain access to university networks where free downloading is often provided. Many universities provide a whole range of domestic or overseas databases. Here is an example from the Northwestern Polytechnical University where the author works (Fig. 3-2).

4. Online documents

Sometimes certain information can be retrieved from documents of previous conferences, previous speeches, product manuals and online lectures. Very often they are in form of Microsoft documents, PowerPoint, or PDF. Both Baidu and Google support search for documents in different formats. Baidu Documents (百度文库, https://wenku.baidu.com) is a good source for information. Google can be accessed overseas.

5. Search engines

Search engines such as Baidu, Google, Bing and Yahoo are good friends of interpreters, especially when interpreters need to search for the translation of certain terminologies from Chinese to English. One good way is to type in the search bar the full terminology in Chinese, then choose the simplest words whose translation the interpreter is certain of, and type the translation of these words in along with the Chinese terminology. For example, the term "柔性直流输电技术", we can almost be certain that "技术" can be translated as "technique" here. So by inputting "柔性直流输电技术 technique", the translation of the whole terminology can be found. But some expressions found in the search engines may not be the authentic expressions. Interpreters need to cautiously determine whether the translation can be trusted.

Search engines can also be used to search for speakers' introduction, previous speeches or relevant photos, audios and videos. They can help interpreters familiarize themselves with the accent and way of speaking of the speakers.

Fig. 3-2 Periodical databases provided by NPU

Source: http://tushuguan.nwpu.edu.cn/test 2019/dzzy 2019/zwsjk 2019.htm(中文)
http://tushuguan.nwpu.edu.cn/test 2019/dzzy 2019/wwsjk 2019.htm(外文)

6. Dictionaries

There are many online dictionaries available for interpreters to use free of charge. Interpreters can choose based on their own preference. Baidu Translation （百度翻译, https://fanyi.baidu.com/) now provide translation of words, phrases, sentences and whole paragraphs from and to various languages. With the emergence of machine learning technology, the accuracy of the translation is now far better than previous times.

7. Clients or the professionals

Some clients prefer to communicate with the interpreters face-to-face in advance after the interpreters confirm to take the job. They would give interpreters paper and electronic materials of previous activities, and relevant information and materials of this activity. These meetings, which are directly attended by clients, are the best channels for interpreters to acquire the topical knowledge before interpreting.

3.2.1.4 Psychological Preparation

After accepting the task, interpreters need to make reasonable time arrangements. They should ensure that there is ample time for preparation. In order to be in the best state when interpreting, interpreters should have enough sleep and rest. If the interpreting location is in another city, interpreters should buy tickets in advance, arrange their itinerary and allow ample time to cope with all possible changes. If the interpreting location is in the city, interpreters should take into account factors such as traffic jams and arrive at the scene half an hour to one hour ahead of time for on-spot preparation. Before departure, interpreters need to check whether they have all the tools or materials at hand, such as laptops, batteries or power lines, wireless network cards, notebooks, multiple pens, telescopes, and various written or electronic materials, including the prepared vocabulary and topical knowledge.

3.2.2 On-Spot Preparation

On-spot preparation refers to the work done after the interpreters arrive at the location. If interpreters have done ample off-spot preparation, on-spot preparation is only to supplement or update some information. If the task is unclear or unknown, and the interpreters cannot prepare off-spot, then interpreters should arrange their time and arrive at the location several hours in advance for on-spot preparations. The amount of preparation is about the same as the off-spot preparation described earlier. Sometimes, due to factors such as coordination or confidentiality between the sponsor, co-sponsor, organizer, participant or speaker, all information or even the arrangement of activities cannot be given to the interpreters until the last moment. Interpreters should actively coordinate and cooperate with the field staff to maximize access to all kinds of information as early as possible.

Interpreters can collect information about the schedule of events, speeches, sponsors, co-sponsors, promotional materials at the sign-in desk of the conference. They can obtain other relevant materials directly from sponsors, co-sponsors or speakers, or go to the conference bulletin to find the English-Chinese comparison of conference names, sponsors, co-sponsors and other information. They should also pay attention to the posters, slogans and various publicity videos or slides being played before the conference.

Before some meetings, some clients would arrange for speakers, especially foreign speakers, to communicate briefly with interpreters. For CI, this is a good chance for interpreters to communicate with the speakers about how often they need to pause for them. In addition, interpreters can politely request the speakers to speak a bit slower. Some guests will take the initiative to communicate with the interpreters. Some may directly give their speeches to interpreters. When convenient, interpreters can also take the chance and consult the clients about some topical knowledge. If the clients are not available, interpreters can consult some guests or people from the audience on certain issues as long as they would not affect the order of the meeting.

For SI, it is necessary to check the location of the interpreting box and the sound effect of the equipment. For CI, interpreters need to find out whether their seat is convenient for them to see the projection or the speaker, and whether the distance between them and the speakers or the audience is reasonable. Interpreter also needs to know whether they are standing or sitting. If they are standing, there needs to be a fixed microphone, because they may need to take notes in the interpreting process. Interpreters also need to check the audio equipment, such as whether the microphone is working properly and whether they can hear the speakers' microphone clearly on their spot.

In a word, no matter off-spot or on-spot, SI or CI, interpreters need to resort to all sources for as much information as possible. There is never perfect interpreting. But the better-prepared the interpreters, the more likely they will succeed, and less mistakes they will make.

Exercises and Practice

3 - 2 - 1 Suppose you now have the chance to take an interpreting job for the International Conference on Artificial Intelligence. What preparation do you need to do? Consider the following questions.

1. What do you need to consider before taking the job? Make a checklist.
2. What off-spot preparation do you need to do? Make a to-do-list.
3. What on-spot preparation do you need to do? Make a to-do-list.

3 - 2 - 2 Discuss with your partner what to do in the following cases.

1. Power failure.
2. The speaker is speaking incessantly.
3. You cannot understand the terminology mentioned.
4. You don't know how to interpret the terminology mentioned.
5. The loudspeaker is making noises

Additional Materials

1. Video:"Coping Tactics"(Video 3-1) from the European Union's interpreters' training course

2. 中华人民共和国主席习近平在金砖国家工商论坛开幕式上的讲话(下)(2017年9月3日,厦门)

President Xi's speech at the opening ceremany of BRICS Business Forum(Part Ⅱ)

中文来源:新华网

http://www.xinhuanet.com/politics/2017-09/03/c_1121596338.htm

译文来源:新华网

http://www.xinhuanet.com//english/2017-09/03/c_129695215.htm

女士们、先生们、朋友们!

Ladies and Gentlemen, Dear Friends,

回首过去,是为了找准前进方向。放眼世界,我们看到世界经济重新恢复增长,新兴市场国家和发展中国家表现突出。新一轮科技革命和产业变革蓄势待发,改革创新潮流奔腾向前。我们有足够的理由相信,这个世界会更好。

Reviewing past progress helps us forge ahead in the right direction. Currently, the global economy has resumed growth, with emerging market and developing countries delivering a strong performance. A new round of technological and industrial revolution is in the making, and reform and innovation are gaining momentum. We have enough reason to believe that our world will be a better place.

同时,我们也看到,全球7亿多人口还在忍饥挨饿,数以千万的难民颠沛流离,无数民众包括无辜的孩子丧身炮火。世界经济尚未走出亚健康和弱增长的调整期,新动能仍在孕育。经济全球化遭遇更多不确定性,新兴市场国家和发展中国家发展的外部环境更趋复杂。世界和平与发展之路还很长,前行不会一路坦途。

On the other hand, more than 700 million people are still living in hunger; tens of millions of people are displaced and become refugees; so many people, including innocent children, are killed in conflicts. The global economy is still not healthy enough and remains in a period of adjustment featuring weak growth, and new growth drivers are yet to emerge. Economic globalization is facing more uncertainties. Emerging market and developing countries find themselves in a more complex external environment. The long road to global peace and development will not be a smooth one.

现在,有人看到金砖国家等新兴市场国家和发展中国家的增长出现起伏,就断言"金砖失色、褪色"。毋庸讳言,受内外复杂环境影响,金砖国家发展难免遭遇不同程度的逆风。但是,金砖国家不断向前发展的潜力和趋势没有改变。我们对此充满信心。

Some people, seeing that emerging market and developing countries have experienced growth setbacks, assert that the BRICS countries are losing their luster. It is true that affected by complex internal and external environments, we BRICS countries have encountered headwinds of varying intensity. But the growth potential and trend of our countries remain unchanged, and we are fully confident about it.

千年潮未落,风起再扬帆。面向未来,金砖国家面临着发展经济、加强合作的重要任务。我们要总结成功经验,勾画合作愿景,踏上新的征程,共同开创金砖合作第二个"金色十年"。

It is time to set sail when the tide rises. Going forward, we BRICS countries have a major task to accomplish, which is growing our economies and strengthening cooperation. We should build on past success, chart the course for future cooperation and embark on a new journey to jointly usher in the second "Golden Decade" of BRICS cooperation.

第一,深化金砖合作,助推五国经济增加动力。近年来,金砖国家凭借大宗商品供给、人力资源成本、国际市场需求等优势,引领世界经济增长。随着五国经济不断发展,资源要素配置、产业结构等问题日渐突出。同时,世界经济结构经历深刻调整,国际市场需求萎缩,金融风险积聚。金砖国家经济传统优势在发生变化,进入到滚石上山、爬坡过坎的关键阶段。

First, we should boost BRICS cooperation to create new impetus for economic growth of our five countries. In recent years, thanks to our strengths in terms of commodities supply, cost of human resources and international market demand, our five countries have driven global growth. As our five economies continue to grow, however, issues concerning resources allocation and industrial structure have become more acute. At the same time, the global economic structure is going through profound changes, evidenced by shrinking global demand and rising financial risks. All this has posed challenges to the traditional strengths of the BRICS economies, taking us to a crucial stage where we must work harder to overcome difficulties.

如何跨越这一阶段? 答案是不能片面追求增长速度,而是要立足自身、放眼长远,推进结构性改革,探寻新的增长动力和发展路径。要把握新工业革命的机遇,以创新促增长、促转型,积极投身智能制造、互联网＋、数字经济、共享经济等带来的创新发展浪潮,努力领风气之先,加快新旧动能转换。要通过改革打破制约经济发展的藩篱,扫清不合理的体制机制障碍,激发市场和社会活力,实现更高质量、更具韧性、更可持续的增长。

How should we get through this stage? Growth rate alone is not the answer. Instead, we should, on the basis of our current conditions and bearing in mind the long-term goal, advance structural reform and explore new growth drivers and development paths. We should seize the opportunity presented by the new industrial revolution to promote growth and change growth model through innovation. We should pursue innovation-driven development created by smart manufacturing, the "Internet Plus" model, digital economy and sharing economy, stay ahead of the curve and move faster to replace old growth drivers with new ones. We should eliminate impediments to economic development through reform, remove systemic and institutional barriers, and energize the market and the society, so as to achieve better quality, more resilient and sustainable growth.

金砖国家虽然国情不同,但处于相近发展阶段,具有相同发展目标。我们应该共同探索经济创新增长之道,加强宏观政策协调和发展战略对接,发挥产业结构和资源禀赋互补优势,培育利益共享的价值链和大市场,形成联动发展格局。我们要用改革创新的实践经验,为其他新兴市场国家和发展中国家抢抓机遇、应对挑战闯出一条新路。

Despite different national conditions, we BRICS countries are at a similar development stage and share the same development goals. We should jointly explore ways to boost innovation-driven growth. This requires us to improve macroeconomic policy coordination, synergize our respective development strategies, leverage our strengths in terms of industrial structure and resources endowment, and create value chains and a big market for shared interests, so as to achieve interconnected development. Basing ourselves on our own practices of reform and innovation, we should blaze a new path which may also help other emerging market and developing countries to seize opportunities and meet challenges.

经济合作是金砖机制的根基。我们应该紧紧围绕这条主线,落实《金砖国家经济伙伴战略》,推动各领域合作机制化、实心化,不断提升金砖合作含金量。今年,我们在新开发银行和应急储备安排建设、电子商务、贸易和投资便利化、服务贸易、本币债券、科技创新、工业合作、政府和社会资本合作等领域取得了一系列成果,拓展了经济合作广度和深度。我们要继续努力,落实以往的成果和共识,让现有机制发挥作用,同时积极探索务实合作新方式新内涵,拉紧联系纽带,让金砖合作行稳致远。

Economic cooperation is the foundation of the BRICS mechanism. With this focus in mind, we should implement the Strategy for BRICS Economic Partnership, institutionalize and substantiate cooperation in various sectors, and continue to enhance the performance of BRICS cooperation. This year, we have made progress in the operation of the New Development Bank and Contingent Reserve Arrangement, and in E-Commerce, trade and investment facilitation, trade in services, local currency bond issuance, scientific and technological innovation, industrial cooperation and public-private partnership, thus expanding and intensifying economic cooperation. We should continue to implement agreements and consensus already reached and better leverage the role of current mechanisms. We should also actively explore new ways and new areas of practical cooperation and strengthen our ties to ensure durable and fruitful BRICS cooperation.

第二,勇担金砖责任,维护世界和平安宁。和平与发展互为基础和前提。要和平不要冲突、要合作不要对抗是世界各国人民共同愿望。在各国一道努力下,世界总体和平得以保持半个多世纪。但是,世界仍不太平,地区冲突和热点问题一波未平、一波又起。恐怖主义、网络安全等威胁相互交织,为世界蒙上一层阴影。

Secondly, we BRICS countries should shoulder our responsibilities to uphold global peace and stability. Peace and development underpin and reinforce each other. People around the world want peace and cooperation, not conflict or confrontation. Thanks to the joint efforts of all countries, global peace has reigned for more than half a century. However, incessant conflicts in some parts of the world and hotspot issues are posing challenges to world peace. The intertwined threats of terrorism and lack of cybersecurity, among others, have cast a dark shadow over the world.

金砖国家是世界和平的维护者、国际安全秩序的建设者。今年,我们举行安全事务高级代表会议和外长正式会晤,建立常驻多边机构代表定期磋商机制,召开外交政策磋商、反恐工作组、网络安全工作组、维和事务磋商等会议,就是要加强在国际和地区重大问题上的沟通和协调,汇聚金砖合力。我们要维护联合国宪章宗旨和原则以及国际关系基本准则,坚定维护多边主义,推动国际关系民主化,反对霸权主义和强权政治。要倡导共同、综合、合作、可持续的安全观,建设性参与地缘政治热点问题解决进程,发挥应有作用。

We BRICS countries are committed to upholding global peace and contributing to the international security order. This year, we have held the Meeting of High Representatives for Security Issues and the Meeting of Ministers of Foreign Affairs/International Relations. We have put in place the regular meeting mechanism for our permanent representatives to the multilateral institutions, and convened the Foreign Policy Planning Dialogue, the Meeting of Counter-Terrorism Working Group, the Meeting of Cybersecurity Working Group, and the Consultation on Peacekeeping Operations. These efforts aim to strengthen consultation and coordination on major international and regional issues and build synergy among the BRICS countries. We should uphold the purposes and principles of the UN Charter and basic norms governing international relations, firmly support multilateralism, work for greater democracy in international relations, and oppose hegemonism and power politics. We should foster the vision of common, comprehensive, cooperative and sustainable security, and take a constructive part in the process of resolving geopolitical hotspot issues and make our due contributions.

我相信,只要坚持综合施策、标本兼治,坚决打击一切形式的恐怖主义,恐怖分子终将无处容身。只要坚持对话协商谈判,为叙利亚、利比亚、巴以等问题的政治解决创造条件,战火终将平息,流离失所的难民定能重返家园。

I am convinced that as long as we take a holistic approach to fighting terrorism in all its forms, and address both its symptoms and root causes, terrorists will have no place to hide. When dialogue, consultation and negotiation are conducted to create conditions for achieving political settlement of issues such as Syria, Libya and the Palestine-Israel conflict, the flame of war can be put out, and displaced refugees will eventually return to their homes.

第三,发挥金砖作用,完善全球经济治理。唯有开放才能进步,唯有包容才能让进步持久。

由于近年来世界经济处于疲弱期,发展失衡、治理困境、公平赤字等问题显得更加突出,保护主义和内顾倾向有所上升。世界经济和全球经济治理体系进入调整期,面临新的挑战。

Thirdly, we BRICS countries should contribute to enhancing global economic governance. Only openness delivers progress, and only inclusiveness sustains such progress. Due to sluggish global growth in recent years, such issues as uneven development, inadequate governance and deficit of fairness have become more acute, and protectionism and inward-looking mentality are on the rise. The global economy and global economic governance system, having entered a period of adjustment, face new challenges.

对经济全球化进程中出现的问题,我们不能视而不见,也不能怨天尤人,而是要齐心协力拿出解决方案。我们要同国际社会一道,加强对话、协调、合作,为维护和促进世界经济稳定和增长作出积极贡献。为此,我们应该推动建设开放型世界经济,促进贸易和投资自由化便利化,合力打造新的全球价值链,实现经济全球化再平衡,使之惠及各国人民。我们五国要相互提高开放水平,在开放中做大共同利益,在包容中谋求机遇共享,为五国经济发展开辟更加广阔的空间。

We should not ignore problems arising from economic globalization or just complain about them. Rather, we should make joint efforts to find solutions. We should work together with other members of the international community to step up dialogue, coordination and cooperation and contribute to upholding and securing global economic stability and growth. To this end, we should promote the building of an open global economy, advance trade and investment liberalization and facilitation, jointly build new global value chains, and rebalance economic globalization. Doing so will bring benefits to people across the world. We five countries should open more to each other, expand converging interests in this process, take an inclusive approach and share opportunities, so as to create even brighter prospects for growing the economies of the five countries.

新兴市场国家和发展中国家的发展,不是要动谁的奶酪,而是要努力把世界经济的蛋糕做大。我们要合力引导好经济全球化走向,提供更多先进理念和公共产品,推动建立更加均衡普惠的治理模式和规则,促进国际分工体系和全球价值链优化重塑。要推动全球经济治理体系变革,反映世界经济格局现实,并且完善深海、极地、外空、网络等新疆域的治理规则,确保各国权利共享、责任共担。

The development of emerging market and developing countries is not intended to move the cheese of anyone but to make the pie of the global economy bigger. We should join hands to steer the course of economic globalization, offer more vision and public goods, make the governance model and rules more balanced and inclusive, and improve and reshape international division of labor and global value chains. We should work to reform the global economic governance system to make it commensurate with the reality of the global economic architecture. We should also improve governance rules for the new domains of deep sea, polar regions, outer space and cyberspace, so as to ensure that all countries share both rights and responsibilities.

第四,拓展金砖影响,构建广泛伙伴关系。作为具有全球影响力的合作平台,金砖合作的意义已超出五国范畴,承载着新兴市场国家和发展中国家乃至整个国际社会的期望。金砖国家奉行开放包容的合作理念,高度重视同其他新兴市场国家和发展中国家合作,建立起行之有效的对话机制。

Fourthly, we should increase the influence of BRICS and build extensive partnerships. As a cooperation platform with global influence, BRICS cooperation is more than about our five countries. Rather, it carries the expectations of emerging market and developing countries and indeed the international community. Guided by the principle of open and inclusive cooperation, we BRICS countries place high premium on cooperation with other emerging market and developing countries and have established effective dialogue mechanisms with them.

一箭易断,十箭难折。我们应该发挥自身优势和影响力,促进南南合作和南北对话,汇聚各国集体力量,联手应对风险挑战。我们应该扩大金砖合作的辐射和受益范围,推动"金砖+"合作模式,打造开放多元的发展伙伴网络,让更多新兴市场国家和发展中国家参与到团结合作、互利共赢的事业中来。

As a Chinese saying goes, "It is easy to break one arrow but hard to break ten arrows bundled together." We should leverage our respective strengths and influence, promote South-South cooperation and North-South dialogue, pool the collective strengths of all countries and jointly defuse risks and meet challenges. We should expand the coverage of BRICS cooperation and deliver its benefits to more people. We should promote the "BRICS Plus" cooperation approach and build an open and diversified network of development partnerships to get more emerging market and developing countries involved in our concerted endeavors for cooperation and mutual benefits.

厦门会晤期间,中方将举行新兴市场国家与发展中国家对话会,邀请来自全球不同地区国家的5位领导人共商国际发展合作和南南合作大计,推动落实2030年可持续发展议程。

During the Xiamen Summit, China will hold the Dialogue of Emerging Market and Developing Countries, where leaders of five countries from different regions will be invited to join the BRICS leaders in discussing global development cooperation and South-South cooperation as well as the implementation of the 2030 Agenda for Sustainable Development.

无论是深化金砖自身合作,还是构建广泛的伙伴关系,人民相互了解、理解、友谊都是不可或缺的基石。我们应该发挥人文交流纽带作用,把各界人士汇聚到金砖合作事业中来,打造更多像文化节、电影节、运动会这样接地气、惠民生的活动,让金砖故事传遍大街小巷,让我们五国人民的交往和情谊汇成滔滔江河,为金砖合作注入绵绵不绝的动力。

Mutual understanding and friendship among peoples are crucial to enhancing BRICS cooperation and building extensive partnerships. We should fully leverage the role of people-to-people and cultural exchanges and encourage extensive public participation in BRICS cooperation. We should hold more events like cultural festivals, movie festivals and sports games that are popular among the people so that the BRICS story will be told everywhere and the exchanges and friendship of the peoples of our five countries will become an inexhaustible source of strength driving BRICS cooperation.

女士们、先生们、朋友们！
Ladies and Gentlemen, Dear Friends,

金砖合作机制不断走深走实的 10 年，也是中国全面推进改革开放、经济社会实现快速发展的 10 年。10 年中，中国经济总量增长 239%，货物进出口总额增长 73%，成为世界第二大经济体，13 亿多中国人民的生活水平实现大幅飞跃，中国为世界和地区经济发展作出的贡献也越来越大。

The past decade has not only seen solid progress in the BRICS cooperation mechanism; it has also witnessed the unfolding of all-round reform and opening up in China and its rapid economic and social development. Over these ten years, China's economic aggregate has grown by 239% and its total volume of exports and imports in goods risen by 73%. China has become the world's second largest economy, the lives of its 1.3 billion-plus people have been significantly improved, and China has made increasingly greater contribution to both regional and global economic development.

不可否认的是，随着中国改革进入攻坚期和深水区，一些深层次的矛盾和问题凸显出来，需要下大决心、花大气力加以破解。中国有句话叫良药苦口。我们采用的是全面深化改革这剂良方。这 5 年来，我们采取了 1500 多项改革举措，推动改革呈现全面发力、多点突破、纵深推进的局面，经济结构调整和产业升级步伐不断加快，经济稳中向好态势不断巩固，经济持续发展的新动能不断积聚。今年上半年，中国经济增长 6.9%，第三产业增加值占国内生产总值的 54.1%，新增城镇就业 735 万人。事实证明，全面深化改革的路走对了，还要大步走下去。

It is true that as China's reform endeavors have entered a crucial stage where tough challenges must be met, some underlying difficulties and problems have surfaced, which must be addressed with resolve and determination. As a Chinese saying goes, "Effective medicine tastes bitter." The medicine that we have prescribed for ourselves is to carry out all-round reform. Over the past five years, we have adopted over 1,500 reform measures covering all sectors, with breakthroughs made in multiple areas, and the reform is being pursued with greater intensity. The pace of economic structural adjustment and industrial upgrading has accelerated. China's economy has maintained steady and sound performance, and new drivers sustaining development have grown in strength. In the first half of this year, China's economy grew by 6.9%, the value added from services accounted for 54.1% of the GDP, and 7.35 million urban jobs were created. All these achievements have proven that deepening all-round reform is the right path that we should continue to follow.

面向未来，中国将深入贯彻创新、协调、绿色、开放、共享的发展理念，不断适应、把握、引领经济发展新常态，推进供给侧结构性改革，加快构建开放型经济新体制，以创新引领经济发展，实现可持续发展。中国将坚定不移走和平发展道路，为世界和平与发展作出新的更大贡献。

Going forward, China will continue to put into practice the vision of innovative, coordinated, green, open and inclusive development. We will adapt to and steer the new normal of economic development, push forward supply-side structural reform, accelerate the building of a new system for an open economy, drive economic development with innovation, and achieve sustainable development. China will stay firmly committed to peaceful development and make even greater contribution to global peace and development.

今年5月，中方成功主办"一带一路"国际合作高峰论坛，29个国家的元首和政府首脑，140多个国家、80多个国际组织的1600多名代表出席，标志着共建"一带一路"倡议已经进入从理念到行动、从规划到实施的新阶段。各国代表在会上共商合作大计，共谋发展良策，达成广泛共识。需要指出的是，共建"一带一路"倡议不是地缘政治工具，而是务实合作平台；不是对外援助计划，而是共商共建共享的联动发展倡议。我相信，共建"一带一路"倡议将为各国实现合作共赢搭建起新的平台，为落实2030年可持续发展议程创造新的机遇。

Last May, China successfully hosted the Belt and Road Forum for International Cooperation, which was attended by 29 heads of state or government and over 1,600 representatives from more than 140 countries and 80-plus international organizations. This ushered in a new stage of translating the Belt and Road Initiative from vision to action and from planning to implementation. Forum participants discussed ways of promoting cooperation and development and reached broad consensus. Let me make this clear: The Belt and Road Initiative is not a tool to advance any geopolitical agenda, but a platform for practical cooperation. It is not a foreign aid scheme, but an initiative for interconnected development which calls for extensive consultation, joint contribution and shared benefits. I am convinced that the Belt and Road Initiative will serve as a new platform for all countries to achieve win-win cooperation and that it will create new opportunities for implementing the 2030 Agenda for Sustainable Development.

工商界是金砖国家经济发展的主力军。10年来，工商界人士将企业发展融入金砖合作，为构建金砖经济伙伴关系作出重要贡献。把工商论坛安排在领导人会晤前夕举行，就是为了听取工商界的意见和建议，共同把厦门会晤办好，把金砖合作建设好。希望你们发挥工商界在信息、技术、资金等方面的优势，开展更多互利共赢、利国利民的务实合作项目，为促进经济社会发展、增进人民福祉作出更大贡献。中国政府将继续鼓励中国企业到其他国家落地扎根，也热忱欢迎其他国家的企业来中国投资兴业。

The business community of the BRICS countries is the main force driving our economic development. Over the last decade, you have incorporated business development into BRICS cooperation, thus making important contribution to forging BRICS economic partnerships. The reason why we are holding the Business Forum on the eve of the Summit is to solicit your views and advice, so that we can work together to make the Xiamen Summit a success and enable BRICS cooperation to deliver. I hope you will leverage your strengths in terms of information, technology and funding to launch more practical and mutually beneficial cooperation projects that benefit our countries and peoples. What you do will help spur economic and social development and improve people's lives. The Chinese government will continue to encourage Chinese companies to operate and take root in other countries, and likewise, we also warmly welcome foreign companies to invest and operate in China.

女士们、先生们、朋友们!
Ladies and Gentlemen, Dear Friends,

金砖国家将迎来更富活力的第二个十年,让我们同国际社会一道努力,让我们的合作成果惠及五国人民,让世界和平与发展的福祉惠及各国民众。
We BRICS countries will enter a second decade of more vibrant growth. Let us work together with other members of the international community. Let our cooperation deliver more benefits to the peoples of our five countries. Let the benefits of global peace and development reach all the people in the world.

最后,我预祝这次工商论坛取得圆满成功!
In conclusion, I wish the Business Forum every success.

谢谢大家。
Thank you!

MODULE II   SKILL-BASED CI TRAINING

Chapter Ⅳ　Information Processing Skills

Learning questions:
- √　What do we listen for and how to extract and analyze information?
- √　What are the different genres of discourses?
- √　How do we train our information processing skills?
- √　How is information stored?

As we have mentioned in previous chapters, information is the key in listening comprehension. When we listen, we listen for the content information instead of specific words or phrases. As CI learners, one of the most important things at the initial stage of learning is to be able to understand the speech, extract information and analyze its logical connections. In this chapter, we will learn about how to extract and analyze information, and how the information is stored.

4.1　Information Processing

4.1.1　Information Extraction and Analysis

The most important way to receive information in interpreting is to listen. As we have talked about in "Active Listening Skills" in interpreting, what we listen for is not the language, but the content information expressed. Of course language is important, without understanding the language, information extraction is hard to achieve. So to excel in CI, learners must first expand their vocabulary, and be well-trained in listening comprehension, especially in the foreign language.

For learners who have already reached certain level in English listening comprehension, they may be able to understand the language, memorize a paragraph, judge what have been said, form their own opinions, notice the speakers' specific word usage or way of speaking, or pick out mistakes in diction, grammar, rhetoric, logic, etc., but these are not what interpreters need to do. Interpreters are very special listeners. Instead of listening with their own judgments, they only need to pay attention to what the speakers are trying to express, extract and analyze the information, and memorize as much details as possible. They need to avoid paying too much attention to other irrelevant matters such as speakers' accent, pronunciation, way of speaking, clothes, gestures, personal manners, etc.

Some students may ask, what exactly is information? How is it different from the language we hear? How do we practice information extraction? In simple words, information is the idea, the meaning or the content expressed. One idea can be expressed in many language forms. So when interpreters listen, they extract the information, but they may not be able to remember exactly which words or phrases the speakers have used. Interpreters collect all of the information, and logically analyze them before storing them in their memory or notes. That is why in the process of interpreting, interpreters not only focus on understanding the language, but also on grasping of the whole idea of the speech.

Information extraction can be trained. One of the best training method is linguistic and information separation exercise, also called oral summary or retelling exercise. It can be divided into two stages: source language retelling and target language retelling. The first training stage is source language retelling, i.e., you listen to a Chinese passage, extract information, and retell in Chinese; or you listen to an English passage and retell in English. The second stage is target language retelling. That means after listening to a passage in Chinese, you need to extract information, switch language code, and retell in English, and vice versa. In retelling exercise, you need to retell the key points, and try to give as much information as possible. This is also a good exercise for memory training. This kind of practice seems simple, but there may be unexpected difficulties, such as remembering all the key points, finding the right expression, organizing the logic, etc. To learn to listen for information, not the language, is the key to successful CI training. Listening for information can also reduce the burden of memory, because memorizing meaning is easier than memorizing words.

1. Source language retelling exercise

Please read/listen to the following passages, and retell in the source language. Pay attention to the logical connections of information, and try not to recite the passages.

Passage 1

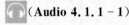(Audio 4.1.1-1)

1960年,哈佛大学的罗森塔尔博士曾在加州一所学校做过一个著名的实验。

新学期开始时,罗森塔尔博士让校长把三位教师叫进办公室,对他们说:"根据你们过去的教学表现,你们是本校最优秀的老师。因此,我们特意挑选了100名全校最聪明的学生组成三个班让你们执教。这些学生的智商比其他孩子都高,希望你们能让他们取得更好的成绩。"三位老师都高兴地表示一定尽力。校长又叮嘱他们,对待这些孩子,要像平常一样,不要让孩子或孩子的家长知道他们是被特意挑选出来的。老师们都答应了。

一年之后,这三个班的学生成绩果然排在整个学区的前列。这时,校长告诉了老师真相:这些学生并不是刻意选出来的最优秀的学生,只不过是随机抽调的最普通的学生。老师们没想到会是这样,都认为自己的教学水平确实高。这时校长又告诉他们另一个真相,那就是,他们也不是被特意挑选出的全校最优秀的教师,也不过是随机抽调的普通教师罢了。正是学校对教师的期待,教师对学生的期待,才使教师和学生都产生了一种努力改变自我,完善自我的进步动力。

　　实际上,这是心理学家进行的一次期望心理实验。他们提供的名单纯粹是随机抽取的。他们通过"权威性的谎言"暗示教师,坚定教师对名单上学生的信心。虽然教师始终把这些名单藏在内心深处,但掩饰不住的热情仍然通过眼神、笑貌、音调滋润着这些学生的心田。积极主动的态度,使学生潜移默化地受到影响,因此变得更加自信,奋发向上的激流在他们的血管中荡漾,于是他们在行动上就不知不觉地更加努力学习,结果就有了飞速的进步。这个令人赞叹不已的实验,后来被誉为"皮格马利翁效应"或"罗森塔尔效应"。"罗森塔尔效应"说明,教师对学生的态度是一种巨大的教育力量,能够改变学生的一生。

——《罗森塔尔效应》节选,来源:百度文库

Passage 2

(Audio 4.1.1-2)

　　大白鲨为何会成为海中一霸? 大家看到了,好莱坞拍的《大白鲨》电影,惊心动魄,而且也令人非常害怕。就说明大白鲨不是一般的鲨鱼,那么大白鲨之所以成为全世界公认的凶猛鲨鱼,是有它特殊的条件的。那么大白鲨之所以能成为海洋中的一霸,原因有这么四点:第一点,它生活在地球上已经有三亿多年的历史了,它有发达的大脑,可以借助电磁场的导航,把各种信息储存到大脑里。它又利用大脑把所有的信息再传递到运动神经系统,凭借着它的非常敏感的嗅觉,就能够快速出击。第二点,就是它的牙齿与众不同,它的牙齿是什么牙齿呢? 是三角形的,而且在三角形牙齿的边缘还有很多锯齿,这样的牙齿一旦咬住了别的小动物,别的小动物是难以脱身的。大白鲨所到之处都是残体和血,说明大白鲨非常凶猛。第三点,大白鲨的游速是非常快的,每小时能够达到70公里,比一般的汽车还要快。第四点,我们认为它的嗅觉是极其灵敏的,尤其是对血腥味非常敏感,敏感度相当大。为什么这么说呢? 因为科学家测定,在一万吨的海水当中即使溶进一克氨基酸,那么大白鲨也会群起而攻之,而且在几公里以外的地方,如果有点血的迹象,流点儿血,大白鲨也会快速地游过去,群起而攻之。

——节选自曹玉茹中央电视台《百家讲坛·海洋生灵——狂鲨》(有删改)

Passage 3

(Audio 4.1.1-3)

　　Most stories of Thanksgiving history start with the harvest celebration of the pilgrims and the Native Americans that took place in the autumn of 1621. Although they did have a three-day feast in celebration of a good harvest, and the local natives did participate, this "first thanksgiving" was not a holiday, simply a gathering. There is little evidence that this feast of thanks led directly to our modern Thanksgiving Day holiday. Thanksgiving can, however, be traced back to 1863 when Pres. Lincoln became the first president to proclaim Thanksgiving Day. The holiday has been a fixture of late November ever since.

—*The Origin of Thanksgiving*, Calendar of Events, Missouri State

Passage 4

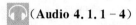(Audio 4.1.1 – 4)

Experts predict nine billion people will live on our planet by 2050. They say by that time demand for food will be two times what it is now. Officials are worried about that prediction because many people already suffer from a lack of food. More than 800 million people go to bed hungry.

A solution to the problem may be as close as our forests. A new report says forests could help reduce hunger and improve nutrition if they are properly managed. Sayay Veoun works at the Cambodian Federation for Bee Conservation. He says some of the best honey in the world comes from forests in southern Cambodia. Healthy forests provide half of the fresh fruit we eat worldwide. They also produce valuable crops like coffee, avocados, cashews and other healthful seeds and nuts.

The growing of crops requires fields. Many fields are created by clearing, or removing, trees. But properly managed fields and forests can exist together.

The report says that forest health and economic value improves when people who live in or near forests are given greater control of them. For example, a project in Ghana aims for proper management of forests and fields together. The people involved hope to grow the Allanblackia plant. The oil from its seed can be used in soap, beauty products and food. Okai Michael Henchard leads the project. He says local people earn money and get trees on their land. The trees provide shade and improve air quality. It can also helps fight climate change.

—From VOA news

Through above exercise, everyone must now be able to tell the difference between language and information. You may notice that when retelling, you may use different words or expressions to express the same ideas. Your attention is on the content rather than which words are used in the source text. In each passages, pieces of information can be extracted. For example, in the first paragraph of Passage 1, we can extract the information of "新学期""罗森塔尔""三名最优秀的老师""100名最优秀的学生""更好""像平常一样". With these information, you can retell without memorizing the original wording of each sentences. For Passage 3, we can extract the information of "Thanksgiving""harvest celebration""pilgrims" "1621""not a holiday, simply a gathering""1863""Lincoln" and "late November". With these key information, we can retell the whole paragraph.

After extracting the information, we also need to logically analyze the information so that they can be stored and clearly expressed. In logical analysis, we first need to build a logical framework, distinguish different layers of information, identify central ideas, main points, sub-points and supportive details, and then analyze the logical connections among them. For example, are they causal-effect, problem-solution, or comparison and contrast in relation? Are they in time order, spatial order, or topical order? Are they parallel in importance or advance by degrees? Are they in the same category or one is inclusive to another?

For example, in Passage 2, we can tell the speaker is talking about the great white shark and how it becomes the world's most ferocious shark. Four reasons are given. These four reasons are in parallel relationship, and together they form a causal-and-effect relationship with the beginning of the passage, which gives the result— the great white shark is the world's most ferocious shark. In Passage 4, we can tell a problem-and-solution relationship at the beginning of the passage, and then a causal-and-effect relationship can be found when explaining why forest is the solution.

2. Source + target language retelling exercise

Please read/listen to the following passages, and retell first in the source language. Analyze the logical connections of information, and try to retell following the logical connections. Then try your best to retell in the target language. You can skip the terminologies that you don't know and check them later.

Passage 1

(Audio 4.1.1-5)

美国华盛顿广场有一座宏伟的建筑,这就是杰弗逊纪念馆大厦。这座大厦历经风雨沧桑,年久失修,表面斑驳陈旧。政府非常担心,派专家调查原因。

调查的最初结果以为侵蚀建筑物的是酸雨,但后来的研究表明,酸雨不至于造成那么大的危害。最后才发现原来是冲洗墙壁所含的清洁剂对建筑物有强烈的腐蚀作用,而该大厦墙壁每日被冲洗的次数大大多于其他建筑,因此腐蚀就比较严重。

问题是为什么每天清洗呢?因为大厦被大量的鸟粪弄得很脏。为什么大厦有那么多鸟粪?因为大厦周围聚集了很多燕子。为什么燕子专爱聚集在这里?因为建筑物上有燕子爱吃的蜘蛛。为什么这里的蜘蛛特别多?因为墙上有蜘蛛最喜欢吃的飞虫。为什么这里的飞虫这么多?因为飞虫在这里繁殖特别快。为什么飞虫在这里繁殖特别快?因为这里的尘埃最适宜飞虫繁殖。为什么这里的尘埃最适宜飞虫繁殖?其原因并不在尘埃,而是尘埃在从窗子照射进来的强光作用下,形成了独特的刺激致使飞虫繁殖加快,因而有大量的飞虫聚集在此,以超常的激情繁殖,于是给蜘蛛提供了丰盛的大餐。蜘蛛超常的聚集又吸引了成群结队的燕子流连忘返。燕子吃饱了,自然就地方便,给大厦留下了大量粪便。

因此解决问题的最终方法是:拉上窗帘。杰弗逊大厦至今完好。有些问题并不像我们看起来的那样复杂,只是我们还没有找到解决问题的简单办法。

——《小故事大道理》之《杰弗逊大厦》,来源:360doc

Passage 2

(Audio 4.1.1-6)

最多变的自卫——章鱼是一个什么样的动物?我们说章鱼在海洋当中是非常厉害的一种动物,而且它是一霸。因为章鱼本身有五大法宝,不像有的动物,自卫能力就只有一种。章鱼的自卫有五大法宝在它身上,不得了,其他动物可不敢欺负它。

它的第一个法宝就是它有八条触手,像带子一样在海中漂浮着,所以有的渔民又把章鱼叫做八带鱼。那么它的八条触手每一条触手上有 300 个吸盘,每一个吸盘的吸力有 100 克(力[①])。大家想想看,比如说我们找一个 20 公斤的,体长 3 米的一个章鱼,它的总的吸附力能够达到 24 万克,也就是 240 公斤,这个可不简单。

第二个法宝,章鱼能够变色,而且章鱼变色的能力在所有的海洋动物当中是首屈一指的,为什么这么说?因为它本身一次可以变出六种颜色,这相当不简单了。如果它碰到了石头,碰到了礁石或者再碰到别的环境,它的身体马上改变颜色,和周围一样,让对方看不出来旁边还有个动物。

第三个法宝,章鱼能够喷射墨汁,原来章鱼身体里有一个墨囊,它能一次、两次,或者连续六次向外喷射墨汁,来保护自己。

第四个法宝就是它的再生能力,如果章鱼碰到劲敌,当然能逃的话它就逃跑,如果逃跑不了,没有退路了,怎么办?它只好把它的八条触手扔出几条给对方,对方一看有吃的了,它可能就先不攻击章鱼了,就把这几条触手先吃了。趁此机会章鱼赶快溜走。它过不了几天又会长出一个新的触手,而且就在它断触手的地方,这个肌肉使劲收缩,而且也不留血,这也是低等动物的一个非常特殊的习性。

第五个法宝,就是它有脱身的绝技。为什么说章鱼有脱身的绝技?我先给大家讲一个小故事。有一位学者拿着一个篮子,这篮子的网眼有 5 厘米,在一个篮子放了一个小章鱼上了电车。上了电车以后,过了没有多长时间,就听见后边座位上的一位绅士歇斯底里地叫起来了。哎呀,这是怎么回事呢?他怎么会叫起来呢?这个先生一看,自己篮子里边的章鱼没了,原来逃出去了,吓坏了后面的那位先生。说明章鱼能够把自己的身体变成饼一样。但是同志们可能要提一个问题,它离开海水怎么能活?我们说章鱼本身有一个套膜腔,在套膜腔里头可以有些海水,它可以用套膜腔里的海水里面的氧,可以供它三两天的生活,所以说章鱼这五大法宝是任何海洋动物都比不了的,要说自卫,章鱼堪称海洋之首。

——节选自曹玉茹中央电视台《百家讲坛:海洋生灵——千奇百怪的自卫》(有删改)

---

① 1 gf(克力) = 9.807×10⁻³ N

Passage 3

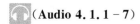(Audio 4.1.1 - 7)

Four best friends met at the hospital since their wives were giving births to their babies. The nurse comes up to the first man and says, "Congratulations, you got twins." The man said, "How strange, I'm the manager of Minnesota Twins." After a while the nurse comes up to the second man and says, "Congratulations, you got triplets." The man was like "Hmmm, strange I worked as a director for the '3 Musketeers'." Finally, the nurse comes up to the third man and says, "Congratulations, you got twins×2." The man is happy and says, "Ironic, I work for the hotel '4 Seasons'." All three of them are happy until they see their last buddy jumping all over the place, cursing God and banging his head on the wall. They asked him what's wrong and he answered, "What's wrong? I work for 7up!"

Passage 4

Experts say that sun and wind are the richest sources of clean, renewable energy. But ocean waves also create powerful, clean energy. So, the U.S Department of Energy has announced a $1.5 million-dollar prize for the winner of a competition on how to capture that energy.

The Department of Energy says that waves and tides along U.S. coasts create about 1,420 terawatt-hours of energy a year. This is equal to the amount of energy produced by more than 330 nuclear power factories.

But today's technologies can only capture about 20 percent of the energy from ocean waves. Jose Zayas is the director of the Wind and Water Power Technologies Office at the Department of Energy. He says 20 percent is too low for an investment in ocean wave energy to be economical. He says it needs to be up in the high 30 percent to 40 percent.

The Department of Energy has launched the Wave Energy Prize competition to encourage development of new technologies. But developing new devices to capture wave energy can be difficult. Wave capture machines must operate in oceans.

Competition organizers expect most of the new ideas to come from established energy companies as well as some universities and research centers. Mr. Zayas says testing the new technologies will be done in several steps using a scaled model. A scaled model is a smaller form of a larger object or structure.

The scaled models will be tested at the United States Navy's largest indoor testing pool near Washington. Machines at the pool can create ocean-size waves. Mr. Zayas says the models will be tested to show how much ocean wave energy they can capture.

The competition will not require the machines to produce electrical power. He says changing the mechanical kinetic energy into electrical energy is easy.

Mr. Zayas says the main goal of the Wave Energy Prize is to develop a new set of power producing technologies for the future. Developers of the best performing devices will receive prizes from $250,000 to as much as $1.5 million.

—From VOA News

4.1.2　Information Processing – Discourse Analysis

As we have mentioned, in information processing, we not only need to focus on the extraction and analysis of the information in each sentences, but also on the logic and structure of the whole text. This is called discourse analysis. Discourse analysis can better help us predict what is to come in interpreting.

4.1.2.1　Logical Structures

1. Chronological or sequential structures

This organizing principle follows a time pattern. It narrates a series of events in the sequence in which they happened, or steps of how certain things are done. It involves putting facts, events, or concepts in order of occurrence. To show in graphs:

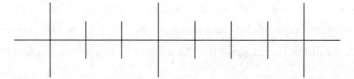

Fig. 4-1　chronological order

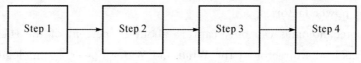

Fig. 4-2　sequential order

2. Spatial structure

This organizing principle follows a directional pattern. That is, the main points proceed from top to bottom, left to right, front to back, inside to outside, east to west, or some other routes.

3. Comparison and contrast structures

This structure shows how two or more ideas or items are similar or different. There are two approaches for this structure: cluster approach and point-by-point approach.

Cluster approach is to introduce one item entirely and then introduce the other one entirely. Then analyze their similarities and differences.

Point-by-point approach is to introduce one aspect of the two items, and compare their similarities and difference, and then move on to the next aspect.

To show in graphs:

Chapter IV Information Processing Skills

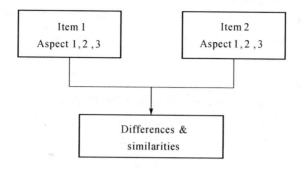

Fig. 4‐3 Cluster approach

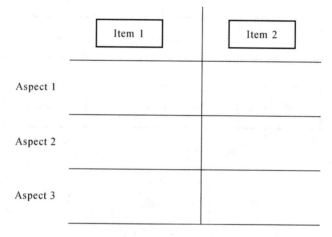

Fig. 4‐4 Point-by-point approach

4. Causal-effect structure

Causal-effect structure organizes main points so as to show a causal-effect relationship. This structure usually starts with the result (effect) of certain event, and then lay out the reasons (causes) for this result. To show in graph:

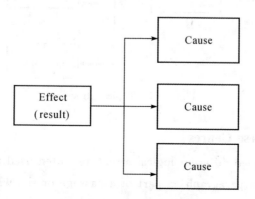

Fig. 4‐5 Causal-effect structure

5. Problem-solution structure

Problem-solution structure is divided into two main parts. First it presents a problem, then it shows how it can be or has been solved and the effects of the solution. This structure is shown in Fig. 4-6.

6. Topical structure

Topical structure results when the speech topic is divided into sub-topics, each of which becomes a main point. This structure is shown in Fig. 4-7.

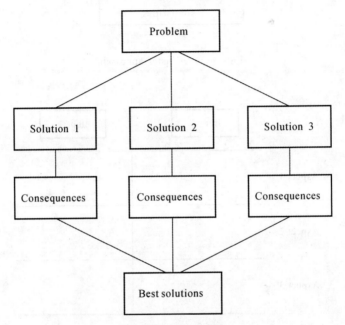

Fig. 4-6 Problem-solution structure

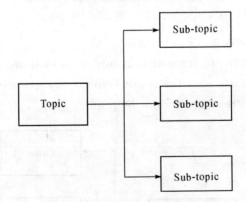

Fig. 4-7 Topical structure

4.1.2.2 Discourse Genres

Just now, we analyzed different logical structures often used in speeches. They can be the logical structure of a paragraph, a part of a passage or the whole passage. Next, let's focus on the analysis of interpreting language and discourse genres.

Chapter IV Information Processing Skills

In interpreting, the language we receive and analyze is mainly spoken language, but it is not exactly the same as the spoken language we use in our daily life, which is very casual with many allegorical sayings, slangs, colloquial and witty words. Language style can be roughly divided into five categories:frozen（庄严体）, formal, general, informal and causal. The spoken language in daily life is rarely frozen or formal, and there are no formal rhetoric or established structures which are unique to formal occasions. The logic and structure is comparatively loose.

The spoken language in interpreting also includes daily spoken language, but more often, the language is in more formal, general or frozen style, and established expressions are often used. The topics involved are also often political, economic, and scientific and technological, and the occasions may include diplomacy, conference, negotiation, technical discussion, product introduction, business communication, legal disputes, cultural exchanges, and academic discussions. This kind of language is more logical, informative and specialized. It has certain discourse structure and pays more attention to wording. It contains a large amount of condensed information and is usually harder to remember. In some cases, notes are needed. So our language in daily life is largely different from that in interpreting. But one thing to note is that the language in interpreting is after all spoken. Though formal, it is not written language.

In interpreting learning, we call it the "working language" of interpreting. Usually in interpreting, the discourses can be divided into four genres: narrative, introductory, argumentative and associative.

1. Narrative（叙述类）

Narrative discourse structure is mainly used in allusions, stories or jokes. In interpreting, it usually has a chronological nature, which means it generally follows a time clue. Different from the narratives in literature works in which several clues may unfold at the same time, and different from the random nature of daily language, the narrative discourse structure in interpreting is mainly manifested in a linear progression of time, supplemented by descriptions of space, scenery, characters, etc. In the beginning, or the introduction part, there is usually an "introductory sentence" to give a sense of "the story is beginning" by using some established expressions, such as "Let me tell you a story""I have heard of such a story""The legend goes..." In this part, the speaker will often illustrate the time, place and main characters of the story, and maybe create some suspense. Following the introduction is the development of the story. Then there is often a climax, and finally the ending. Generally speaking, very few narrative discourse would violate this general structure.

The narrative structure is logically clear, and is usually easier for interpreters to remember. Interpreters can easily tell where the speakers are in discourse, and many times they can predict what is to come. The narrative structure can be shown in Figure 4-8.

◉ **Discourse analysis exercise**

Please analyze the following passages with what we have learned about the narrative structure, and then retell the passages in the source language.

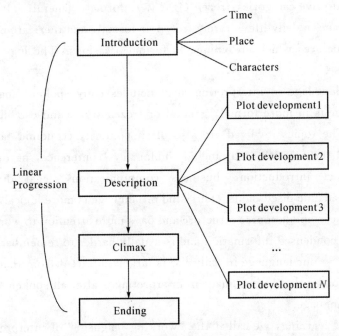

Fig. 4-8 Narrative structure

Passage 1

最致命的自卫——水母。在讲这个之前,给大家讲一个有意思的事情。什么事情呢?就是在一家天然的海滨浴场,大人们已经游完泳了,休息了。还有好多小朋友,他们兴致不减,互相戏耍打闹。在这个时候,其中有一个小朋友,他游在最前边,看到了一个像小伞一样的东西往自己这边游。其中有一个岁数稍微大一点的,也就是十四五岁的这个孩子他游得非常快,游到那儿以后,他就抓住了这个非常漂亮的"绸带",手抓住以后不要紧,他"哇"的一声叫了起来。这时候就看到最先摸到漂亮"绸带"的这个少年,已经失去了游泳的能力。大家赶快把他送到了医院,幸亏抢救及时,最后他的胳膊上全都是一条一条的红印,那么大家去想这到底是什么动物?我们今天说的是水母,原来水母是这么可怕。

——节选自曹玉茹中央电视台《百家讲坛·海洋生灵——千奇百怪的自卫》(有删改)

Passage 2

When I was young, I went looking for gold in California. I never found enough to make me rich, but I did discover a beautiful part of the country. It was called the Stanislaus.

By the time I reached the Stanislaus, all the people were gone. As I walked through the empty town that summer day so long ago, I realized I was not alone after all. A man was smiling at me as he stood in front of one of the little houses. Still smiling, the man opened the door of his house and motioned to me. I went inside, and could not believe my eyes. I saw a bright rug on the shinning wooden floor. Pictures hung all around the room and on little tables there were seashells, books and china vases full of flowers. A woman had made this house into a home.

The pleasure I felt in my heart must have shown on my face. The man read my thoughts. "Yes." he smiled:"It is all her work. Everything in this room has felt the touch of her hand." I looked around. When my eyes reached the corner of the room near the fireplace. He broke into a happy laugh. I went to a little black shelf that held a small picture of the most beautiful woman I had ever seen. "She was nineteen on her last birthday that was the day we were married. When you see her, oh, just wait until you meet her!""Where is she now?" I asked. "Oh, she is away." the man sighed putting the picture back on the little black shelf. "She went to visit her parents. They live forty or fifty miles from here. She has been gone two weeks to date.""When will she be back?" I asked. "Well, this is Wednesday." He said slowly, "She will be back on Saturday, in the evening.""I'm sorry, because I will be gone by then," I said. "Gone? No, why should you go? Don't go. She will be so sorry. You see, she likes to have people come and stay with us." I decided to stay. The man told me his name was Henry.

That night Henry and I talked about many different things but mainly about her. The next day passed quietly. Thursday evening, we had a visitor. He was a big gray hair miner named Tom. "I just came for a few minutes and ask when she is coming home." He explained. The next day, Friday, another old miner came to visit. Saturday finally came. I found I was looking at my watch very often. I was glad to see his two friends Tom and Joe coming down the road as the sun began to set. The old miners were carrying guitars. They also brought flowers and a bottle of whiskey. They put the flowers in vases and began to play some fast and lovely songs on their guitars. Henry's friends kept giving him glasses of whiskey which they made him drink. When I reached for one of the two glasses left on the table, Tom stopped my arm. "Drop that glass and take the other one." He whispered. He gave the remaining glass of whiskey to Henry just as the clock began to strike midnight.

Henry emptied the glass. His face grew whiter and whiter. "Boys," He said, "I am feeling sick. I want to lie down!" Henry was asleep almost before the words were out of his mouth. In a moment his two friends had picked him up and carried him into the bedroom. They closed the door and came back. They seemed to be getting ready to leave. So I said:

"Please don't go, gentlemen. She will not know me; I am a stranger to her." They looked at each other. "His wife has been dead for nineteen years!" Tom said. "Dead?" I whispered. "She went to see her parents about six months after she got married, on the way back, on a Saturday evening in June, when she was almost here, Indians captured her. No one ever saw her again. Henry lost his mind. He thinks she is still alive. When June comes, he thinks she has gone on her trip to see her parents. Then he begins to wait for her to come back. On the Saturday night she is supposed to come home. We come here to be with him. We put a sleeping drug in his drink so he will sleep through the night. Then he's all right for another year. We have done this every June for nineteen years." He said, "The first year there were twenty-seven of us. Now just the two of us are left." He opened the door of the pretty little house, and the two old men disappeared into the darkness of the Stanislaus.

—Adapted from *"The Californian's Tale"* written by Mark Twain

2. Introductory（介绍类）

The introductory, or descriptive genre, is often seen in the introduction to scientific or technological products, commodities, people, scenic spots, corporations, organizations, etc. The clues of this genre are mainly developed according to the law of human cognition: before formal introduction, there is often an introductory paragraph, in which the speakers sometimes use some rhetorical devices to attract the attention of the audience. In the introduction part, the description is mostly done from the surface to the inside, from the superficial to the deep, basically in line with the way of thinking of most people. The "main line" can sometimes follow a spatial or temporal order. There is usually a summary at the end of the text.

Texts from the introductory genre contain a large amount of information. Interpreters may need to take some notes to memorize all of the information. But the content is usually easy to understand except for some terminologies. The introductory structure can be shown in Figure 4-9.

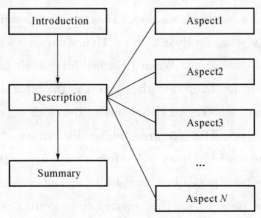

Fig 4-9 Introductory structure

Chapter Ⅳ　Information Processing Skills

⊙**Discourse analysis exercise**

Please analyze the following passages with what we have learned about the introductory structure, and then retell the passages in the source language.

Passage 1

　　西北工业大学(以下简称西工大)坐落于陕西西安,是一所以发展航空、航天、航海(三航)等领域人才培养和科学研究为特色的多科性、研究型、开放式大学,是国家"一流大学"建设高校(A类),隶属于工业和信息化部。新中国成立以来,西工大一直是国家重点建设的高校,1960年被国务院确定为全国重点大学,"七五""八五"期间均被国务院列为重点建设的全国15所大学之一,1995年首批进入"211工程",2001年进入"985工程",是"卓越大学联盟"成员高校,先后获得"全国文明单位""全国创先争优先进基层党组织""全国毕业生就业典型高校""全国文明校园"等荣誉称号和表彰奖励。学校秉承"公诚勇毅"校训,弘扬"三实一新"(基础扎实、工作踏实、作风朴实、开拓创新)校风,扎根西部、献身国防,历史上书写了新中国多个"第一",今天在创建一流大学和一流学科上续写新的辉煌。

　　学校办学资源富集,学科特色鲜明。现有学生31 000余名,教职工4000余人,占地面积近5400亩,设有23个专业学院和国际教育学院、教育实验学院、西北工业大学伦敦玛丽女王大学工程学院。拥有67个本科专业,34个硕士学位一级授权学科,21个博士学位一级授权学科,21个博士后流动站。其中,材料科学、工程学、化学、计算机科学、物理学等5个学科群进入ESI国际学科排名前1%,形成了以三航学科群为引领,3M(材料、机电、力学)学科群、3C(计算机、通信、控制)学科群、理科学科群和人文社科学科群协调发展的学科体系,为建设世界一流学科奠定了良好的基础。

　　学校坚持引培并重,打造人才高地。实施从青年教师到杰出学科带头人全过程的"翱翔人才工程",构建青年教师成长支持体系,建设层级合理的人才梯队。完善准长聘机制,激发人才活力。打造优质中小幼服务,为人才解决后顾之忧。设立校内人才特区、海外工作特区,形成高端人才聚集的环境和效应。学校现有两院院士(含外聘)34人、长江学者44人、万人领军计划人才20人、国家杰出青年基金获得者20人、国家教学名师奖获得者4人;现有国家自然科学基金委创新研究群体2个、国家级教学团队7个、教育部创新团队7个、国防创新团队8个。

　　学校立德树人,精心育才。"以学生为根、以育人为本、以学者为要、以学术为魂、以责任为重"的办学理念深植人心,着力培养具有家国情怀、追求卓越、引领未来的领军人才。历史上,铸造、航空宇航制造工程、飞行力学、航空发动机、水中兵器、火箭发动机等6个学科的全国第一位工学博士由我校培养。在我校为国防科技事业发展和国民经济建设输送的20万多名校友中,有48位省部级以上领导和64位将军,48位两院院士,还有6位中国十大杰出青年。在航空领域,一半以上的重大型号总师、副总师为我校校友。中国航空工业成立60周年纪念表彰了10位"航空报国特等金奖",6位西工大校友获此殊荣,在中航工业先后授予的6名"中青年自主创新领军人才"中西工大校友占到4位;在航天领域,从早年的"航天三少帅"中的张庆伟和雷凡培,到中国探月工程总设计师吴伟仁等,一大批西工大杰出校友担任集团公司、院所、企业党政领导干部及副总师以上职务,相继为我国航天事业的飞速发展做出了突出贡献;航海领域同样有大批的杰出校友活跃在船舶工业、水中兵器行业的重要管理岗位与核心技术岗位上,英才辈出,不胜枚举。大批西工大学子成为行业精英、国之栋梁,在人才培养领域形成了独有的"西工大现象"。

——节选自西北工业大学网站(数据截至 2019 年 12 月)

Passage 2

Apple Inc. is an American multinational technology company headquartered in Cupertino, California, that designs, develops, and sells consumer electronics, computer software, and online services.

Its hardware products include the iPhone smartphone, the iPad tablet computer, the Mac personal computer, the iPod portable media player, the Apple Watch smart watch, and the Apple TV digital media player. Apple's consumer software includes the OS X and iOS operating systems, the iTunes media player, the Safari web browser, and the iLife and iWork creativity and productivity suites. Its online services include the iTunes Store, the iOS App Store and Mac App Store, and iCloud.

Apple was founded by Steve Jobs, Steve Wozniak, and Ronald Wayne on April 1, 1976, to develop and sell personal computers. It was incorporated as Apple Computer, Inc. on January 3, 1977, and was renamed as Apple Inc. on January 9, 2007, to reflect its shifted focus toward consumer electronics. Apple joined the Dow Jones Industrial Average on March 19, 2015.

—Excerpt from Wikipedia

3. Argumentative(论证类)

This genre is commonly used in interpreting and is one of the typical discourse structures of the working language of interpreting. This discourse structure is highly logical, with "argument + supportive evidence" as its main structure. Generally speaking, with frequent use of logical connectors, this genre has a clear structure and rigorous logic. Of course, speakers may sometimes stray away from the topic.

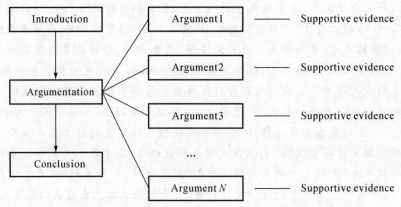

Fig. 4-10 Argumentative structure

Chapter IV Information Processing Skills

The argumentative genre is comparatively more challenging for interpreters than the other genres. Generally speaking, the argumentative genre is closer to written language. The language is often formal, with their own unique and formal established structures. In most cases, they are composed of long compound sentences, which may contain a large amount of information and are harder to understand. This brings considerable difficulties to interpreters. Very often, interpreters need to resort to note-taking to memorize all of the information. The structure of the argumentative genre is shown in Figure 4 – 10.

⊙**Discourse analysis exercise**

Please analyze the following passages with what we have learned about the argumentative structure, and then retell the passages in the source language.

Passage 1

中国新一轮的改革涵盖政治、经济、文化、社会、生态文明五大方向,涉及15个方面、60多个领域,共形成300多项重要举措。改革的范围之广、程度之深、难度之大可谓前所未有。大家可能最想知道的是,这一轮改革能否再获成功,续写辉煌?改革将给世界带来什么?我愿明确告诉大家,我们对于中国改革的成功充满自信。

——自信来自于中华民族5000年自强不息的优秀传统和博大精深的文明底蕴。中华民族曾历经无数危难,面对各种考验,却始终百折不挠,生生不息,一个重要的原因就是我们这个民族勇于自我革新,敢于自我超越。中国人在任何时候都不怕改革,乐于改革,善于改革。

——自信来自于中国业已选择的正确道路。新中国成立65年来,我们经过上下求索,找到了一条完全符合中国国情并且得到全体人民拥护的发展道路,这就是中国特色社会主义道路。实践已经并将继续证明,只要坚持这一方向,不偏离这条道路,中国就能保持发展活力,获得发展动力。

——自信来自于中国共产党的坚强有力领导。作为执政党,中国共产党拥有8600万党员。这是中国发展最独特的优势和最重要的资源。只要8600万党员团结一心,就能迸发出无与伦比的强大正能量,就能在改革进程中无坚不摧,无难不克。

——自信来自于中国业已打下的坚实基础和积累的丰富经验。改革开放以来,中国从贫穷走向富裕,从摸着石头过河到形成系统理论支撑和完整政策体系。我们不仅清晰地把握了自身存在的各种问题,也完全具备了解决这些问题的能力。

——自信来自于中国巨大的发展空间与潜力。中国是一个拥有13亿人口和960万平方公里领土的大国,发展空间极为广阔,发展潜力远未发掘。目前,中国的城乡差距、中西部与东部差距还很大,这既是中国面临的重大课题,更是未来发展的希望所在。随着改革的深入,中国的巨大需求将波浪式持续释放,长久地推动中国经济保持强劲发展势头。

——自信来自于中国奉行的互利共赢开放战略。中国改革最成功的一条经验就是,改革与开放并行推进,通过改革扩大开放,又通过开放促进改革。中国的改革成果将更多惠及世界,同时也会从世界不断汲取改革的动力。

——节选自王毅外长在世界经济论坛2014年年会上的演讲《中国新发展 世界新机遇》

Passage 2

It gives me a great pleasure to join you for this important initiative as the UN marks its 70th anniversary.

Education is very close in my heart. My father grew up in a very small village in China. In those days, not many villagers could read. So my father opened a night school to teach them how to read. With his help, many people learned to write their own names; with his help many people learned to read newspapers for the first time; with his help, many women were able to teach their children how to read.

As his daughter, I know what education means to the people, especially those without it. After generations of hard work, China has come a long way in education. I myself am a beneficiary of that progress. Otherwise I would never become a soprano and a professor of musical. I am following my father's footsteps by teaching at China's Conservatory of Music to help continue China's success story. I want to thank Director-General Bokova and UNESCO for naming me the Special Envoy for Women and Girls Education. I am truly honored to work with the UN and do something about Global Education. I have visited many schools around the world. I've seen first-hand on how much we can do for education.

Education is about women and the girls. It is important for girls to go to school because they will become their children's first teacher someday. But women still account for over half of the world's poor in population and 60% of adults who can't read.

Education is crucial in the addressing such inequalities. In China, Spring Bud Education Program has helped over 3 million girls go back to school. Many of them have finished university education and they are doing well at work.

Education is about equality. In poor countries and regions, the number of school dropouts is astonishing. We call for more educational resources to these places.

Education is about the young people. Young people are the future. Education is important because it not only gave young people knowledge and skills but also help them become responsible citizens. As the UNESCO special envoy and the mother myself my commitment to education for all will never change.

Many years ago my father made a small difference in his village. Together we can make a big difference in the world. I was once asked about my Chinese dream. I said I hope all children especially girls can have access to good education. This is my Chinese dream. I believe one day education first will no longer be a dream, it will be a reality enjoyed by every young woman on this planet.

——节选自彭丽媛出席联合国"教育第一"全球倡议高级别会议讲话

4. Associative（联想类）

The associative genre is the type of speech with no specific topic. It is like free association. The speaker may speak about one topic, then jump to the next relevant one based on association, and then to the next. The logic and structure are quite loose. It is close

Chapter Ⅳ Information Processing Skills

to our daily language, and is often seen in casual meetings or conversation before and after the formal meetings. Though seemingly illogical, there are some hidden logical traces that can be found. The topics associated from the original one can be similar or contradictory in nature. This genre can challenge interpreters' memory, but the language is usually simple conversational language. The structure of the argumentative genre is shown in Figure 4 - 11.

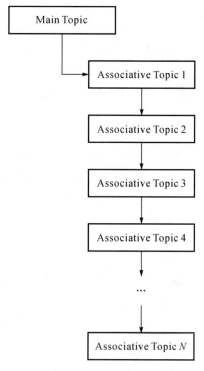

Fig 4 - 11 Associative structure

⊙ **Discourse analysis exercise**

Please analyze the following discourse with what we have learned about the associative structure, and then retell the discourse in the source language.

　—Chinese company: I hope we can do some business with you.

　—Buyer: I'm sure we will. No problem.

　—Chinese company: Excellent.

　—Buyer: We do need to consider the environmental issues.

　—Chinese company: I'm sorry?

　—Buyer: I was wondering about the waste water flowing back to the river.

　—Chinese company: We have a very good system in place which conforms to regional standards.

　—Buyer: Yes, but if you increase your production for extra demand, we have to consider upgrading the water system. (Interpreter tries to cut in) I have a friend who makes and installs water filtering system. (Interpreter tries to cut in) As far as the water filtering system goes, it's probably one of the best companies in the world. It's all state-of-art stuff.

He does a lot of work in Scandinavia where they have some pretty tough regulations when it comes to the environment. I can tell you. (Interpreter tries to cut in) He also does a lot of work in Eastern Europe where they have some very big environmental problems to deal with. (Interpreter tries to cut in) Just let me finish, it's not that I think you've got a problem at the moment, but if you do increase your production. (Interpreter tries to cut in) The other thing is that Mike, he always delivers on time and he always stick to the original price. You wouldn't have to worry about a thing. Why don't I get Mike to give you a call? He's indeed a wonderful guy. You'll like him. Actually...

—Transcribed from the video "Coping Tactics" from the European Union's interpreters' training course (Video 3-1)

Exercises and Practice

4-1-1 Read/Listen to the following passages. Extract information from them and analyze their logical structures. Choose the right logical structure for each passage. Then work with your partner, and retell these passages either in the source language or the target language.

A. Chronological structure

B. Spatial structure

C. Causal-effect structure

D. Problem-solution structure

E. Comparison and contrast structure

F. Topical structure

(　　)1. Passage 1

(　　)2. Passage 2

(　　)3. Passage 3

(　　)4. Passage 4

Passage 1

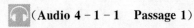(Audio 4-1-1 Passage 1)

The rivalry between Microsoft and Apple to dominate the technological industry and markets has seen major developments in the industry. Their achievements have been tremendous in the past years, and in 2012, according to the Fortune list, Apple was perched at position 17 while Microsoft was at 37. Apple Incorporated was initially known as Apple computer Incorporated mainly focuses on the production and designing of electronics like Smartphone while Microsoft develops, produces licenses, and supports software applications for computers.

One of the similarities between the two companies is based on their founders; they are both founded on the ideas of genius self-motivated businessmen. Both companies have Tablet devices; as Apple manufactures iPad, Microsoft produces Surface. They are both designed with a touch screen, they are of the same thickness, both were secretly unveiled, and they both fall in the premium group in the tablet souk.

In the electronic sector, Apple is well known for designing personal computers and entertainment devices like iPod. The products have gone through a series of advancement to meet the needs of the consumers. On the contrary, Microsoft is known in relation to its operating systems and applications, like Windows and the Office. Apple has also ventured in software and boasts of producing iLife and the famous multimedia software.

—Source Unknown

Passage 2

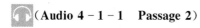(Audio 4-1-1　Passage 2)

The Eiffel Tower is the most-visited paid monument in the world; 6.91 million people ascended it in 2015. The tower is 324 metres (1,063 ft) tall, about the same height as an 81-storey building, and the tallest structure in Paris. Its base is square, measuring 125 metres (410 ft) on each side. Excluding transmitters, the Eiffel Tower is the second tallest free-standing structure in France after the Millau Viaduct.

The tower has three levels for visitors, with restaurants on the first and second levels. The top level's upper platform is 276 m (906 ft) above the ground—the highest observation deck accessible to the public in the European Union. The climb from ground level to the first level is over 300 steps, as is the climb from the first level to the second. Although there is a staircase to the top level, it is usually accessible only by lift.

—From Wikipedia

Passage 3

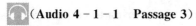(Audio 4-1-1　Passage 3)

二战期间,一支部队在森林中与敌军相遇并发生激战,最后两名战士与部队失去了联系。他们之所以在激战中还能互相照顾、彼此不分,是因为他们是来自同一个小镇的战友。两人在森林中艰难跋涉,互相鼓励、安慰。十多天过去了,他们仍未与部队联系上,幸运的是,他们打死了一只鹿,依靠鹿肉又可以艰难度过几日了。可也许因战争的缘故,动物四散奔逃或被杀光,这以后他们再也没看到任何动物。仅剩下的一些鹿肉,背在年轻战士的身上。这一天他们在森林中遇到了敌人,经过再一次激战,两人巧妙地避开了敌人。就在他们自以为已安全时,只听到一声枪响,走在前面的年轻战士中了一枪,幸亏在肩膀上。后面的战友惶恐地跑了过来,他害怕得语无伦次,抱起战友的身体泪流不止,赶忙把自己的衬衣撕下包扎战友的伤口。

晚上,未受伤的战士一直叨念着母亲,两眼直勾勾的。他们都以为他们的生命即将结束,身边的鹿肉谁也没动。天知道,他们怎么过的那一夜。第二天,部队救出了他们。

事隔30年,那位受伤的战士安德森说:"我知道谁开的那一枪,他就是我的战友。他去年去世了。在他抱住我时,我碰到了他发热的枪管,但当晚我就宽恕了他。我知道他想独吞我身上带的鹿肉活下来,但我也知道他活下来是为了他的母亲。此后30年,我装着根本不知道此事,也从不提及。战争太残酷了,他母亲还是没有等到他回来,我和他一起祭奠了老人家。他跪下来,请求我原谅他,我没让他说下去。我们又做了二十几年的朋友,我没有理由不宽恕他。"

一个人,能容忍别人的固执己见、自以为是、傲慢无礼、狂妄无知,却很难容忍对自己的恶意诽谤和致命的伤害。但唯有以德报怨,把伤害留给自己,让世界少一些不幸,回归温馨、仁慈、友善与祥和,才是宽容的至高境界。

——小故事大道理之《把伤害留给自己》,来源:360doc

Passage 4

(Audio 4-1-1　Passage 4)

The World Economic Forum warned that there would be more plastic than fish in the world's oceans by 2050. Globally, production of plastics exceeds 300 million tons per annum and only a small percentage of this is recycled. At least 8 million tons of plastic are dumped in the ocean every year, a large proportion ultimately ends up in one of the five major ocean gyres; drawn in by winds and ocean currents.

Pollution of the environment with plastic is a global environmental problem. There is extensive evidence that entanglement in plastics can cause injury and death to a wide range of marine organisms. From coral reefs smothered in plastic bags, to turtles gagging on straws, to whales and seabirds that starve because their bellies are so full of plastic that there's no room left for real food.

Over the past few years, scientists and researchers have created a variety of compostable plastic substitutes. Following the launch of the New Plastic Economy Innovation Prize in 2017, innovators worldwide have been invited to take part in The Circular Materials Challenge. The University of Pittsburgh team applies nano-engineering to create a recyclable material that can replace complex multi-layered non-recyclable packaging. Working together, Full Cycle Bioplastics, Elk Packaging, and Associated Labels and Packaging make a compostable high-performance material from renewable materials, agricultural by-products and food waste to pack a broad range of products from granola bars and crisps to laundry detergent.

Innovation is necessary, but the key priority is to focus on reducing the quantity of plastic waste generated by society. It is changing our own behaviors, choices and actions that will save our oceans, and the most important challenge is to improve the way we design, manage, recycle and re-use plastic.

—From VOA news

Chapter IV　Information Processing Skills

4-1-2　Analyze the discourse structure of the following passages and determine which genres they belong to. Then work with your partner, and retell these passages either in the source language or the target language.

A. Narrative
B. Introductory
C. Argumentative
D. Associative

(　)1. Passage 1
(　)2. Passage 2
(　)3. Passage 3

Passage 1

13亿人口的大国快速走向现代化,这是一幅多么波澜壮阔的历史画卷,更是中华民族对人类文明进步的最大贡献。我们不仅要对自己的国家和民族负责,也愿对世界承担应尽的义务。中国新一轮改革既符合中国人民的利益,也符合世界各国的需求。我们将加快转变经济发展方式,强化提质增效升级,跨越中等收入陷阱,实现可持续发展。而一个深化改革、日益繁荣的中国对世界意味着:

——中国将为世界发展提供更多"中国机遇"。

一是市场机遇。在全球有效需求不足背景下,中国的市场吸纳力却在不断扩容。中国人去年一年就购买了2100万辆汽车,超过全球汽车销量的1/4。中国的年进口总额已接近2万亿美元,预计今后5年将进口超过10万亿美元商品。

二是投资机遇。在实体经济面临融资难题背景下,中国企业成为国际投融资新的生力军。去年中国非金融类对外直接投资已超过900亿美元。新一轮改革将鼓励企业和个人对外投资,推动中国对外投资迈入新阶段。

三是增长机遇。在世界经济增速低迷背景下,中国作为一个规模超过9万亿美元的经济体,去年仍实现了7.7%的快速增长,在G20国家中继续名列前茅。而且这一增长是在加快调整经济结构进程中实现的,是实实在在、真金白银的增长。据推算,只要中国保持7%的增长率,就将拉动全球经济增长一个百分点。新一轮改革将使中国保持较长时间的中高速增长,这对世界经济无疑是重大利好。

四是合作机遇。在全球治理改革举步维艰背景下,中国新一轮改革将维护开放型世界经济和自由贸易体制,有利于经济全球化的健康发展,有助于各国经济政策的相互协调。

——节选自王毅外长在世界经济论坛2014年年会上的演讲《中国新发展　世界新机遇》

Passage 2

Harvard University is a private, Ivy League research university in Cambridge, Massachusetts, established 1636, whose history, influence and wealth have made it one of the world's most prestigious universities.

Established originally by the Massachusetts legislature and soon thereafter named for John Harvard (its first benefactor), Harvard is the United States' oldest institution of higher learning.

The University is organized into eleven separate academic units—ten faculties and the Radcliffe Institute for Advanced Study—with campuses throughout the Boston metropolitan area: its 209-acre (85 ha) main campus is centered on Harvard Yard in Cambridge, approximately 3 miles (5 km) northwest of Boston; the business school and athletics facilities, including Harvard Stadium, are located across the Charles River in the Allston neighborhood of Boston and the medical, dental, and public health schools are in the Longwood Medical Area. Harvard's \$37.6 billion financial endowment is the largest of any academic institution.

Harvard's alumni include eight U.S. presidents, several foreign heads of state, 62 living billionaires, 335 Rhodes Scholars, and 242 Marshall Scholars. To date, some 150 Nobel laureates, 18 Fields Medalists and 13 Turing Award winners have been affiliated as students, faculty, or staff.

—Excerpt from Wikipedia

Passage 3

有一则故事说,一个穷人与妻子、六个孩子,还有女儿女婿,共同生活在一间小木屋里,局促的居住条件让他感到活不下去了,便去找智者求救。他说,我们全家这么多人只有一间小木屋,整天争吵不休,我的精神快崩溃了,我的家简直是地狱,再这样下去,我就要死了。智者说,你按我说的去做,情况会变得好一些。穷人听了这话,当然是喜不自胜。智者听说穷人家还有一头奶牛、一只山羊和一群鸡,便说,我有让你解除困境的办法了,你回家去,把这些家畜带到屋里,与人一起生活。穷人一听大为震惊,但他是事先答应要按智者说的去做的,只好依计而行。

过了一天,穷人满脸痛苦地找到智者说,智者,你给我出的什么主意?事情比以前更糟,现在我家成了十足的地狱,我真的活不下去了,你得帮帮我。智者平静地说,好吧,你回去把那些鸡赶出房间就好了。过了一天,穷人又来了,他仍然痛不欲生,他哭诉说,那只山羊撕碎了我房间里的一切东西,它让我的生活如同噩梦。智者温和地说,回去把山羊牵出屋就好了。过了几天,穷人又来了,他还是那样痛苦,他说,那头奶牛把屋子搞成了牛棚,请你想想,人怎么可以与牲畜同处一室呢。"完全正确,"智者说,"赶快回家,把牛牵出屋去!"

故事的结局是这样的:过了半天,穷人找到智者,他是一路跑着来的,满脸红光,兴奋难抑,他拉住智者的手说:"谢谢你,智者,你又把甜蜜的生活给了我。现在所有的动物都出去了,屋子显得那么安静,那么宽敞,那么干净,你不知道,我是多么开心啊!"

一个人生活的幸福与否,从来没有一个恒定的标准,你的处境虽然很糟糕,但还不是最糟糕的,还没有到绝望的时候,你需要做的是调整你的心态,鼓起生活的信心,改变眼下的处境,至少,不要退到你已经见识过的比现在还糟糕的境地。

——小故事大道理之《我的处境并不算最糟糕的》,来源:360doc

4.2 Information Storage

After the information is extracted and analyzed, the next step in CI is to store the information. Of course, these steps are accomplished in an instant. There are mainly two ways to store the information, memory and note-taking. They will be discussed in details respectively in Chapter Ⅶ and Chapter Ⅷ. In this chapter, we will mainly focus on how the information is processed in information storage.

4.2.1 Memory—Information Visualization

In consecutive interpreting, information analysis can help interpreters better memorize the information received. In the process of information analysis, there is a good way to enhance our memory even more—information visualization.

Our daily experience and common sense tell us that vivid and rich audio or visual materials are usually easier to remember while materials with empty or dull contents are easily forgotten. Many psychological experiments also show that "imagery" plays a very important role in memory. Generally speaking, our memory of imagery materials is better than that of language materials, and our memory of visual materials is better than that of audio materials.

Even though interpreters cannot choose the content or format of the source language, changing verbal information to imageries can still help them enhance the memory of the source information. This process is called information visualization. In this process, interpreters draw a mental picture in their mind as they listen to the source language, memorize it, and then reproduce in the target language by using this mental picture. Information visualization can often be used when the speakers are describing events or processes, or introducing products, people, scenic spots, groups, organizations, enterprises, etc. By visualization the content, interpreters can better process the information in a more comprehensive way, avoid focusing on certain words, and express in a clearer way.

⊙**Information visualization exercise**

Please read/listen to the following passages, memorize through information visualization, and retell in the source language.

Passage 1

(Audio 4.2.1 - 1)

那么我今天给大家讲的第二个题目,是鲸为什么不是鱼? 因为一般在我们生活当中,习惯上都会叫它"鲸鱼"。因为什么呢? 因为它的形状看起来跟鱼是一样的,但是我们现在讲,鲸不是鱼,它是哺乳动物。为什么呢? 那么我们现在就来说明一下。先请大家看一下这个图,这就是一条须鲸的外形图。那么从这个整体形状来看,我们觉得,它还是跟鱼一样的样子,当然个

大一点。那么它跟鱼有什么区别?第一,鱼一般大多数长有鳞片,鲸它身上没有鳞片。第二,我们知道鱼是靠什么呼吸的?鱼它是用鳃呼吸的,是不是?那么鲸呢?它不是用鳃呼吸,它是用肺呼吸的。那么用肺呼吸,那就意味着它必须要从水里面出来,到水外面来呼气跟吸气,所以它需要一个构造,那个构造就是呼吸孔。然后我们再来看看,在鱼的身体两边,它有胸鳍跟腹鳍,就是鱼划水的那个器官。那么在鲸来讲,它只有在身体前面有一对,过去也有人把它叫胸鳍,其实不对,因为什么?实际上它不是一个鳍,它实际上就相当于我们的前肢,变成它现在的样子,相当于动物的前肢,或者相当于我们的手,所以它不是一个鳍。所以,现在我们给它一个专业的名称,这个就叫鳍肢。也就是说,它的前肢变成了鳍肢,然后它的后肢没有了,因为它在水里生活,后肢没有了。第三,大家还注意鱼,它在游泳的时候怎么游的?鱼游泳的时候,尾巴是不是左右摆动,鱼的尾鳍是这样子,直的,它是左右摆动;那鲸呢?你们看到过海豚游泳,它是上下地摆动,它尾叶跟尾柄上下摆动。第四,鱼如果要繁殖的时候,它生的是什么?鱼子,卵,叫产卵;鲸生的就是小鲸鱼。那么小鲸鱼生下来,就要吃奶,它要哺乳。那么鱼呢,它就没有哺乳。所以这个也证明鲸,它是哺乳动物,跟鱼不同。最后,哺乳动物跟鱼还有一个差别,就是鱼它是变温动物,就是它身体的温度不是恒定的,它是根据环境温度的改变而改变的,而鲸它是恒温动物。它一般是大概三十五六(摄氏)度体温,保持恒温。

——节选自曹玉茹中央电视台《百家讲坛·海洋生灵——巨无霸——鲸》

Passage 2

(Audio 4.2.1 - 2)

One December night, a long long time ago, a family sat around the fireplace in their home. A golden light from the fire filled the room.

The mother and father laughed at something their oldest daughter had just said. The girl was seventeen, much older than her little brother and sister who were only five and six years old. A very old woman, the family's grandmother, sat knitting in the warmest corner of the room. And a baby, the youngest child, smiled at the fire's light from its tiny bed.

This family had found happiness in the worst place in all of New England. They had built their home high up in the White Mountains, where the wind blows violently all year long. The family lived in an especially cold and dangerous spot. Stones from the top of the mountain above their house would often roll down the mountainside and wake them in the middle of the night.

But this family was never lonely. People traveling through the mountains in wagons, always stopped at the family's door, for a drink of water and a friendly word. Lonely travelers crossing the mountains on foot would step into the house to share a hot meal.

On that December evening, the wind came rushing down the mountain. The family fell silent for a moment, but then they realized that someone was really knocking at their door.

The oldest girl opened the door and found a young man standing in the dark.

"This fire is just what I needed," the young man said, "the wind has been blowing in my face for the last two hours. I wanted to reach the valley tonight. But when I saw the light in your window. I decided to stop. I would like to sit and enjoy your fire and your company for a while." As the young man took his place by the fire, something like heavy footsteps was heard outside. It sounded as if someone was running down the side of the mountain taking enormous steps.

The father looked out of one of the windows.

"That old mountain has thrown another stone at us again. He sometimes shakes his head and makes us think he will come down on top of us." the father explained to the young man.

"But we are old neighbors," he smiled, "and we manage to get along together pretty well. Besides, I have made a safe hiding place outside to protect us in case a slide brings the mountain down on our heads." As the father spoke, the mother prepared a hot meal for their guest.

While he ate, he talked freely to the family as if it were his own.

This young man did not trust people easily. Yet on this evening, something made him share his deepest secret with these simple mountain people. The young man's secret was that he was ambitious. He did not know what he wanted to do with his life yet. But he did know that he did not want to be forgotten after he died. He believed that sometime during his life, he would become famous and be admired by thousands of people.

"So far," the young man said, "I have done nothing. If I disappeared tomorrow from the face of the Earth, no one would know anything about me. But I cannot die until I have reached to my destiny. Then let death come."

The family also talked about their ambition, secret and how they would want their death to be.

The young man stared into the fire. "Old and young," he said, "we dream of graves and monuments. I wonder how sailors feel when their ship is sinking; and they know they would be buried in the wide and nameless grave that is the ocean."

A sound rising like the roar of the ocean shook the house. Young and old exchanged one wild look. Then the same words burst from all their lips. "The Slide! The Slide!" They rushed away from the house into the darkness to the secret spot that father had built to protect them from the mountain slide.

The whole side of the mountain came rushing toward the house like a waterfall of destruction. But just before it reached the little house, the wave of earth divided in two and went around the family's home.

Everyone and everything in the path of the terrible slide was destroyed except the little house.

The next morning, smoke was seen coming from the chimney of the house on the mountain. Inside, the fire was still burning. The chairs were still drawn up in a half circle around the fireplace. It looked as if the family had just gone out for a walk.

Some people thought that the stranger had been with the family on that terrible night.

But no one ever discovered who the stranger was. His name and way of life remained a mystery. His body was never found.

—Adapted from "*The Ambitious Guest*" written by Nathaniel Hawthorne

4.2.2 Information Storage Trough Note-taking

Another important way of information storage is note-taking. Note-taking and information processing are closely related. Note-taking is a way for the interpreters to record information on paper in the form of simple linguistic symbols, such as words, abbreviations, graphs, special symbols and other non-linguistic symbols so as to reduce the memory load. The note-taking process is not simply a "listening-recording" process, but a process of "listening-analysis-processing-recording". Points, logical relationship between information points and discourse information are analyzed and processed into various forms of language codes or symbols convenient for recording. Logical analysis is the core of note-taking. It not only decides whether the interpreters can record accurately and completely, but also whether the interpreters can understand the notes and reproduce the information in the target language accurately and completely.

The process of note-taking is actually a thinking process. The result of note-taking—notes—is a simple representation of the result of this thinking process on paper. Note-taking in CI can not only help interpreters concentrate and maintain their attention and improve their listening comprehension, but also help them better analyze and sort out the information points and the structure of discourse, and dramatically increase their memory of the source information.

Exercises and Practice

4-2-1 Answer the following questions.

1. How are information stored?
2. What is information visualization?
3. What is the relationship between information processing and note-taking?

4-2-2 Please read/listen to the following passages, memorize through information visualization, and retell in either the source language or the target language, or both.

Passage 1

(Audio 4-2-2 Passage 1)

那么下一个问题,就是鲸的空中动作。大家从电影上,或者海洋公园表演看到鲸,我们就注意到,它有很多的空中动作,那么这个空中动作,我们把它归纳起来,大概有这么几种:一种叫做跃水,也就是说,它整个身体或者大部分身体跳出水面,然后啪嗒一下又摔到水里,或者又掉下来掉到水里去,下去的时候"啪——"溅起一大片水花,这种情况叫跃水。

第二个空中动作,叫"乘浪"。乘浪也是很有意思的,就是船在往前走的时候,船头里面它会形成一种浪,叫做压浪,这是一个专门名字,叫压浪,那么海豚它就具有这个本事,它会坐在这个,或者躺在这个浪上面,由这个浪把它带着走,所以我们把它的名称叫做乘浪,就是像乘船一样,它是乘浪。那么我们出去看海,曾经在甲板上看到,船头水面上有海豚,靠在船头就贴在上面,你船在走它也在走。我前面讲了,海豚游泳是靠怎么动作的?就是尾叶上下摆,乘浪的时候它不动的,尾巴不动。也就是它不需要自己推进,坐着这个浪它就往前走,这叫"乘浪"。

第三种叫滑水,滑水一般就是说,它在游泳,往前加速度,加到一定速度,把身子竖起来,然后在水上滑一段时间。

第四个动作,叫"空中转体"。空中转体,也就是说,整个跳起来,在空中可以沿着身体的长轴这么旋转,它可以转多少圈,它可以转14圈,跳起来转14圈,这个也是非常惊人的。

——节选自曹玉茹中央电视台《百家讲坛·海洋生灵——巨无霸——鲸》

Passage 2

(Audio 4-2-2 Passage 2)

It was raining as I got off the train in Nashville Tennessee, a slow grey rain. I was tired, so I went straight to my hotel. A big heavy man was walking up and down in the hotel lobby. Something about the way he moved made me think of a hungry dog looking for a bone. He had a big fat red face and a sleepy expression in his eyes. He introduced himself as Major Wentworth Caswell from a fine southern family. Caswell pulled me into the hotel's bar room and yelled for a waiter. We ordered drinks.

While we drank, he talked continually about himself, his family, his wife and her family. He said his wife was rich. He showed me a handful of silver coins that he pulled from his coat pocket. By this time, I had decided that I wanted no more of him. I said goodnight. I went up to my room and looked out of the window. It was 10 o'clock but the town was silent. "A nice quiet place," I said to myself as I got ready for bed, "just an ordinary sleepy southern town." I was born in the south myself, but I live in New York now. I write for a large magazine. My boss had asked me to go to Nashville. The magazine had received some stories and poems from a writer in Nashville named Azalea Adair. The editor liked her work very much. The publisher asked me to get her to sign an agreement to write only for his magazine. I left the hotel at 9 o'clock the next morning to find Miss Adair. It was still raining. As soon as I stepped outside, I met Uncle Caesar. He was a big old black man with fuzzy grey hair. Uncle Caesar was wearing the strangest coat I had ever seen. It must have been a military officer's coat. It was very long and when it was new it had been grey. But now rain, sun and age had made it a rainbow of colors, only one of the buttons was left. It was yellow and as big as a 50-cent coin. Uncle Caesar stood near a horse-sent carriage.

He opened the carriage door and said softly, "Step right in, sir, I'll take you anywhere in the city."

"I want to go to 861 Jasmine Street," I said. And I started to climb into the carriage, but the old man stopped me.

"Why do you want to go there, sir?"

"What business is it of yours?" I said angrily.

Uncle Caesar relaxed and smiled. "Nothing, sir, but it's a lonely part of town. Just step in and I'll take you there right away."

—Excerpt from "*A Municipal Report*" written by O. Henry

Passage 3

(Audio 4-2-2 Passage 3)

科学家通过对鲨鱼胃里检查,剖开它的胃一看,它的胃里边等于就是杂货铺,里边什么都有,都有什么呢?像鱼类、海鸟、海龟,有海豹、海狮,有皮靴,还有钢盔,还有记录本,可以说什么都有。鲨鱼之所以见什么都吞什么,并不见得是吃它,而是有三个原因促使它这么做:一个原因那就是故意挑逗它,这个时候它见什么都吃,也不管能不能消化得了,甚至定时炸弹它也敢吞吃;另外一个原因呢,那就是声音,非常剧烈的声音,使它震怒,而见到什么也吞吃什么;除此以外还有一个原因,那就是异乎寻常的味道的刺激,当然这里包括血液,也包括一些其他异乎寻常的味道,那么这三种原因促使它见到什么吞什么。

下边我再给大家讲一个有关鲨鱼吞吃定时炸弹的故事,这个也是一个真实的故事。在20世纪60年代,在大西洋的洋面上,有一艘军舰正在行驶,这个船长就说,今天下午我们发射一枚深海定时炸弹,这个时候军舰旁边有条大白鲨,就在船的周围游动着,当然这个时候有些船员们就说,说你这大白鲨,我知道你非常凶猛,但是我们这钢板制成的军舰你怎么也不会咬掉它一块,因为大家不可能认为它会咬掉这个船板。船长看看表,时间到了,告诉射击手,赶快发射一枚定时炸弹,这定时炸弹到了深水下边,眼看这条大白鲨一个猛子扎了下去,把这个定时炸弹吞到了嘴里,而且马上它又出来,又在水面上出现。这个时候船长和其他的船员们都吓得面如土色,不得了,所以船长就命令舵手赶快加足马力,赶快躲开身怀定时炸弹的这条大鲨鱼。这个时候只看这条大白鲨又一次冲进了深海里,只听"轰"的一声爆炸了,船上的人安然无恙。当时从船上发射出来那种巨响激怒了大白鲨,大白鲨不顾一切就把定时炸弹吞到了嘴里,幸亏它又回到了深海里,否则的话,船毁人亡,后果不堪设想。

还有一个故事。在加勒比海上急速地行驶着一条海盗船,这条海盗船为什么要急急忙忙地在加勒比海上逃命呢?因为后边有一艘英国兵舰在追赶着它,那么这英国兵舰为什么要追它?原因就是海盗船偷窃了英国海域里的科学资料,偷窃完这资料以后,他们就想赶快逃命。可是在这个时候,英国兵舰已经追到了,正在万分紧要的时候,这个海盗船的船长把这个很珍贵的记录本扔到了海里。那么这个时候他们已经被捕了,被带到牙买加皇家港受审,那么在审判的过程当中呢,结果有两种不同的意见:一边认为这个船长应该被判处死刑,为什么呢?因为他破坏了国际航海法;可是另外一部分人就反对,他的罪行你不可能给他判处死刑,那么怎么办?只好休庭,这个疑难案件不能解决,可是我们的大鲨鱼却解决了这个疑难的案件。怎么回事呢?就在这时候,又有一艘英国的船只入港了,他们在赫坦岛的外海捕到了一条鲨鱼,通过解剖以后,就看到有一个非常完整的记录本,这个记录本就是海盗船船长当时扔下去的。那么在铁的事实面前,原来持反对意见的人也放弃了原来的观点,那么这个船长被判处死刑,后来这条鲨鱼名声大噪,所有的英国人几乎都认识了这条鲨鱼,而且这个鲨鱼吞食的这个记录本,作为"鲨鱼之书",现在保存在金斯敦的牙买加学院内,永远地保存着。

给大家讲这个故事的原因就是,因为鲨鱼是见什么吃什么,也不管它消化得了或消化不了，它都吃，这是它的一个特殊的习性。那么这个习性还有什么呢？就是如果它实在消化不了，它可以在十天半个月以后又可以从口中吐出来，这又是它与其他海洋动物不一样的。

——节选自曹玉茹中央电视台《百家讲坛·海洋生灵——鲨鱼》

Additional Materials

1. Foreign Secretary William Hague's Statement at the Geneva Conference on Syria on January 22, 2014

英国外交大臣威廉·黑格 2014 年 1 月 22 日在日内瓦会议上就叙利亚问题的讲话
来源：可可英语网
http://www.kekenet.com/kouyi/201401/274278.shtml

Thank you very much Secretary General.
非常感谢秘书长。

We meet today with the urgent task of implementing the Geneva communiqué agreed 18 months ago, as a roadmap to end the conflict in Syria.
今天，我们开会讨论一项紧迫的任务，即实施 18 个月前达成一致的《日内瓦公报》，该公报是结束叙利亚冲突的路线图。

At that time, 15,000 people had been killed and there were 87,000 registered Syrian refugees in the region. These numbers seemed appallingly high at the time.
当时，叙利亚已有 1.5 万人被杀害，而该地区登记在案的叙利亚难民有 8.7 万人，这些数字在当时看起来已经高得惊人。

But the failure to implement the Geneva communiqué has meant that at least 110,000 other innocent people have now died, and 2.3 million more people have had to flee as refugees-including a staggering one million children.
但未能实施《日内瓦公报》则意味着现在另有至少 11 万无辜平民已经死亡，另有 230 万人被迫逃离该国成为难民，其中儿童难民的数量达到惊人的 100 万。

These facts should be seared into our consciences. They are a devastating reminder of the human cost of this war, and they give overriding urgency to the task before us.
这些事实在拷问着我们的良心，有力地提醒我们这场战争所造成的人类的生命损失，并且使摆在我们面前的这一任务具有压倒一切的紧迫性。

For we can be absolutely certain that if this peace process fails, then thousands more innocent Syrians will pay the price. I urge both Syrian delegations to approach these negotiations in that spirit—recognizing that the entire future of Syria is at stake.
我们绝对可以肯定，如果这一和平进程失败的话，还将有成千上万无辜的叙利亚人成为战争的牺牲品。我敦促叙利亚双方代表本着这样的精神进行谈判,即双方需要认识到,叙利亚的整个未来正处于极其危险之中。

And the Syrian government bears a particular responsibility for this crisis and can do the most to end it. I call on them to commit themselves to the aim of a mutually agreed settlement; and to stop actions on the ground which undermine the negotiations.

而叙利亚政府则对本次危机负有特别重要的责任,并且可以尽一切所能结束危机。我呼吁双方致力于达成彼此同意的解决办法的目标,并为此停止可能破坏谈判的行动。

At a time of relentless attacks on their homes and their families, the National Coalition have agreed to participate in this Conference, which was not an easy decision for President al-Jarba and the National Coalition leadership and I commend them for taking this step and for endorsing today the Geneva Communiqué as their basis of our work. They have our full support in doing that.

当其家园和家属都在遭受无情攻击的时候,全国联盟就已经同意参加本次会议,而这对于主席贾尔巴和全国联盟的领导层来说并不是轻易能够做出的决定。他们能够采取这一步骤并且现在赞同《日内瓦公报》,将其作为他们参与我们这项工作的基础,对此我表示赞赏,我们对他们的这种行为给予全力支持。

And we should be absolutely clear that the Syrian conflict did not begin with terrorism. This began with ordinary people calling for greater political and economic freedom, who were met with brute force and oppression rather than the offer of peaceful change. And there must be accountability for the appalling crimes committed in this conflict, including those reported by distinguished jurists this week.

我们还应绝对清楚这一点,即叙利亚冲突并不是开始于恐怖主义,而是开始于普通民众,他们要求获得更大的政治和经济自由,但没有获得和平变革,反而遭到了残酷的打击和压迫。对于这场冲突中所发生的骇人听闻的罪行,包括本周由重要的法学家所报告的那些罪行,都必须进行问责。

And it was because of that repression that those protests escalated into a mass uprising and civil war, and it is this instability that has created a foothold for extremists. But they are in a tiny minority compared to the millions of Syrians who have taken no part in this conflict and who want and deserve lives of dignity, and safety, and freedom.

正是因为镇压,抗议活动升级为一场大规模的起义和内战;而正是这种不稳定成了产生极端分子的土壤。但是相对于几百万叙利亚人来说,极端分子只是极少数,大多数叙利亚人并没有参与这场冲突,他们希望的是过上有尊严、有安全、有自由的生活,这也是他们应该享有的。

The only way to end the bloodshed and to deal with extremist threats, is to reach an inclusive political settlement that takes into account the needs and aspirations of all Syria's communities with a Syrian-led political process, leading to a transition enabling the Syrian people independently and democratically to determine their future.

停止流血和应对极端分子威胁的唯一途径,是需要通过政治途径进行解决:一个由叙利亚人领导的政治进程,包含叙利亚各方需求和愿景并使之实现,最终成功政治过渡,使叙利亚人能够独立地、民主地决定他们的未来。

All of us who have endorsed the Geneva Communiqué know what the goal is: a transitional governing body in Syria with full executive powers, formed by mutual consent, which means no one included without the agreement of the others, including a President who has destroyed his own legitimacy.

我们所有人都赞同《日内瓦公报》。我们知道该公报的目标是,在叙利亚建立一个具有充分的行政权力、经各方协商组成的过渡管理机构。这意味着未经其他方的同意,任何人将不会进入该机构,这也包括一个破坏了自身合法性的总统。

And we know what the steps are that are needed to reach that goal, including a firm timetable for a Syria-led transition for a future for Syria that is genuinely democratic and pluralistic; and ceasefire agreements enabling immediate and full humanitarian access. We have provided £500 million pounds in aid as the United Kingdom and pledged £100m more but aid must be able to reach the people who need it most. The deliberate obstruction of humanitarian aid is utterly unacceptable and a flagrant disregard of the UN Security Council presidential statement of last October. The UN estimates that 2.5 million people inside Syria are currently receiving no or extremely limited assistance, including 250,000 people trapped in besieged or hard-to-access areas. Urgent efforts are required to improvement this situation.

我们知道要达到该目标所要采取的步骤,包括为叙利亚主导的、向真正民主多元的未来的过渡制定一个明确的时间表,和能够立即全面进行人道主义援助的停火协议。英国已经提供了5亿英镑的援助,并承诺再援助1亿英镑,但是援助必须能够到达最需要援助的人民手中。对人道主义援助的蓄意阻挠是完全不可接受的,这种阻挠行为是对去年10月的联合国安理会主席声明的公然挑衅。据联合国估计,叙利亚境内目前有250万人没有得到任何援助或者所得到的援助极其有限,其中有25万人处于包围之中或者难以接近的区域。现在急需采取行动改善这种状况。

The transition in Syria should also include full participation for women, as set out in the Geneva communiqué. As the United Kingdom we would have liked to see a formal role for Syrian women's groups and civil society at this meeting. But I welcome the Secretary General's and Mr Brahimi's strong support for the inclusion of women in both delegations. There can be no lasting settlement in Syria that does not involve Syria's women at every stage of the process and as the UK we will work to achieve their full participation in this process.

根据《日内瓦公报》的精神,叙利亚的过渡还应包括妇女的全面参与。对于英国来说,我们本希望看到叙利亚妇女团体和民间团体能以正式的身份参与此次会议。不过我对会议秘书长和卜拉希米先生为将妇女纳入双方代表团进行强有力的支持表示欢迎。如果不能将叙利亚妇女纳入每一个进程阶段,就不可能产生持久的解决办法。对于英国,我们将在这一进程中努力实现妇女的全面参与。

These talks are only the start of a process, so will require commitment and courage, but I urge both sides to remain at the negotiating table. And to them I say, this is your opportunity to put an end to the devastation of your country. Now is the time to choose to save a generation of Syrian children from violence and trauma; to end the sieges being laid to ancient towns and cities; to begin to repair the rich fabric of Syrian society; and to spare millions of refugees the prospect of years of exile, homelessness and deprivation.

这些会谈只是进程的开始,需要人们有决心和勇气来参与。但是我敦促双方将谈判进行下去。我想对他们说,这是你们结束你们国家破败局面的一个机会。现在是选择拯救一代叙利亚儿童免于暴力和创伤的时候,是结束古老城镇摆脱围攻的时候,是开始修复叙利亚社会的各种组织结构的时候,是使数百万难民不再继续背井离乡、无家可归、极度贫困生活的时候。

We have no illusions about how difficult and challenging this process is likely to be but we should all do everything possible to help the people of Syria achieve peace.

我们对这一进程的困难程度和挑战性非常清楚。但是我们应该尽一切可能帮助叙利亚人民实现和平。

2. The full text of the Chinese ambassador to Australia MA Zhaoxu's signed article on The Australian Financial Review on Jan 31, 2014—"China is Australia's land of opportunity"

2014年1月31日,中国驻澳大利亚大使马朝旭在当地主流媒体《澳大利亚金融评论报》发表题为《澳大利亚经济的新机遇》的署名文章

中文来源:人民网

http://australia.people.com.cn/n/2014/0208/c364496-24300199.html

译文来源:可可英语网

http://www.kekenet.com/kouyi/201402/274949.shtml

澳大利亚经济的新机遇

上周中国国家统计局发布数据显示,2013年中国国内生产总值(GDP)增长了7.7%。这个数字从全球范围看,保持了中高速增长。全年城镇新增就业人数超过1300万,是历年最多的。去年中国进口额接近2万亿美元,中国企业对外直接投资也超过了900亿美元。这一成绩来之不易,是在国际金融危机余波未平、世界经济尚待复苏和中国经济转型升级的背景下产生的。在世界经济不确定因素较多、国际市场对主要经济体宏观政策动向异常敏感的情况下,中国稳定财政、货币政策,保持合理的流动性,向国际市场发出了明确的稳定预期的信号,这也是中国对世界经济发展的负责任之举。

Last week China released economic data for 2013, which shows GDP grew by 7.7 per cent, a mid-to-high growth rate in global terms. More than 13 million new urban jobs were created, more than in any previous year. Total imports approached ＄US 2 trillion.

Overseas direct investment by Chinese enterprises exceeded ＄US 90 billion. Given the lingering international financial crisis, the unrecovered world economy and China's effort of economic restructuring, such a "score report" is a hard-won achievement. Moreover, with uncertainties in the global economy and unusual sensitivities of the international market to macro-policy developments in major economies, China's stable fiscal and monetary policies as well as reasonable liquidity have sent a clear signal of stability to international market expectations. This is an act of responsibility by China in the interest of the world economy.

新公布的数据也释放出中国经济增长结构优化,以及这种转变对世界和澳大利亚经济带来巨大机遇的积极信息。根据中国国家统计局的数据,第三产业占中国 GDP 比例从 2012 年的 44.6％上升为 2013 年的 46.1％,首次超过以工业、采矿业、建筑业为代表的第二产业。中国的经济已由过去依靠制造业的"单轮驱动"发展到如今制造业、服务业双增长的"双轮驱动",服务业正成为中国经济长期持续健康发展与优化升级的新引擎和新动力。中澳服务业合作正处于快速发展时期。中国已连续 3 年成为澳最大的服务产品出口市场。2012—2013 财年双边服务贸易近 85.3 亿澳元,其中,澳对华出口 66.6 亿澳元。

The figures also mean an upgrading of China's economic growth and show that huge opportunities may arise for the global and the Australian economy. China's service sector accounted for 46.1 per cent of the country's GDP in 2013, up from 44.6 per cent in 2012, outperforming the industrial sector for the first time. The service sector has become a new growth engine, setting economic growth on a healthier, long-term trajectory. China-Australia co-operation in the service sector is moving forward fast. China has been Australia's largest export market for service products for three years in a row. Our two-way trade in services reached ＄8.5 billion and Australia exported ＄6.7 billion worth of service products to China in 2012—2013.

中国已成为澳大利亚最大的留学生来源国、第二大海外游客来源国,也是增长最快的旅客市场。一些有战略眼光的澳大利亚企业已经敏锐捕捉到了商机。澳新银行在去年 11 月正式登陆上海自贸区。西太银行(Westpac)大中华区总裁魏安德(Andrew Whitford)认为,澳洲企业应当考虑将进驻上海新自贸区作为与中国投资者产生联系的一种方式。

China is Australia's largest source of international students, second-largest source of inbound tourists as well as the fastest-growing inbound tourism market. Far-sighted Australian enterprises have been capitalising on opportunities provided by the new momentum. ANZ won approval for a sub-branch in the Shanghai Free Trade Zone last November. Andrew Whitford, Westpac's head of Greater China, said Australian companies should establish themselves in the new zone as there are "enormous opportunities".

2013 年,中国中西部地区 GDP 总量占全国的 44.4％,比 2012 年提高 0.2 个百分点。中国农村居民人均纯收入实际增长 9.3％,比城镇居民人均可支配收入实际增速高 2.3 个百分点,增速连续四年快于城镇,城乡居民人均收入倍差由上年的 3.10 缩小为 3.03。这些数据表明长期困扰中国经济发展的城乡失衡、区域失衡问题正得到逐步缓解,中国庞大的中西部和农村市场潜力正不断释放。我们看到,澳企业正日益积极地参与到中国西部地区的发展中来。我相信这将帮助澳在中国经济转型中占得先机。

In 2013, the GDP of central and western parts of China was 44 per cent of China's total, up by 0.2 per cent on the previous year. The per capita net income of rural residents grew by 9.3 per cent in real terms, 2.3 per cent higher than that of urban residents. The income gap between urban and rural residents shrank from 3.10 in 2012 to 3.03. This trend for four consecutive years is a sign that regional development disparity has been easing, unleashing huge market potential for the vast hinterland areas. Australian enterprises have been increasingly active in the development of central and western China, which will help Australia gain a head start in China's economic restructuring.

中国对澳能源资源等需求依然强劲稳健。尽管 2013 年中国经济增速与 2012 年持平,较过去有所下降,但总体增量却比以前要大得多。中国 GDP 总量已经达到 9.18 万亿美元,连续 4 年成为世界第二大经济体。一个总量更大、增长质量更高、增长速度更稳的中国经济将为世界、为澳大利亚带来更多机遇。2013 年,中国城镇化率同比提高 1.16%,达 53.73%,并有望在未来十年保持年均 1.2% 的提升速度。中国仍需进行大量的基础设施建设。同时,中国对外贸易与投资不断扩大,未来五年,中国对外投资规模将达到 5000 亿美元。这对于澳能源资源的开发与出口、农产品国际市场的开拓等,无疑都是好消息。

Despite a softening of its economy, with 2013 growth the same as 2012, China still has robust demand for Australian energy and resources. China's economic aggregate is now on a much larger base than before, with a GDP of US＄9.18 trillion, the second largest economy for four years running. A larger, better-quality and more stable Chinese economy will bring even more opportunities to the world. The urbanization rate rose by 1.16 per cent to 53.73 per cent in 2013 which shows China still has a large demand for infrastructure building. China's outbound trade and investment will continue to expand with outbound investment expected to reach ＄US 500 billion over five years. This is good news to Australian businesses in energy, resources and agriculture.

2014 年是世界经济走向复苏的重要年份,也是中澳经贸合作升级发展的关键一年。中澳双方应该携手努力,发掘合作潜力,为两国人民带来更多实实在在的利益。

This year is going to be vital to world economic recovery. It will also be an important year for upgrading China-Australia economic ties. Both nations should work together to seize new opportunities and fully tap co-operation potential.

Chapter Ⅴ Code-Switching Skills

Learning questions:
√ *How are English sentences and passages different from the Chinese ones?*
√ *What are the strategies involved in C – E(Chinese-English) code-switching?*

In this part, we will study the differences between English and Chinese sentences and the different cohesive devices used between them. We will learn the skills involved in dealing with these differences in CI. We will also learn how to better deal with the fuzzy or culturally-loaded information in CI. Since the skills work both ways, i.e., E – C(English-Chinese) and C – E(Chinese-English), here in this chapter, we will mainly focus on one direction, Chinese to English consecutive interpreting.

5.1 Code-Switching Skills—Sentence Level

As we have talked about in "the Process of Interpreting", code-switching is a process where the language code is switched from the source language to the target language. Here we are mainly talking about code-switching from Chinese to English. Chinese and English are largely different in syntax and discourse, and some strategies must be used in interpreting.

5.1.1 Parataxis vs. Hypotaxis

As we have mentioned in Chapter Ⅱ, Chinese way of language organization is parataxis while English is hypotaxis. That means Chinese sentences are formed on the basis of meaning rather than structure and the logical connections are very often implied. English, on the contrary, uses structure to express meaning. This is the most fundamental difference between Chinese and English. In C – E code-switching, one of the strategies is to add connectives in the English sentences. The following are some examples.

[1] 好好学习,天天向上。
[2] 天气寒冷,河水都结了冰。
[3] 我们尊重知识分子是对的。没有革命知识分子,革命就不会胜利。
[4] 坚持变革创新,理想就会变为现实。
[5] 请大家畅所欲言,进一步完善相关的制度规定。
[6] 李克强总理多次强调:"要让创新创造的血液在全社会自由流动,让自主发展的精神

在全体人民中蔚然成风,释放民智民力,打造中国经济未来增长的新引擎。"

In the examples above, the logical connections in Chinese sentences are implied. In C-E interpreting, we need to add the connectives and sometimes subjects to make these logical relations more explicit.

[1]　好好学习,(才能)天天向上。
Study hard, and make progress every day.
If one studies hard, she/he will make progress every day.

[2]　天气寒冷,(以至于)河水都结了冰。
It was so cold *that* the river froze.

[3]　我们尊重知识分子是对的。(因为)没有知识分子,革命就不会胜利。
It's the right thing to do to respect the intellectuals, *for* without them, we cannot triumph in the revolution.

[4]　(如果我们)坚持变革创新,(我们的)理想就会变为现实。
If we persist in our reform and innovation, *we will* be able to turn our ideals into reality.

[5]　请大家畅所欲言,(以便我们)进一步完善相关的制度规定。
Please speak freely so *that we can* further improve the relevant regulations.

[6]　李克强总理多次强调:"要让创新创造的血液在全社会自由流动,(并)让自主发展的精神在全体人民中蔚然成风,(我们要)释放民智民力,(并)打造中国经济未来增长的新引擎。"
Premier Li Keqiang reiterated several times, "We must let the blood of innovation flow freely in our whole society, and make self-development a habit in the general population. *We must* unleash the wisdom of the general population, *and* make it the new engine of the future economic development."

5.1.2　Topic vs. Subject

Chinese is a topic-prominent language while English is a subject-prominent language. In Chinese, the part in front of predicate is not necessarily the subject. Many Chinese sentences have no subject at all. Chinese frequently use the structure of "topic + comment (TC)". English, however, must have a subject in a complete sentence (except imperatives). Most English sentences are in a "subject + verb + object (SVO)" structure. Let's look at some examples.

[1]　打雷了,下雨了。
[2]　只要不懈努力,就一定能打赢这场反贪战争。
[3]　打针比吃药有效。/开车打电话会造成交通事故。
[4]　关于入河排污的问题,有一套符合国家规定的系统。
[5]　衣服洗好了。/今天星期一。/他的英语说得很好。
[6]　近三十年的实践已经充分证明,我们进行改革开放的方向是正确的,信念是坚定的,步骤是稳妥的,方式是渐进的,取得的成就是巨大的。

From the above examples, we can see that Chinese sentences often have implied subject, multiple subjects or no subject at all, and the subject is not necessarily pronouns, nouns or noun phrases. Example [1] has no subject at all. Example [2] has an implied subject. In the two sentences in example [3], the subjects are verb phrases. Example [4] and [5] are "topic+comment" structures. Grammatically speaking, example [4] has no subject. Example [6] has multiple subjects.

So in Chinese-English code-switching, one of the first priorities is to find the subject or the implied subject in Chinese sentences, and the following strategies can be used.

⊙**Add subject when there is no subject or an implied subject.**

[1] 打雷了,下雨了。

It is thundering and raining.

[2] 只要(我们)不懈努力,就一定能打赢这场反贪战争。

As long as *we* work unremittingly, *we* will certainly win the war against corruption.

⊙**Change subject to nouns or noun phrases when they are not.**

[3] 打针比吃药有效。

Injection works better than *medicine*.

Getting injections is more effective than *taking medicine*.

开车打电话会造成交通事故。

Making phone calls while driving can cause traffic accidents.

⊙**Change TC structure to SVO structure by adding subjects or predicates.**

[4] 关于入河排污的问题,有一套符合国家规定的系统。

On the issue of waste water flowing back to the river, *we have* a system in place which conforms to national standards.

[5] 衣服洗好了。

The clothes *are* washed.

今天星期一。

Today *is* Monday.

他的英语说得很好。

He *speaks English* very well.

⊙**Choose only one subject when there are multiple subjects and put the rest in clauses.**

[6] 近三十年的**实践**已经充分证明,我们进行改革开放的方向是正确的,**信念**是坚定的,**步骤**是稳妥的,**方式**是渐进的,**取得的成就**是巨大的。

The practice in the past 30 years has eloquently proved that *the direction* of our reform and opening-up is right, *our conviction* is firm, *our steps* are steady, *our approach* is gradual and *our achievements* are huge.

5.1.3 Dynamic vs. Stative

Dynamic (动态) expression means, in expression, more verbs or verb phrases are used. Static (静态) expression means more nouns or noun phrases are used. Generally speaking, Chinese tends to use dynamic expressions while English tends to use more stative expressions. Here are some examples.

[1] 她**做饭**做得很好。
She's a very good *cook*.

[2] 精品之所以"**精**",就在于其**思想精深**、**艺术精湛**、**制作精良**。
The true value of a masterpiece lies in its *intellectual depth*, *artistic exquisiteness* and *skillful production*.

[3] **一想到**那个场景,我就起鸡皮疙瘩。
The thought of that scene gives me goosebumps.

[4] **少**说空话,**多**干实事。
There must be less empty talk and more actual work.

[5] 医生**迅速到达**,并非常仔细地**检查**了病人,因此病人很快就**得救**了。
(Compare:医生的迅速到达和对病人非常仔细的检查使病人快速得救。)
The doctor's *extremely quick arrival* and uncommonly *careful examination* of the patient brought about his very *speedy recovery*.
(Compare:The doctor arrived extremely quickly and examined the patient uncommonly carefully; the result was that he recovered very quickly.)

[6] 他们**违反**在赫尔辛基达成的协议,在国内**侵犯**基本人权,因此受到了各地热爱自由的人们的**谴责**。
(Compare:他们对在赫尔辛基达成的协议的违反和在国内对基本人权的侵犯受到了各地热爱自由的人们的谴责。)
The *abuse* of basic human rights in their own country in *violation* of the agreement reached at Helsinki earned them *condemnation* of freedom-loving people everywhere.
(Compare:Freedom-loving people everywhere condemned them because they violated the agreement reached at Helsinki and abused human rights in their own country.)

Based on this feature, in C – E interpreting, the nominalization of some verbs or verb phrases can sometimes make the interpreting simpler and more idiomatic. And vice versa for E – C interpreting.

5.1.4 *Active vs. Passive*

Active voice and passive voice are two ways of expression in language. Active voice emphasizes on the executor of the act. Passive voice emphasizes on the result of the act. For example, the sentence, "My brother broke the teapot." is in active voice and emphasizes on the person—"my brother". The sentence, "The teapot was broken." is in passive voice and emphasizes on the result that it's broken. Comparatively speaking, Chinese uses more active voice while English uses more passive voice.

In English, there are two types of passive voice:syntactic passive(结构被动式)and notional passive(意念被动式). Syntactic passive is in the form and structure as being "passive" while notional passive, though not in the form and structure as being "passive", offers a passive notion.

1. Syntactic passive in English

a. No need to state the executor of the act

Eg. An additional 10% quantity discount is allowed for orders over $3,000.

b. The executor is unknown

Eg. Her purse *was stolen* at the train station.

c. Unwilling to state the executor

Eg. He was reported and arrested very soon.

2. Notional passive in English

a. Passive meaning expressed in active form

Eg. The sign reads well.

Eg. The rice is cooking.

b. Copula + prepositional phrase

Eg. The building is under construction.

3. Code-switching strategies in interpreting

a. Chinese sentences without a subject

Eg. 请听众关闭手机。

The audience *are requested* to switch off their cellphones.

Eg. 正在处理这些问题。

The issues *are being* dealt with.

Eg. 要加快改革的步伐。

Great efforts should *be made* to speed up the reform.

b. Sentences of generic persons (泛指人称句)

Eg. 过去人们普遍认为人越胖越健康。

It was generally believed that the fatter a man was, the healthier he was.

Eg. 人家给她一个银行里的职位。

She *was offered* a job in a bank.

c. TC structures

Eg. 人民群众日益增长的物质文化需求应该得到政府的关注。

The growing material and cultural needs of the broadest masses of people should always *be identified and realized* by the government through persistent endeavors.

Eg. 1964年10月，中国爆炸了第一颗原子弹，这把基辛格吓了一跳。

Kissinger *was alarmed* by the explosion of China's first atom bomb in October, 1964.

Eg. 这个问题正在研究。

This problem is being considered (by us).

d. Chinese sentences with "由""被""把""让""叫""给""受""挨""遭""加以""予以""为……所""被……所""是…的"

Eg. 工作已由他完成了。

The work *has been done* by him.

Eg. 眼镜**给**打碎了。
　　The glasses *were broken*.

Eg. 这个问题必须**予以**处理。
　　This matter *must be dealt with*.

Eg. 汽车**让**洪水冲跑了。
　　The cars *were washed away* by the flood.

Eg. **被**人**被**游击队消灭了。
　　The enemy *was wiped out* by the guerrillas.

Eg. 我**教**雨淋了。
　　I *was caught* in the rain.

Eg. 他们去年**遭**了旱灾。
　　They *were hit* by a drought last year.

Eg. 你**把**她吓哭了。
　　She *was scared* to tears (by you).

Eg. 她**被**花言巧语**所**陶醉。
　　She *is intoxicated* with sweet words.

Eg. 历史**是**人民创造**的**。
　　History *is made* by the people.

There are also some established passive structures in English that we need to pay attention to.

- It is hoped/reported/said/supposed that...
- It must be admitted/pointed out that...
- It will be seen from this that...
- It is asserted/believed/well known/generally considered that...
- It will be said that...
- It was told that...

5.1.5　Position of Attributives and Adverbials

5.1.5.1　Attributives（Modifiers）

The attributives in Chinese sentences are front-loaded, which means, the structure is usually "modifier(s)+center word". English, however, is back-loaded, with the structure of "(short) modifier(s)+center word+(long) modifier(s)". Let's look at the following example. The center word is highlighted.

(Chinese)
女**孩子**
长头发**女孩子**
漂亮的长头发**女孩子**

一个漂亮的长头发**女孩子**

一个漂亮的个子高高的长头发**女孩子**

一个穿着高跟鞋的漂亮的个子高高的长头发**女孩子**

朝我们挥手的一个穿着高跟鞋的漂亮的个子高高的长头发**女孩子**

微笑着朝我们挥手的一个穿着高跟鞋的漂亮的个子高高的长头发**女孩子**

(English)

Girl

Girl with long hair

beautiful **girl** with long hair

one beautiful **girl** with long hair

one beautiful and tall **girl** with long hair

one beautiful andtall **girl** with long hair and high-heel shoes on

one beautiful and tall **girl** with long hair and high-heel shoes on who is waving at us

one beautiful and tall **girl** with long hair and high-heel shoes on who is waving at us with a smile

As can be seen from the examples above, in code-switching between Chinese and English, we need to pay special attention to the position of the center words and their modifiers. In C – E interpreting, we need to identify the center words and interpret them first, and then put the long modifiers after the center words, in the forms of prepositional phrases, non-predicate verb phrases, attributive clauses, appositional clauses, and adverbial clauses.

In E – C interpreting, especially simultaneous interpreting, the interpreting of attributive clauses can turn out to be challenging because the center words appear first while in Chinese, the center words need to be put last. For CI, interpreters may have the time to reorganize the sentences to make them sound more idiomatic, but in SI, interpreters may not have the luxury of time. A good strategy to use here is to repeat the center words. Even though it may sound a bit wordy, it works, especially for SI.

Eg. I feel sorry for the famous people who live their lives in the glare of publicity.

我真同情那些名人，他们要在众目睽睽之下生活。

Eg. Nobody is going to buy a house whose front door opens onto a grave yard.

没人会愿意买这样一栋房子，它的大门对着坟场。

5.1.5.2 Adverbials

Due to different ways of language organization (please refer to Parataxis vs. Hypotaxis), Chinese and English also use adverbials differently. Chinese sentences focus more on meaning, and the logical connections are often implied without even using adverbials, while English sentences focus on forms, and adverbials are often used as logical connectors. The following are some examples.

[1]　工作了两个小时**才**写出了几句话，**之后**他就放弃了，去看电影了。
After working for two hours, he only wrote a few sentences. He gave up *afterwards*, *and* went to see a movie. (Time adverbial)

[2]　外面下雨了，我们得带把伞。
We need to bring an umbrella, *for* it's raining outside. (Cause Adverbial)

[3]　热爱生活，生活也会厚爱你。
If you love your life, life will love you back. (Conditional Adverbial)

[4]　我安装了电脑，让她能在家办公。
I set up the computer so *that* she could work from home. (Purpose Adverbial)

5.1.6 Focus of Negations

Chinese and English have different focus of negations（否定焦点）. In code-switching between Chinese and English, we need to pay attention to this difference; otherwise, the interpreting in the target language may sound awkward and unidiomatic. Generally speaking, English prefers to put the focus of negations in the front, usually in the main clause.

Eg. I **don't** think that she would be of much help.
我觉得她**帮不上**什么忙。

Eg. I **didn't** work because I needed the money.
我当时工作**不是因为**需要钱。

Eg. I'm **not** here to argue with you.
我来这儿**不是**为了和你争吵。

There are two special uses of negations that we need to be careful about.

（1）**"Negation word＋enough/too" to express positive meaning.**

Eg. We cannot prepare enough for this conference.
　　为了这个会议，我们准备再多都不为过。

（2）**"No more... than..." to show negation in both.**

Eg. I can no more speak Japanese than he can speak English.
　　我说不了日语，就像他说不了英语一样。

In C - E code-switching, one of the strategies is to change the way of expression (negative expression or positive expression).

Eg. 我一天都没回家。(Negative expression)
　　I was not home the whole day. (Negative expression)
　　I was out the whole day. (Positive expression)

Eg. 这个理由站不住脚。(Negative expression)
　　This explanation does not hold water. (Negative expression)
　　This explanation is pretty thin. (Positive expression)

Exercises and Practice

5 - 1 - 1 Interpret the following sentences. Pay attention to the implied logical connections.
1. 他很穷,但是给他多少钱,他也不会出卖祖国。
2. 工作非常不易,我们很感激他。
3. 天气很好,我们决定举行露天招待会。
4. 中国是一个有五千年文明历史的国家,从历史文化来了解和认识中国,是一个重要的视角。
5. 这是我个人的想法,不见得恰当。谢谢!

5 - 1 - 2 Interpret the following sentences. Add subject or predicate if necessary.
1. 噪声控制工程师所使用的测量设备品种繁多,令人眼花缭乱。
2. 下雨了,赶快回家。
3. 多吃水果对身体有益。
4. 我们这周六一家人去动物园玩。
5. 科学所涵盖的领域很广。

5 - 1 - 3 Interpret the following sentences. Decide whether to use dynamic or stative expressions.
1. 你一定很不善于学习,要不然就是教你的人很不会教。
2. 过去我也常常有点喜欢胡思乱想。
3. 他失业以后,就很不合群了。
4. 石蕊试纸(Litmus paper)可用于检测溶液中是否含有酸。
5. 最令人吃惊的是,事情拖了很久,大大超过了我原来设想的两周。

5 - 1 - 4 Interpret the following sentences. Pay attention to the use of passive or active voices.
1. 注意看看信的地址是否写对了。
2. 有人听见呼救的声音。
3. 要制造飞机,就必须仔细考虑空气阻力问题。
4. 众所周知,中国人很久以前就发明了指南针。
5. 敌人的阴谋教我们揭穿了。

5 - 1 - 5 Interpret the following sentences. Pay attention to the position of attributives, adverbials and negations.
1. 那个手拿黑包正朝我们走来的高个子年轻人是我的大学同学。
2. 代表们在西安参观了兵马俑,然后去了大雁塔,之后回到酒店。
3. 我觉得他不可靠。
4. 你不走,我也不走。你走,我就走。
5. He is no more a singer than a dancer.

5.2 Code-Switching Skills—Discourse Level

As we have mentioned, interpreters are not just interpreting single sentences. Most of the time, they are interpreting a short or long passage. If they only pay attention to each single sentence without connecting them logically, the audience will be confused. There are also some fuzzy or culturally-loaded information that the interpreters need to properly deal with.

5.2.1 Cohesion and Coherence

One of the common rules in Chinese-English translation is "explicitation (显性化)". This is also determined by the different ways of language organization between Chinese and English.

Generally speaking, a discourse is not simply a compilation of sentences. To achieve communication purposes, a discourse is an organic whole with sentences connected by different cohesion and coherence devices. Coherence is the ways a text makes sense to readers and writer through the relevance and accessibility of its configuration of concepts, ideas and theories. Cohesion is the grammatical and lexical relationship between different elements of a text which hold it together. There are five cohesion and coherence devices that can be used in C-E interpreting.

1. Conjunctions

There are four types of conjunctions: additive, adversative, causal and temporal. The following example can demonstrate all four types of relations.

Eg. For the whole day he climbed up the steep mountainside, almost without stopping.

[1] *And* in all this time he met no one. (Additive)

[2] *Yet* he was hardly aware of being tired. (Adversative)

[3] *So* by the night time the valley was far below him. (Causal)

[4] *Then*, as dusk fell, he sat down to rest. (Temporal)

2. Lexical cohesion

There are two types of lexical cohesion: reiteration and collocation.

⊙ Reiteration

Reiteration is a form of lexical cohesion which involves repetition, synonym or near synonym, superordinate and a general noun.

Eg. *Pollution* of our environment has occurred for centuries, but it has become a significant *health problem* only within the last century. Atmospheric *pollution* contributes to respiratory disease, and to lung cancer in particular. Other *health problems* directly related to air pollutants include heart disease, eye irritation and so on.

⊙ Collocation

Collocation refers to the cohesion that is achieved through the association of lexical items that regularly co-occur. These lexical items or words tend to occur in similar environments. For instance: hair/comb, reader/writer, door/window, chair/table, north/south, peace/war, bee/honey, etc.

Eg. Why does this little *boy* wriggle all the time? *Girls* don't wriggle.

3. Reference

There are three types of reference: personal, demonstrative and comparative.

Chapter V Code-Switching Skills

◉ **Personal**

Eg. English is considered an international language. *It* is a spoken by more than 260 million people all over the world.

◉ **Demonstrative**

Eg. How do you like a cruise in *that* yacht?

◉ **Comparative**

Eg. The little dog barked *as noisily as* the big one.

4. Substitution

There are three types of substitution: nominal, verbal and clausal.

◉ **Nominal**

Eg. The little dog barked as noisily as the big *one*.

Eg. The size of the kitchen is the same as *that of* the dining room.

Eg. Winter is often so damp. *The same* is true for the summer.

◉ **Verbal**

Eg. I finally called on him. I have wanted to *do (so)* for a long time.

◉ **Clausal**

Eg. —Is there going to be a thunder storm?

　　—It says *so*.

5. Ellipsis

There are three types of ellipsis: nominal, verbal and clausal.

◉ **Nominal**

Eg. Here are thirteen cards. Take any (—)①. Now give me any three (—).

Eg. Smith was the first person to leave. I was the second (—).

◉ **Verbal**

Eg. Have you been losing weight? Yes, I have (—).

◉ **Clausal**

Eg. I kept quiet because Mary gets embarrassed if anyone mentions about John's name. I don't know why (—).

6. Discourse markers

Discourse markers are the connectors in a discourse which show the semantic relation among sentences. They are an important coherence device in a discourse. The following table (Table 5 – 1) lists some frequently used discourse markers and their functions.

Table 5 – 1　Discourse Markers and Their Functions

Function	Discourse Markers
Introducing the subject	I'd like to start by... Let's begin by... First of all, I'll... Starting with...

---

① (—): This part is omitted.

Continued Table

Function	Discourse Markers
Getting attention and curiosity	Have you ever seen/heard of...? You've probably seen countless times... You may have wondered... Before we start, let me ask you a question. Before we start, let's look at a picture/video. Before we start, let me show you a chart.
Finishing one subject	Well, I've told you about... That's all I have to say about... We've looked at... So much for...
Starting another subject	Now we'll move on to... Let me turn now to... Next... Turning to... I'd like now to discuss... Let's look now at...
Analyzing a point and giving suggestions	Where does this lead us? Let's consider this in more detail... What does this mean for...? Translated into real terms...
Outlining the structure and sequencing	I'll talk about it from three parts/perspectives/aspects:... I have broken my presentation down into X parts... I have divided my presentation into X parts... In today's presentation, I'll first introduce... then... and finally... I'll concentrate on the following points:... Firstly... secondly... thirdly... lastly... First of all... then... next... after that... To start with... later... to finish up...
Dealing with questions	If you have any questions, I will be happy to answer them as we go along. Please feel free to ask me any questions. Perhaps we can leave any questions you have until the end. Please feel free to interrupt me if you have any questions. By the end of my presentation, there will be ten minutes for Q & A. There will be plenty of time for questions and discussion at the end of my presentation.

Continued Table

Signaling the ending	In conclusion, to conclude... To summarize, in summary, to sum up... In a word... So now...
Summarizing and concluding	To sum up, just now, we have talked about... So now, let me summarize what we have talked about today. So now, let me recap the three points I have made today. OK, now let's answer the question I asked at the very beginning. Let me restate my three main views... Today we have talked about... I think now it is clear that... Today we tried to understand... now I think it's clear... Finally, let me remind you of... If I can just sum up the main points... In conclusion, if we want to... we need to... To conclude, to solve this problem, we need... As a result, we suggest that... I would recommend that... From what we have discussed, you can see that...
Giving an example	For example... A good example of this is... As an illustration,... To give you an example... To illustrate this point...

5.2.2 *Fuzzy or Culturally-loaded Information*

5.2.2.1 **Fuzzy Information**

Fuzziness is a commonly seen phenomenon in all languages. There are two main types of fuzziness: lexical fuzziness and semantic fuzziness. Lexical fuzziness includes words of time, age, color, temperature, taste, etc. They usually have no clear boundaries. For example, when "hot" or "warm" are used, there is not an exact temperature range for how much is considered hot and how much is considered warm. Semantic fuzziness can be seen in some wording in sentences, such as "大约，左右，也许，大概，若干" in Chinese, and "about, probably, almost, in a sense, to a degree, roughly, more or less" in English.

There is a necessity for fuzziness in communication. According to different communication purposes, there are five main categories of fuzziness.

1. To generalize

Eg. 我们店有草莓、菠萝、桃子、葡萄……**诸如此类**的水果。

Our shop has strawberries, pineapples, peaches, grapes and *fruits like that*.

2. To increase flexibility (often used in diplomacy and negotiations)

Eg. 您所提及的污水治理问题,我们会采取**一定的**措施。

As for the waste water treatment issue you have mention, we will *take certain measures*.

3. To indicate politeness

Eg. 这个条款**好像**应该修改一下。

It seems this clause should be revised.

Eg. 在更改收货地址之前通知一下供货方,这样**似乎**会更好点。

It *seems better* to notify the supplier before changing the shipping address.

4. To increase effect

Eg. 我们的价格是**最优惠的**。其他供货商都以**大幅度涨价**,而我们价格变化不大。

Our price is *most favorable*. Other suppliers all have *dramatically* increased their prices while ours haven't changed *much*.

5. To fill up empty information

Eg. 下次来的时候记着带……**那个什么**……记着带合同。

Remember to bring... *what's that... you know...* the contract with you next time you come.

5.2.2.2 Culturally-Loaded Information

As we have talked about in Cross-Cultural Communication Skills in Chapter Ⅲ, language and culture cannot be separated, and language is often heavily culturally-loaded. This causes great difficulties for interpreters. With over 5,000 years of history, this is especially true for Chinese.

Generally speaking, there are two types of culturally-loaded words in Chinese. The first type comes from tradition. Examples are: the 24 solar terms of Chinese (二十四节气) such as the Grain Rain (谷雨) and the Waking of Insects (惊蛰); some traditional food such as Jiaozi (饺子), Zongzi (粽子); traditional clothing such as cheongsam (旗袍), and traditional etiquettes such as kowtow (磕头).

The second type comes from some expressions used in the modern society in China. Examples are: moderately well-off society (小康社会), left-behind children (留守儿童), the Hope Project (希望工程), high blood sugar, high blood fat, and high blood pressure (三高), etc.

In interpreting, there are mainly three strategies in dealing with culturally-loaded words.

1. Substitution (替换)

When an English term can be found directly, we can use substitution in interpreting.

Eg. 庙,庵,观 temple

女婿 son-in-law

亲家 the in-laws

不折腾 no Z-turns

2. Explanation or free translation（释义或意译）

When the information cannot be translated literally, we can use explanation or free translation.

Eg. 戴绿帽子 Cheat on somebody

亲家 Relatives by marriage

不折腾 no flip-flop/ don't get sidetracked/ no major changes

比赛中要讲公平。

Stress must be put on fairness in competition.

人才更趋于年轻化、专业化、国际化。

Talents tend to be younger, more specialized and more globalized.

3. Transliteration（音译）

Some Chinese terms are used directly and can be understood by people of other languages.

Eg. 风水 Fengshui

阴阳 Yinyang

饺子 Jiaozi

4. Combination of strategies（混译）

With the deepening of globalization and popularization of internet language, some mixed words with both Chinese and English elements appear. Many of them are even recognized internationally and can be used directly.

Eg. 不作不死 no *zuo* no die

（中国）宇航员 Taikonaut (*Taikong*＋-naut)

Exercises and Practice

5-2-1　Revise the following passage. Use cohesion and coherence devices to make it sound more coherent.

The ancient Egyptians were masters of preserving dead people's bodies by making mummies of them. Mummies several thousand years old have been discovered nearly intact. The skin, hair, teeth, fingernails and toenails, and facial features of the mummies were evident. It is possible to diagnose the disease they suffered in life, such as smallpox, arthritis, and nutritional deficiencies. The process was remarkably effective. Sometimes apparent were the fatal afflictions of the dead people: a middle-aged king died from a blow on the head, and polio killed a child king. Mummification consisted of removing the internal organs, applying natural preservatives inside and out, and then wrapping the body in layers of bandages.

5-2-2　Interpret the following sentences. Pay special attention to the culturally-loaded

information.
1. 美化环境从我做起。
2. 他最近走桃花运。
3. 技术评估必须经得起时间检验,要过好三道关——质量关、人情关、功利关。
4. 随后的发展也相当顺利,可以说是"一心同德"谋事业,"一往直前"大发展,"一鼓作气"求跨越。
5. 著名的"两弹一星"功勋奖章的23名获得者中有21名是归国学者。

Additional Materials

1. New Regulation in U.S. Immigration: Green Cards Are Harder to Obtain for People Relying on Public Benefits
美国移民新规:依赖公共福利者难获绿卡
来源:中国日报网
http://ex.chinadaily.com.cn/exchange/partners/80/rss/channel/language/columns/oy49x2/stories/WS5d539ddba310cf3e35565b72.html

US President Donald Trump's administration is to make it more difficult for poorer legal migrants to extend their visas or gain permanent resident status (a green card).
美国政府将加大贫困合法移民申请续签签证或获得永久居民身份(绿卡)的难度。

The rule targets migrants who rely on public benefits, such as food aid or public housing, for more than a year.
这项规定针对的是那些依赖食品券和公共住房等公共福利生活超过一年的移民。

Their applications will be rejected if the government decides they are likely to rely on public assistance in future.
如果政府认为他们未来可能依赖公共援助,其申请将被拒绝。

The rule change would reinforce "ideals of self-sufficiency," officials said.
有官员表示,这一规则的改变将强化"自给自足的理念"。

Anyone who relies on one or more publicly funded social safety net benefits, such as Medicaid or food stamps, is known as a "public charge."
任何依赖一项或多项公共社会保障福利(如医疗补助计划或食品券)的人都被视为"公共负担"。

According to this rule, an immigrant will be designated as a "public charge" if that person "receives one or more designated public benefits for more than 12 months in the aggregate within any 36-month period."

根据规定,在任意36个月内,"累计领取一项或多项指定公共福利超过12个月"的移民将被视为"公共负担"。

The new regulation, known as a "public charge rule," was published in the Federal Register on Monday and will take effect on October 15.
这项"公共负担"新规于周一(8月12日)发表在《联邦公报》上,将于10月15日生效。

Immigrants who are already permanent residents in the US are unlikely to be affected by the rule change.
已经是美国永久居民的移民不太可能受到新规的影响。

Undocumented immigrants would not be affected—unless an avenue opens up for them to apply for green cards or visas since they are largely ineligible for public aid.
非法移民不会受到影响,除非他们有机会申请绿卡或签证,因为他们大部分没有资格获得公共援助。

It also does not apply to refugees and asylum applicants.
这项新规也不适用于难民和庇护申请人。

But applicants for visa extensions, green cards or US citizenship will be subject to the change.
但申请续签签证、绿卡或美国公民身份的人将受此影响。

Those who do not meet income standards or who are deemed likely to rely on benefits such as Medicaid (government-run healthcare) or housing vouchers in future may be blocked from entering the country.
那些收入不达标或被认为未来可能依赖医疗补助计划(政府医疗保健)或住房券等福利的人可能被禁止入境。

Those already in the US could also have their applications rejected.
已经身在美国的人,申请也可能会被拒绝。

An estimated 22 million legal residents in the US are without citizenship, and many of these are likely to be affected.
据估计,美国约有2200万合法居民没有公民身份,其中许多人可能会受到影响。

Civil rights groups have said the move unfairly targets low-income immigrants. The National Immigration Law Center (NILC) has said it will sue the Trump administration to stop the regulation from taking effect.

民权组织表示,此举专门针对低收入移民,有失公允。美国国家移民法律中心表示,将起诉特朗普政府,以阻止该规定生效。

But the White House said the current system favors immigrants with family ties rather than those who "are self-sufficient and do not strain our public resources."

但白宫方面表示,目前的移民体系更青睐在美国有家庭关系的移民,而不是那些"自给自足、不会造成公共资源紧张"的移民。

Since his inauguration, Mr. Trump has cut the number of refugees admitted to the US each year. The White House blocked a Senate compromise immigration proposal in January 2018 in part because it did not include changes to the legal immigration system.

自就职以来,特朗普每年都在削减进入美国的难民人数。2018年1月,白宫否决了参议院的移民提案,部分原因是提案未包括对合法移民体系的改革,而这一提案是此前两党妥协的结果。

Now the administration is making it more difficult for less affluent individuals to obtain legal US residency—or perhaps even enter the country at all.

如今,特朗普政府加大了经济能力较差的个人获得美国合法居留权的难度,他们甚至可能根本无法入境。

This sets up an election clash next year between a president sharpening and broadening his immigration rhetoric and Democrats, many of whom have said they believe all immigrants, legal or otherwise, should be eligible for public aid.

这将在明年的美国总统大选中引发一场冲突,一方是正在强化和扩大其移民言论的总统,另一方是民主党人。许多民主党人曾表示,他们认为所有移民,无论合法与否,都应有资格得到公共援助。

President Trump has made immigration a central theme of his administration. This latest move is part of his government's efforts to curb legal immigration.

特朗普总统将移民问题作为政府的中心议题。这是其减少合法移民数量的最新举措。

"To protect benefits for American citizens, immigrants must be financially self-sufficient," a White House statement read after the rule change was announced.

在新规公布后,白宫发表声明称:"为了保护美国公民的利益,移民必须在经济上自给自足。"

It said two-thirds of immigrants entering the US "do so based on family ties rather than on skill or merit."

声明称,三分之二的移民"基于家庭关系,而不是技能或优势"进入美国。

Ken Cuccinelli, the acting director of the US Citizenship and Immigration Service, announced the regulation at a press conference on Monday.
周一(8月12日),美国公民及移民服务局代理局长肯·库奇内利在新闻发布会上宣布了这一规定。

He said finances, education, age, and the level of an applicant's English-language skills will all be considered in green card applications. "No one factor alone" will decide a case, he added.
他说,经济、教育、年龄和申请者的英语水平都将被视为绿卡申请的考量因素。他补充说,"不会单凭某一个因素"决定一个申请是否通过。

"We expect people of any income to stand on their own two feet," Cuccinelli said on Monday.
他表示:"我们希望所有收入阶层的人们都能够自食其力。"

The Trump administration has also cracked down on illegal immigration. Last week, about 680 people were arrested in Mississippi on suspicion of being undocumented migrants.
特朗普政府也对非法移民进行打击。上周,密西西比州约有680人因涉嫌非法移民而被捕。

The number of would-be migrants apprehended at the US southern border with Mexico has been rising over the last two years.
过去两年,在美国南部与墨西哥边境被捕的潜在移民人数一直在上升。

However, the number of undocumented immigrants in the US is falling, according to recent analysis from the Pew Research Center.
然而,皮尤研究中心最新分析显示,美国的非法移民人数正在下降。

In May, President Trump put forward proposals for a new skills-based immigration system, designed to favor younger, better educated, English-speaking workers.
今年5月,特朗普总统提出了一项以技能为基础的新移民体系提案,旨在吸引更年轻、受教育程度更高、会说英语的人移民美国。

The 837-page rule applies to those seeking to come to or remain in the United States via legal channels and is expected to impact roughly 382,000 people seeking to adjust their immigration, according to the Department of Homeland Security. However, immigration advocates say millions of people could be affected by the regulation.
根据美国国土安全部的数据,这项长达837页的规定适用于那些寻求通过合法途径来美国或定居美国的人,预计将影响约38.2万打算调整移民身份的人。然而,移民支持者表示,这一新规可能影响到数百万人。

New York Attorney General Letitia James announced Monday evening that she plans to sue to block the rule.
纽约司法部长莉蒂夏·詹姆斯周一晚间宣布,她计划提起诉讼,阻止这项规定实施。

Immigrant advocates have argued that the rule goes beyond what Congress intended and would discriminate against those from poorer countries, keep families apart and prompt legal residents to forgo needed public aid, which could also impact their US citizen children.
移民维权人士辩称,该规定超出了国会的本意,是对来自较贫穷国家移民的歧视,使家庭分离,还会导致合法居民放弃必要的公共援助,或将影响其美国公民子女。

They also said it would penalize even hard-working immigrants who only need a small bit of temporary assistance from the government.
他们还表示,即使是辛勤工作、只需要政府提供少许临时援助的移民,也会处于不利境地。

About one in seven adults in immigrant families reported that either the person or a family member did not participate in a non-cash safety net program last year because of fear of risking his or her green card status in the future, an Urban Institute study found.
美国城市研究所调查发现,在移民家庭中,约七分之一的成年人表示,由于担心将来失去绿卡,去年自己或家人没有参加非现金保障计划。

2. Certificates Needed for a Permit for Qomolangma(想攀登珠峰?你还得有这些证明!)
来源:搜狐网
https://www.sohu.com/a/335201633_100191005

All climbers seeking a permit for Qomolangma must have prior high altitude mountaineering experience and demonstrable training, a high-level commission for the Nepalese government has ruled.
尼泊尔政府管辖的高级委员会规定,凡是想获准攀登珠穆朗玛峰的人,必须有高海拔登山经历并受过硬核的培训。

The recommendation was issued by the body charged with looking at the issue of high-altitude safety after one of the deadliest seasons in recent years on Qomolangma, which was blamed on inexperience and crowding near the summit.
在珠峰上出现了近年来最致命的高海拔安全问题后,负责调查这一问题的机构发布了上述建议。登山安全问题被归咎于经验不足和山顶附近过于拥挤。

Eleven climbers were killed or went missing on the 8,850-metre[①] mountain in May, nine on the Nepalese side and two on the Tibetan side.

[①] 中国国家测绘局测量的珠峰岩面高(裸高即地质高度)为 8 844.43 m。

今年 5 月，11 名登山者在海拔 8850 米①的珠峰上死亡或失踪，9 名在尼泊尔境内的南坡遇难，2 名在中国西藏的北坡遇难。

The Nepalese panel—made up of government officials, climbing experts and agencies representing the climbing community—was set up after climbers and guides criticized officials for allowing anyone who paid $11,000 to attempt to climb Qomolangma. Some veteran guiding companies had long warned of the dangerous consequences of inexperience and crowds on the summit slopes.

尼泊尔的这一委员会由政府官员、登山专家和登山团体代表机构组成。在该委员会成立之前，登山者和导游们批评尼泊尔官员允许任何能支付 1.1 万美元（约合人民币 7.7 万元）的人攀登珠峰。一些经验丰富的导游公司早就警告过缺乏经验和山顶拥挤的危险后果。

"Climbers to Qomolangma and other 8,000-metre mountains must undergo basic and high altitude climbing training," the panel said in the report it submitted to the government.

委员会在提交给政府的报告中写道："攀登珠穆朗玛峰和其他海拔 8000 米以上山峰的人必须接受基本的登山训练和高海拔登山训练。"

It said that those hoping to climb Qomolangma must have climbed at least one Nepalese peak of more than 6,500-metres before getting a permit. Climbers must also submit a certificate of good health and physical fitness and be accompanied by a trained Nepalese guide.

委员会称，想攀登珠穆朗玛峰的人必须至少攀登过一座海拔 6500 米以上的尼泊尔山峰才能得到登山许可。登山者还必须提交健康和体能证明，并由受过训练的尼泊尔导游陪同。

Mira Acharya, a member of the panel, said: "Climbers died due to altitude sickness, heart attack, exhaustion or weaknesses, and not due to traffic jams." She said the compulsory provision of guides for each climber was to discourage solo attempts, which put lives at risk.

委员会的其中一名成员米拉·阿查里雅说："登山者是由于高原反应、心脏病、精疲力竭和体弱而死亡，不是因为交通堵塞而死亡。"她说，强制规定每一名登山者都要有导游陪同，目的是阻止有人独自登山，独自攀登会有生命危险。

The panel's report also proposes a fee of at least $35,000 for those wanting to climb Qomolangma, and $20,000 for other mountains higher than 8,000m.

委员会的报告还提议，对想攀登珠峰的人收取至少 3.5 万美元的费用，对想攀登海拔 8000 米以上其他山峰的人收取 2 万美元的费用。

Nepal is home to eight of the world's 14 highest mountains, and mountain climbing is a key source of employment and income for the poor nation.

世界最高的 14 座山峰中,尼泊尔就占了 8 座。登山是这个较为贫穷的国家的重要就业渠道和收入来源。

The numbers attempting the climb in May led to bottlenecks in the "death zone," where very low oxygen levels put lives at risk. Oxygen cylinders ran out while as many as 100 people waited in the queue.

5 月登珠峰人数过多导致了"死亡地带"出现拥堵,那里极低的氧气水平威胁到了登山者的生命安全。在多达 100 人排队登顶的过程中,有些人用光了自己的氧气储备。

The issues were underlined by Simon Lowe, the managing director of UK-based Jagged Globe, who said this year's crowding had aggravated an underlying issue of lack of experience.

英国公司 Jagged Globe 的总经理西蒙·洛强调了这一问题,他表示今年珠峰的拥堵加重了缺乏经验的潜在问题。

"That is incompetent climbers being led by incompetent teams," Lowe said. "If you go up with a bare minimum bottles of supplementary oxygen and stand in a queue for ages that is going to cause problems."

"这里指的是不合格的团队带领的不合格的登山者,"洛说道,"如果你只带了最小量的备用氧气瓶上山,又在队伍里长时间地等待,那肯定是要出问题的。"

Without reforms such as those suggested by the panel, Lowe said guiding on the mountain by responsible companies could become untenable.

洛指出,如果没有委员会建议的这些改革,负责任的公司的登山导游工作将会做不下去。

Nepal issued 381 permits for Qomolangma for this year's climbing season, which tends to culminate in May, when the daylight and weather are the most forgiving.

今年登山季,尼泊尔签发了 381 份攀登珠峰的许可证。珠峰攀登通常都在 5 月达到高峰,那时候的日照和天气条件都是最佳的。

Ghanshyam Upadhyaya, a senior tourism ministry official, said the recommendations would be implemented. "The government will now make the required changes in laws and regulations guiding mountain climbing," he told Reuters.

旅游部的高级官员甘希亚姆·乌帕德希雅说,这些建议将会被实行。他告诉路透社说:"现在政府将会对指导登山的法律法规做出所需的改动。"

Chapter Ⅵ   Interpreting Figures

Learning questions:
√ *How to note down and interpret long complicated figures?*
√ *How to interpret round figures?*

In consecutive interpreting, figures (numbers) are frequently used to support a point or illustrate a situation. It can be said that figures are almost inevitable in interpreting. It is also the reason why in this book, we talk about interpreting figures before talking about other key CI skills such as memory training and note-taking.

For many interpreters, figures are a huge barrier in interpreting, mainly due to different ways of expression between Chinese and English and the limit of short-term memory. According to a survey, over 65% of interpreters think that a large part of their work pressure comes from interpreting figures. Some interpreters even fear figures.

Figure interpreting, however, can be trained. With the right skills and ample training, interpreters can interpret figures faster and more accurately, and with more confidence. In this chapter, we will mainly talk about some basic skills in interpreting figures, and do some training in single figures and sentences with figures.

6.1   Basic Skills in Interpreting Figures

6.1.1   The Basics About Figures

Figures, especially English figures, are harder to understand and note down. When interpreting figures, we need to pay special attention to the following issues.

6.1.1.1   The Reading of Chinese and English Figures

The precondition of recognizing and interpreting figures quickly and accurately is to be able to read them fluently. For Chinese students, the reading of numbers in English is a major difficulty. Learners need to start practicing reading figures from two digits, then move on to three, four, five or more digits. Among them, the two-digit and three-digit reading is the basis for reading all the numbers.

The biggest difference between English and Chinese figures lies in the different ways they are read. It is also one of the main reasons for the difficulty in interpreting figures. Of course, there are rules to follow in order to quickly read out the big numbers in English and

Chinese. Counting from right to left, English uses a three-digit unit while Chinese uses a four-digit unit. In English, the name of each unit from small to large (right to left) is: thousand, million, billion and trillion. In Chinese, the name of each unit from small to large is: ten thousand (万), one hundred million (亿) and trillion (万亿).

For example: 2367492103.

In English, it is divided based on the three-digit unit (separated by commas): 2,367,492,103. It reads: two billion, 3 hundred and sixty-seven million, four hundred and ninety-two thousand, and one hundred and three.

In Chinese, it is divided based on the four-digit unit: 23/6749/2103. It reads: 二十三亿六千七百四十九万两千一百零三。

Note that commas are required for English figures that are more than three digits. The slashes in Chinese, however, are not. They are only used here to indicate the unit division in figures.

6.1.1.2 Distinguishing "-teen" and "-ty"

Many learners have a difficult time distinguishing the sound "-teen" and "-ty". A good way to distinguish the two sounds is through stresses (重读) and phonemes (音素). Words that end with "-teen" have two stresses. That means stress needs to be put on "-teen", and the phoneme in "-teen" is [iː]. It is usually pronounced long and clear. Words that end with "-ty" have only one stress, and the stress is not put on "-ty". The phoneme in "-ty" is [i], which is pronounced short and fast.

6.1.1.3 Different Reading of Figures in American and British English

In interpreting, we may face speakers from different countries. Their way of speaking can vary even when they are speaking the same language. One good example would be the different pronunciation and diction between American and British English. The difference between the two can also be seen in their way of reading figures. There are three main differences:

For four digit figures (especially simple round numbers), British people would prefer the use of "thousand" while Americans prefer "hundred". For example, 2,400, it reads "two thousand and four hundred" in British English while "twenty-four hundred" in American English.

For ten digit figures, British people may prefer the use of "thousand million" while Americans prefer the use of "billion". For example, 3,000,000,000, British way of reading would be "three thousand million" while the American way would be "three billion".

Between the second and third digit, British people would use "and" while Americans tend not to. For example, 356 would be read "three hundred and fifty-six" in British English and "three hundred fifty-six" in American English.

Of course, each individual speaks differently, and the above differences may not apply to all British or American speakers.

6.1.2 Note-taking Methods in Figure Interpreting

Noting figures down accurately can be challenging for learners, especially with the long and complicated ones. Even when the figures are noted down, it is not easy to interpret them accurately. Here we will introduce three effective methods in noting and interpreting figures, namely: comma-and-slash method, missing digit supplement method and interpreting formulas.

6.1.2.1 Comma-and-Slash Method (点三杠四法)

The comma-and-slash method is mainly used for noting long and complicated figures. It is specially designed for E - C and C - E interpreting, based on the different division of figures in reading. As we have discussed earlier, English figures are divided by unit of three while Chinese are divided by four. In English, we use commas to indicate units while in Chinese, we use slashes. So in interpreting, the note-taking and interpreting process can be as follows:

1. Chinese to English

(1) Hearing Chinese figure: 十一亿两千五百八十三万四千一百六十七.

(2) Noting down on paper: $11^{亿}2583^{万}4167$, or 11/2583/4167.

(3) Adding commas from right to left in unit of three: $1,1^{亿}25,83^{万}4,167$.

(4) Marking the units with "thousand (th), million (m), billion (b), or trillion (tr)" from right to left: $1,_b1^{亿}25,_m83^{万}4,_{th}167$.

(5) Reading the figure out in English: one billion one hundred and twenty-five million eight hundred and thirty-four thousand (and) one hundred and sixty-seven.

2. English to Chinese

(1) Hearing English figure: two billion three hundred and twenty-five million nine hundred and sixty-one thousand two hundred and one.

(2) Notingdown on paper: $2^b325^m961^{th}201$, or 2,325,961,201.

(3) Adding slashes from right to left in unit of four: 2,3/25,96/1,201.

(4) Marking the units with "万(w), 亿(y), 万亿(wy)" from right to left: $2,3/_{亿}25,96/_{万}1,201$.

(5) Reading the figure out in Chinese: 二十三亿两千五百九十六万一千两百零一.

6.1.2.2 Missing Digit Supplement Method (缺位补零法)

Many times, long and complicated figures may not be as complete as the above examples. They are often missing a few digits, and if these digits are not supplemented, comma-and-slash method cannot be applied. Otherwise, mistakes will occur. In interpreting, we need to be extra careful with figures that are missing digits. The missing digit supplement method is designed for these figures. When digits are missing, we need to supplement them with zeros before using the comma-and-slash method. The note-taking and interpreting process can be as follows:

1. Chinese to English

(1) Hearing Chinese figure: 五亿零三十二万零四十五.

(2) Noting down on paper: 5亿32万45, or 5/32/45.

(3) Adding 0 to the missing digits according to Chinese division: 5亿0032万0045.

(4) Adding commas from right to left in unit of three: 5亿00,32万0,045.

(5) Marking the units with "thousand (th), million (m), billion (b), or trillion (tr)" from right to left: 5亿00,$_m$32万0,$_{th}$045.

(6) Reading the figure out in English: five hundred million three hundred and twenty thousand and forty-five.

2. English to Chinese

(1) Hearing English figure: two hundred billion fifty-three million two thousand and ninety.

(2) Noting down on paper: 200^{b}53^{m}2th90, or 200,53,2,90.

(3) Adding "0" to the missing digits according to English division: 200^{b}053^{m}002th090.

(4) Adding slashes from right to left in unit of four: 200^{b}0/53^{m}00/2th090.

(5) Marking the units with "万(w), 亿(y), 万亿(wy)" from right to left: 200^{b}0/$_亿$53^{m}00/$_万$2th090.

(6) Reading the figure out in Chinese: 两千亿五千三百万两千零九十.

Note that no matter it is three-digit or four-digit division, "0" should be added **from left to right** in each unit.

6.1.2.3 Interpreting Formulas（公式法）

Formulas are designed for the interpreting of short numbers. In many cases, they are actually more frequently seen in interpreting than those long and complicated numbers. These formulas should be internalized by interpreters as part of their skill set, and be used as if conditioned reflex.

1. C-E formulas

一万＝10 thousand.

十万＝100 thousand.

百万＝1 million.

千万＝10 million.

一亿＝100 million/ 0.1 billion.

十亿＝1 billion.

百亿＝10 billion.

千亿＝100 billion.

万亿＝1 trillion.

2. E-C formulas

1 thousand ＝千.

10 thousand＝万.

Chapter VI Interpreting Figures

100 thousand=十万.
1 million=百万.
10 million=千万.
100 million=亿.
1 billion=十亿.
10 billion=百亿.
100 billion=千亿.
1 trillion=万亿.

6.1.3 Figure-Related Expressions

6.1.3.1 Ordinal Numbers

Ordinal numbers（序数词）are used to indicate order. Except for a few special ordinal numbers (such as "first", "second" and "third"), most of the ordinal numbers are formed by adding "-th" after corresponding cardinal numbers（基数词）. But usually "the" is added in front, such as "the fourth" "the tenth" "the fifteenth".

For larger numbers, ordinal numbers are often replaced by cardinal numbers. To indicate order, the word "number" can be added in front, such as "number 321" (often abbreviated to No. 321).

6.1.3.2 Fractions, Decimals, and Multiples

1. Fractions（分数）

Fractions are formed by combining cardinal numbers and ordinal numbers. The denominators are expressed in ordinal numbers and the numerators are expressed in cardinal numbers. And when the numerator is bigger than one, the denominator must be in plural form. For example, 1/3 reads one third; 5/7 reads five sevenths; 1/2 reads a (one) half; 3/4 reads three quarters; 3 1/2 reads three and a half.

For more complicated fractions, the structure of "cardinal number over cardinal number" is often used. For example, 31/75 reads thirty-one over seventy-five.

2. Decimals（小数）

The decimal point is read "point". The numbers after the decimal point must be read individually. The numbers before the decimal point are read as cardinal numbers. If the number before the decimal point is 0, it is read "zero" or "not", or it is not read at all. For example:

1.3536 reads one point three five three six;

0.251 reads zero/not point two five one, or point two five one;

17.23 reads seventeen point two three.

3. Multiples（倍数）

Besides some set terms such as "double" "triple" and "quadruple", multiples are often expressed by using "time" or "-fold". For example:

A is four times as large as B. / A is four times larger than B. / A is four times the size/ number/length of B. （A 是 B 的 4 倍）

A increases fourfold/ four times/ by a factor of four/ by 300％. （A 增加到原来的 4 倍）

A decreases by four times/ by 75％. / There is a fourfold decrease in A. / A is four times smaller than before. （A 减少到原来的 1/4）

6.1.3.3　Fuzzy Figures

Fuzzy figures are often used in spoken language，both in Chinese and in English. Here are some examples：

几个：a few, some, a number of, several.

十几个：around a dozen, more than ten, less than twenty.

几十个：dozens of, several dozens.

几十年：decades, a few decades.

五十好几：well over fifty.

好几百个的：hundreds of.

成千上万的：thousands of.

几十万的：hundreds of thousands of.

几千万的：millions of.

亿万的：hundreds of millions of.

6.1.3.4　Trends and Values

1. Trends

增加：increase, rise, grow, go up.

增长到：increase to, go up to, be up to, rise to, reach, expand to.

增长了：increase by, go up by.

大幅上升，飙升：increase dramatically/largely, surge up, hike up, jump up, shoot up, soar, zoom up, skyrocket.

爬升：climb, pick up.

下降：decrease, decline, drop, fall, go down, reduce.

大幅下降，猛跌：decrease dramatically, plunge, be slashed, tumble.

稍降：be trimmed, dip, slip.

超过：surpass, exceed, be more than, be over, outpace.

2. Values

达到：reach, amount to, come to, stand at, be up to, arrive at, hit.

总计：total, add up to, amount to.

占：account for, make up, take up.

多达：be as many as, be as much as, be up to.

大约：about, around, roughly, approximately, some, in the neighborhood of, more or less, or so.

少于：less than, fewer than, under, below, within.

多于：more than, over, above... and more.
差不多：close to, nearly, almost.

Exercises and Practice

6-1-1 Listen to the following long figures, note them down and read them out in both Chinese and English using the comma-and-slash method or the missing digit supplement method, or both.

1. English figures. (Audio 6-1-1 En)

478,291,032	3,518,921,113	10,112,348,214
8,009,011,230	818,320,091	1,004,020,000
42,000,190,012	7,034,000,000	1,823,021,000,329

2. Chinese figures. (Audio 6-1-1 CN)

9/0372/9941	906/4017/4658	21/9823/4101
9/0092/0038	801/0001/0219	300/0000/1900
1/0092/3250/1001	51/0028/0000	6/8012/0099

6-1-2 Listen to the following short figures, note them down and interpret them using interpreting formulas.

1. English to Chinese. (Audio 6-1-2 EC)

20 million	90 billion	256 thousand
6 billion	21 thousand	102 billion
7 trillion	690 million	5 million

2. Chinese to English. (Audio 6-1-2 CE)

6万	8亿	930亿
67亿	5000万	7000亿
4万亿	11万	501万

6-1-3 Interpret the following figures or expressions.

1. 8.112,3   0.823
2. 2 4/5   34/91
3. 第87   第3
4. 35是7的5倍。
5. 总值增加到原来的6倍。
6. 数值降低到原来的1/5。
7. The value increased by 6 times.
8. The total number reduced by threefold.

6.2 Figure Interpreting Training

With the basic knowledge of figures and the note-taking and interpreting methods in mind, we can now start the training of figure interpreting. To accurately interpret figures, we first need to be able to understand and read figures before we can even talk about interpreting figures. Then, a large amount of training is needed in both interpreting just figures and interpreting sentences with figures. Here in this book, we can only provide a limited amount of training. Much more work needs to be done after class.

6.2.1 Interpreting Figures

6.2.1.1 Understanding Figures

Exercise 1: Listen to the following figures in Chinese and write them down. (Audio 6.2.1.1 E1)

  2341 3881 9016
  34781 79312 65173
  610901 780913 600892
  6530012 5430918 7690010
  23768016 70019068 16028041
  780002571 300900180 532074190
  5097319840 9754490218 5231057259
  76310098609 81000642908 90075210005
  501853006420 100861100856 714208420086

Exercise 2: Listen to the following figures in English and write them down. (Audio 6.2.1.1 E2)

  8702 7313 6219
  32919 70012 83210
  829012 721392 390012
  7462309 8235632 3002983
  48920093 79120321 10002383
  821082230 298457338 893600281
  3109300721 4092083274 4652050982
  37260003729 53900835230 54200801021
  543010046278 132009273092 632800002315

6.2.1.2 Reading Figures

Exercise: Mark the following figures with commas or slashes, and read them out in both English and Chinese.

  1049 8139 5432 7301
  48756 10485 74042 74639
  748592 100583 842802 920870
  3847201 7947902 4300031 1375832
  46352901 48560372 90028421 10932453

Chapter VI   Interpreting Figures

464900702	430820002	730763112	630004241
1089300211	4730028472	4600003742	1305837000
30482803831	26472002850	64322080001	10492743881
728497623098	223119763711	320990221035	500064003590

6.2.1.3 Interpreting Figures

Exercise 1: Listen to the following long figures and interpret them using the skills we have learned in Section 6.1.

1. Chinese to English. (Audio 6.2.1.3 E1 CE)

7932/1786	4543/9013	1/3095/1239	7/3221/3400
32/1908/8091	780/2132	10/6091/6510	1/7102/8900/3110
2309/0078	6/8821/0009	90/0009/0003	670/0981/0012
460/7812/0000	89/0000/3210	68/0000/0010	1/0000/0338/0900
670/8900/0218	901/2100/8899	2003/0098	20/8000/0099/0201

2. English to Chinese. (Audio 6.2.1.3 E1 EC)

901,891,210	1,679,561	12,789,651	12,908,740,127
984,771,675	2,890,560,183	639,226,100	1,249,806,281,117
68,001,012	4,360,007,011	800,006,001	441,500,003,081
761,000,890	2,057,084,000	9,000,000,011	8,568,000,000
690,033,457	620,011,772,668	8,566,319	5,990,001,681,008

Exercise 2: Listen to the following short figures and interpret them using the skills we have learned in Section 6.1.

1. Chinese to English. (Audio 6.2.1.3 E2 CE)

4.81 万	6.29 亿	517 亿	3.11 亿
20.88 亿	3000 万	9000 亿	259.1 万
7.1 万亿	29.01 万	810.8 万	21 万亿
3670 亿	6104 万	0.86 亿	6400.1 亿
0.18 万	910.3 亿	306 万	2001.5 万

2. English to Chinese. (Audio 6.2.1.3 E2 EC)

10.6 million	67.54 billion	809 thousand	900 million
7.19 billion	67.2 thousand	573.8 billion	3 billion
9.7 trillion	359 million	6.09 million	55.8 million
457.9 thousand	87.3 million	700 billion	21.99 billion
875.12 million	44 thousand	82.8 million	577.1 billion

6.2.2 Interpreting Sentences with Figures

Learning to interpret just figures is not enough, we need to be able to distinguish figures in sentences, understand related expressions, and be able to express values, trends and etc. in a sentence. Figures are almost inevitable in interpreting, no matter what type of speech it is, what topic it involves, where it happens and what occasion it is for. In interpreting training, we need to pay special attention to figures and expressions or sentences with figures.

Exercise 1: Listen to the following sentences, take notes if necessary, and retell the sentences in the source language. Pay special attention to the figures involved. (Audio 6.2.2 E1 CN, Audio 6.2.2 E1 En)

1. 全省经济继续在上升通道的合理区间稳健运行。完成生产总值1.77万亿元,增长9.7%。地方财政收入1890亿元,增长13.6%。

2. 城乡居民收入分别为24 366元和7932元,增长9%和11.8%。城镇登记失业率3.41%,物价上涨1.6%,明显低于控制目标。单位GDP能耗预计下降3.3%,四项污染物减排指标全面完成计划。

3. 全省引进内资4980亿元、外资41.8亿美元,分别增长19%和13.5%。进出口总额增长36%,其中出口139.3亿美元,增长36.2%,外贸依存度继续提高。

4. 全市生产总值15 722亿元,增长10%;一般公共预算收入2390亿元,增长15%;全社会固定资产投资11 654亿元,增长15.1%;社会消费品零售总额增长6%;外贸进出口增长4.2%。

5. 城镇登记失业率3.6%;居民消费价格涨幅1.9%;城乡居民收入分别增长8.7%和10.8%。

6. 全面放开中小城市户籍,投资139.3亿元建设重点示范镇和文化旅游名镇,新开工保障性安居工程43.4万套,基本建成保障性住房31.59万套,其中棚改8.44万套,全省25.3万户群众乔迁新居,100.22万农村居民进城落户,26.75万农民工子女免费入学。

7. 28个县城过境公路改造和沿黄河公路建设全面实施,31个文化旅游名镇旅游收入达33.2亿元。

8. 陕南搬迁开工住房6万户、完工5.3万户,陕北开工4万户、完工3.2万户,秦岭北麓和渭北旱塬开工1.42万户、完工1.15万户,延安灾后重建任务全面完成,全省建成新型农村社区236个,114万人脱贫。

9. 农村生态环境综合整治深入实施,42个县的122个乡镇、872个行政村示范项目全面完成,受益群众超过130万人。

10. 淘汰落后和过剩产能341.4万吨、3700万米,节约标准煤172万吨,超额完成国家任务。造林绿化497.6万亩①,保护恢复湿地146万亩,退耕还林56万亩。

11. In 2001, China's GDP reached 9.593,3 trillion yuan, almost tripling that of 1989, representing an average annual increase of 9.3 percent.

12. Efforts will be made to quadruple the GDP of the year 2000 by 2020.

13. As compared with the same period last year, the price of rice, wheat, maize and soybean rose by 16.2%, 18.1%, 22.8% and 29.5% respectively.

14. I propose a 450 million initiative to bring mentors to over 1 million disadvantaged junior high students and children of prisoners.

15. I propose a new $600 million program to help an additional 300,000 Americans

---

① 1亩=666.7平方米。

receive treatment over the next 3 years.

16. My budget will commit an additional $400 billion over the next decade to reform and strengthen Medicare.

17. I'm proposing 1.2 billion in research funding so that America can lead the world in developing clean, hydrogen-powered automobiles.

18. The 89% Christian share of the US population just after WWⅡ meant that America held about 130 million Christians.

19. The 82% share of Christians in today's much larger population means there are now about 230 million American Christians.

20. We had a $147 billion trade relationship in 2002 and we anticipate that that relationship will increase by 20% in 2003.

Exercise 2: Listen to the following sentences, take notes if necessary, retell the sentences in the source language, and then interpret in the target language. Pay special attention to the figures involved. (Audio 6.2.2 E2 CN, Audio 6.2.2 E2 En)

1. 从1979年的不足25亿美元,发展到今天的1000多亿美元,增长了几十倍。

2. 从2000年开始,连续三年全球的资金流量下滑,到2002年,已下降到6510亿美元。

3. 截止到2002年年底,中国的上网计算机总数已达到2083万台,上网用户总人数为5910万人,在全世界排名第二位。

4. 中央和地方政府共同投资68亿元建设地方疾病预防控制机构。

5. 每年投入2亿多元资金,专项用于艾滋病防治。

6. 中央和地方政府共同投资22.5亿元,重点加强中西部地区的血站建设。

7. 初步分析结果表明,目前中国现有艾滋病病毒感染者约有84万人,其中艾滋病病人约8万例。

8. 经过几年的推进,基本养老保险的参保职工已由1997年末的8671万人增加到2001年末的10 802万人。

9. 领取基本养老金人数由2533万人增加到3381万人,平均月基本养老金也由430元增加到556元。

10. 1998年至2001年,仅中央财政对基本养老保险补贴支出就达到861亿元。

11. The earth's moon is located an average of 239,000 miles from the earth. It has a diameter of 2,136 miles, and its gravity is one-sixth that of earth's.

12. Except Xinjiang, output value of the secondary industry of other Chinese provinces occupies more than 40% of its GDP, while output value of the tertiary industry occupies more than 30% in most of the provinces.

13. Steel production this week totaled 327,289 metric tons, down 1.4% from 332,103 tons a week earlier, but up 9.8% from 298,100 tons in the same week of 2003.

14. The number of savings of urban and rural residents have increased over 71.4 percent from 21.6 billion yuan in 1978 to 1,520.35 billion yuan in 1993.

15. Unemployment has risen to over three million for the first time in six years and analysts expect the jobless total to rise by a further 40,000 this month. Manufacturing

output has meanwhile steadied, after a zero point five percent decrease last month.

16. With over 40,000 US-invested enterprises, the paid-in value of the total US investment in China now stands at 43 billion US dollars. Of the top 500 US companies, more than 400 have come to China, and most of them are making a handsome profit.

17. China's GDP in 1997 amounts to US $ 902 billion. This figure ranks No. 7 behind USA (US $ 7819.3 billion), Japan (US $ 4223.4 billion), Germany (US $ 2115.4 billion), France (US $ 1393.8 billion), Britain (US $ 1278.4 billion) and Italy (US $ 1146.2 billion). From 1979 to 1997, China's average annual growth rate is 9.8 percent, 6.5 percentage points higher than that of the world.

18. In 1999, China's gross domestic product (GDP), which came to only 362.41 billion yuan in 1978, amounted to 7,955.3 billion yuan, 20-fold increase over 1978. China ranks No. 7 in terms of total supply and demand and No. 1 in terms of economic growth rate.

19. China hit 9.1 percent in GDP growth in 2003, despite the impact of SARS epidemic, a record since the Asian Financial Crisis in the late 1990s.

20. China contributed to about four percent of the world's total GDP in 2003 by consuming 7.4 percent of the oil, 31 percent of the coal, 27 percent of steel, 25 percent of alumina and 40 percent of the cement, worldwide.

Translation for Reference (参考译文) (for Exercise 2)

1. From merely 2.5 billion US dollars in 1979 to over 100 billion today, the increase is of dozens of times.

2. Global investment flows in 2002 fell for the third consecutive year to US $ 651 billion dollars.

3. By the end of 2002, China already had 20.83 million computers with internet connection and the total number of netizens reached 59.1 million, ranking second in the world.

4. The central and local governments have allocated 6.8 billion Yuan to establish and improve the disease prevention and control mechanism in the province.

5. Each year more than 200 million yuan are used as a special fund for HIV/AIDS prevention, care and treatment.

6. The central and local governments have invested 2.25 billion yuan, mainly in strengthening the blood stations in the middle and western regions.

7. Initial analysis shows that currently, China has about 840,000 HIV/AIDS infections, including about 80,000 HIV/AIDS patients.

8. After several years of implementation of the program, employees participating in the old-age insurance program increased from 86.71 million in late 1997 to 108.02 million by the end of 2001.

9. The number of those enjoying the basic old-age pension also increased from 25.33 million to 33.81 million, with the average monthly basic pension per person growing from 430 yuan to 556 yuan.

10. From 1998 to 2001, the subsidy outlay for basic old-age insurance from the central finance alone reached the grand total of 86.1 billion yuan.

11. 月亮离地球约有 23.9 万英里①远,其直径为 2136 英里,重力为地球的 1/6。

12. 除新疆以外,中国其他省份的工业值占 GDP 的百分之四十几,而第三产业的产值在大部分省份中占有的比值均超过 30%。

13. 本周钢产量总数为 32 万 7289 吨,比上一周的 33 万 2103 吨下降 1.4%,而与 2003 年同一周的数据 29 万 8100 吨比较增加了 9.8%。

14. 城乡居民的储蓄从 1978 年的 210 亿 6000 万元增加到 1993 年的 15 203 亿 5000 万元,上升 71.4 个百分点。

15. 失业人数六年来首次突破 300 万人。专家预测本月失业人数约新增 4 万人,而制造业产量继上个月下跌百分之零点五之后已趋稳定。

16. 今天,美国在华投资设立企业超过 4 万家,实际投资 430 亿美元。美国 500 强企业中,已有 400 多家进入中国,大多数企业获利丰厚。

17. 1997 年中国的国内生产总值达到 9020 亿美元,在世界排名第七,仅次于美国(78 193 亿美元)、日本(42 234 亿美元)、德国(21 154 亿美元)、法国(13 938 亿美元)、英国(12 784 亿美元)和意大利(11 462 亿美元)。从 1979 年到 1997 年,中国的国内生产总值年平均增长率为 9.8%,比世界平均值高出 6.5 个百分点。

18. 1999 年,中国的国内生产总值达到 79 553 亿元,相比 1978 年的 3 624.1 亿元,增长了 20 倍。中国在总供给和需求方面排名世界第七,而在经济增长率上排名第一。

19. 尽管有非典的影响,2003 年中国的国内生产总值增长率达 9.1%,创 18 世纪 90 年代后期亚洲金融危机以来的最高纪录。

20. 2003 年中国的 GDP 是世界总 GDP 的 4%,消耗了世界 7.4% 的油,31% 的煤,27% 的钢,25% 的氧化铝,以及 40% 的水泥。

Exercises and Practice

6-2-1 Listen to the following figures, write them down, mark them with commas or slashes, and read them out in both English and Chinese. (Audio 6-2-1 CN, Audio 6-2-1 En)

2384	8310
82012	90122
102912	832101
3948510	7456112
72090012	24380104
129178100	250021843
3132700274	4570190821
91123201032	56100230483
732090017251	189012394119

---

① 1 英里≈1.61 千米。

6-2-2　Listen to and interpret the following figures.

1. English to Chinese.（Audio 6-2-2 EC）

Country	Area（km²）	Population
Estonia	45,277	1,340,000
Finland	338,417	5,352,000
France	632,834	6,545,000
Greece	131,957	11,310,000
Hungary	93,030	10,010,000
Ireland	70,282	4,420,000
Italy	301,333	60,020,000
Luxembourg	2,586.3	493,500
Macedonia	25,713	2,048,000
Moldova	33,800	3,560,000

2. Chinese to English.（Audio 6-2-2 CE）

3850/2004	9/7271/0048	98/3765/0081
4/8590/0002	30/0029/8570	234/8993
49/2800/2940	980/0300/3021	6/5638/9402
2/0040/0000	9/0029/0000/2410	82/0000/1253
215/4009/4311	809/0032/0009	654/2001/0090

6-2-3　Interpret the following short figures.

1. English to Chinese.（Audio 6-2-3 EC）

29.1 million	21 billion	209.1 billion
7.19 billion	45 thousand	102 million
1.3 trillion	289.1 million	0.3 billion

2. Chinese to English.（Audio 6-2-3 CE）

3万	8.4亿	29.88万
18.5亿	3000万	500万
36万亿	0.3万	901万

6-2-4　Interpret the following sentences with figures.（Audio 6-2-4 CN，Audio 6-2-4 En）

1. 经济运行保持在合理区间。国内生产总值增长6.6%,总量突破90万亿元。经济增速与用电、货运等实物量指标相匹配。居民消费价格上涨2.1%。国际收支基本平衡。

2. 城镇新增就业1361万人、调查失业率稳定在5%左右的较低水平。近14亿人口的发展中大国,实现了比较充分的就业。

3. 精准脱贫有力推进,农村贫困人口减少1386万,易地扶贫搬迁280万人。

4. 其他预期目标包括：居民消费价格涨幅3%左右;国际收支基本平衡,进出口稳中提质;宏观杠杆率基本稳定,金融财政风险有效防控;农村贫困人口减少1000万以上,居民收入增长与经济增长基本同步;生态环境进一步改善,单位国内生产总值能耗下降3%左右,主要污染物排放量继续下降。

5. 乡村振兴战略有力实施,粮食总产量保持在 1.3 万亿斤①以上。新型城镇化扎实推进,近 1400 万农业转移人口在城镇落户。

6. In 2001, 225 million square meters were completed. Furthermore, there were 292 million square meters started in 2001.

7. For example, in Shanghai during the first 9 months of 2001, resale house transactions totaled 119,096 units.

8. Total transaction area was 1,012 million square meters, reaching 12.9 billion RMB.

9. The main projected targets for economic and social development this year include: a GDP growth of 6 - 6.5 percent, over 11 million new urban jobs, a surveyed urban unemployment rate of around 5.5 percent, and a registered urban unemployment rate within 4.5 percent.

10. China's total volume of trade in goods exceeded 30 trillion yuan, and its utilized foreign investment totaled US $138.3 billion, ranking China first among developing countries.

Additional Materials

1. Excerpt from the Press Conference on the National Economic Situation by the State News Office (国新办国民经济情况新闻发布会节选) (2011 - 07 - 13)

上半年,国民经济保持平稳较快增长。

National economy maintained steady and fast growth in the first half of 2011.

上半年,面对复杂多变的国际形势和国内经济运行出现的新情况、新问题,党中央、国务院积极实施积极的财政政策和稳健的货币政策,不断加强和改善宏观调控,经济运行总体良好,继续朝着宏观调控的预期方向发展。

In the first half of 2011, faced with the complicated and volatile international environment and the emerging challenges in domestic economic development, the Central Party Committee and the State Council firmly carried out the pro-active fiscal policy and prudent monetary policy, continuously strengthened and improved macro control. As a result, the national economy showed a good momentum of development, and kept moving towards the expected direction of macro control.

初步测算,上半年国内生产总值 204 459 亿元,按可比价格计算,同比增长 9.6%;其中,一季度增长 9.7%,二季度增长 9.5%。分产业看,第一产业增加值 15 700 亿元,增长 3.2%;第二产业增加值 102 178 亿元,增长 11.0%;第三产业增加值 86 581 亿元,增长 9.2%。从环比看,二季度国内生产总值增长 2.2%。

---

① "斤"为市制计量单位,1 斤 = 500 g。

According to the preliminary estimation, the gross domestic product (GDP) of China was 20,445.9 billion yuan for the first half of this year, a year-on-year increase of 9.6 percent at comparable prices. Specifically, the growth of the first quarter was 9.7 percent, and 9.5 percent for the second quarter. The value added of the primary industries was 1,570.0 billion yuan, up by 3.2 percent; the secondary industries 10,217.8 billion yuan, up by 11.0 percent; and the tertiary industries 8,658.1 billion yuan, up by 9.2 percent. The gross domestic product of the second quarter of 2011 went up by 2.2 percent on a quarterly basis.

一、农业生产总体稳定,夏粮生产获得丰收。全国夏粮产量12 627万吨,比上年增产312万吨,增长2.5%。上半年,猪牛羊禽肉产量3722万吨,同比增长0.2%,其中猪肉产量2443万吨,下降0.5%。

1. Agricultural Production Went on Steadily and the Summer Grain Production Achieved a Good Harvest. The total output of summer grain was 126.27 million tons, an increase of 3.12 million tons, up by 2.5 percent year-on-year. In the first half of this year, the total output of pork, beef, mutton and poultry reached 37.22 million tons, a year-on-year growth of 0.2 percent. The output of pork reached 24.43 million tons, down by 0.5 percent.

二、工业生产平稳增长,企业效益继续增加。上半年,全国规模以上工业增加值同比增长14.3%。分登记注册类型看,国有及国有控股企业同比增长10.7%;集体企业增长9.6%;股份制企业增长16.1%;外商及港澳台投资企业增长11.1%。分轻重工业看,重工业同比增长14.7%,轻工业增长13.1%。分行业看,39个大类行业均实现增长。分地区看,东部地区同比增长12.4%,中部地区增长17.8%,西部地区增长17.3%。上半年,规模以上工业企业产销率达到97.8%,比上年同期提高0.1个百分点。6月份,规模以上工业增加值同比增长15.1%,环比增长1.48%。

2. Industrial Production Realized a Steady Growth with Further Improved Economic Efficiency. In the first half of this year, the total value added of the industrial enterprises above designated size was up by 14.3 percent year-on-year. An analysis by types of ownership showed that the value added growth of the state-owned and state holding enterprises went up by 10.7 percent; collective enterprises by 9.6 percent; share-holding enterprises by 16.1 percent; and enterprises funded by foreign investors or investors from Hong Kong, Macao and Taiwan province by 11.1 percent. The year-on-year growth of the heavy industry was up by 14.7 percent, and the light industry by 13.1 percent. All the 39 industrial divisions registered year-on-year growth. The growth in eastern, central and western regions was up by 12.4 percent, 17.8 percent and 17.3 percent respectively. In the first half of this year, the sales ratio of industrial enterprises above designated size was 97.8 percent, or 0.1 percentage point higher than that in the same period of last year. In June, the total value added of the industrial enterprises above designated size was up by 15.1 percent year-on-year, or up by 1.48 percent month-on-month.

1—5月份，全国规模以上工业企业实现利润 19 203 亿元，同比增长 27.9%。在 39 个大类行业中，37 个行业利润同比增长，2 个行业同比下降。1—5月份，规模以上工业企业主营业务成本占主营业务收入的比重为 84.7%，比一季度提高 0.3 个百分点。5月份，规模以上工业企业主营业务收入利润率为 6.2%。

In the first five months of this year, the profits made by industrial enterprises above designated size stood at 1,920.3 billion yuan, up by 27.9 percent year-on-year. Among the 39 industrial divisions, 37 of them registered year-on-year increase in profits, and 2 divisions witnessed reduction. In the first five months of this year, the costs of primary activities of the industrial enterprises above designated size accounted for 84.7 percent of the turnover from their primary activities, which was 0.3 percentage point higher than that in the first quarter of 2011. In May, the profit rate of industrial enterprises above designated size from their primary activities was 6.2 percent.

三、固定资产投资保持较快增长，房地产投资增速较快。上半年，固定资产投资（不含农户）124 567 亿元，同比增长 25.6%。其中，国有及国有控股投资 43 050 亿元，增长 14.6%。分产业看，第一产业投资同比增长 20.6%，第二产业投资增长 27.1%，第三产业投资增长 24.7%。分地区看，东部地区投资同比增长 22.6%，中部地区增长 31.0%，西部地区增长 29.2%。从环比看，6月份固定资产投资（不含农户）下降 1.04%。

3. Investment in Fixed Assets Kept a Fast Growth and Investment in Real Estate Sector Increased Rapidly. In the first half of this year, the investment in fixed assets (excluding rural households) was 12,456.7 billion yuan, a year-on-year growth of 25.6 percent. Specifically, the investment in the state-owned and state holding enterprises reached 4,305.0 billion yuan, a rise of 14.6 percent. The investment in the primary industries, the secondary industries and the tertiary industries went up by 20.6 percent, 27.1 percent and 24.7 percent respectively. In term of different areas, the growth in eastern, central and western regions was 22.6 percent, 31.0 percent and 29.2 percent respectively. In June, the investment in fixed assets (excluding rural households) went down by 1.04 percent month-on-month.

上半年，全国房地产开发投资 26 250 亿元，同比增长 32.9%。其中，住宅投资 18 641 亿元，增长 36.1%。全国商品房销售面积 44 419 万平方米，同比增长 12.9%。其中，住宅销售面积增长 12.1%。上半年，房地产开发企业本年资金来源 40 991 亿元，同比增长 21.6%。6月份，全国房地产开发景气指数为 101.75。

In the first half of 2011, the investment in real estate development was 2,625.0 billion yuan, a year-on-year growth of 32.9 percent. Specifically, the investment in residential buildings reached 1,864.1 billion yuan, up by 36.1 percent. The floor space of commercial buildings sold in the first half of 2011 reached 444.19 million square meters, a year-on-year growth of 12.9 percent. Specifically, the growth of residential buildings was up by 12.1 percent. In the first half of this year, the sources of funds for real estate development enterprises from the current year reached 4,099.1 billion yuan, up by 21.6 percent year-on-year. In June, the national real estate climate index was 101.75.

四、市场销售稳定增长,汽车、房地产相关商品销售放缓。上半年,社会消费品零售总额 85 833 亿元,同比增长 16.8%。其中,限额以上企业(单位)消费品零售额 39 034 亿元,增长 23.7%。按经营单位所在地分,城镇消费品零售额 74 450 亿元,同比增长 16.9%;乡村消费品零售额 11 383 亿元,增长 16.2%。按消费形态分,餐饮收入 9579 亿元,同比增长 16.2%;商品零售 76 254 亿元,增长 16.9%。在商品零售中,限额以上企业(单位)商品零售额 36 108 亿元,同比增长 24.2%。其中,汽车类增长 15.0%,增速比上年同期回落 22.1 个百分点;家具类增长 30.0%,回落 8.5 个百分点;家用电器和音像器材类增长 21.5%,回落 7.3 个百分点。6 月份,社会消费品零售总额同比增长 17.7%,环比增长 1.38%。

4. Sales at Domestic Markets Enjoyed a Steady Growth and the Sales of Motor Vehicles and Real Estate Related Commodities Slowed Down to Some Extent. In the first half of this year, the total retail sales of consumer goods reached 8,583.3 billion yuan, a year-on-year rise of 16.8 percent. Specifically, the retail sales of the enterprises (units) above designated size stood at 3,903.4 billion yuan, up by 23.7 percent. Analyzed by different areas, the retail sales in urban areas reached 7,445.0 billion yuan, up by 16.9 percent, and the retail sales in rural areas stood at 1,138.3 billion yuan, up by 16.2 percent. Grouped by consumption patterns, the income of catering industry was 957.9 billion yuan, up by 16.2 percent; and retail sales of goods was 7,625.4 billion yuan, up by 16.9 percent. In particular, the retail sales of the enterprises (units) above designated size reached 3,610.8 billion yuan, a year-on-year growth of 24.2 percent. Specifically, the sales of motor vehicles rose by 15.0 percent, or 22.1 percentage points lower than that in the same period of last year; that of furniture grew up by 30.0 percent, or 8.5 percentage points lower; and that of household appliances and audio-video equipment went up by 21.5 percent, or 7.3 percentage points lower. In June, the total retail sales of consumer goods rose by 17.7 percent year-on-year, or 1.38 percent month-on-month.

五、城乡居民收入稳定增长,农村居民收入增长较快。上半年,城镇居民家庭人均总收入 12 076 元。其中,城镇居民人均可支配收入 11 041 元,同比增长 13.2%,扣除价格因素,实际增长 7.6%。在城镇居民家庭人均总收入中,工资性收入同比名义增长 11.5%,转移性收入增长 9.9%,经营净收入增长 31.2%,财产性收入增长 20.4%。农村居民人均现金收入 3706 元,同比增长 20.4%,扣除价格因素,实际增长 13.7%。其中,工资性收入同比名义增长 20.1%,家庭经营收入增长 21.0%,财产性收入增长 7.5%,转移性收入增长 23.2%。

5. Urban and Rural Residents' Income Increased Steadily with a Higher Growth for Rural Residents. In the first half of this year, the per capita total income of urban households was 12,076 yuan. Specifically, the per capita disposable income of urban population was 11,041 yuan, a year-on-year growth of 13.2 percent, or a real growth of 7.6 percent after deducting price factors. Of the per capita total income of urban households, the year-on-year growth of wage income was 11.5 percent; transferred income 9.9 percent; net

income from business operation 31.2 percent; and 20.4 percent from property income. The per capita cash income of rural population was 3,706 yuan, up by 20.4 percent year-on-year, or 13.7 percent growth in real terms. Specifically, the rural growth of wage income was 20.1 percent; household operation income 21.0 percent; property income 7.5 percent; and 23.2 percent from transferred income.

当前,经济发展面临的国内外环境依然十分复杂,不稳定、不确定因素较多。下阶段要坚持宏观经济政策取向不动摇,继续保持政策的连续性、稳定性,继续把稳定物价总水平放在宏观调控的首要位置,增强政策的针对性、灵活性、有效性,进一步处理好保持经济平稳较快发展、调整经济结构和管理通胀预期的关系,加大改革创新力度,加快经济结构调整和发展方式转变,促进经济又好又快发展。

The external and internal environment for China's economic development is still rather complicated with numerous instabilities and uncertainties. In the next phase, we should adhere firmly to the macro-control policies, maintain their continuity and stability, give first priority of work to the stabilization of overall price level and improve the relevance, flexibility and effectiveness of policies. We should also persist in balancing the relationship among a steady and comparatively rapid economic development, adjustment of economic structures and management of the inflation expectation; promote reform and innovation; and speed up adjustment of economic structures and transformation of economic development mode in order that we achieve a sound and fast growth.

2. Boris Winning the Election and Becoming the Prime Minister of United Kingdom(鲍里斯当选英国首相)

来源:中国日报网

http://language.chinadaily.com.cn/a/201907/24/WS5d37ef3ba310d83056400be8.html

Boris Johnson has won the United Kingdom's leadership election 92,153 votes to 46,656, becoming prime minister and leader of the ruling Conservative Party.

鲍里斯·约翰逊以 92 153 票对 46 656 票在近日的英国选举中获胜,成功当选英国首相和执政的保守党领袖。

Johnson had been widely expected to win ever since Theresa May, the nation's outgoing prime minister, announced on May 24 that she was resigning following heavy criticism of her handling of the UK's exit from the European Union.

自英国即将离任的首相特雷莎·梅 5 月 24 日宣布辞职以来,外界普遍预计鲍里斯·约翰逊将赢得大选。此前,外界对特雷莎·梅处理英国脱欧问题的方式提出了严厉批评。

In a short but impassioned acceptance speech, Johnson thanked his leadership opponent Jeremy Hunt and May. He said that the party will "deliver Brexit, reunite the country and defeat" the leader of the opposition Labor Party Jeremy Corbyn.

在简短但充满激情的胜选感言中,鲍里斯·约翰逊感谢了他的竞选对手杰里米·亨特和首相特雷莎·梅。他表示,工党将"实现脱欧,团结国家",并且"击败"反对党工党领袖杰里米·科尔宾。

"That's what we are going to do," Johnson said, "We know that we can do it, the people in our country know that we can do it, and I know that we will do it."

"这就是我们要做的,"鲍里斯·约翰逊说,"我们知道我们能做到,英国人民知道我们能做到,我知道我们会做到。"

Johnson and Hunt were the last people standing in the leadership battle that had initially involved 10 hopefuls and was ultimately decided in a postal vote open to the party's 160,000 members.

鲍里斯·约翰逊和杰里米·亨特在这场首相争夺战中走到了最后。这场角逐最初有10名候选人参加,最终结果由保守党16万名成员通过邮寄投票决定。

Johnson takes over as party leader immediately and will be sworn in as prime minister on Wednesday.

鲍里斯·约翰逊将立即接任保守党领袖,并将于周三(7月24日)宣誓就任首相。

He was an outspoken critic of May and says he will take the UK out of the EU on Oct 31, with or without a deal with the political bloc.

他曾直言不讳地批评特雷莎·梅,并表示无论是否与欧盟达成协议,他都将在10月31日让英国退出欧盟。

Following the result, May congratulated Johnson and said he will have her "full support from the back benches".

选举结果公布后,特雷莎·梅向鲍里斯·约翰逊表示祝贺,并表示约翰逊将得到她的"全力支持"。

Donald Trump said on Twitter:"Congratulations to Boris Johnson on becoming the new Prime Minister of the United Kingdom. He will be great!"

美国总统唐纳德·特朗普发推说:"祝贺鲍里斯·约翰逊成为英国新任首相。他会很棒的!"

Johnson entered politics as a member of Parliament in 2001, and later served two terms as Mayor of London.

鲍里斯·约翰逊2001年以议员身份进入政界,之后担任了两届伦敦市长。

The homicide rate in London—which includes murder and manslaughter—fell from 22 per million to 12 per million people during his time as mayor.

伦敦的凶杀犯罪率——包括谋杀和过失杀人——在他担任市长期间从每百万人中22起下降到每百万人中12起。

Police numbers in London rose slightly, from 31,460 to 32,125, between March 2008 and March 2016. Across England and Wales in that period the number of officers fell by 17,603.

2008年3月至2016年3月期间,伦敦的警察人数有所提升,从31 460人增至32 125人。在此期间,英格兰和威尔士的警察人数则减少了17 603人。

There was an increase in the number of affordable homes built—101,525 by the end of March 2016, of which the Greater London Authority contributed to 94,001.

截至2016年3月底,伦敦保障性住房增加了101 525套,其中大伦敦市政府建设保障性住房94 001套。

One of his most famous transport initiatives was the so-called "Boris Bike" cycle scheme, introduced in July 2010.

他最著名的交通倡议之一是被称作"鲍里斯自行车"的自行车计划,于2010年7月推出。

Mr. Johnson regularly promoted the hire bikes by riding them himself and the number of rentals reached more than 10.3 million during his last year as mayor.

鲍里斯·约翰逊经常通过自己的骑行来推广这种出租自行车,在他担任市长的最后一年,出租自行车的使用次数超过了1030万次。

Johnson reentered Parliament in 2016, when he established himself as a leading figure in the "Vote Leave" campaign in the EU referendum.

他在2016年重新进入议会,当时他在"脱欧"运动中确立了自己的领导地位。

During the Brexit campaign, he came under sustained criticism from those in favor of Remain, for his claims about the benefits of leaving and what he called "taking back control".

在英国脱欧运动期间,由于他对于脱欧好处的言论以及他所谓的"夺回控制权"说法,鲍里斯不断受到留欧派人士的抨击。

And he has continued to advocate a harder form of Brexit, sharply criticizing both the deal that Mrs. May agreed and her whole approach to the negotiations with the EU.

同时他一直倡导更为强硬的脱欧方式,尖锐批评特雷莎·梅提出的脱欧协议以及她与欧盟谈判的整个方式。

Johnson was strongly tipped to take over as prime minister when the leave campaign won. However, his political ally Michael Gove dashed his chances by publicly questioning Johnson's ability to lead.

脱欧阵营获胜时,外界强烈猜测鲍里斯·约翰逊将接任首相一职。然而,他的政治盟友迈克尔·戈夫公开质疑其领导能力,使这一机会化为泡影。

Theresa May then succeeded David Cameron as prime minister and appointed Johnson as foreign secretary. Johnson once again positioned himself as a potential leadership candidate when he resigned over May's handling of Brexit negotiations, paving the way for an ultimately successful run for the office of prime minister.

特雷莎·梅随后接替戴维·卡梅伦成为英国首相,并任命约翰逊为外交大臣。鲍里斯·约翰逊因特雷莎·梅处理英国脱欧谈判的方式而辞职时,他再次将自己定位为潜在的首相候选人,为最终成功当选铺平了道路。

Chapter Ⅶ Memory

Learning questions:
√ *What is memory and what are the different types of memory?*
√ *Why is memory important in consecutive interpreting?*
√ *How to train to expand our memory?*

Different user groups in different settings naturally have different needs and expectations from their interpreters from different training backgrounds. Andrè Kaminker, a well-known interpreter, was said to receive rounds of applause after consecutive interpreting for an hour without taking any notes. However, most interpreters' memory can be seriously stretched when note-taking is not available, prohibited or discouraged for reasons of confidentiality.

The study of human memory has been a subject of science and philosophy for thousands of years and has become one of the major topics of interest within cognitive psychology and interpreting. But what exactly is memory? How are memories formed? This chapter offers a brief look at what memory is, how it works, what the affecting factors are and how it is trained to expand its capacity.

7.1 Introduction to Memory

7.1.1 What Is Memory

What exactly is memory? Essentially, memory is a complex process that involves acquiring, encoding, storing, and recalling information. In terms of interpreting, it involves the process of active listening (information acquiring), information processing (decoding and encoding), storing and information retrieving. As can be seen, information processing is a crucial step in memorizing. That is the reason why some of the training methods in this chapter partly overlaps with Chapter Ⅳ, Information Processing Skills.

Human memory involves the ability to both preserve and recover information we have learned or experienced. In order to form new memories, information must be changed into a usable form, which occurs through the process known as encoding. Once the information has been successfully encoded, it must be stored in memory for later use. Much of this stored memory lies outside of our awareness most of the time, except when we actually need to use it. The retrieval process allows us to bring stored memories into conscious awareness. To use the information that has been encoded into memory, it first has to be retrieved.

However, this is not a flawless process. There are many factors that can influence how memories are retrieved such as the type of information being used and the retrieval cues that are present. Sometimes we forget or misremember things. Sometimes things are not properly encoded in memory in the first place. Memory problems can range from minor annoyances like forgetting a few words to major diseases that affect the quality of life and the ability to function.

7.1.2 Types of Memory

Some memories are very brief, just seconds long, and allow us to take in sensory information about the world around us. Some are a bit longer. These memories mostly consist of the information we are currently focusing on and thinking about. Some memories can be much longer, lasting days, weeks, months, or even decades. Most of these long-term memories lie outside of our immediate awareness, but we can draw them into consciousness when they are needed.

While several different models of memory have been proposed, the stage model of memory is often used to explain the basic structure and function of memory. Initially proposed in 1968 by Atkinson and Shiffrin, this theory outlines three separate stages of memory: sensory memory, short-term memory, and long-term memory.

Sensory memory is the earliest stage of memory. During this stage, sensory information from the environment is stored for a very brief period of time, generally for no longer than a half-second for visual information and 3 or 4 seconds for auditory information. We attend to only certain aspects of this sensory memory, allowing some of this information to pass into the next stage—short-term memory.

Short-term memory (STM), also known as active memory, is the information we are currently aware of or thinking about. In Freudian psychology, this memory would be referred to as the conscious mind. Paying attention to sensory memories generates information in short-term memory. Most of the information stored in active memory will be kept for approximately 20 to 30 seconds. Memory in interpreting often lasts for a short time. Once the interpreting assignment is over, the interpreter moves on to another one, often with different context, subject and speakers. While many of our short-term memories are quickly forgotten, attending to this information allows it to continue to the next stage—long-term memory.

Long-term memory (LTM) refers to the continuing storage of information. In Freudian psychology, long-term memory would be called the preconscious and unconscious. This information is largely outside of our awareness but can be used when needed. Some of this information is fairly easy to recall, while other memories are much more difficult to access. Long-term memory occurs when we have created neural pathways for storing ideas and information which can then be recalled weeks, months, or even years later. To create these pathways, you must make a deliberate attempt to encode the information in the way you intend to recall it later. Long-term memory is a learning process. In interpreting, it is an important part of the interpreter's acquisition of knowledge, because information stored in LTM may last for minutes to weeks, months, or even an entire life.

In consecutive interpreting, all three types of memory are involved. Sensory memory may be used for interpreters to capture sounds, form words and understand meaning; short-term memory is used to memorize information in a sentence or a passage, and long-term memory is used to retrieve linguistic and topical knowledge. Sometimes, in interpreting, the combined use of short-term memory and long-term memory can also be called working memory. The relationship among all types of memory can be seen in Fig. 7-1. Even though the interpreters may seem to mostly rely on their short-term memory in interpreting, long-term memory is also crucial in speech comprehension and memory recall. Although short-term memory is crucial at the stage of comprehension in CI, adequate understanding requires the efficient coordination of other components, a central executive and a robust knowledge base. Research in developmental psychology suggests that a domain knowledge which is "highly organized with many strong connections among the items within the base" not only shows easier activation of related items within the knowledge base, it also speeds up the processing of domain-specific information. In other words, "the more people know about a topic, the easier it is for them to learn and remember new information about it." Although mnemonics will help during memory retrieval, students must expand their knowledge base, in terms of both linguistic and world knowledge.

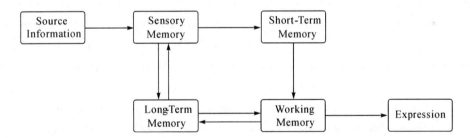

Fig. 7-1 Relationship among different types of memory

7.1.3 Memory Capacity

Memory capacity mainly refer to the capacity of short-term memory. One of the prominent features of short-term memory is its limited and expandable information capacity. Atkinson and Shiffrin believe that short-term memory information is stored in a channel. When the channel is fully occupied by information, it is difficult for new information to enter, or the new information is likely to squeeze out the earliest information. With continuous input of new information, this replacement occurs constantly because the storage space of short-term memory is always limited. In fact, the number of items it can store at one time is limited to 7±2 items (objects, numbers, letters, etc.) that are not related to each other. In 1956, George Armitage Miller, a professor at Harvard University, published a paper entitled "Magic Numbers, Seven Plus or Minus Two: The Limit of Our Information Processing Ability", which proved the limit of the number of short-term memory items. This theory has been widely accepted.

However, although the capacity of short-term memory is limited, it can be expanded, because 7±2 can be 7±2 syllables, 7±2 words, 7±2 phrases or 7±2 short sentences. In interpreting, it is also the short-term memory that is the focus of our memory training. To expand memory capacity, the concept of "chunking" is proposed. The so-called "chunks" refers to a unit of information, and "chunking" is the process that combines several small units of information into larger ones. Chunks have the capacity of expansion. The capacity of short-term memory can be expanded by increasing the information in each chunk. For example, it may be difficult to remember someone's identification number 612379198010013××6, but if it is divided into chunks according to a certain meaning, such as 612379 (area code), 19801001 (date of birth), and 3××6 (identification number), it will be easier to remember, because each chunk is meaningful and is within the 7±2 limit. Another example, look at the following words: desk, apple, bookshelf, red, plum, table, green, pineapple, purple, chair, peach, yellow. Spend a few seconds reading them, then look away and try to recall and list these words. How did you group the words when you listed them? Most people will list using three different categories: color, furniture, and fruit.

Another way of memory organization is known as the semantic network model. This model suggests that certain triggers activate associated memories. A memory of a specific place might activate memories about related things that have occurred in that location. For example, thinking about a particular campus building might trigger memories of attending classes, studying, and socializing with peers. So to expand our memory, we need to find the right trigger words. These trigger words are also very often the ones we put down in our note-taking. Semantic network model can also be used on the basis of chunking. Finding the right trigger word for each chunk can help us remember more.

The theory of the limitation and expansibility of short-term memory capacity and semantic network model provide powerful guidance for interpreting practice. In the process of receiving information in interpreting, whether it is "listening" or "viewing", the information units of the source language are various, such as words, phrases, sentences or paragraphs. So that means it can be 7±2 words, phrases, sentences or paragraphs. To ease our memory load in interpreting, it is crucial to remember unit of meaning, or message, instead of each single word. For long paragraphs, interpreters need to expand their memory capacity of each chunk from words to sentences or even a short passage. Usually, the larger the interpreters' linguistic and topical knowledge base, the larger their memory chunks, and the more they can remember. Only through expanding the information in each chunk and integrate all the information and store them as a whole, can we better store and retrieve them.

The following is an example. It is an excerpt from the remarks made by President Obama at the United Nation Conference on Sept. 3, 2009.

"We must remember that the greatest price of this conflict is not paid by us. It's not paid by politicians. It's paid by the Israeli girl in Sderot who closes her eyes in fear that a rocket will take her life in the middle of the night. It's paid for by the Palestinian boy in Gaza who has no clean water and no country to call his own. These are all god's children. And after all the politics and all the posturing, this is about the right of every human being to live with dignity and security. And that is why, even though there will be setbacks and false starts and tough days, I will not waver in my pursuit of peace."

This may look like a long passage to remember, but we can chunk it into several information units:

[1] We must remember that the greatest price of this conflict is not paid by us. It's not paid by politicians.

[2] It's paid by the Israeli girl in Sderot who closes her eyes in fear that a rocket will take her life in the middle of the night.

[3] It's paid for by the Palestinian boy in Gaza who has no clean water and no country to call his own.

[4] These are all god's children.

[5] And after all the politics and all the posturing, this is about the right of every human being to live with dignity and security.

[6] And that is why, even though there will be setbacks and false starts and tough days, I will not waver in my pursuit of peace.

In each unit, we can find some trigger words to help us remember.

[1] We must remember that the greatest price of this conflict is not paid by us. It's not paid by politicians. (paid not by us, not politicians)

[2] It's paid by the Israeli girl in Sderot who closes her eyes in fear that a rocket will take her life in the middle of the night. (by Israeli girl)

[3] It's paid for by the Palestinian boy in Gaza who has no clean water and no country to call his own. (by Palestinian boy)

[4] These are all god's children.

[5] And after all the politics and all the posturing, this is about the right of every human being to live with dignity and security. (right to live)

[6] And that is why, even though there will be setbacks and false starts and tough days, I will not waver in my pursuit of peace. (not waver, pursuit of peace)

The passage also follows the logic line of "not... but... so..." Thus, through chunking, finding trigger words and linking them following a logic line, our memory load can be reduced and it will be easier for us to remember all of the information above.

7.1.4 Memory Curve

As we have mentioned, short-term memory only last a few seconds to 30 seconds, one minute the longest, and the information we can hold in this very short period of time drop dramatically after only a matter of seconds. According to L. R. Peterson's experiment, testees can accurately recall 80% of information when the time interval is 3 seconds. As time interval increases, the accuracy drops dramatically, falling to only 55% at 6 seconds and 10% at 18 seconds. This short-term memory curve can be seen in Figure 7-2.

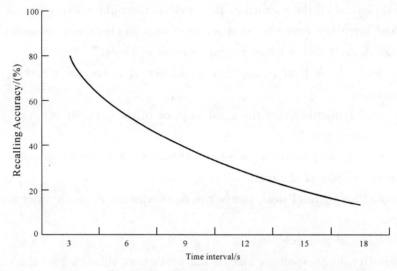

Fig. 7-2 Short-term memory curve

This shows that short-term memory can only last a very short period of time, and only through constant repeating and reminding can we keep the information. This feature also makes interpreting especially challenging and note-taking necessary. Note-taking can help activate passive memory and store as much information as possible. Note-taking is what we will learn in the next chapter. But note-taking is not everything in interpreting, without good memory capacity, note-taking is not enough.

As for long term memory, the famous Ebbinghaus Forgetting Curve depicts that memory retention rate drops dramatically within just a day, as can be seen in Fig. 7-3. This also makes it challenging for interpreters since interpreters need to constantly expand their vocabulary and topical knowledge and store them in long-term memory for future use. This also means that interpreters need to constantly train themselves and refresh their linguistic and topical knowledge.

Due to the fact that the capacity of long-term memory is almost limitless and it takes years of accumulation to expand it, for this course, the training focus is on expanding the capacity of short-term memory.

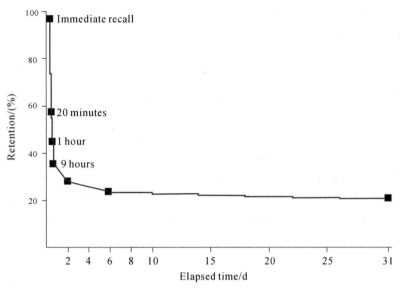

Fig. 7 – 3   The Ebbinghaus Forgetting Curve

7.1.5 Factors Influencing Memory in CI

Interpreting is a highly stressful work. Interpreters need to be fully concentrated for a certain period of time, very often for several hours, and they may need to keep working in this state for days. Even experienced interpreters with good memory capacity may be affected by this schedule. Interpreters are also greatly limited by their own memory capacity, which vary from person to person, and is mainly determined at birth if without training. Other than these, memory can also be affected by many other factors, both internally and externally.

1. Interpreters' language abilities

This is the interpreters' innate ability that may affect their memory. Language abilities directly affect understanding, and understanding affect memory. Time and effort spent on analyzing the language in listening and searching for words in expression can both greatly affect how much time and energy one can put on memorizing.

2. Interpreters' information processing skills

As we have discussed in Chapter IV, from listening to expressing, from decoding to encoding, information processing skills play an important role, which in turn may affect memory. Less effort can be put on memorizing if too much energy is put on analyzing information.

3. Interpreters' physical health

Interpreters' physical condition may directly affect their concentration. It's hard to memorize anything without good concentration. Interpreters should always try to work in their best physical state. If they are too ill to interpret, they should notify the client ahead of time or politely request for being replaced.

4. Interpreters' psychological status

Interpreters need to handle both the pressure from the heavy work in interpreting and the pressure from public speaking. It's very natural for interpreters to feel stressed, especially for the inexperienced ones. A highly-stressed mind will not be able to effectively process information, let alone memorize the information. That is why many people would feel that their mind would become completely blank when they are nervous. This is the reason why public speaking skills are also crucial in interpreting.

5. Interpreters' background knowledge

We all have the experience that the more familiar we are with something, the easier it will be for us to remember its related information. When interpreters can relate what they hear with their own personal experience or their background knowledge of something, it will be easier for them to remember. This means if condition allows, interpreters should always be well-prepared for each assignment, both in vocabulary and related expressions, and in the topical knowledge (background knowledge of a topic).

6. Interpreting environment

Interpreting environment is the external factor that may affect the memory of interpreters. It mainly refers to the distractions at the interpreting site, including the noise from outside, sounds from the audience, people moving about and etc. But it can also include unreasonable arrangement of seating or failure of equipment. These distractions can all greatly affect interpreters' concentration and memory. This is why anti-distraction training is necessary in CI training.

7. Memorizing methods

The way we memorize information vary from person to person. Generally speaking, there are three encoding methods in the memorizing process: sound encoding, visual encoding and semantic encoding. Sound encoding is the most mechanical one. For short information, this method is often used, but the memory from this method usually cannot last long. Semantic encoding is a frequently used way in interpreting and in our daily life. When we understand the meaning, it's easier to remember, and the more logical the information, the easier it will be remembered. Visual encoding, though not used as often, can often effectively help us remember. Psychologically speaking, it is considered one of the most effective ways to remember. Psychologists believe that visual memory and semantic memory are stored separately. It is advised to use more visual memory in CI to help us reduce the load of semantic memory. For more information about visual memory, please refer back to Chapter Ⅳ, Section 4.2.1.

Exercises and Practice

7-1-1 Talk with your partner(s) and explain to them what memory is and what the different types of memory are.

7-1-2 Discuss with your partner(s) how different types of memory work in consecutive interpreting and what may affect our memory in CI.

7-1-3 Analyze the following passages and memorize them through chunking and locating trigger words.

1. Now, like all of you, my responsibility is to act in the interest of my nation and my people, and I will never apologize for defending those interests. But it is my deeply held belief that in the year 2009—more than at any point in human history—the interests of nations and peoples are shared. The religious convictions that we hold in our hearts can forge new bonds among people, or they can tear us apart. The technology we harness can light the path to peace, or forever darken it. The energy we use can sustain our planet, or destroy it. What happens to the hope of a single child—anywhere—can enrich our world, or impoverish it.

—Remarks by the U.S. President to the United Nations General Assembly, September 23, 2009

2. 今年是亚欧会议成立20周年。20年前,亚洲和欧洲领导人以远见卓识,联手缔造了亚欧会议机制,开创了亚欧平等对话、全面合作、共同应对挑战的新时代。20年来,通过共同努力,亚欧各方政治互信不断增强,经贸和人文合作更加密切,在维护地区和平稳定、促进经济发展繁荣、加强文明交流互鉴方面都取得长足进展。比如,中欧已是彼此的最大贸易伙伴,去年贸易额接近7000亿美元。现在的亚欧,各领域合作达到前所未有的高度。

—Premier Li Keqiang's Speech Made at the 11th ASEM Summit

7.2 Training Methods

Though largely determined by personal abilities, memory can be trained. The following are some commonly used methods in CI memory training. Some of the training methods are very much similar to those for information processing. No matter which type of method you are using, it's key to remember that only when you understand can you remember.

7.2.1 Training Method—Word Repeating

Memory training starts at word level, which is considered the smallest unit in chunking. Word repeating exercise is to repeat (recite) as many given words as possible in source language. It is a very good way to train to expand our memory capacity.

As we have mentioned earlier, our memory capacity is 7 ± 2 items (words). These words can be related or totally unrelated. They can be shorter or longer. They can be daily objects or academic expressions. Our word repeating training usually starts with 5 words, and from shorter, familiar objects; and then move onto longer, more complicated items or concepts. Time intervals can also be added after listening and before repeating to increase difficulty. To better remember all the words, learners need to try their best to find correlation between all the words if possible, and memorize them in groups. Or they can try to visualize the items and the relationship between all of them, forming a mental picture.

Now, let's start with five words in Chinese. Read or listen to the words in the following exercises, try to memorize and repeat all of them. You don't need to repeat them in the exact same order.

Exercise 1:FIVE Chinese words.（Audio 7.2.1 E1）
1.水果　商店　老太太　自行车　晚餐
2.剪刀　苹果　卫生纸　遥控器　创可贴
3.消毒水　互联网　航空　加压舱　停业
4.苹果手机　新闻发布会　航空母舰　卫星　手表
5.教育　平板电脑　流行歌曲　太阳系　手套

Exercise 2:FIVE Chinese words with 10 seconds time interval after reading or listening.（Audio 7.2.1 E2）
1.地球　计算机　奥巴马　恐怖主义　新闻联播
2.面条　五角大厦　打印机　名片　翻译
3.黑洞　拳击　蓝牙　基因工程　嫌疑犯
4.背包　笔记本电脑　打印机　螺旋桨　昆虫
5.无人驾驶汽车　四旋翼　潜艇　化学工程师　金属

Most people can handle five words in Chinese. Now let's try six words.

Exercise 3:SIX Chinese words.（Audio 7.2.1 E3）
1.网络　文章　电话　国家　世界　手机
2.美国　图片　电影　大学　学生　电脑
3.记者　科技　程序　语言　工具　汽车
4.计算机　传真　电视　食品　影片　数码相机
5.3D打印　PM2.5　传真机　马达　游轮　芯片

Exercise 4:SIX Chinese words with 10 seconds time interval after reading or listening.（Audio 7.2.1 E4）
1.孩子　歌曲　声音　小说　银行　建筑
2.嗅觉　安检　雾霾　虫洞　冥王星　地壳运动
3.物理　实验室　讲座　安全教育　雕塑　校园
4.办公室　数学竞赛　接力赛　油画　细菌　高考
5.力学　牛顿定律　劳动奖章　国庆节　数学竞赛　摄影展

Many learners may already have some difficulty remembering all six Chinese words. Let's just try a few exercises with seven Chinese words.

Exercise 5:SEVEN Chinese words.（Audio 7.2.1 E5）
1.水果　计算机　遥控器　晚餐　新闻联播　名片　面条
2.设备　指纹　研究员　威胁　气候变化　本地化　场景
3.谎话　编辑　冲突　参与者　良性肿瘤　咖啡机　邮件

Chapter Ⅶ Memory

 4. 手势 伤口 抗生素 游戏机 平板电脑 沙发 药物

 5. 衣服 图书 病毒 武器 笔记本 地图 股票

Exercise 6:SEVEN Chinese words with 10 seconds time interval after reading or listening. (Audio 7.2.1 E6)

 1. 足球 房屋 杂志 屏幕 操作系统 黄金 引擎

 2. 药品 日记 电池 玻璃 石油 电源 飞机

 3. 家具 电子邮件 车辆 光盘 植物 电器 玩具

 4. 相片 笔记本电脑 啤酒 导弹 戒指 证件 卫星

 5. 办公室 无人机 瑜伽 水下航行器 联合国 电子文档 游行

Many people may feel that they are stretching their memory for seven words. Right now, we are repeating Chinese words. For native Chinese speakers, understanding these words is not an issue. All we need to do is focusing on memorizing them. Now, let's move on to some exercise in English. We will also start with five words.

Exercise 7:FIVE English words. (Audio 7.2.1 E7)

 1. morning restaurant glass wallet watch

 2. class head test laugh breakfast

 3. meteor mind-control biology barcode alarm

 4. psychology selfie solar-system phobia planet

 5. basketball glasses engine camera hard drive

Exercise 8:FIVE English words with 10 seconds time interval after reading or listening. (Audio 7.2.1 E8)

 1. pill spoon penguin protein workout

 2. chip lenses rocket bit coins PM2.5

 3. dinner table library mug missile submarine

 4. aircraft carrier tank truck sedan AK47

 5. airplane monorail refrigerator sofa TV

In repeating English words, we need to divide part of our attention to the understanding of these words. This may greatly affect our memory. That is why many learners already feel that they can barely remember four of them. But to test our memory, let's try six words.

Exercise 9:SIX English words. (Audio 7.2.1 E9)

 1. Coke hamburger comedy popcorn shower elevator

 2. sugar global-warming orbit bacteria standard drug

 3. equator astronaut microbiology injury majority obstacle

 4. jumpsuit cellphone wood chocolate milk newspaper behavior

 5. basketball micro-chip birthday cake casualty environment sensor

Exercise 10:SIX English words with 10 seconds time interval after reading or listening. (Audio 7.2.1 E10)

1. pillow   newspaper   workout   sugar   wallet   glass
2. Peaches   chopsticks   fast food   explosion   bowl   atomic bombs
3. helicopters   handgun   poker game   mahjong   noodles   rice wine
4. traffic-light   keyboard   lenses   nature   waves   surface
5. crystal   smart-phone   mirror   health   link   engineer

In English word repeating, many people feel that the most they can remember are six words, and this is when they can understand each word easily.

Word repeating exercise is a very good way for learners to quickly check on their memory capacity. Some may be five words, some six or seven, or even more. Learners need to have a good knowledge about their own memory capacity, and train accordingly. Ideally, learners should train to remember 8+ words in Chinese and 7+ words in English. In training, the difficulty of the words can also be gradually increased. We can also add some numbers, dates or proper names to the list to increase the difficulty. Time intervals can also be increased.

7.2.2 Training Method—Passages Retelling

This is an exercise that we have done in Chapter Ⅳ when we discuss information extraction and analysis. Without information extraction and analysis, memorization can hardly be achieved. Memory training is done on the basis of information processing, and passage retelling exercise is frequently used because it involves both information processing and memorization.

As we have discussed, we often categorize the passages according to their discourse structures (chronological, spatial, comparison and contrast, causal-effect, problem-solution, and topical) or genres (narrative, introductory, argumentative, and associative).

Passage retelling exercise starts with simpler narrative passages, which usually follow a chronological structure and can be easily visualized; then move on to argumentative and associative passages which often have strong logical connections; and then to introductory passages which may have many parallel structures, list of items and etc. and are usually heavily-loaded with information. Passage retelling exercise also starts with source language retelling, then move on to source+target language retelling, and then to target language retelling (which is similar to interpreting without note-taking). The length of each passage range from a few minutes to 15 minutes the most. We need to note that retelling does not mean word-for-word repeating. Retelling means to retell the key ideas, and try to recall as much information from the passage as possible.

In passage retelling, understanding is the key. Visualization (refer to Chapter Ⅳ, Section 4.2.1) and association by logic can also help with our memorization.

Chapter Ⅶ　Memory

Exercise: Retell the following passages first in the source language, and then in the target language.

Passage 1 (Narrative)

(Audio 7.2.2 P1)

The man walked down the trail on a cold, gray day. This was his first winter in Alaska. He was wearing heavy clothes and fur boots. But he still felt cold and uncomfortable. The man was on his way to a camp near Henderson Creek. His friends were already there. He expected to reach Henderson Creek by six o'clock that evening. It would be dark by then. His friends would have a fire and hot food ready for him.

A dog walked behind the man. The man continued to walk down the trail. He came to a frozen stream called Indian Creek. He began to walk on the snow-covered ice. It was a trail that would lead him straight to Henderson Creek and his friends.

As he walked, he looked carefully at the ice in front of him. Once, he stopped suddenly, and then walked around a part of the frozen stream. He saw that an underground spring flowed under the ice at that spot. It made the ice thin. If he stepped there, he might break through the ice into a pool of water. To get his boots wet in such cold weather might kill him. His feet would turn to ice quickly. He could freeze to death.

At about twelve o'clock, the man decided to stop to eat his lunch. He made a fire, beginning with small pieces of wood and adding larger ones. He sat on a snow-covered log and ate his lunch. He enjoyed the warm fire for a few minutes. Then he stood up and started walking on the frozen stream again.

A half hour later, it happened. At a place where the snow seemed very solid, the ice broke. The man's feet sank into the water. It was not deep, but his legs got wet to the knees. He would have to build a fire now to dry his clothes and boots.

He walked over to some small trees. They were covered with snow. He put several large pieces of wood on the snow, under one of the trees. On top of the wood, he put some grass and dry branches. He pulled off his gloves, took out his matches, and lighted the fire. He fed the young flame with more wood. As the fire grew stronger, he gave it larger pieces of wood.

He worked slowly and carefully. At sixty degrees below zero, a man with wet feet must not fail in his first attempt to build a fire. While he was walking, his blood had kept all parts of his body warm. Now that he had stopped, cold was forcing his blood to withdraw deeper into his body. His wet feet had frozen. He could not feel his fingers. His nose was frozen, too. The skin all over his body felt cold.

Now, however, his fire was beginning to burn more strongly. He was safe. He sat under the tree and thought of the old men in Fairbanks. The old men had told him that no man should travel alone in the Yukon when the temperature is sixty degrees below zero. Yet here he was. He had had an accident. He was alone. And he had saved himself. He had built a fire.

Those old men were weak, he thought. A real man could travel alone. If a man stayed calm, he would be all right. The man's boots were covered with ice.

He leaned back against the tree to take out his knife. Suddenly, without warning, a heavy mass of snow dropped down. His movement had shaken the young tree only a tiny bit. But it was enough to cause the branches of the tree to drop their heavy load. The man was shocked. He sat and looked at the place where the fire had been.

The old men had been right, he thought. If he had another man with him, he would not be in any danger now. The other man could build the fire. Well, it was up to him to build the fire again. This time, he must not fail.

The man collected more wood. He reached into his pocket for the matches. But his fingers were frozen. He could not hold them. He began to hit his hands with all his force against his legs.

After a while, feeling came back to his fingers. The man reached again into his pocket for the matches. But the tremendous cold quickly drove the life out of his fingers. All the matches fell onto the snow. He tried to pick one up, but failed.

The man pulled on his glove and again beat his hand against his leg. Then he took the gloves off both hands and picked up all the matches. He gathered them together. Holding them with both hands, he scratched the matches along his leg. They immediately caught fire. He held the blazing matches to a piece of wood. After a while, he became aware that he could smell his hands burning. Then he began to feel the pain. He opened his hands, and the blazing matches fell on to the snow. The flame went out in a puff of gray smoke. The man looked up. The dog was still watching him. The man got an idea. He would kill the dog and bury his hands inside its warm body. When the feeling came back to his fingers, he could build another fire. He called to the dog. The dog heard danger in the man's voice. It backed away. The man called again. This time the dog came closer. The man reached for his knife. But he had forgotten that he could not bend his fingers. He could not kill the dog, because he could not hold his knife.

The fear of death came over the man. He jumped up and began to run. The running began to make him feel better. Maybe running would make his feet warm. If he ran far enough, he would reach his friends at Henderson Creek. They would take care of him.

It felt strange to run and not feel his feet when they hit the ground. He fell several times. He decided to rest a while. As he lay in the snow, he noticed that he was not shaking. He could not feel his nose or fingers or feet. Yet, he was feeling quite warm and comfortable. He realized he was going to die.

Well, he decided, he might as well take it like a man. There were worse ways to die. The man closed his eyes and floated into the most comfortable sleep he had ever known.

The dog sat facing him, waiting. Finally, the dog moved closer to the man and caught the smell of death. The animal threw back its head. It let out a long, soft cry to the cold stars in the black sky. And then it tuned and ran toward Henderson Creek... where it knew there was food and a fire.

—Adapted from the story *To Build a Fire* written by Jack London

Passage 2 (Narrative)

(Audio 7.2.2 P2)

曾经问一位企业家朋友,他成功的秘诀是什么。他毫不犹豫地告诉我,第一是坚持,第二是坚持,第三还是坚持。我心里暗笑。没想到朋友又"狗尾续貂"了一句,"第四是放弃"。

放弃?作为一个成功的企业家怎么可以轻言放弃?该放弃的时候就要放弃,朋友说,如果你确实努力再努力了,还不成功的话,那就不是你努力不够的原因,恐怕是努力方向以及你的才能是否匹配的事情了。这时候最明智的选择就是赶快放弃,及时调整,及时调头,寻找新的努力方向,千万不要在一棵树上吊死。

据说乾隆皇帝曾经在殿试的时候给举子们出了一个上联"烟锁池塘柳",要求对下联。一个举子想了一下就直接回答说对不上来,另外的举子们还都在苦思冥想时,乾隆就直接点了那个回答说对不上的举子为状元。因为这个上联的五个字以"金木水火土"五行为偏旁,几乎可以说是绝对,第一个说放弃的考生肯定思维敏捷,很快就看出了其中的难度,而敢于说放弃,又说明他有自知之明,不愿意把时间浪费在几乎不可能的事情上。"童话大王"郑渊洁曾经说过:"每个人都有自己的最佳才能区,除非他是白痴,要拿自己的长处和别人的短处竞争,打得过就打,打不过就跑。"

这句看似"懦弱"的话说得很有道理。首先要"打",打过了才知道自己的短处和长处,才知道自己是否是人家的对手,努力了之后在取胜无望的情况下作战略性撤退,不作无谓的牺牲,是智者所为。"打不过就跑",是最容易走向成功的捷径。

——小故事大道理之《走向成功的捷径"打不过就跑"》,来源:360doc

Passage 3 (Argumentative)

(Audio 7.2.2 P3)

发展之路没有终点,只有新的起点。"往者不可谏,来者犹可追。"世界正处在快速变化的历史进程之中,世界经济正在发生更深层次的变化。我们要洞察世界经济发展趋势,找准方位,把握规律,果敢应对。

——我们正面临增长动能的深刻转变。当前,改革创新成为各国化解挑战、谋求发展的方向。结构性改革的正面效应和潜能持续释放,对各国经济增长的促进作用进一步显现。新一轮科技和产业革命形成势头,数字经济、共享经济加速发展,新产业、新模式、新业态层出不穷,新的增长动能不断积聚。

——我们正面临全球发展方式的深刻转变。随着时代进步,发展的内涵正在发生深刻变化。创新、协调、绿色、开放、共享的发展理念日益深入人心,实现更加全面、更有质量、更可持续的发展,是国际社会共同追求的目标。落实2030年可持续发展议程,应对气候变化等全球性挑战,成为国际社会重要共识。

——我们正面临经济全球化进程的深刻转变。过去数十年,经济全球化对世界经济发展作出了重要贡献,已成为不可逆转的时代潮流。同时,面对形势的发展变化,经济全球化在形式和内容上面临新的调整,理念上应该更加注重开放包容,方向上应该更加注重普惠平衡,效应上应该更加注重公正共赢。

——我们正面临全球经济治理体系的深刻转变。世界经济格局的演变对全球经济治理体系提出了更高要求。坚持多边主义,谋求共商共建共享,建立紧密伙伴关系,构建人类命运共同体,是新形势下全球经济治理的必然趋势。

——Excerpt from President Xi Jinping's Keynote Address "*Seizing the Opportunity of a Global Economy in Transition and Accelerating Development of the Asia-Pacific*" at the APEC CEO Summit in Da Nang, November 10, 2017

Passage 4 (Argumentative)

(Audio 7.2.2 P4)

In many cases, girls tend not to do as well at math and science as boys. There are several reasons for this. The first and most important reason is that they aren't encouraged to play with toys that build up interest in math and science problems and that build skills for problem solving or understanding how things work. Girls are encouraged to play with toys that foster language and human relations skills. As a result, they can grow up not knowing how an engine works or how to build a model from directions.

Second, studies have shown that many teachers don't expect girls to be good at math. Even female math and science teachers pay more attention to boys in class and tend to call on boys more often. Because teachers don't expect girls to excel, they don't try very hard, and soon girls are far behind boys in these studies.

Finally, girls don't have many role models to look up to. Not very many math and science teachers are women, especially in the later grades. When the media picture mathematicians and scientists, they usually picture men. As a result, girls aren't inspired to choose these fields as careers.

In summary, several factors work together in the home, in schools, and in society at large to send a subtle message to girls. Girls almost always get the message; as a result, very few girls excel at math and science.

——Source unknown

Passage 5 (Introductory)

(Audio 7.2.2 P5)

Those tiny little hairs above our eyes that many women pluck or paint play a very important role in keeping moisture out of our eyes.

Just like an umbrella keeps our bodies dry from rain, our hairy eyebrows keep our eyes dry from rain or sweat. When it's pouring with rain outside or when sweat runs down our foreheads, our eyebrows divert the flow of water or sweat away from our eyes. Our eyebrows angle the rain or sweat around to the sides of our faces, leaving our eyes fairly dry. By catching the water or sweat, our eyebrows not only allow us to see more clearly but also keep the salt in the sweat from burning or irritating our eyes.

Eyebrows have other roles also. As one of our most expressive facial features, eyebrows help us determine how people are feeling without having to ask them. If a person's eyebrows are drawn in a frown, the chances are that they are angry or upset.

What is more, over the years, eyebrows have been having an increasing impact on our concepts of beauty or fashion. Big, thick and hairy eyebrows tend to be considered unattractive, while thin, plucked eyebrows are said to be more attractive.

(Source: http://yingyu.xdf.cn/200801/150695.html)

Passage 6 (Introductory)

(Audio 7.2.2 P6)

在海里边尤其是深海,有很多动物能发光,能发光的动物等于它本身带着一个灯,自己照明。在海中遨游,恰似龙灯飞舞,群星闪烁,非常好看。那么这么多的发光动物,到底它怎么能够保护自己呢？正在这时,有一条非常凶猛的大鱼,看着这个亮光就游过来了,就想吃掉这条发光的鱼。因为它看到一个亮光,游过来以后,灯光灭了,因为这个灯光,鱼本身能控制。那么好,当时就灭了,灭了以后,这条凶猛的大鱼只好悻悻地游走了。到底谁在耍魔术？怎么回事？原来是一种发光鱼,发光鱼的原理是什么呢？我们说它身体里有一种腺细胞(gland cell)的分泌液,含有一种磷脂(phospholipid),这个磷脂就叫荧光素(fluorescein),那么荧光素在催化剂荧光酶的作用下,会和血液中的氧化合,那么发出一种荧光,也叫冷光。这种能发光的鱼是谁呢？是一种叫鮟鱇鱼的鱼(anglerfish)。这个鮟鱇鱼可不是一般的鱼类,它是在水深1600米的地方,生活着的一种能够发光的鱼类。它怎么就能发出光来呢？刚才我说了,腺细胞的分泌液含有一种磷脂。但是有一点它发出的光是怎么发的？是这样,因为它身体里头有背鳍(dorsal fin),它的第一背鳍棘长出一个钓竿,在钓竿的顶上有一个肉穗,就能发出各种各样的光色来。而且这个肉穗在水中漂浮着,不知情的小鱼就以为它是一条小虫都过来吃,这样一过来吃不要紧,它马上大嘴一张,小鱼小虾全流进了它的嘴里。这个鮟鱇鱼长得什么模样？是一个又大又圆又扁这么一个样子,尾鳍不长,它的口非常大。在口的周围还有很多短短的触须。如果有大鱼过来以后,它马上把光色去掉,灭掉以后,别的鱼看不到它自己在这里,那么就保护了它。

那么这个发光的动物它有几个作用：第一就是它要集中光线,又要调整强度。这说明这条鱼本身是能控制它的发光器的；第二点,就是发光鱼本身它的发光的部位,一般在它的眼睛、下颚、身体两侧,在它的腹面,这样发出来的光可以说能够照到前面、两侧、下面和腹部,这样对它本身鱼类是有很大的好处的;第三点,发光鱼所发出的光的颜色是不一样的。正因为它发出的颜色不一样,才使自己能够按照颜色找到它的同类。所以说我们认为这在鱼类发光当中,是起着极其重要的作用的。还有一点,就是这个发光鱼在仿生学方面起到什么作用?我们现在用的日光灯,就是仿照冷光灯做的。而且它就是一种冷光灯,它的功率小,效率大,亮度也大。它的寿命是普通的灯寿命的七到八倍。我们用冷光灯在矿井下照明,不易使瓦斯爆炸,也保证了安全。

——节选自曹玉茹中央电视台《百家讲坛·海洋生灵——千奇百怪的自卫》

7.2.3　Training Method—Shadowing Exercise

Shadowing exercise is a training method to repeat after the speakers in the same language almost simultaneously. In a sense, when we are repeating after the speakers, we are like their shadows, repeating the exact same words in the same manner.

Shadowing exercise can help learners adapt to the "multi-purpose" mode of interpreting, and have the ability to deal with multiple tasks such as listening, understanding, memorizing, speaking, retelling, monitoring and so on. It is often used in simultaneous interpreting training, but it can also be used for memory training in CI. It can also be used for learners to improve their pronunciation and intonation.

Initially, the time delay can be 1 second, or one word. That means we repeat immediately after the speakers start speaking. Then we can add the time delay to 3 – 5 seconds, or a few words. And after training for a while, we can add the time delay to even longer, even the length of a sentence.

As for the language, we can train with both Chinese or English. For Chinese native speakers, shadowing exercise in Chinese may not be as challenging as in English because we have no difficulty in understanding Chinese, and understanding is the key to memorizing. So we often start the training with Chinese, and then move on to English.

As for the speed of utterance, we can start the training with special English, i.e., English read in a slower speed, and then move on to standard English, and then to English or Chinese with faster utterance speed.

All sorts of news, TV or radio programs, talk shows, and public speaking can be used in shadowing exercise. Learners should even foster a habit of doing the shadowing exercise in our daily life and do it when we are listening to a conversation on a bus, watching a TV program at home, or almost anywhere possible.

Sometimes when learners are doing shadowing exercise, they only mechanically repeat the sound of what they hear without understanding. This should be avoided. One way to test understanding is to retell what has been repeated after the exercise and try to recall as much information as possible.

In addition, distractions can also be added in the training to add difficulty. This will be discussed later in this chapter.

Chapter VII Memory

Exercise: Listen to the following passages and do the shadowing exercise with 1-second time delay and 3-second time delay respectively.

Passage 1

(Audio 7.2.3 P1)

Ancient Conditions Around the Dead Sea Could Signal a Drier Future

The Dead Sea is losing about a meter of water each year.

The sea is on the border of Israel and Jordan. It is the lowest place on Earth meaning its surface is farther below sea level than any other place. And the sea's surface is getting lower because of below average rainfall in the area.

Now, an international team of geologists is seeking to understand how climate changes, over 200,000 years, have affected the area. They also may have found that a severe drought deeply changed the Dead Sea thousands of years ago.

The scientists have been studying soil sediment that shows dry seasons and wet seasons over thousands of years.

Marwan al-Raggad studies hydrology, or how water moves on the Earth. He is a member of a team studying the Dead Sea area. He said the group is looking at rocks and soil to find evidence of the climate in the area thousands of years ago. He said he is trying to develop a clear idea of the current conditions in order to "forecast the future climate of the Dead Sea area".

Recently, the team gathered samples from the eastern shore of the Dead Sea and from rivers and streams that flow into it.

Yael Kiro is a geochemist with the Lamont-Doherty Earth Observatory in New York City. She says her group is seeking a better understanding of the area's climate.

"We want to learn what's going on in the Dead Sea in terms of how much water [is coming] from the eastern side and what is the composition of water and what is the composition of sediments. We can't understand without this, the changes that we see in the Dead Sea and therefore we can't understand the climate without knowing what is going on here."

Members of the group said they are finding evidence of a huge drought thousands of years ago. The lack of rains was so severe that it dried up 80 percent of what today is a very salty lake.

Stephen Goldstein also is with the Lamont-Doherty Earth Observatory. He said understanding the past can help plan for the future.

"What happened in the past tells us something about what's possible in the future. And what happened in the past in this area is that the water that people are using now and need now stopped running."

Scientists with the observatory say that the area may have faced two periods of extremely dry conditions. One was 120,000 years ago, the other as recent as 10,000 years ago. During those periods, rainfall dropped to one fifth of its current level. The area is already considered arid, or very dry.

Kiro and Goldstein were among the authors of a study that provided evidence of past periods of extreme drought in the Dead Sea. The study was published in Earth and Planetary Science Letters.

The authors said their findings could be important as current climate models predict that the area may be in another historic dry period.

I'm Mario Ritter.

—from VOA Special English

Passage 2

(Audio 7.2.3 P2)

应习近平邀请 法国总统等外国领导人将出席第二届中国国际进口博览会

第二届中国国际进口博览会将于11月5日至10日在上海举行。应国家主席习近平邀请,法国总统马克龙、希腊总理米佐塔基斯、牙买加总理霍尔尼斯、塞尔维亚总理布尔纳比奇将出席博览会开幕式及相关活动。

应习近平邀请 法国总统将访华

应国家主席习近平邀请,法兰西共和国总统埃马纽埃尔·马克龙将于11月4日至6日来华出席第二届中国国际进口博览会开幕式并对中国进行国事访问。

雄安新区:未来之城奋进书写新答卷

设立河北雄安新区,是以习近平同志为核心的党中央作出的一项重大的历史性战略选择。2017年2月和2019年1月,习近平总书记先后在河北安新县和雄安新区考察调研,嘱托这里要有"世界眼光、国际标准、中国特色、高点定位"。两年多来,河北省牢记嘱托,高起点规划、高标准建设,今年河北雄安新区从以规划为中心向以建设为中心转换,这座未来之城将逐渐绽放光彩。

来到雄安新区,不同于一般大城市的"水泥森林",这里建筑不高,视野开阔,绿地成荫。像雄安政务服务中心、白洋淀等地方还成为游客的热门打卡地。这跟两年多来,雄安新区先谋后动的规划思路密不可分。

2019年是雄安新区总体规划落地实施的开局之年,也是新区全面建设之年。这里是京雄城际铁路施工现场,也是雄安新区设立后首个开工的重大交通项目。2019年1月,习近平总书记在雄安新区考察时,现场连线雄安站建设工地。

目前,6700余名建设者、200多台大型机械设备正昼夜不停施工作业,雄安站宏大的基础已初步显现。未来通车后,北京与雄安将实现半小时通达。

植树造林也紧锣密鼓,"千年大计"从打造"千年秀林"开始。雄安新区的生态建设正在大力推进。不仅建成雄安森林大数据系统,造林面积也不断扩大,今年新增6万亩。未来雄安新区的森林覆盖率达到40%。

白洋淀是华北地区的"晴雨表",被喻为"华北之肾"。2017年2月,习近平总书记在这里考察时强调,建设雄安新区,一定要把白洋淀修复好、保护好。目前,以控源、截污、治河、补水为重点的6大类45个白洋淀治理工程项目全面建设。

同时,政务服务水平全面提升。雄安新区设立两年多来,大批企业进驻,疏解北京非首都功能的作用正得到加强。新区本级注册登记企业3100多家,其中大多来自北京。

一系列改革措施也正在雄安落地。新区政务服务中心"一枚印章管到底"流程全面贯通,实现"一门覆盖、一窗受理、一网通办、一帮到底",流程更简、效率更高。

从铁路、市政等基础设施建设,到生态环境的修复保护;从公共服务的不断完善,到社会管理的制度创新。眼下,住房、教育、医疗等公共服务体系逐步打造,高端高新产业发展和智能城市建设稳步推进。雄安新区这座未来之城将更具承载力、集聚力和吸引力,将更加绽放光彩。

全国粮食丰收已成定局

秋粮产量占全年粮食总产量的70%以上。农业农村部最新农情调度显示,随着秋粮收获大头落地,全年粮食丰收已成定局,为保供给、稳物价、增信心,提供有力支撑。

我国秋粮作物品种多,从北到南覆盖广。目前,秋粮收获已近九成,北方收获基本进入扫尾阶段,南方双季晚稻收获过三成。

今年秋收画卷的突出亮点是产能提升,增产提质。全国新建高标准农田8000万亩;农田有效灌溉面积超过10.2亿亩;深松整地等高产技术广泛推广;优质稻谷、大豆面积持续增加。

伴随着秋粮收获,秋冬种也随即展开。秋冬种面积占全年农作物的1/4。目前,冬小麦和冬油菜的播种都已超过七成,总体进展顺利。今年秋冬种的突出亮点是,继续推进农业供给侧结构性改革,力争冬小麦面积稳定在3.3亿亩以上,优质专用麦比例比上年提高2个百分点,冬油菜面积稳定在1亿亩以上。

—from CCTV News, Oct 30, 2019

7.2.4 Training Method—Short CI Without Note-taking

Interpreting without note-taking is also a good way to train our memory. It is also a good way to help us stay focus on the message rather than words. Different from passage retelling in the target language, interpreting without note-taking requires more accuracy and completeness of information, and the training materials are usually much shorter.

When we say "short" CI, it usually refers to a sentence or a short paragraph, ranging from 10 seconds to 90 seconds. Learners can start training from shorter ones and gradually move on to longer ones. The process is gradual. As Baxter said, at this stage, students should be reassured that they should aim to do the minimum well, rather than trying to do the maximum shoddily. At this stage, memory training is the focus. Diction and grammar are secondary. But this training can also give the trainer and learners the best window of opportunity to spot areas for improvement in their rendition and public speaking. For beginners, they can also start from source language retelling before interpreting.

Exercise 1: Interpret the following Chinese sentences or paragraphs into English without Note-taking. (Audio 7.2.4 E1)

1. 改革开放是中国人民和中华民族发展史上一次伟大革命,正是这个伟大革命推动了中国特色社会主义事业的伟大飞跃!

2. 我们党作出实行改革开放的历史性决策,是基于对党和国家前途命运的深刻把握,是基于对社会主义革命和建设实践的深刻总结。

3. 中华民族迎来了从站起来、富起来到强起来的伟大飞跃! 中国特色社会主义迎来了从创立、发展到完善的伟大飞跃! 中国人民迎来了从温饱不足到小康富裕的伟大飞跃!

4. 必须坚持走中国特色社会主义道路,不断坚持和发展中国特色社会主义。必须坚持以发展为第一要务,不断增强我国综合国力。

5. 亚洲是当今世界最具发展活力和潜力的地区之一,同时面临政治互信不足、经济发展不平衡、安全和治理问题突出等共同挑战,实现持久和平和共同繁荣任重道远。

6. 我们用几十年时间走完了发达国家几百年走过的工业化历程。在中国人民手中,不可能成为了可能。我们为创造了人间奇迹的中国人民感到无比自豪、无比骄傲!

7. 北京世界园艺博览会以"绿色生活,美丽家园"为主题,旨在倡导人们尊重自然、融入自然、追求美好生活。

8. 生态文明建设已经纳入中国国家发展总体布局,建设美丽中国已经成为中国人民心向往之的奋斗目标。中国生态文明建设进入了快车道,天更蓝、山更绿、水更清将不断展现在世人面前。

9. 我们要维持地球生态整体平衡,让子孙后代既能享有丰富的物质财富,又能遥望星空、看见青山、闻到花香。

10. 面对生态环境挑战,人类是一荣俱荣、一损俱损的命运共同体,没有哪个国家能独善其身。唯有携手合作,我们才能有效应对气候变化、海洋污染、生物保护等全球性环境问题,实现联合国2030年可持续发展目标。只有并肩同行,才能让绿色发展理念深入人心、全球生态文明之路行稳致远。

Exercise 2: Interpret the following English sentences or paragraphs into Chinese without Note-taking. (Audio 7.2.4 E2)

1. Seventy-five years ago, more than 150,000 Allied troops were preparing on this island to parachute into France, storm the beaches of Normandy, and win back our civilization.

2. The world again faces simultaneous humanitarian crises. This time there are four: in the Syrian Arab Republic, the Philippines, the Central African Republic, and South Sudan. These crises are testing WHO's emergency performance.

3. We should be ambitious with these strategies and plans, but also pragmatic and realistic. As we have learned since the start of this century, sustainable health improvements depend on a well-functioning health system. We must build the capacities of countries, not overburden them.

4. On behalf of all Americans, I offer a toast to the eternal friendship of our people, the vitality of our nations, and to the long, cherished, and truly remarkable reign of Her

Majesty the Queen.

5. In nine years, the United States will celebrate the 250th anniversary of our founding—250 years since the day we declared our independence. It will be one of the great milestones in the history of the world. But what will America look like as we reach our 250th year? What kind of country will we leave for our children?

6. On D-Day, the Queen's beloved father King George the Sixth delivered a stirring national address. That day, he said, "After nearly five years of toil and suffering, we must renew that crusading impulse on which we entered the war and met its darkest hour... Our fight is against evil and for a world in which goodness and honor may be the foundation of the life of men in every land."

7. We should be absolutely clear that the Syrian conflict did not begin with terrorism. This began with ordinary people calling for greater political and economic freedom, who were met with brute force and oppression rather than the offer of peaceful change.

8. Our obligation is to serve, protect, and defend the citizens of the United States. We are also taking strong measures to protect our nation from radical Islamic terrorism. According to data provided by the Department of Justice, the vast majority of individuals convicted of terrorism and terrorism-related offenses since 9/11 came here from outside of our country.

9. As promised, I directed the Department of Defense to develop a plan to demolish and destroy ISIS—a network of lawless savages that have slaughtered Muslims and Christians, and men, and women, and children of all faiths and all beliefs. We will work with our allies, including our friends and allies in the Muslim world, to extinguish this vile enemy from our planet.

10. I'll never forget, on my first trip to Berlin as Secretary of State, meeting with a group of young Germans. They told me something I never knew about the city where I'd spent time growing up in the aftermath of World War Two. Throughout the city, they've placed "stumbling stones" to mark where Jews were murdered in the streets and other victims of the Holocaust. Every day, passers-by remember what happened—and equally important—they never forget or deny it.

⊙ Interpreting Reference for Exercise 1

1. The reform and opening up is the great revolution in the development history of the Chinese nation that propelled a quantum leap forward in the cause of socialism with Chinese characteristics.

2. The Party made the historic decision of going for reform and opening-up, based on a profound grasp of the future of the Party and of the country, and on an in-depth review of the experience gained in socialist revolution and development.

3. The Chinese nation has achieved a tremendous transformation from standing up, growing rich to becoming strong. Socialism with Chinese characteristics has achieved a

tremendous transformation from establishment, development to improvement. The Chinese people have achieved a tremendous transformation from the days of scarcity to a life of moderate prosperity.

4. We must stay on the path of socialism with Chinese characteristics, and uphold and develop socialism with Chinese features. We must continue to take development as the top priority and enhance our composite national strength.

5. Asia is one of the most dynamic regions with great development potential. Asian countries also face some common challenges such as inadequate political trust, uneven economic development and prominent security and governance impediments. Our journey to lasting peace and common prosperity will be a long and arduous one.

6. In just a few decades, we have completed an industrialization process that took developed countries several hundred years. The Chinese people have achieved what was once impossible. We are immensely proud of our fellow country men and women who have worked an unprecedented miracle.

7. The Beijing World Horticulture Expo, as indicated by its theme "Live Green, Live Better", aims to promote respect for nature and a better life in harmony with nature.

8. Ecological conservation has become part of China's overall plan for national development. Building a beautiful China is an inspiring goal for the Chinese people. As China steps up its conservation efforts, the world will see a China with more blue skies, lush mountains and lucid waters.

9. We must maintain the overall balance of the Earth's eco-system, so that our children and children's children will not only have material wealth but also enjoy starry skies, green mountains and sweet flowers.

10. In the face of environmental challenges, all countries are in a community with destinies linked, and no country can stay immune. Only together can we effectively address climate change, marine pollution, biological conservation and other global environmental issues and achieve the UN 2030 Agenda for Sustainable Development. Only concerted efforts can drive home the idea of green development and bring about steady progress in the ecological conservation of the globe.

⊙ Interpreting Reference for Exercise 2

1. 75年前，超过15万名盟军在这个岛上准备降落到法国，突袭诺曼底海滩，夺回我们的文明。

2. 全世界再次面对同时发生的人道主义危机。这回是发生在叙利亚阿拉伯共和国、菲律宾、中非共和国和南苏丹的四场危机。这些危机考验着世卫组织的突发事件处理能力。

3. 我们的战略和计划，要有雄心，但同时也要务实和切合实际。自本世纪初以来，我们已经认识到，可持续的卫生改进取决于运转良好的卫生系统。我们必须建设各国的能力，而不是给它们过重的负担。

4. 我谨代表所有美国人民，为我们两国人民的永恒友谊干杯，为我们两国的活力干杯，为女王陛下久负盛名的卓越统治干杯。

5. 九年后,美国将庆祝国家诞生 250 周年——自宣布独立以来的 250 年。它将是世界历史上伟大的里程碑之一。但是,当 250 周年来临时,美国会是什么样子? 我们将为我们的孩子留下一个怎样的国家?

6. 在诺曼底登陆日,女王敬爱的父亲,乔治六世国王发表了激动人心的全国讲话。那天他是这么说的,"在经历了近 5 年的艰苦奋战后,我们必须重新唤起当年那种英勇无畏,敢于冲锋陷阵的精神以迎接至暗时刻的到来……我们的斗争是为了抗争邪恶与改变世界,在新世界中,善良和荣誉是所有国家人民生活的基础。"

7. 我们还应绝对清楚这一点,即叙利亚冲突并不是开始于恐怖主义,而是开始于普通民众,他们要求获得更大的政治和经济自由,但没有获得和平变革,反而遭到了残酷的打击和压迫。

8. 我们必须服务、保护、守卫美国的公民。对恐怖组织我们也会采取强硬手段。根据司法部提供的数据,自"9·11"恐袭以来,绝大多数在美国实施恐袭的人,都来自这个国家之外。

9. 正如我保证过的一样,我下令国防部提出计划,摧毁 ISIS 组织——一帮目无法纪的野蛮人,残害穆斯林和基督徒,以及各种信仰的男女和儿童。我们会和盟友合作,包括来自穆斯林世界的朋友们,一起让这些邪恶的敌人,从我们的地球上消失。

10. 我永远不会忘记在我作为国务卿首次出访柏林时与一批年轻德国人的会面。他们告诉我一些我从未听说过的有关该城市的事情,而我是在第二次世界大战后在那里长大的。他们在整个城市放置了"绊脚石",以标出犹太人和大屠杀的其他受害者当街被杀害的位置。每天,过路的人都会记住发生过什么——同样重要的是——他们永远不会忘记或否认发生过的事。

7.2.5 Distractions

No matter it is word repeating, passage retelling, shadowing exercise or CI without note-taking, we can add some distractions to increase difficulty. Anti-distraction training is necessary because no interpreter can work without any distraction.

Distractions usually come in two ways: internal distractions and external distractions. Internal distractions mainly come from the interpreters themselves, such as their health condition, note-taking, listening comprehension, etc. External distractions mainly refer to the noise at scene, people moving about, interruptions from the speakers or the audience, or the way the speakers speak that may affect interpreters' understanding.

Based on the two different types of distractions, we can also train accordingly.

(1) Note-taking is one major internal distraction. When doing the above exercises, we can write down some non-relevant things like figures, names or draw some pictures. Figures are often used as distractions. We can start from writing from 1 to 100, then write from 100 to 1. To add difficulty, we can also write only the odd numbers or even numbers from small to large, or the other way around. After doing the exercise, make sure to check whether the numbers are written correctly.

(2) Noise is one of the major distractions externally. When training, we can ask some

other students to work as distractions and intentionally try to distract the person doing the exercise. For example, they can cough, taking phone calls, stand up and walk pass the person, or speak to each other. No matter what they do, they must cause certain distraction, but they should not overdo it.

Anti-distraction training is crucial in CI training, especially in the stage of memory training. But to reach desired effect, learners must check the accuracy of their repetition or retelling. Only when they can do it accurately can we gradually add more distractions and add the difficulty of the exercise.

Exercises and Practice

7-2-1　Read or listen to the words in the following exercises, try to memorize and repeat all of them (not necessarily in the exact same order). Add time delay if needed. (Audio 7-2-1 CN, Audio 7-2-1 En)

1. 软件　有限公司　设计　环境　科技　服务器
2. 频道　房地产　委员会　贷款　消费者　上市策略
3. 股份公司　社会主义　多媒体　机场　手续费　法律责任　信用
4. 知识产权　工程师　人民政府　糖尿病　流程　信仰　邮政编码
5. tribe, procedure, mass media, exhibition, discount
6. dormitory, Singapore, market economy, intellectual property, museum
7. blood pressure, export, press conference, Thailand, infrastructure, bank account
8. public servant, expiration date, merchant, climate, refrigerator, court room

7-2-2　Retell the following passages first in the source language, and then try your best to retell in the target language. Add distraction if possible when listening.

Passage 1

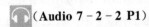(Audio 7-2-2 P1)

One day, our neighbor Keno Carter rode his horse over to our house. He had another horse with him. He rode to me and said: "You have helped me a lot during the year. You've been a good boy. Now, here is the horse I promised. It is yours." At first, I just stood with my mouth open and looked. The horse was a white female. A mare with brown spots. I have never seen anything so beautiful and she was mine, all mine.

"She is a kind animal. Remember this, boy. You can lose her love easily. If you become angry, if you hurt her, she will never obey or love you. You should teach her very gently. It is your job to feed her, clean her and give her water. Put her at the end of a long rope and let her play. Call her name and gently pull on the rope. She will soon learn to come to you when she wants water or food." He talked for half an hour telling me how to train my horse.

When he finished, I said: "Can I have her now? I want to begin right away." He left me

Chapter VII Memory

and went to town with my father. I walked away with my horse. The first thing I did was to give her a name. I named her Queen. She liked me, I knew it because she obeyed me and seemed to enjoy it.

From then on, I was with my horse every day. I taught her to run around in a circle, to go one way then turn around and go another. I broke a piece of wood from a tree and used it as my training stick. My small sisters wanted to help me. I let them do some little things but I gave the orders.

A week later, I started to teach her to carry me. This was slow work. I began by gently putting my arm on her back. If she did not like it, I slowly moved my arm away. When she let me leave my arm there, I placed the cloth on her back. I slowly got up and sat on the cloth, then I got down again. I did this hundreds of times. I wanted to hurry and ride her, but I remembered what Keno Carter said about being slow and gentle. I learned how to wait. At last, she let me ride her, just for a few minutes at first, then for a longer time. When she got tired and started to jump, I got off. One thing about Queen, she was my horse and she did not let my sisters or anyone else ride her. It was always like that, just Queen and me.

One day, the circus came to town. I wanted to see only one thing, the horses. I went to the tent where the trainer lived. I talked to him. He let me watch him train the circus horses. I learned a lot. I trained Queen until she was better than all of them. She could soon stand up on her back legs, go down on her front legs and even lie down and roll over.

I started to teach Queen another trick, a difficult and dangerous trick. But I was sure I could do it. I saw the circus horse do it first. He stepped over a clown who lay on the ground. He ran back and forth and did not touch the clown with his feet. The trainer told me how to teach Queen. First, I got pieces of wood and put them on the ground. I led Queen over them. If she touched one of them, I told her it was wrong and did not give her any sugar. When she learned how to do this, I was ready to let her step over a clown. I did not have a clown. But I did have two sisters. They were happy to be part of my circus act. They lay down on the ground and let Queen step over them.

My Queen did it like the circus horses. This act was our secret. We did not tell anyone about it, not even my mother. It would be a surprise. We decided to show my parents that Saturday night. I cleaned Queen until she shone. I fixed her hair like they do in the circus with the bright blanket across her back and a flower behind her ear. Queen was ready. My sisters put on their best dresses. We were all ready.

Saturday evening, when dad came home from work, we showed him our trick. When dad saw the act, he stopped and looked. His eyes grew wide, his face turned white. My mare was running back and forth, her head high jumping over the bodies of my two sisters lying on the ground. I was standing proudly, nearby was the trainer stick in my hand. I thought the look on my father's face was surprise, but it was not. It was fear and anger.

"Stop," he shouted, "stop that." He ran to me and pulled the stick from my hand. He hit me on the seat of my pants. The girls got up and brushed the dirt from their dresses.

We tried to tell him how we had trained the horse. But dad was too angry to listen.

"Don't you know that this is dangerous?" He said breathing fast, "You might have killed your sisters." And he hit my bottom good and hard.

I learned something useful from the punishment I got for that horse trick. I learned about the pain in my heart when people did not understand me. I learned that some mothers and fathers do not train their boys as carefully as I trained my horse. Perhaps, they do not have the time. Perhaps, they do not have any reasons.

When dad finished hitting me, he explained to mother why he had punished me. Then, I told my story. I told both of them how long and carefully I had taught my horse to walk over the girls. I showed my father that I could really control Queen. Then, I said something that hurt him very much.

"I taught my mare that trick," I said, "I have taught her all she knows and I never hit her, not once." Mother gave dad one of her special looks. There was a long silence. I stood there in the middle of the yard gently touching the seat of my pants. I wondered why my dad suddenly looked like a small boy.

—Adapted from short story *Lessons from a Pony* written by Lincoln Steffens

Passage 2

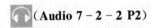（Audio 7-2-2 P2）

三种错误的饭后习惯

医生提醒人们，随着人们生活水平的逐渐提高，人们的保健意识也随之增强了，许多人认为饭后吃点水果是现代生活的最佳搭配。无论是在餐厅、饭店，还是在家里就餐，许多人都喜欢饭后吃点水果爽口，其实这是一种错误的生活习惯，因为饭后马上吃水果会影响消化功能。医生解释说，由于食物进入胃以后，必须经过一到两个小时的消化过程，才能缓慢排出。如果人们在饭后立即吃进水果，就会被先期到达的食物阻滞在胃内，致使水果不能正常地在胃内消化，在胃内时间过长，从而引起腹胀、腹泻或便秘等症状。如果人们长期坚持这种生活习惯，将会导致消化功能紊乱，因此，人们最好在饭后一到两个小时再吃水果。

医生还提醒说，人们还要注意改正饭后饮茶和饭后散步的错误习惯。

饭后立即饮茶，茶水会冲淡胃液，影响胃内食物的正常消化。茶水中含有的单宁酸还会促使胃内的物质凝固，影响蛋白质的吸收，从而增加了胃的负担。对此，医生建议人们，在饭后一小时内最好不要饮茶，应待饭后一小时胃内食物消化得差不多时再饮用茶水，这样对消化功能和物质凝固也不会产生太大的影响。

"饭后百步走，活到九十九"，这种说法也是不科学的。人的胃在饭后是处于充盈状态的，即使是非常轻微的运动也会使胃受到震动，从而增加胃肠负担，影响消化功能。对此，医生建议，饭后适当休息三十分钟，待胃内的食物适当消化后，再活动较为适宜，这样也不会对消化系统产生太大的影响。

—Source unknown

Chapter Ⅶ　Memory

Passage 3

🎧（Audio 7-2-2 P3）

　　我想大家都吃过海蟹(sea crab)，那么海蟹本身是弱小的，它没什么反抗能力，但是它有一点，它那个大螯夹(pincers)非常厉害，也就是它会用它的大螯夹来去和敌人拼搏。那么海蟹它自己想，我自己没有多大能力，我也不想成为这种强壮动物口中的美餐。那么我自己怎么办？我就用一个小技巧，我也不能失败。它有它的高招，什么呢？首先我们说，螃蟹的眼睛我们管它叫柄眼，为什么呢？因为它的眼睛长在柄上，一个长形的柄上。那么这个柄，它的基部有一个开关，等于有一个活动的关节。那么它也可以竖起来，当竖起来的时候，这个螃蟹本身就等于安上了一个瞭望哨，柄竖起来了，眼睛竖起来了，这两个眼睛等于是一个瞭望哨。不需要它的时候，它就可以把它藏在眼窝里边，连同柄一起藏在眼窝(eye socket)里边。有时候就通过沙冒出来，自己藏在沙里边去，就指着两个眼睛来眼观六路。所以我们觉着呢，螃蟹就是用这种办法。除这以外，螃蟹还有一个高招，它自己无能为力，但是它找一个有能力的当它的"护身符"。它找谁呢？找海葵(sea anemones)，因为海葵本身也有刺丝胞(stinging cells)，也能够往外放射那种毒刺。如果碰到敌害的话，怎么办？它就用它的步足，用螃蟹的步足来托起海葵到处游走。别看它狐假虎威，但是得利的也就是保证能够安全的，还是螃蟹受益，它用这种办法。因为别的动物都不敢惹这个海葵，但是它有它的步足，能够拖着它游走，所以螃蟹是用这种办法来去保卫自己的。

　　　　——节选自曹玉茹中央电视台《百家讲坛·海洋生灵——千奇百怪的自卫》

7-2-3　Listen to the following passages and do the shadowing exercise with 1-second time delay and 3-second time delay respectively. Add distractions if possible.

Passage 1

🎧（Audio 7-2-3 P1）

South Sudan's Refugee Crisis Affects Ugandan Health System

　　The huge increase in the number of refugees entering northern Uganda from South Sudan has affected the country's already-weak health care system.

　　VOA recently visited the Adjumani area in northern Uganda. Health centers there are also near refugee settlements for South Sudanese. But the health centers are unable to care for all of the pregnant women in the area.

　　Experts estimate that Uganda has one doctor for every 24,000 of its citizens. It has about one nurse for every 11,000 people. Most health care workers are in cities.

　　Because of war and violence in neighboring countries, the country now has 1.2 million refugees.

　　The United Nations says more refugees entered Uganda than any other part of the world in 2016 as civilians fled conflict and hunger in South Sudan. The flow of refugees into Uganda has continued this year.

Ester Ponne Charles is a refugee. She arrived in northern Uganda eight months ago. She also was pregnant.

"If you do not have money, you may lose your life and the child too. Because there they want money. Without money, even medicine, you buy even the gloves yourself, everything in the hospital. So those are the challenges we are facing. Those ones who cannot even afford any coin, so they will just end up losing their life."

Aid agencies and the government have worked to set up temporary health centers in the refugee settlements to help women.

One refugee settlement called Maaji now has 15,000 refugees. However, there are no doctors and only eight medical officers and nurses for the settlement.

Tako Stephen provides medical care at health center three in Maaji. However, there are limits to what medical workers can do for pregnant women at the center.

"We are unable to conduct planned deliveries here because of the setup of the place. The place is very small," he said. "We only conduct emergency deliveries and yet there are very many pregnant mothers here. So they have to walk all the way from here up to Maaji Two for deliveries."

Some of the women are sent to another health center. Odaru Judith is a nursing officer at the center. She says the number of babies born at the center has increased from 29 to 75 a month.

But, there is little space for patients, she says.

"Our general ward is very small," says Judith. "It has only 10 beds, but the number of deliveries we have in a day, the average is five, and when you take the labor room, it is so squeezed and small that it only fits one bed and at times you have three deliveries at a time, so making it very difficult. You will not even have a place where you can squeeze at least a carpet for a mother to deliver."

In January, the government and United Nations agencies promised to spend $1 million for women's health in the refugee camps. But the U.N. Population Fund says the camps will need four times that amount.

I'm Jill Robbins.

—From VOA Special English

Passage 2

(Audio 7-2-3 P2)

王岐山与南非副总统举行会谈并共同主持召开中南国家双边委员会第七次全体会议

国家副主席王岐山31日在人民大会堂与南非副总统马布扎举行会谈,并共同主持召开中南国家双边委员会第七次全体会议。

王岐山表示,中国和南非同为重要发展中大国和新兴市场国家,互为重要的战略伙伴。两国关系意义已超越双边范畴,战略和全球影响不断上升。去年以来,习近平主席同拉马福萨总统实现历史性互访,达成重要共识,为两国关系发展提供了引领。双方政治互信不断增强,在经贸投资、人文交流等领域合作成果丰硕,走在中非合作前列。

王岐山说,中南国家双边委员会对深化两国全面战略伙伴关系发挥了非常重要的作用。下一阶段,我们要加强顶层设计,巩固政治互信,坚定支持彼此核心利益和重大关切,提升战略协作水平。要共享发展机遇,持续提升务实合作水平,打造一批新的合作亮点。要夯实人文交流,携手维护多边主义,维护好发展中国家共同利益,树立发展中大国团结协作典范。

王岐山表示,中方愿同南非和非洲国家一道,加强共建"一带一路"倡议、论坛北京峰会"八大行动"同非盟《2063年议程》以及非洲各国发展战略深入对接,推动中非全面战略合作伙伴关系不断迈上新台阶,构建更加紧密的中非命运共同体。引领金砖合作沿着第二个"金色十年"轨道不断前进。

马布扎祝贺中华人民共和国成立70周年,祝愿中国经济社会建设取得更大成就。南非视中国为可信赖的伙伴和朋友。南非重视在国际地区问题上同中国的协调合作,将以最符合两国关系发展的方式看待和处理中方关切。

会谈前,王岐山为马布扎举行欢迎仪式,全国政协副主席何维等出席。

军乐团奏南、中两国国歌,王岐山陪同马布扎检阅了中国人民解放军仪仗队。

5G商用服务今天正式启动

今天(10月31日),工业和信息化部和中国移动、中国电信、中国联通三大运营商以及中国铁塔公司正式启动5G商用。三大运营商同步发布了5G套餐,从明天起,个人手机用户就可以使用5G通信服务。三大运营商5G套餐资费大同小异。价格从128元起步到599元共分五到七档,套餐总体单价低于4G套餐单价,部分套餐按上网速度定价,低价低速、高价高速。

今年6月6日,工业和信息化部发放5G牌照,运营商陆续开始5G用户预约。目前,移动、电信、联通三家预约5G业务的用户已经超过1000万。

第二届世界顶尖科学家论坛闭幕

以"科技,为了人类共同命运"为主题的第二届世界顶尖科学家论坛今天(10月31日)在上海闭幕。65位世界顶尖科学家就基础科学、新兴前沿领域的问题进行了热烈讨论,并对科技与人类的未来发展进行了猜想。

为期3天的世界顶尖科学家论坛,65位获得诺贝尔奖、沃尔夫奖、斯卡克奖、图灵奖等的世界顶尖科学家通过莫比乌斯论坛、青年科学家论坛以及8场主题峰会,对基础科学、新兴前沿等领域进行了热烈讨论,畅想和预判未来20年科学、宇宙和人类的样态。科学家们聚焦关注自己领域的发现和探索,科技的进步和想象让我们看到人类的无限可能。

—From CCTV News, Oct 31, 2019

7-2-4 Interpret the following sentences without note-taking. (Audio 7-2-4 CN, Audio 7-2-4 En)

1. 上周中国国家统计局发布数据显示,2013年中国国内生产总值(GDP)增长了7.7%。这个数字从全球范围看,保持了中高速增长。全年城镇新增就业人数超过1300万,是历年最多的。

  2. 我们看到,澳企业正日益积极地参与到中国西部地区的发展中来。今年是世界经济走向复苏的重要一年,也是中澳经贸合作升级发展的关键一年。中澳双方应该携手努力,发掘合作潜力,为两国人民带来更多实实在在的利益。

  3. 40年的实践充分证明,中国发展为广大发展中国家走向现代化提供了成功经验、展现了光明前景,是促进世界和平与发展的强大力量,是中华民族对人类文明进步作出的重大贡献。

  4. 相互尊重和信任是国与国应有的相处之道。我们要遵循联合国宪章确立的宗旨和原则,尊重各国主权独立、领土完整,尊重各国自主选择的政治制度和发展道路。

  5. 中方将继续在和平共处五项原则基础上深化同各国的友好合作,通过和平方式处理同有关国家的领土主权和海洋权益争端。我们将坚持开放共赢,同各国分享发展机遇。中方愿同各方用好共建"一带一路"国际合作平台,为共同发展持续注入强大动能。

  6. As we are seeing, getting and using better information can set off a chain of events, with improved health outcomes as the end result. We have seen this most dramatically in Niger, one of the poorest countries in the world, where the availability of high-quality data was instrumental in reducing child mortality by a stunning 43%.

  7. We can be absolutely certain that if this peace process fails, then thousands more innocent Syrians will pay the price. The Syrian government bears a particular responsibility for this crisis and can do the most to end it. I call on them to commit themselves to the mutually agreed settlement; and to stop actions on the ground which undermine the negotiations.

  8. Every year on the anniversary of the liberation of the Auschwitz concentration camp, we commemorate the victims of the Holocaust. We recall the suffering of millions of innocent people, and highlight the perils of anti-Semitism and hatred of any kind.

  9. As Secretary-General of the United Nations, I hold high the banner of empowering women and girls, promoting their health and defending their rights. The International Day of Zero-Tolerance for Female Genital Mutilation is an opportunity to confront this persistent problem—and to find hope that it can end.

  10. On behalf of President Obama and the American people, I am delighted to extend best wishes to the many people around the world who celebrate the arrival of the Lunar New Year on January 31. In this festive time, we should all take a moment to pause and reflect on the shared humanity that ties us together—not just here in America, but around the world.

Additional Materials

  1. Video:"Memory"(Video 7-1) from the European Union's interpreters' training course
  2. 《乘风破浪,坚定前行》——国务委员兼外交部长王毅在2019年国际形势与中国外交研讨会开幕式上的演讲(2019年12月13日,北京)(节选)
  "Braving Waves and Sailing Forward with Resolve." Address by H. E. Wang Yi, State

Councilor and Minister of Foreign Affairs at the Opening of Symposium onThe International Situation and China's Foreign Relations in 2019, Beijing, 13 December 2019(Excerpt)

中文来源:外交部网站
(https://www.fmprc.gov.cn/web/ziliao_674904/zyjh_674906/t1724297.shtml)
译文来源:外交部英文网站
(https://www.fmprc.gov.cn/mfa_eng/wjdt_665385/zyjh_665391/t1724306.shtml)

各位专家,各位朋友:
Members of the academia, friends,

大家好! 在岁末年初之际,很高兴和大家再次相聚。
Good morning! It gives me great pleasure to join you again at the turn of the year.

今年是国际形势与中国外交研讨会举办30周年。30年来,研讨会见证了国际形势的风云变幻,亲历了中国外交走过的不平凡历程。在各位专家学者的积极参与和大力支持下,研讨会已成为交流讨论国际形势和中国外交的重要平台,在国内外拥有越来越大的影响力,也为我国的外交工作提供了许多有价值的意见和建议。在此,我首先要向在场的所有专家学者们表示衷心的感谢!

This year marks the 30th anniversary of this symposium on the international situation and China's foreign relations. Over the past three decades, the symposium has witnessed the changes in the international landscape and the extraordinary journey of Chinese diplomacy. Thanks to your active participation and strong support, the symposium has enjoyed growing influence both at home and abroad. It has evolved into an important platform for discussions on international developments and China's diplomacy and a valuable source of insights and suggestions for China's foreign policy. For this, I wish to express my sincere thanks to all the experts and scholars present today.

2019年,对中国来说,是举国同庆、继往开来的一年。我们隆重庆祝了中华人民共和国成立70周年。回顾70年波澜壮阔的发展历程,我们更加认识到新中国发展成就来之不易,更加坚定了走中国特色社会主义道路的决心,更加提升了实现"两个一百年"奋斗目标、实现中华民族伟大复兴的信心。我们胜利召开党的十九届四中全会。这次会议全面总结了中国特色社会主义制度和国家治理体系的核心内涵、建设成就和显著优势,首次明确提出坚持和完善中国特色社会主义制度、推进国家治理体系和治理能力现代化的总体目标,为推动中华民族伟大复兴提供了更加坚实的制度保障。一个稳定、安全、繁荣的中国昂首屹立在世界东方,不断为人类的和平与发展事业作出新的贡献。

For China, 2019 is a year of national celebration and of building on past achievements to forge into the future. We warmly celebrated the 70th anniversary of the founding of the People's Republic of China. Looking back on the momentous journey China has traversed in the past seven decades, we understand better than ever how New China has come a long way to what it is today. This has made us even more determined to follow the path of socialism with Chinese characteristics and more confident about achieving the two centenary goals and the rejuvenation of the Chinese nation. We successfully held the fourth plenary session of the 19th Central Committee of the Communist Party of China (CPC). The Plenum made a full exposition of the core tenets, achievements, and remarkable advantages of the socialist system with Chinese characteristics and China's governance system. It put forward for the first time the overarching goal of upholding and improving the socialist system with Chinese characteristics and modernizing China's system and capacity for governance, thus laying a stronger institutional foundation for realizing national rejuvenation. A stable, secure and prosperous China is standing tall and proud in the east of the world, poised to make new contributions to the cause of peace and development of humankind.

2019年,对世界而言,是乱象丛生、挑战上升的一年。多边主义和单边主义之争更加尖锐,保护主义和民粹主义逆流涌动,强权政治和霸凌行径四处横行。在这样的背景下,大国博弈明显升温,全球治理步履维艰,世界经济持续低迷。从亚洲到中东,从欧洲到拉美,一系列的热点此起彼伏,一连串的国家动荡频发,传统与非传统安全威胁交织蔓延,国际治理面临严峻挑战。但同时也要看到,和平与发展仍然是当今时代的主题,全球化和多极化依然在曲折中负重前行,新一轮科技革命和产业变革正在破茧而出。人类社会的未来走向何方,将取决于各国在合作与对抗、多边与单边、开放与封闭等重大课题上能否作出正确抉择。

For the world, 2019 is a year of turbulence and mounting challenges. Multilateralism and unilateralism are locked in a bitter contest, protectionism and populism have been on the rise, and the world is seeing a rampage of power politics and bullying. Big power rivalry has intensified, global governance is confronted with more difficulties, and global growth remains sluggish. From Asia to the Middle East, from Europe to Latin America, flashpoints keep flaring up, countries are plunged into turmoil, and traditional and non-traditional security threats are becoming more intertwined. All these are posing severe challenges to global governance. That said, we must also see that peace and development remain the prevailing trend of our times. Globalization and multipolarization are moving forward despite twists and turns. And a new round of scientific and technological revolution and industrial transformation is gathering momentum. Whether countries make the right choice between cooperation and confrontation, multilateralism and unilateralism, openness and isolation will largely shape the future of human society.

2019年,面对错综复杂的国际形势,中国外交在以习近平同志为核心的党中央领导下,全面总结70年成功经验和优良传统,不忘为人民谋幸福的初心,勇担为人类进步作贡献的使命,继续开拓进取,奋发有为,在乱局中引领方向,在挑战中克难前行,取得了一系列新进展,形成了一大批新成果,既为国家发展建设提供了有力支撑,也为世界和平进步作出了重要贡献。

In 2019, facing the complex international situation, China has forged ahead with its foreign relations under the leadership of the CPC Central Committee with Comrade Xi

Jinping at the core. We comprehensively summed up the successful experience and fine traditions of the past 70 years, and reaffirmed our original aspirations to bring happiness to the Chinese people and contribute to progress for humanity. Charting the course forward and overcoming difficulties and challenges, we achieved new advances and new outcomes in China's foreign relations in wide-ranging areas. Such progress has not only bolstered China's development but also made important contributions to world peace and progress.

一年来,我们积极运筹同主要大国关系,为保持国际局势总体稳定不断注入正能量。

Over the past year, China has vigorously developed its relations with other major countries, injecting positive energy into overall global stability.

今年是中俄建交70周年。习近平主席对俄罗斯进行历史性访问,两国元首就进一步深化中俄全面战略协作伙伴关系达成重要共识,签署了关于加强全球战略稳定的联合声明,"一带一路"建设和欧亚经济联盟对接顺利进行,能源、航空、航天、互联互通等领域战略性大项目稳步推进。本月初,中俄元首通过视频连线见证中俄东线天然气管道投产通气。中俄关系正在两国元首引领下,携手迈向守望相助、深度融通、开拓创新、普惠共赢的新时代,为维护世界和平稳定发挥着更为关键和重要的作用。

This year marks the 70th anniversary of the diplomatic relations between China and Russia. During President Xi Jinping's historic visit to Russia, the two Presidents reached important agreement on further deepening the comprehensive strategic partnership of coordination, and signed a joint statement on strengthening global strategic stability. Smooth progress has been made in synergizing the Belt and Road Initiative and the Eurasian Economic Union and in implementing major strategic projects in areas of energy, aviation, space and connectivity. Early this month, the two Presidents witnessed via video link the launch of the east-route natural gas pipeline between the two countries. Under the watch of the two Presidents, the China-Russia relationship is entering a new era of mutual support, deep convergence, continuous innovation and mutual benefit, playing a more crucial role in maintaining world peace and stability.

今年是中美建交40周年。经过40年发展,中美两国经济利益高度融合,各领域交往日益密切,两国共同应对全球性挑战的需要不断上升。但同时,中美之间也存在需要正视和解决的深层次问题,正在对两国关系的未来带来越来越严峻的挑战。今年以来,我们本着对两国人民、对国际社会负责任的态度,继续寻求同美方进行建设性对话。同时坚决抵制美方的各种霸凌行径,努力维护中美三个联合公报确立的各项原则。两国最高领导人在大阪实现会晤,明确要推进以协调、合作、稳定为基调的中美关系。

This year also marks the 40th anniversary of diplomatic ties between China and the United States. Over the past 40 years, China and the US have become deeply inter-connected through shared economic interests, and thriving exchanges in all areas. Internationally, there is ever greater need for the two countries to jointly address global challenges. At the same time, there exist some deep-seated issues between the two sides that need to be tackled head-on. These issues have presented growing challenges to the future of China-US relations. Acting in the interest of the two peoples and as a responsible member of the international community, China has continued to pursue constructive dialogue with the US this year. We have also taken firm actions to counter US bullying and uphold the principles enshrined in the three China-US joint communiqués. At their meeting in Osaka, the two Presidents expressed a clear-cut commitment to advance China-US relations based on coordination, cooperation and stability.

今年的中欧交往十分密切,习近平主席的出访从欧洲亮丽开场、在欧洲圆满收官,李克强总理出席中欧领导人会晤、中国-中东欧国家领导人会晤,中国-中东欧合作实现首次扩员。中欧地理标志协定谈判按期完成,中欧民航合作协定顺利签署。德、法、意等欧洲主要大国领导人先后访华,中欧就加强全球治理、坚持多边主义、维护自由贸易等重大问题达成广泛共识,向世界发出中欧加强战略合作、应对全球挑战的明确信号。

This year has also witnessed close interactions between China and Europe. Europe was the destination of both President Xi Jinping's first and last overseas visit this year. Premier Li Keqiang attended the China-EU Summit and the China-CEEC Heads of Government Summit. The membership of China-CEEC cooperation was enlarged for the first time. China and the EU concluded negotiations on an agreement on geographical indications as scheduled and signed the agreements on civil aviation cooperation smoothly. Leaders of Germany, France and Italy visited China respectively. China and the EU also reached extensive consensus on major issues from strengthening global governance, upholding multilateralism to safeguarding free trade. This has sent a clear message of China and Europe enhancing strategic cooperation and jointly addressing global challenges.

一年来,我们全面加强同周边国家关系,为促进地区形势趋稳向好作出积极贡献。

Over the past year, China has comprehensively strengthened its ties with neighboring countries, bringing greater stability to the region.

习近平主席同莫迪总理在印度金奈成功举行第二次会晤,两位领导人进行了长时间、深层次战略沟通,决定深化各领域务实合作,促进文明间交流互鉴,为保持中印关系平稳向好发展定下了基调,为打开中印互利合作新局面开辟了前景。习近平总书记在中朝建交70周年之际对朝鲜进行历史性访问,有力巩固和传承了中朝传统友谊。中日双方就改善和发展两国关系达成十点共识,两国领导人确定努力构建契合新时代要求的中日关系,推动两国关系重回正轨并取得新发展。《中国-东盟自贸区升级议定书》全面生效,"南海行为准则"案文第一轮审读提前完成,准则磋商全面推进,中国东盟关系进入全方位发展新阶段。习近平主席访问中亚国家并出席上海合作组织和亚信"双峰会",中国与中亚国家关系以及上合组织发展迈上新台阶。

President Xi Jinping and Indian Prime Minister Narendra Modi successfully held their second summit in Chennai. The two leaders had long and in-depth discussions on issues of strategic significance. They agreed to enhance practical cooperation across the board and promote exchanges and mutual learning between the two civilizations. The summit set the tone for the steady and sound growth of China-India relations and opened new prospects for mutually beneficial cooperation between the two countries. General Secretary Xi Jinping paid a historic visit to the Democratic People's Republic of Korea (DPRK) on the occasion of the 70th anniversary of China-DPRK diplomatic relations. The visit has given a new boost to the traditional friendship between the two countries. China and Japan reached a ten-point consensus on improving and growing the bilateral relations. Leaders of the two countries agreed to work for a China-Japan relationship consistent with the needs of the new era, bringing the relationship back on track for new progress. The China-ASEAN FTA Upgrading Protocol has fully entered into force. The first reading of the Code of Conduct (COC) in the South China Sea has been completed ahead of schedule, and COC consultations are making solid progress. All this has ushered China-ASEAN relations into a new stage of all-round development. President Xi Jinping visited Central Asia and attended the SCO summit and CICA summit, taking China's relations with Central Asian countries and the development of the SCO to a new level.

我们还积极引领和推动亚太区域合作迈出重要步伐。不久前,区域全面经济伙伴关系协议(RCEP)15个成员国结束全部文本谈判,正式签署协议提上议程,世界上人口数量最多、成员结构最多元、发展潜力最大的区域自贸安排呼之欲出。本月底,中国将主办第八次中日韩领导人会晤,在中日韩合作进入20周年之际为东亚合作与发展注入新的活力。

China also played a pivotal role in bringing about important progress in regional cooperation in the Asia-Pacific. Not long ago, the 15 participating countries of the Regional Comprehensive Economic Partnership (RCEP) concluded all the text-based negotiations, and a timeline has been drawn up for its formal signing. A regional free trade area boasting the largest population, most diverse membership and greatest potential is in the making. Later this month, China will host the eighth China-Japan-ROK (CJK) leaders' meeting. As we mark the 20th anniversary of CJK cooperation, the meeting is set to inject new impetus into cooperation and development in East Asia.

一年来,我们继续高举互利共赢旗帜,为构建开放型世界经济提供新的动力。

Over the past year, China has consistently advocated win-win cooperation, energizing the building of an open world economy.

中方成功举办第二届"一带一路"国际合作高峰论坛,40位国家和国际组织领导人齐聚一堂,150个国家、92个国际组织近6000名代表共襄盛举,达成283项重要成果。今年又有16个国家和国际组织同我国签署共建"一带一路"合作文件,文件总数升至199份。中巴经济走廊、中老铁路、雅万高铁、中欧班列等重大项目给沿线各国带去大量发展机遇,共建"一带一路"踏上高质量发展新征程。第二届中国国际进口博览会盛况空前,共有181个国家、地区和国际组织、3800多家企业与会参展,超过50万名境内外采购商齐聚一堂,成交金额达710多亿美元,较去年增长23％。习近平主席在开幕式主旨演讲中揭示经济全球化是不可逆转的时代潮流,倡议共建开放合作、开放创新、开放共享的世界经济,宣布中国对外开放5方面重大举措,得到各国一致高度评价。

China successfully hosted the second Belt and Road Forum for International Cooperation, which was attended by 40 national leaders and heads of international organizations, and nearly 6,000 representatives from 150 countries and 92 international organizations. The forum produced 283 important outcomes. This year, China has signed documents on Belt and Road cooperation with 16 countries and international organizations, bringing the total number of such cooperation documents to 199. Flagship projects such as China-Pakistan Economic Corridor, China-Laos Railway, Jakarta-Bandung High-Speed Railway and China-Europe Railway Express have created substantial development opportunities for the participating countries, and brought the Belt and Road cooperation into a new phase of high-quality development. The second China International Import Expo attracted an impressive gathering of 181 countries, regions and international organizations, more than 3,800 exhibitors and over 500,000 buyers from home and abroad. Business deals worth more than US$71 billion were concluded, up by 23％ from last year. In his keynote speech at the opening ceremony of the Expo, President Xi Jinping pointed out that economic globalization is an irreversible trend of the times. He called for the building of an open world economy featuring cooperation, innovation and mutual benefit, and announced the major opening-up initiatives China would take in five areas. His speech drew a warm response across the audience.

我们还继续深化同广大发展中国家之间的"南南合作"。中非合作论坛北京峰会成果落实协调人会议在北京成功举行,对非"八大行动"框架下880多个合作项目和融资支持进展过半,峰会成果落实工作全面铺开,呈现出"早见效、高标准、惠民生"的可喜态势。中拉、中阿关系继续走稳走实,各领域合作布局不断深化完善。

China has deepened South-South cooperation with fellow developing countries. The Coordinators' Meeting on the Implementation of the Follow-up Actions of the FOCAC Beijing Summit was successfully held in Beijing. More than half of the 880 plus cooperation projects and the financing support have been delivered under the framework of the eight major initiatives on China-Africa cooperation. The follow-up actions of the FOCAC Summit, which have been in full swing, have been held to high standards and produced early and encouraging results to the benefit of our peoples. China's relations with Latin American and the Caribbean countries and Arab countries continue to make steady and solid progress, with deeper and better-structured cooperation in all fields.

一年来,我们坚守国际公平正义,成为维护多边主义和国际关系民主化的中流砥柱。

Over the past year, China has firmly defended fairness and justice in the international arena, serving as a pillar for multilateralism and greater democracy in international relations.

面对单边主义和霸权主义逆流,我们旗帜鲜明站在历史演进的正确一边,站在绝大多数国家的共同利益一边。从二十国集团领导人峰会到金砖国家领导人会晤,从亚洲文明对话大会到中法全球治理论坛,从博鳌亚洲论坛到东亚合作领导人系列会议,中国坚定维护以联合国为核心的国际体系,坚定维护以国际法为基础的国际秩序,坚定维护以世界贸易组织为基石的多边贸易体制。习近平主席倡导共商共建共享的全球治理观,呼吁各国携手构建人类命运共同体,得到越来越多国家的响应和支持。我们深入参与全球应对气候变化、反恐防恐、维护网络安全等领域国际合作,认真履行应尽的国际责任和义务,为共同应对全球性挑战作出了重要贡献。中国同法国、联合国在G20峰会期间专门举行应对气候变化会议,中法还签署了《生物多样性保护和气候变化北京倡议》。中国籍候选人高票当选联合国粮农组织总干事,首次担任联合国秘书长特使和联合国系统驻地协调员,在联合国事务中发挥越来越大作用。

In the face of unilateralist and hegemonic moves, China has firmly stood on the right side of history and on the side of the common interests of the overwhelming majority of countries. From the G20 Summit to the BRICS Summit, from the Conference on Dialogue of Asian Civilizations to the China-France Seminar on Global Governance, from the Boao Forum for Asia to the leaders' meetings on East Asian cooperation, China has taken a consistent and unwavering stand, namely, firmly upholding the UN-centered international system, safeguarding the international order underpinned by the international law, and promoting the multilateral trading regime centered on the WTO. President Xi Jinping's call for extensive consultation, joint contribution and shared benefits in global governance and for building a community with a shared future for mankind has been embraced and supported by more and more countries. China is deeply engaged in international cooperation in such areas as climate change, combating and preventing terrorism and cyber-security. China has honored its international responsibilities and duties, and made important contributions to global efforts against global challenges. During this year's G20 Summit, China held a meeting on climate change together with France and the UN. China and France also signed the Beijing Call for Biodiversity Conservation and Climate Change. In the election for the FAO Director-General, the Chinese candidate won by a wide margin. And for the first time, Chinese nationals have been appointed Special Envoy of the UN Secretary-General and UN Resident Coordinator. All this speaks to the increasing role played by China in UN affairs.

一年来,我们主动承担大国责任,为政治解决地区和热点问题发挥建设性作用。

Over the past year, China has stepped up to its responsibility as a major country, playing a constructive role in the political settlement of regional flashpoints.

在朝鲜半岛问题上,我们始终坚持维护半岛和平稳定、坚持通过对话协商解决问题,坚持并行推进构建半岛永久和平机制和实现半岛完全无核化,主张解决好各方尤其是朝方在安全和发展方面的正当关切。在中东问题上,我们坚持维护伊朗核问题全面协议的有效性和权威性,坚持对话协商化解分歧,为巴勒斯坦、叙利亚等热点问题的政治解决仗义执言。我们还首次举办中东安全论坛,提出促进中东安全的中国方案,受到地区国家普遍欢迎。在阿富汗问题上，我们开展穿梭斡旋，推动阿富汗各派别、中阿巴、中美俄对话，举行首次中美俄巴(基斯坦)四方会议，更深入参与阿富汗和平和解进程。我们积极推动印度和巴基斯坦这两个共同邻邦缓解冲突，恢复对话，管控分歧。我们在缅甸和孟加拉国之间劝和促谈，鼓励双方通过对话协商妥善解决当前存在的问题。

On the issue of the Korean Peninsula, China has always been committed to safeguarding peace and stability of the Peninsula and resolving the issue through dialogue and consultation. China has been working to promote synchronized progress in the establishment of a permanent peace mechanism and complete denuclearization of the Peninsula. In this process, China maintains that the concerns of all parties, the DPRK's legitimate concerns over its security and development in particular, should be properly addressed. On the question of the Middle East, China is committed to upholding the effectiveness and authority of the Joint Comprehensive Plan of Action (JCPOA), and resolving differences through dialogue and consultation. China has advocated the political settlement of the Palestinian and Syrian issues and other regional hotspots. China held the first Middle East Security Forum, and its proposals on Middle East security were welcomed by countries in the region. As part of its shuttle diplomacy on Afghanistan, China facilitated the intra-Afghan dialogue, the China-Afghanistan-Pakistan trilateral dialogues and the China-Russia-US consultation, and hosted the first China-Russia-US-Pakistan four-party meeting in intensified efforts to expedite peace and reconciliation in Afghanistan. China called on its two neighbors, India and Pakistan, to deescalate conflict, resume dialogue and manage differences. China promoted peace talks between Myanmar and Bangladesh, and urged them to properly resolve existing issues through dialogue and consultation.

一年来，我们坚定捍卫国家核心利益，为国内发展稳定和祖国统一大业作出应有贡献。

Over the past year, we have firmly defended our core national interests, contributing our due share to China's development, stability and national reunification.

我们坚决贯彻"一国两制"方针，支持香港特区政府尽快止暴制乱、恢复秩序，同插手干预香港事务、干涉中国内政的外部势力进行坚决斗争，坚决斩断企图在香港制造"颜色革命"的黑手。我们有力回击反华势力在新疆问题上的攻击抹黑，一年来邀请上千名各国外交官、媒体、学者赴新疆实地参访、了解真相。针对一些西方国家在联合国人权理事会、联合国大会第三委员会等场合挑起事端，我们澄清事实，以正压邪，中国的正义立场赢得国际社会的压倒性支持。我们继去年同多米尼加、布基纳法索、萨尔瓦多建交和复交后，今年又同所罗门群岛建交，同基里巴斯复交，使我国建交国总数上升至180个，"一个中国"的共识在国际上更加巩固。

We have firmly implemented the policy of "one country, two systems", and supported the Hong Kong SAR government in curbing violence and restoring order. We have fought resolutely against external forces interfering in Hong Kong and in China's internal affairs, and pushed back the dark hand instigating a "color revolution" in Hong Kong. We have given a robust response to the slanderous attacks by anti-China forces over Xingjiang. In

Chapter Ⅶ Memory

2019, up to 1,000 diplomats, journalists and scholars were invited to visit Xinjiang and see the situation there through their own eyes. Facing provocations by some Western countries at the UN Human Rights Council and the Third Committee of the General Assembly, China refuted and prevailed over groundless accusations with clear facts, and its just position has won overwhelming support from the international community. Last year, China established or resumed diplomatic relations with the Dominican Republic, Burkina Faso and El Salvador. This year, China established relations with the Solomon Islands, and resumed relations with Kiribati. As the number of countries having diplomatic ties with China increased to 180, the one-China consensus is more widely embraced than ever before in the international community.

(For full text, please check the websites provided.)

Chapter VIII Note-taking

Learning questions:
✓ What is note-taking and how to balance note-taking with memory?
✓ How to take notes?

As discussed in previous chapters, interpreters use their "working memory" in interpreting. Yet this memory is quite limited. If the speakers speak for 5 or 10 minutes without stopping, it is very hard for interpreters to remember all of them. If the speech involves numbers or names, it is even more difficult for interpreters to remember. In this case, note-taking becomes necessary. In this chapter, we will learn some basic knowledge of note-taking and the proper ways to take notes in CI. We will also train intensively on note-taking.

8.1 Introduction to Note-taking

8.1.1 What Is Note-taking?

Note-taking is the process of noting down the key information of what is being said on paper. However, it is not a simple process of listening and noting, but listening, processing and noting. It is not a process of recording information mechanically, but a complex cognitive process involving many factors. It requires interpreters to listen, understand and memorize information, organize and select information, and encode and write down the information in a very short time.

To complete the task of note-taking, interpreters need to first deal with the time issue. In general, the writing speed is 0.2 - 0.3 words per second, while the speaking speed is 2 - 3 words per second. That is to say, in the continuous information flow, interpreters should always maintain intensive attention. Interpreters also need to coordinate the relationship between understanding and information storage, and extract, organize and write down the information immediately understood.

We need to keep in mind that note-taking is different from shorthand writing or stenography (速记). The main purpose of stenography is to improve the writing speed. It has a complete system of symbols, which are used by stenographers to record the speakers' speech word-for-word. After the stenographers complete the writing task, it takes a long time for them to decode the symbols and sort out the meaning. Stenography is similar to the function of a recorder. Note-taking, on the other hand, is a process to note down only the key information, which can later remind interpreters of the entire message.

8.1.2 Three Balances in Note-taking

8.1.2.1 Memory vs. Note-taking

Generally speaking, note-taking is to aid memory. That means, interpreters need to take understanding as their priority. Only when they understand can they remember. Focusing too much on note-taking can distract the interpreters and affect understanding. According to Baxter, before learners have a full and automated grasp of the basic tasks require of them, note-taking can represent an additional effort... a hindrance rather than an aid. For this reason, note-taking explanations and demonstrations should come as late as possible in CI training. And even after note-taking has been officially introduced to CI training, it is advisable for learners to be timely reminded of the crucial skill of active listening whenever there are signs of an inadequate grasp of the source text structure and key points.

The use of memory and note-taking in interpreting activities is a closely related interactive process. Interpreters analyze, process, memorize and note down the source information as soon as they hear it. Without analyzing, processing and memorizing the information obtained, note-taking cannot be carried out; the memory of the interpreters may also be greatly tested if interpreters rely solely on their memory without note-taking.

In general, it is advised for interpreters to use 60% to 70% of their efforts on understanding and memory, and 30% to 40% of their efforts on note-taking. But the balance between memory and note-taking depends on the characteristics of the interpreting activities, the interpreting habits of interpreters, and the memory capacity of interpreters. In interpreting short discourse, passage with strong logical connections, less new information, and fewer numbers and proper nouns, the interpreters may be more inclined to use memory; in interpreting longer discourse with heavier information, passages with more trivial information or parallel structures, interpreters may take more notes. In addition, when the topics are familiar to the interpreters, they may use notes to reduce the burden of memory. When the topics are relatively unfamiliar, interpreters may need to concentrate on listening and understanding, and rely more on their memory because it is less distracting than note-taking. New interpreters are more likely to use notes, while experienced interpreters are more accustomed to using their memory. Therefore, when to and how much notes are taken vary from person to person, from time to time, and from job to job. Interpreters need to constantly adjust and balance of the use of their memory and note-taking.

8.1.2.2 Script/PowerPoint Slides vs. Note-taking

Usually for the benefit of the interpreters and the speakers, many speakers would provide their speech script to the interpreters so that they can prepare in advance. This is definitely a good thing for the interpreters, but it can also cause some new problems. The speakers are very often unpredictable. Sometimes they may add new information on the basis of the speech script; sometimes, due to time constraints, they may greatly shorten their speech; sometimes they may simply stray away from their script. When the speakers add new content, it's not easy to know when they will return to their speech script. If rely too much on note-taking, interpreters may easily lose track of where the speakers are at in their script. So how to balance script with notes?

It is suggested when printing out the speakers' script, a certain gap should be left between each line, so that interpreters can make notes where necessary, and when the speakers return to their original script, interpreters can easily find where they are at in the script. In addition, interpreters can highlight the first a few words of each paragraph just in case the speakers decide to jump to a certain paragraph directly. This is very useful when the speakers suddenly shorten their speech or change the order of the paragraphs.

Interpreters should always listen carefully even when they have the speech script at hand. If they somehow lose track of the script, instead of searching throughout the entire script to find where the speakers are at, they should focus on listening and take notes if necessary. If possible, hand the notes to their partners to help them find the place.

Some speakers like to use PowerPoint slides, and they may provide them to the interpreters in advance. Some even translate the slides into Chinese or English in advance for the convenience of the audience. In this case, the interpreters still need to print out the content of the slides on paper, instead of relying completely on the speakers' slides and reading or sight interpreting the content on the screen when the speakers are speaking. This is because the speakers may turn to the next page when the interpreters haven't finished reading or interpreting. If the interpreters depend entirely on the slides instead of their notes or their listening comprehension, they can be caught off guard.

8.1.2.3 Note-taking in the Source Language vs. Note-taking in the Target Language

The third balance is between note-taking in the source language and in the target language. There is no right or wrong in which language to take notes in. Some prefer the source language, some the target language, some mix the two, depending on the interpreters' note-taking habit and their noting system.

No matter the source language or the target language, we need to remember that we are noting down the key information rather than noting down every word possible, because there is simply no time for interpreters to note down every word and it can greatly affect their listening comprehension. Yet, for learners, noting down the key information is difficult to achieve, as most people tend to write down what they hear without processing. That is why note-taking training is necessary.

When taking notes in English, some people like to note down the first a few letters of each word. This practice should be avoided because they may not be able to recall what they have noted down. Abbreviations can be used, but only when they make sense to the interpreters or when they can help spell out the original words. Due to the fact that it is easier for us to recognize and remember in Chinese, in English to Chinese interpreting, sometimes note-taking in the target language is suggested. For one thing, it can train learners to grasp the meaning of the source language rather than focusing on each single word. For another, by note-taking in the target language, the conversion is basically completed in the process of note-taking, and it will be easier for interpreters to organize their thinking in expression.

Generally speaking, interpreters take notes in whichever language that is the fastest, that comes to their mind first, or that can best help them recall the message. Learners need to find the note-taking method that suits them the best, and gradually make the transition from noting down as many words as possible to noting down only the key information.

8.1.3 Common Misconceptions

For CI learners, there are many misconceptions about note-taking. We need to first have the correct understanding of note-taking before we can start the training.

1. Misconception 1

"The most important part of CI training is note-taking, and as long as we master note-taking, we can do interpreting."

In fact, as we have mentioned, note-taking is only a supplement to our memory. It is to aid our memory, not the end purpose. In CI training, listening comprehension, information processing and memory training are also crucial. They actually lay the foundation for note-taking.

2. Misconception 2

"In note-taking, we should note down as many words or sentences as possible."

As we have talked about, in note-taking, we need to first process the information while listening before we can take notes. That means we note down the key information rather than every word possible. This is the best way to help interpreters analyze the logical connection and express clearly and quickly.

3. Misconception 3

"In note-taking, we should use as many symbols and abbreviation as possible."

Symbols and abbreviations indeed can help us save a lot of time in note-taking, especially in noting down the logical connections, but interpreters should not rely too much on them. In interpreting, it is also not advisable for interpreters to create symbols or abbreviation on-spot, for they may not remember what they stand for. Learners should gradually accumulate symbols and abbreviation that they can clearly remember and use with ease, and combine them with the use of words.

8.1.4 Tools to Use in Note-taking

For interpreters, tools are like their weapons. The two main note-taking tools are their notebooks and their pens.

1. Notebooks

For notebooks, it is advised to use spiral notebooks instead of regular notebooks. More often, interpreters prefer to use the spiral notebooks that opens from bottom to top instead of from right to left. But it really depends on the interpreters' personal habit.

The size of the notebooks can be as small as the interpreters' hands or larger ones with hard covers. Usually it is not advisable for them to exceed the size of 15 cm×20 cm.

2. Pens

For pens, it is advised to use push-down pens rather than the ones with caps or switch-open pens. Interpreters should also keep multiple pens as back-up.

Exercises and Practice

8-1-1 Discussion with your partner on how to balance note-taking with memory.

8-1-2 Discuss with your partner what to do if the speakers stray off their script or their PowerPoint slides. How to prepare for such occasions?

8-1-3 Explain to your partner why the following statements are incorrect.

1. Note-taking equals stenography.
2. As long as you learn note-taking, you can do interpreting.
3. In note-taking, you need to note down as many words as possible.
4. In note-taking, you need to use as many symbols as possible.

8.2 Note-taking Method

8.2.1 What to Note Down?

Notes are structured and condensed idea-by-idea recall cues for the meaning, reflecting the interpreter's analysis of the speech and support the interpreter's memory. With adequate training, interpreters can capture the most effective cues at the best timing. So what exactly are these cues? What do we note down?

As we have mentioned, note-taking is based on understanding, analyzing and processing the source language. Interpreters note down some condensed and easy-to-remember words, acronyms, or symbols after quickly analyzing the information, dividing the meaning units （意群）, and locating the key information. That is to say, in CI, note-taking is done on the basis of meaning units. In each meaning unit, interpreters, in their own ways, may note down some key information points to help them recall this meaning unit. These points are the "cues" we have mentioned. Besides these key information points, we also need to note down the logical connections between the meaning units. Other than these, there are still a large number of necessary details that are hard to memorize, such as a list of things, figures, names, proper names and so on. They may not have strong logical connections between them, yet they take up a large amount of space in our memory. These details also need to be noted down. So to summarize, we need to note down:

(1) **Memory cues**: processed or condensed key information points (words, acronyms, symbols, etc. in notes) that can help recall the meaning units.

(2) **Logic lines**: the logical connections between meaning units (symbols, lines, arrows, words or abridged words, etc. in notes).

(3) **List of items**: necessary details that need to be noted down (words, abridged words, acronyms, symbols, etc. in notes). In notes, they are often listed vertically.

(4) **Figures**: numbers, trends or number-related information (numbers, symbols, arrows, etc. in notes).

(5) **Names and proper names**: names of people, locations, organizations, meetings, products, etc. (words, acronyms, etc. in notes).

(6) **Terminologies**: terms from different fields (words, acronyms, etc. in notes).

8.2.2 Note-taking Principles

To take notes more effectively, there are some general principles to follow:

(1) **Division of attention**: more listening comprehension, less note-taking. As we have mentioned, the attention should be put more on listening, understanding and memorizing than on note-taking.

(2) **Principle of least effort—simplification**: use simplified Chinese characters (reduce the strokes of Chinese characters), abridged English words, acronyms, Chinese radicals (部首) or other simplified words, phrases or sentences to express complicated meaning. Use the language that takes less time to write. For example, "中" is easier to write than "Chinese", while "but" is easier to write than "但是". However, in E - C interpreting, avoid noting down the first a few letters of each word throughout your notes. It is easily forgotten and it can be very hard for interpreters to recall the entire message.

(3) **Principle of least effort—generalization**: note-taking does not mean to note down every word you hear. we only note down highly generalized or condensed key points or information. Every word, phrase or sentence should help you recall the message of the meaning unit or the entire sentence or paragraph.

(4) **Borrowing previous information**: in CI, very often, some information can be repetitive. We can save much time by using arrows or lines to indicate repetitive information rather than writing them down one more time.

(5) **Using symbols properly**: symbols are visual information that are usually easy to remember and recognize. If used properly, they can help interpreters save much time and energy. Each interpreter may have their own symbol system, but it doesn't mean the more

symbol, the better the note-taking. Too many symbols may be hard to read and interpret. Interpreters also should not invent symbols on-spot in CI. They should use familiar symbols that they can easily recognize. Symbols will be talked in more details in later section.

8.2.3 Note-taking Layout

Note-taking in CI is different from note-taking in classrooms. The way we take notes differs not only in what we note down, but also how we do it, that is, the layout of our notes on paper. Generally speaking, there are three main principles:

1. Vertical layout

Unlike taking note in classrooms where we write horizontally until the end of each line, Note-taking in CI usually has a vertical layout. That means, after each meaning unit, we switch to the next line. So each line may have only a few words. This vertical layout can show the logical connections more clearly, and it is easier to read. A list of items (words, phrases or meaning units) should also be listed out vertically (using a bracket or line to indicate relation) to facilitate reading.

Because of this unique way of writing, we can arrange our notes in the following ways:

⊙**On small spiral notebooks**

(1) No dividing line(Fig. 8 – 1).

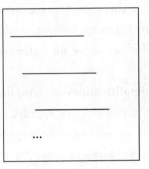

Fig. 8 – 1 Sample 1

(2) Dividing line on the left, used for noting down logical connectors(Fig. 8 – 2).

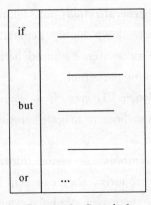

Fig. 8 – 2 Sample 2

Chapter Ⅷ   Note-taking

(3)Dividing line on the right, used for noting down additional or left-out information, or for emphasizing the importance of some information or giving further explanation(Fig. 8-3).

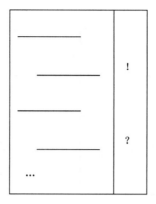

Fig. 8-3   Sample 3

⊙**On larger spiral notebooks**
(1)Dividing line in the middle(Fig. 8-4).

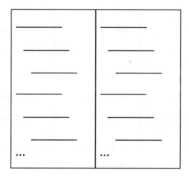

Fig. 8-4   Sample 4

(2)Dividing line in the middle; and dividing line on the left of each section, used for noting down logical connectors(Fig. 8-5).

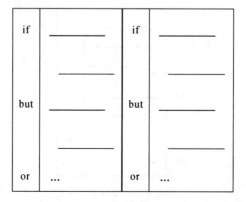

Fig. 8-5   Sample 5

(3) Dividing line in the middle; and dividing line on the right of each section, used for noting down additional or left-out information, or for emphasizing the importance of some information or giving further explanation (Fig. 8 – 6).

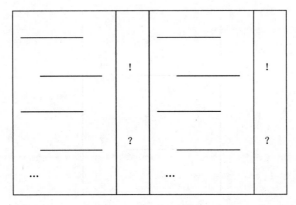

Fig. 8 – 6　Sample 6

(4) Two dividing lines (Fig. 8 – 7).

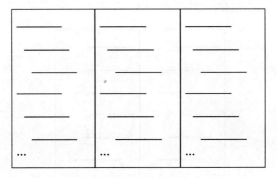

Fig. 8 – 7　Sample 7

(5) Two dividing lines, one on the left and one on the right, used for logical connectors (on the left), and for additional or left-out information, or for emphasizing the importance of some information or giving further explanation (on the right) (Fig. 8 – 8).

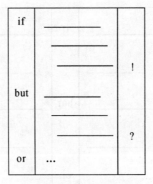

Fig. 8 – 8　Sample 8

2. Indentation

In CI note-taking, it is recommended to start writing from the left, and indent the following lines if they are commentary or a sub-point of the previous one (as shown in previous notebook layout samples). Very often after a few indented sentences, it is back to the very left when new information begins.

3. Clear division

In CI Note-taking, when the speaker pauses for the interpreter, or when there is a clear stop in meaning, we usually would mark it with a line to indicate the completion of a part. Some interpreters would even mark the stop of each complete sentence.

To better understand the above principles, let's look at an example:

中外合资是一种互补互惠的合作关系,外国在华投资可以最大限度地发挥各自优势。我国幅员辽阔、资源丰富、劳动力低廉、消费市场潜力大。此外,我们还有稳定的政治社会环境和优惠的投资政策。

In this example, there are three sentences (marked by periods), each with several meaning units. We can divide the meaning units this way:

中外合资是一种互补互惠的合作关系,/ 外国在华投资可以最大限度地发挥各自优势。// 我国幅员辽阔、/ 资源丰富、/ 劳动力低廉、/ 消费市场潜力大。// 此外,我们还有稳定的政治社会环境 / 和优惠的投资政策。

If we write each meaning unit in one line and number them, it looks like this:

1. 中外合资是一种互补互惠的合作关系,
2. 外国在华投资可以最大限度地发挥各自优势。
3. 我国幅员辽阔、
4. 资源丰富、
5. 劳动力低廉、
6. 消费市场潜力大。
7. 此外,我们还有稳定的政治社会环境
8. 和优惠的投资政策。

The first two meaning units have a causal-effect relationship, so we can indent the second one. Line 3 to line 6 are parallel in structure. And line 7 and 8 are also in parallel structure. As we have mentioned, when listing parallel items, we note them down vertically, using a line or a bracket to indicate relationship. Between each sentence, we use a "/" to indicate completion of meaning. After the above analysis, we can write the passage this way:

中外合资是一种互补互惠的合作关系,
　　外国在华投资可以最大限度地发挥各自优势。/

| 我国 | 幅员辽阔、
| | 资源丰富、
| | 劳动力低廉、
| | 消费市场潜力大。/

| 此外,我们还有 | 稳定的政治社会环境
| | 和优惠的投资政策。/

Note that the above is only the logical analysis of this passage, it is not the actual note in CI. By using simplified words and symbols, a note in CI may look like this:

It is not recommended to write like this (horizontal layout, using all Chinese characters):

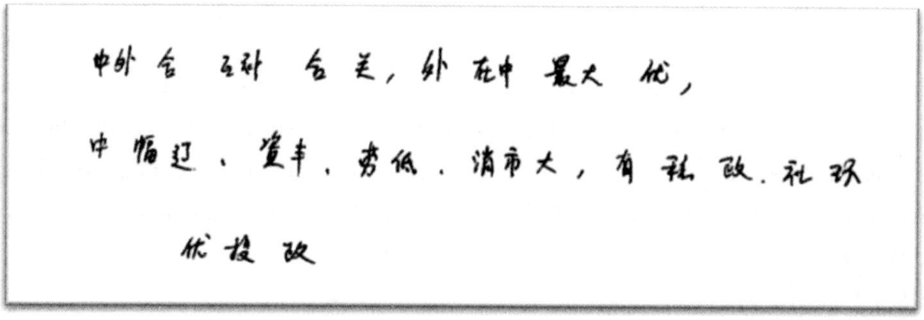

Chapter Ⅷ Note-taking

[handwritten notes image]

Or like this (horizontal layout, with no indication of logical connections or division):

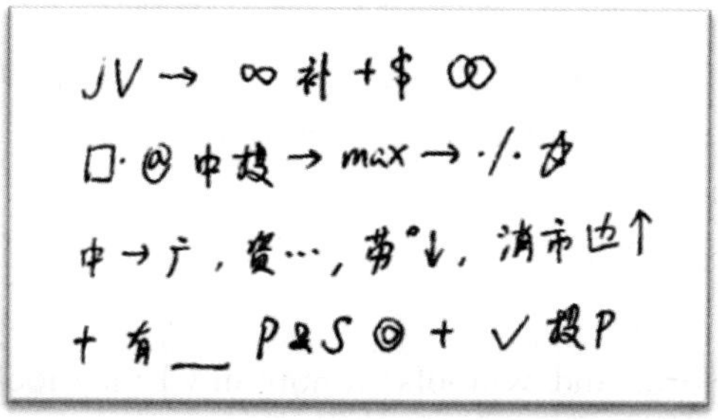

[handwritten notes image]

Here is another example:
Today I say to you that the challenges we face are real. They are serious and they are many. They will not be met easily or in a short span of time. But know this, America—they will be met.

In this example, there are four sentences (marked by periods), each with several meaning units. We can divide the meaning units this way:
Today I say to you / that the challenges we face are real. // They are serious / and they are many. // They will not be met easily / or in a short span of time. // But know this, America /— they will be met. //

If we write each meaning unit in one line and number them, it looks like this:
1. *Today I say to you*
2. *that the challenges we face are real.*
3. *They are serious*
4. *and they are many.*
5. *They will not be met easily*
6. *or in a short span of time.*
7. *But know this, America*

8. — *they will be met*.

Line 2 is to provide details for line 1. Line 3 and line 4 are parallel in structure, and they are commentary on the first two. Line 5 and 6 are also parallel, and they are also commenting on the first two meaning units. Line 7 indicates a change of direction in meaning. Line 8 is to give details of line 7. After the above analysis, we can write the passage this way:

Today I say to you
    that the challenges we face are real.
       | *They are serious*
       | *and they are many.* /

They will not be met | *easily*
                          | *or in a short span of time.* /
But know this, America
    —*they will be met.* /

By using simplified words and symbols, a note in CI may look like this:

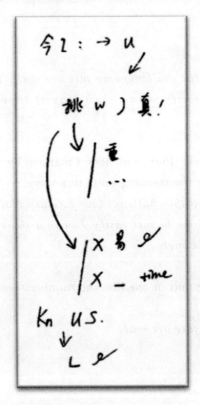

It is not recommended to write like this (horizontal layout, with no indication of logical connections or division):

> 今1: → U, 挑 w) 真!, 重, ⋯
> They × of 务, × - ∧ time. 知 → they L ♡

Or like this (noting down only the first a few letters of each word, using all English):

> Today 1 say → u
> cha w face real
> They → / ser
>   many
> × met easi
> × shor sp time
> kno Ame
> They wil met

8.2.4 Symbols and Abbreviations in Note-taking

Symbols and abbreviations are used in CI to reduce the memory load of interpreters. Each interpreter may have their own note-taking system. They may have their own symbol system which other people may not be able to understand. It's always recommended for learners to acquire or create their own symbol and abbreviation systems that they familiarize themselves with.

Here in this section, we will introduce some frequently used CI note-taking symbols and abbreviations. They are for reference only.

8.2.4.1 Symbols

Symbols are shapes or designs that represent something. They can be used alone or in combination with other symbols, or words or characters. They can be shapes, special designs, symbols from mathematics, biology, human behavior, chemistry, etc. They can be punctuation marks or Chinese radicals. They can be used to represent nouns, verbs, adjectives, adverbs and logical connections. They are shown in Table 8-1 to Table 8-5.

Table 8-1 Symbols of Different Shapes or Special Designs

Symbol	Meaning	Explanation or Examples
□	Country, state, nation, national, 国, 国家	The symbol resembles the radical of the Chinese character "国".
△	1. City, urban, 城市; 2. Represent, 代表 (v.)	As a city is part of a country, a triangle is part of a square.
▽	Village, suburb, rural areas, 农村, 乡村, 郊区	The upside-down triangle is to indicate the opposite of city.
○	People, human, person, -man, -er, -st, 人	It looks like the head of a person. It can be used in combination with other Chinese characters. Eg: 中○: 中国人, e○: economist
△○	1. Citizen; 2. Representative, 代表 (n.)	
▽○	farmer 农民	
○	Area, location, 地区	Opposite to "○", it is a circle on the bottom. It looks like circling out a small piece of land. It can also be used to indication location. Eg: 飞○: 机场, 广○: 广场
∧	Supervise, lead, head, top, above, summit, superior, most, utmost, supreme, 领导, 顶, 最, 最高	It is also used with a word to indicate superlative degree.
∨	Below, beneath, inferior, 下, 最低	
∧○	Leader, supervisor, 领导人, 上级	
□∧○	National leader, 国家领导人	
∨○	Subordinator, 下属	
⌀	World, global, international, universal, 世界, 国际, 全球	It looks like a globe.
…□ or □s	Many countries	
□&□	Country and country, 国与国	
□/□	Between the two countries, 两国之间	
⊡	Domestic, 国内	
□·	Foreign, overseas, abroad, 国外	
⊡·	At home and abroad, 国内外	
⇐	Import, 进口	

Continued Table

Symbol	Meaning	Explanation or Examples
⊟▶	Export，出口	
△̂	Capital city，首都	
hîgh	Highest，最高	
☆	Important, great, excellent, outstanding, remarkable, promising，杰出，重要	
☆̂	Most important，最重要的	
○	Overall, complete, all, entire, integrated, intact, integrity, united，整体，所有，完整，团结	
○°	Everyone，所有人	
○□	All countries，所有国家	
领○	Territorial integrity，领土完整	
主领|○	Sovereignty and territorial integrity，主权与领土完整	
Ⓟ	Product，产品，成品	It indicates it is something that has been completed.
⊙	Meeting, conference，会议	It looks like a round table.
⌒	Summit，峰会	
⊕	Hospital, medical care，医院，医疗	
◎	Environment, surroundings，环境	It looks like a ring（环）.
♯	1. End, stop，停止 2. only，仅	1. When we are asked to enter our ID number on our phone, we are often asked to end with a "♯". 2. "♯"sounds like "仅".
×♯	Not only，不仅	
*	Feature，特点	
♀	Female，女性	This is a sign from biology.
♂	Male，男性	
@	At，在，位于	
%	Percentage，百分位	
&.	And，和	
U	Make a toast, agree on, agreement, treaty, contract，举杯，协议，达成协议	It looks like a wineglass.

Continued Table

Symbol	Meaning	Explanation or Examples
∩	Enter，进入	It looks like a door.
∽	1. Relate to, associate with，关联； 2. Replace，替换	
∞	1. Exchange, communicate，交换，交流； 2. Interaction, relation, relationship，关系； 3. Forever，永远，永恒	
⊥	1. dispute，分歧； 2. Pressure，压力	
→|	So far，到目前为止，迄今	
◠	Develop, developing，发展，发展中	It looks like a rising sun.
⊙	Developed，发达	The sun is above the horizon.
⊖	Undeveloped，不发达	The sun is under the horizon.
◠□	Developing country，发展中国家	
⊙□	Developed country，发达国家	
)	Face，面对	It looks like a person's face.
:	1. See, concern, pay attention to，看到，关注 2. Say，说	1. It looks like two eyes. 2. ":"（colon）is used before quotation marks in Chinese.
⌐	step up 上一个台阶	
⌙	In the past, past，过去	
∟	In the future, future，未来	
⊠	Never before, unprecedented 前所未有	
⋯	For a long time 很久以来	
⌶	Foresee，预言，预见	
⌴	Potential，潜力	
⌻	Traditional culture，传统文化	
.d	Yesterday，昨天	The dot is used to indicate time.
d.	Tomorrow，明天	
..d	The day before yesterday，前天	
d..	The day after tomorrow，后天	
.y	Last year，去年	
y.	Next year，明年	

Continued Table

Symbol	Meaning	Explanation or Examples
.w	Last week，上周	
w.	Next week，下周	
∞	Abandon, solve, overcome，摒弃，解决，去除，战胜	
☺ :)	Good, happy, pleasant，好，高兴	
☹ :(	Not good, unhappy, unpleasant，不好，不高兴	
Q	1. Say, talk, discuss，说； 2. inflation，通货膨胀	1. QQ is a popular app where people talk to each other; 2. It looks like a balloon.
…Q	Everyone has their opinions. 众说纷纭	
K	OK, understand, agree，理解，同意	
×	No, not good, cannot, wrong, veto，不，不好，不行，错的，否决	Eg. ×足：不足
√	Good, OK, feasible, correct, good for, approve，好的，可行的，可以，正确的，有益的，认可	
♡	Love, care, care about, concern，爱，关心	
→	1. Lead to, result in, cause, in order to，导致，为了 2. Leave for，去，赴	
←	Due to, since, because, from，由于，来自	
↑	Increase, rise，增加，上升	
↑↑	Increase dramatically, soar，急剧增加，大幅度上升，猛增	
↓	Decrease, fall，减少，降低	
↓↓	Decrease dramatically, plunge，急剧下降，大幅度减少，暴跌	
↗	Increase gradually, on the rise，逐步上升，缓慢增长	
↘	Decrease gradually, slow down，逐步降低，慢慢减少，减慢	
↔	Two way，双向	

Continued Table

Symbol	Meaning	Explanation or Examples
⇒	Push forward, promote, 推动, 推进	
⇐	Hinder, delay, 阻碍, 推迟	
—	1. long, 长 2. steady, 平稳, 稳定, 稳固 3. base, basis, 基础 4. right now, 现在, 当下	4. Eg. p̄ : current policy
ˉ	Short, temporary, 短, 短暂	
≡	1. Ensure, safeguard, guarantee, insist on, 保障, 坚持 2. determination, perseverance, 恒心, 决心	
H or ⌐	Host, chair (v.), 主持	It looks like a chair.
h°	Host, chair, chairman (n.), 主持人, 主席	
△	Target, goal, purpose, 目标, 意图	
◎	Contact, cooperation, 接触, 合作	
•/	On the one hand, 一方面	
/•	On the other hand, 另一方面	
•/•	Both sides, 双方, 两方面	
<	Open up, open, 开放	
~	Far, far away, 遥远	It reminds us of 1~1000.
⤸	Not far, close, 不遥远	
∼∼	Path, way, method, 道路, 方法	
♂	Fruit, achievement, 成果, 成绩	It looks like an apple.

Table 8-2 Mathematical Symbols

Symbol	Meaning	Explanation or Examples
+	And, additionally, furthermore, besides, more, add, 此外, 额外, 增加, 更多	It is also used with a word to indicate comparative degree. Eg.: 高+: 更高; 灵+: 更加灵活
−	Minus, decrease, 减少, 减去	
×	Cross, 交叉	
÷	Except, 除了	
>	More than, 大于, 多于	

Continued Table

Symbol	Meaning	Explanation or Examples
<	Less than, 小于, 少于	
⊖	Majority, most part, most of, 大部分, 大多数	
=	Equal, equal to, means, 平等, 等于, 意味着	
≠	Unequal, does not equal to, does not mean, 不平等, 不等于, 不意味着, 不代表	
++	Better, stronger, 更好, 更强	
--	Worse, weaker, 更差, 更弱	
>>	Far more, 远大于	
<<	Far less, 远小于	
><	Conflict, 冲突	
≈	About, approximately, 大约	
≡	Always means, 永远意味着	
Σ	Sum, total, 总和	
∈	Belongs to, is a part of, 属于	
π	Policy, politics, 政策	"π" and "po" are close in pronunciation.
∠	Angle, perspective, 角度	
∵	Because, 因为	
∴	So, therefore, as a result, 所以	
2	To, two, mutual, bilateral, 二, 双, 互	Eg. 2边:双边

Table 8-3 Punctuation Marks

Symbol	Meaning	Explanation or Examples
?	Doubt, question, problem, 质疑, 问题	
!	Show emphasize, extremely important, 表强调, 非常重要	
…	1. Many, 许多 2. Etc, 等等	
:	Express, say, show, claim, comment, think, 表示, 说, 指出, 声明, 评论, 认为	
"	Show quotes, 表示引言	
《	Name of book, 书名	Eg.《红:《红楼梦》

Continued Table

Symbol	Meaning	Explanation or Examples
{ ([|	Include, consist of, comprise, incorporate, 包括	
/	Pause, stop, 暂停, 停	It is often used at the end of a sentence or paragraph to indicate completion.

Table 8-4 Chinese Radicals

Symbol	Meaning
扌	Measure, 措施
饣	Food, 食物, 饮食
疒	Disease, 疾病
疒°	Patient, 病人
氵	River, lake, pond, water, 河流, 湖, 水
冫	Ice, cold, 冰, 冰冷
纟	Organize, organization, 组织
宀	Home, 家
忄	Fast, quick, rapid, 快
钅	Metal, 金属
冖	Military, 军, 军队
廴	Construct, build, 建, 建设
阝	Listen, 听
𥫗	Manage, management, 管, 管理
𭕄	Study, learn, school, college, university, 学习, 学校
饣	Health, healthy, 健康

Table 8-5 Common Currencies

Symbol	Meaning
$	Dollar, 美元
¥	RMB, yuan, 人民币
£	Pound, 英镑
€	Euro, 欧元

8.2.4.2 Abbreviations

An abbreviation is a short form of word or phrase, made by leaving out some of the letters or by using only the first letter of each word. In CI, we can abbreviate by using only the first letter of a word, using the first two to five letters of a word (most often the first three letters), or using only the consonants of a word. For phrases, we can use the first letter of each word in a phrase. They are also called acronyms. They are most often used for names of organizations, countries, cities or some fixed expressions. Here we will only list a few from each category (Table 8-6 to Table 8-9). For more abbreviations, please refer to the appendix of this book.

Table 8-6   First Letter or One Letter Abbreviation

I	I, me
u	you
w	we
V	victory
G	government
P	policy
S	society
w.	with
w/o	without

Table 8-7   First a Few Letters

esp	especially
eco	economy, ecology
tec	technology
Hi-t	high-technology
edu	education
info	information
infra	infrastructure
co-op	cooperation
doc	doctor, document
demo	demonstration
Adm	administration
gov	government
prof	professor
corp	corporation
univ	university

Table 8-8 Leaving only the Consonants

Ssm	Socialism	
bz	business	Here "z" is used instead of "ss" to indicate pronunciation.
nz	news	Same as above.
trv	travel	
tx	tax	
rm	room	
dpmt, dept	department	
xp	experience	
pls, plz	please	
acpt	accept	
acdg	according	
ads	address	
bldg	building	

Table 8-9 Acronyms

ASAP	as soon as possible
R&D	research and development
CPC	The Communist Party of China
DPRK	Democratic People's Republic of Korea
JV	Joint Venture
HR	Human Resources
SAR	Special Administrative Region
UN	United Nation
UNESCO	United Nations Educational, Scientific, and Cultural Organization
WTO	World Trade Organization
WHO	World Health Organization
APEC	The Asia-Pacific Economic Cooperation
EU	European Union
HK	Hong Kong
TW	Taiwan
BJ	Beijing

Exercises and Practice

8-2-1 What do we note down in CI? Tick out the correct ones.
- ☐ every word
- ☐ key points
- ☐ names
- ☐ repetitive information
- ☐ figures
- ☐ logical connectors
- ☐ list of items
- ☐ terminologies
- ☐ complete sentence
- ☐ meaning units
- ☐ unnecessary details

8-2-2 Discuss with your partner the main principles of note-taking.

8-2-3 Discuss with your partner the main principles for note-taking layout.

8-2-4 Analyze the following short passages, write each meaning units in one line, and analyze the logical connections between them.

1. 中国已成为澳大利亚最大的留学生来源国、第二大海外游客来源国,也是增长最快的旅客市场。一些有战略眼光的澳大利亚企业已经敏锐捕捉到了商机。澳新银行在去年11月正式登陆上海自贸区。

2. Everywhere we look, there is work to be done. The state of the economy calls for action, bold and swift, and we will act—not only to create new jobs, but to lay a new foundation for growth. We will build the roads and bridges, the electric grids and digital lines that feed our commerce and bind us together.

3. The time has come to reaffirm our enduring spirit; to choose our better history; to carry forward that precious gift, that noble idea, passed on from generation to generation: the God-given promise that all are equal, all are free and all deserve a chance to pursue their full measure of happiness.

4. 今年是新中国成立70周年,是全面建成小康社会、实现第一个百年奋斗目标的关键之年。做好政府工作,要在以习近平同志为核心的党中央坚强领导下,以习近平新时代中国特色社会主义思想为指导,全面贯彻党的十九大和十九届二中、三中全会精神。

8.3 Note-taking Training

8.3.1 Sight Note-taking (视记) Training—Accumulating and Creating Your Own Abbreviations and Symbols

Sight note-taking means to transcribe a piece of reading material into notes. That is to say, rather than listening and taking notes, we read and take notes.

CI note-taking training starts from sight note-taking. Since our focus is on how to better take notes, we first take out the element of listening comprehension. By using reading materials, we can have more time processing the information and use the principles, methods and the symbols we have learned. It also gives learners a good opportunity to create their own symbols and formulate their own note-taking systems. It is recommended for learners to reach a certain amount of accumulation and familiarity with the symbols before moving onto note-taking through listening.

Exercise 1: Read the following speech and transcribe it into CI notes.

全国同胞们，

尊敬的各位国家元首、政府首脑和联合国等国际组织代表，

尊敬的各位来宾，

全体受阅将士们，

女士们、先生们，同志们、朋友们：

今天，是一个值得世界人民永远纪念的日子。70年前的今天，中国人民经过长达14年艰苦卓绝的斗争，取得了中国人民抗日战争的伟大胜利，宣告了世界反法西斯战争的完全胜利，和平的阳光再次普照大地。

在这里，我代表中共中央、全国人大、国务院、全国政协、中央军委，向全国参加过抗日战争的老战士、老同志、爱国人士和抗日将领，向为中国人民抗日战争胜利作出重大贡献的海内外中华儿女，致以崇高的敬意！向支援和帮助过中国人民抵抗侵略的外国政府和国际友人，表示衷心的感谢！向参加今天大会的各国来宾和军人朋友们，表示热烈的欢迎！

女士们、先生们，同志们、朋友们！

中国人民抗日战争和世界反法西斯战争，是正义和邪恶、光明和黑暗、进步和反动的大决战。在那场惨烈的战争中，中国人民抗日战争开始时间最早、持续时间最长。面对侵略者，中华儿女不屈不挠、浴血奋战，彻底打败了日本军国主义侵略者，捍卫了中华民族5000多年发展的文明成果，捍卫了人类和平事业，铸就了战争史上的奇观、中华民族的壮举。

中国人民抗日战争胜利，是近代以来中国抗击外敌入侵的第一次完全胜利。这一伟大胜利，彻底粉碎了日本军国主义殖民奴役中国的图谋，洗刷了近代以来中国抗击外来侵略屡战屡败的民族耻辱。这一伟大胜利，重新确立了中国在世界上的大国地位，使中国人民赢得了世界爱好和平人民的尊敬。这一伟大胜利，开辟了中华民族伟大复兴的光明前景，开启了古老中国凤凰涅槃、浴火重生的新征程。

在那场战争中，中国人民以巨大民族牺牲支撑起了世界反法西斯战争的东方主战场，为世界反法西斯战争胜利作出了重大贡献。中国人民抗日战争也得到了国际社会广泛支持，中国人民将永远铭记各国人民为中国抗战胜利作出的贡献！

女士们、先生们，同志们、朋友们！

经历了战争的人们，更加懂得和平的宝贵。我们纪念中国人民抗日战争暨世界反法西斯战争胜利70周年，就是要铭记历史、缅怀先烈、珍爱和平、开创未来。

那场战争的战火遍及亚洲、欧洲、非洲、大洋洲，军队和民众伤亡超过1亿人，其中中国伤亡人数超过3500万，苏联死亡人数超过2700万。绝不让历史悲剧重演，是我们对当年为维护人类自由、正义、和平而牺牲的英灵、对惨遭屠杀的无辜亡灵的最好纪念。

战争是一面镜子，能够让人更好认识和平的珍贵。今天，和平与发展已经成为时代主题，但世界仍很不太平，战争的达摩克利斯之剑依然悬在人类头上。我们要以史为鉴，坚定维护和平的决心。

为了和平，我们要牢固树立人类命运共同体意识。偏见和歧视、仇恨和战争，只会带来灾难和痛苦。相互尊重、平等相处、和平发展、共同繁荣，才是人间正道。世界各国应该共同维护以联合国宪章宗旨和原则为核心的国际秩序和国际体系，积极构建以合作共赢为核心的新型国际关系，共同推进世界和平与发展的崇高事业。

为了和平，中国将始终坚持走和平发展道路。中华民族历来爱好和平。无论发展到哪一步，中国都永远不称霸、永远不搞扩张，永远不会把自身曾经经历过的悲惨遭遇强加给其他民族。中国人民将坚持同世界各国人民友好相处，坚决捍卫中国人民抗日战争和世界反法西斯战争胜利成果，努力为人类作出新的更大的贡献。

中国人民解放军是人民的子弟兵，全军将士要牢记全心全意为人民服务的根本宗旨，忠实履行保卫祖国安全和人民和平生活的神圣职责，忠实执行维护世界和平的神圣使命。我宣布，中国将裁减军队员额30万。

女士们、先生们，同志们、朋友们！

"靡不有初，鲜克有终。"实现中华民族伟大复兴，需要一代又一代人为之努力。中华民族创造了具有5000多年历史的灿烂文明，也一定能够创造出更加灿烂的明天。

前进道路上，全国各族人民要在中国共产党领导下，坚持以马克思列宁主义、毛泽东思想、邓小平理论、"三个代表"重要思想、科学发展观为指导，沿着中国特色社会主义道路，按照"四个全面"战略布局，弘扬伟大的爱国主义精神，弘扬伟大的抗战精神，万众一心，风雨无阻，向着我们既定的目标继续奋勇前进！

让我们共同铭记历史所启示的伟大真理：正义必胜！和平必胜！人民必胜！

——习近平 2015 年 9 月 3 日阅兵式讲话

（来源：中国青年网 news.youth.cn/gn/20150903_7076967.htm）

Exercise 2：Read the following speech and transcribe it into CI notes.（来源：中国青年网 news:youth.cn/gn/20150903_7076967.htm）

Hi everybody. On Thursday, I traveled to Pittsburgh for the White House Frontiers Conference, where some of America's leading minds came together to talk about how we can empower our people through science to lead our communities, our country, and our world into tomorrow.

Plus, we had some fun. I had a chance to fly a space flight simulator where I docked a capsule on the International Space Station. I met a young man who'd been paralyzed for more than a decade—but thanks to breakthrough brain implants, today, he can not only move a prosthetic arm, but actually feel with the fingers.

It's awe-inspiring stuff. And it shows how investing in science and technology spurs our country towards new jobs and new industries; new discoveries that improve and save lives. That's always been our country's story, from a Founding Father with an idea to fly a kite in a thunderstorm, to the women who solved the equations to take us into space, to the engineers who brought us the internet. Innovation is in our DNA. And today, we need it more than ever to solve the challenges we face. Only through science can we cure diseases, and save the only planet we've got, and ensure that America keeps its competitive advantages as the world's most innovative economy.

That's why it's so backward when some folks choose to stick their heads in the sand about basic scientific facts. It's not just that they're saying that climate change a hoax or trotting out a snowball on the Senate floor. It's that they're also doing everything they can to gut funding for research and development, the kinds of investments that brought us breakthroughs like GPS, and MRIs, and put Siri on our smartphones.

That's not who we are. Remember, sixty years ago, when the Russians beat us into space, we didn't deny Sputnik was up there. We didn't haggle over the facts or shrink our R&D budget. No, we built a space program almost overnight and beat them to the moon. And then we kept going, becoming the first country to take an up-close look at every planet in the solar system, too. That's who we are.

And that's why, in my first inaugural address, I vowed to return science to its rightful place. It's why in our first few months, we made the largest single investment in basic research in our history. And it's why, over the last eight years, we've modernized the government's approach to innovation for the 21st Century. We've jumpstarted a clean energy revolution and unleashed the potential of precision medicine. We've partnered with the private sector and academia, and launched moonshots for cancer, brain research, and solar energy. We've harnessed big data to foster social innovation and invested in STEM education and computer science so that every young person—no matter where they come from or what they look like—can reach their potential and help us win the future.

That's what this is about—making sure that America is the nation that leads the world into the next frontier. And that's why I've been so committed to science and innovation—because I'll always believe that with the right investments, and the brilliance and ingenuity of the American people, there's nothing we cannot do.

Thanks everybody. Have a great weekend.

—Obama's weekly speech on radio

There can be literally endless versions of notes for the above two exercises. As long as they are logically clear, easy to read, simple to write, and can help the interpreters easily recall most of the information, they are workable notes. The following are notes for part of the exercises, only for reference.

全国同胞们，
　　尊敬的各位国家元首、政府首脑
　　和联合国等国际组织代表，

尊敬的各位来宾,

全体受阅将士们,

女士们、先生们,同志们、朋友们:

今天,是一个值得世界人民永远纪念的日子。70 年前的今天,中国人民经过长达 14 年艰苦卓绝的斗争,取得了中国人民抗日战争的伟大胜利,宣告了世界反法西斯战争的完全胜利,和平的阳光再次普照大地。

在这里,我代表中共中央、全国人大、国务院、全国政协、中央军委,向全国参加过抗日战争的老战士、老同志、爱国人士和抗日将领,向为中国人民抗日战争胜利作出重大贡献的海内外中华儿女,致以崇高的敬意!向支援和帮助过中国人民抵抗侵略的外国政府和国际友人,表示衷心的感谢!向参加今天大会的各国来宾和军人朋友们,表示热烈的欢迎!

为了和平,我们要牢固树立人类命运共同体意识。偏见和歧视、仇恨和战争,只会带来灾难和痛苦。相互尊重、平等相处、和平发展、共同繁荣,才是人间正道。

世界各国应该共同维护以联合国宪章宗旨和原则为核心的国际秩序和国际体系，积极构建以合作共赢为核心的新型国际关系，共同推进世界和平与发展的崇高事业。

It's awe-inspiring stuff. And it shows how investing in science and technology spurs our country towards new jobs and new industries; new discoveries that improve and save lives.

That's always been our country's story, from a Founding Father with an idea to fly a kite in a thunderstorm, to the women who solved the equations to take us into space, to the engineers who brought us the internet.

Chapter Ⅷ　Note-taking

And today, we need it more than ever to solve the challenges we face. Only through science can we cure diseases, and save the only planet we've got, and ensure that America keeps its competitive advantages as the world's most innovative economy.

And that's why, in my first inaugural address, I vowed to return science to its rightful place. It's why in our first few months, we made the largest single investment in basic research in our history. And it's why, over the last eight years, we've modernized the government's approach to innovation for the 21st Century.

8.3.2 Note-taking Training—Sentences (C-E)

[1]我们要共建开放合作的世界经济。面对矛盾和摩擦,协商合作才是正道。只要平等相待、互谅互让,就没有破解不了的难题。

We need to build an open and cooperative world economy. In the face of contradictions and frictions, consultation and cooperation are the right way. As long as we treat each other equally, understand each other and yield to each other, there is no problem that cannot be solved.

[2]我们应当坚持以开放求发展,坚决反对保护主义、单边主义。

We should persist in pursuing development through openness and resolutely oppose protectionism and unilateralism.

[3]共建开放创新的世界经济,各国应该加强创新合作,推动科技同经济深度融合。

To build an open and innovative world economy, countries should strengthen innovation cooperation and promote the deep integration of science and technology with the economy.

[4]站在新的历史起点,中国开放的大门只会越开越大。我们将坚持以开放促改革、促发展、促创新,持续推进更高水平的对外开放。

Standing at a new historical starting point, China will only open its door wider and wider. We will continue to promote reform, development and innovation through opening up, and keep promoting a higher level of opening up.

[5]中国支持对世界贸易组织进行必要改革,增强多边贸易体制的权威性和有效性。

China supports the necessary reform on the World Trade Organization to enhance the authoritativeness and effectiveness of the multilateral trading system.

[6]中国将秉持共商共建共享原则,坚持开放、绿色、廉洁理念,努力实现高标准、可持续目标,推动共建"一带一路"高质量发展。

China will adhere to the principle of "achieving shared growth through discussion and collaboration", keep pursuing the ideas of openness, green and integrity, and strive to achieve the goal of high standards and sustainability, and promote the construction of high quality development on the basis of the "Belt and Road Initiative".

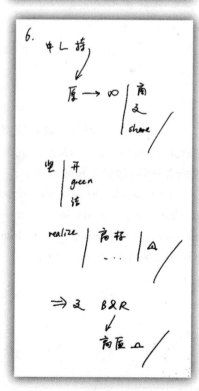

[7] 法国总统马克龙表示,中国改革开放 40 多年来取得举世瞩目的成就,堪称人类历史上最伟大的事件,成为当代国际秩序的重要转折点之一。

French President Emmanuel Macron said that China has made remarkable achievements in the reform and opening up over 40 years, which is the greatest event in human history and one of the most important turning points of the contemporary international order.

[8] 精简、有效、灵活的世卫组织必须具有战略性,其所开展的工作必须具有高度选择性。

A lean, effective, and flexible WHO must be strategic and highly selective in the work it undertakes.

[9] 借此机会,我还要特别感谢常年关注我的新闻界的朋友们,感谢我的赞助商和合作伙伴,很荣幸和你们共事。

I'd also like to take this opportunity to thank my friends in the media, my sponsors, and partners. I am honored to have worked with all of you.

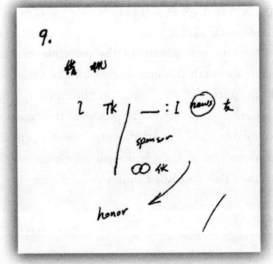

[10]教育要倡导公平公正。在很多贫困国家和地区,辍学比例很高。我们呼吁,加大对这些地区的教育投入。

Education is about equality. In poor countries and regions the number of school dropouts is astonishing. We call for more educational resources to these places.

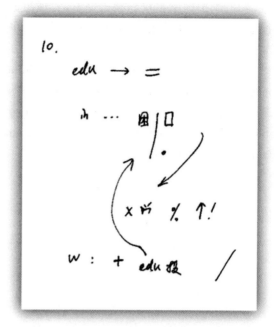

[11]新时代属于每一个人,每一个人都是新时代的见证者、开创者、建设者。只要精诚团结、共同奋斗,就没有任何力量能够阻挡中国人民实现梦想的步伐!

The new era belongs to everyone, and we are all its witnesses, creators and builders. No force can stop Chinese people's march toward realizing their dreams as long as we unite as one and strive together!

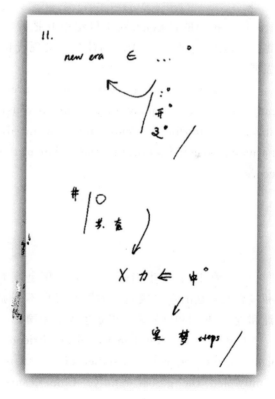

[12] 维护国家主权和领土完整，实现祖国完全统一，是全体中华儿女的共同愿望，是中华民族根本利益所在。

It is the shared aspiration of all Chinese people and in the fundamental interests of the Chinese nation to safeguard China's sovereignty and territorial integrity and realize China's complete reunification.

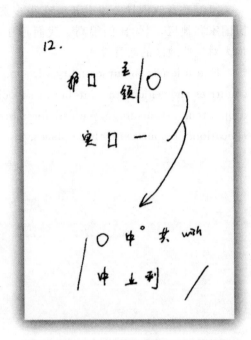

[13] 我们的目标是，到本世纪中叶把我国建成富强民主文明和谐美丽的社会主义现代化强国。

Our goal is to build China into a great modern socialist country that is prosperous, strong, democratic, culturally advanced, harmonious, and beautiful by the middle of the century.

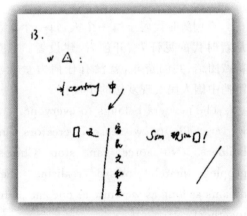

[14] 女士们、先生们、朋友们！中国是亚洲和世界大家庭的重要成员。中国发展离不开亚洲和世界，亚洲和世界繁荣稳定也需要中国。

Ladies and Gentlemen, dear Friends, China is an important member of the Asian family and the global family. China cannot develop itself in isolation from the rest of Asia and the world. On their part, the rest of Asia and the world cannot enjoy prosperity and stability without China.

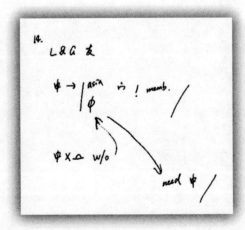

[15]经济运行保持在合理区间。国内生产总值增长 6.6%,总量突破 90 万亿元。

The main economic indicators were kept within an appropriate range. Gross domestic product (GDP) grew by 6.6 percent, exceeding 90 trillion yuan.

[16]对外开放全方位扩大,共建"一带一路"取得重要进展。首届中国国际进口博览会成功举办。

Opening up was expanded on all fronts, and joint efforts to pursue the Belt and Road Initiative (BRI) made significant headway. The first China International Import Expo was a success.

[17]今年 1 月,日本政府通过了核物质核反应堆管理法的修正案。德国 2020 年前要关闭全部核电站,而欧美许多国家则加强了对核电站的安全研究。

In January this year, the Japanese government adopted new amendment to the law on the regulation of nuclear source materials, nuclear fuel materials and reactors. Germany has decided to shut down all its nuclear power plants by the year of 2020. And many European countries and the United States have stepped up their research on the safety of nuclear power stations.

[18] 改进空气质量需要政府、企业、公众和媒体共同努力,仅仅依靠测试数据还是不够的。我们也呼吁企业减少污染,并积极参加空气的改善工作。

To improve air quality requires the concerted efforts of the government, the enterprises, the public and the media. It is not enough to just monitor air pollution, we call on the enterprises to reduce pollution and be actively involved in activities to improve air quality.

[19] 中国和日本都是缺少能源的国家,大量能源依靠进口,中国愿意和日本加强在核电和其他新能源方面的交流与合作,彼此学习,共同吸取教训,提高开发新能源的能力。

Both China and Japan lack energy sources. Our two countries both rely heavily on imports to meet our domestic energy demand. We hope to step up exchanges and corporation with Japan in nuclear power and fields related to the new energy. So we can learn from each other and together learn the lessons from the accidents, and improve our capacity in developing new energies.

[20] 中国发展核电的政策是要在极端安全的前提下发展,并且要着力于第三代核电站的设计和建设。

The top priority in China on the development of nuclear power station is safety. We have been focusing on the design and construction of the third generation nuclear power stations.

[21] 中国在 100 多个国家建立了大约 350 所孔子学院,这都是经外方邀请后成立的,现在还有很多邀请,但是一时不能够完全满足。

China has established about 350 Confucius Institutes in more than 100 countries. And they are all established at the invitation of the foreign countries. And there are some standing invitations which are yet not able to meet.

[22] 汉语是使用人口最多的语言,但是使用国家却很少,只有中国和新加坡。而一些语言,比如英语,有 170 多个国家流行,西班牙语有 30 多个国家流行。

Although Chinese language has the biggest number of users around the world, only China and Singapore have made Chinese language their common language. Over 170 countries use English, and over 30 countries use Spanish.

[23] 城乡居民收入稳定增长,农村居民收入增长较快。上半年,城镇居民家庭人均总收入 12 076 元。其中,城镇居民人均可支配收入 11 041 元。

Urban and rural residents' income increased steadily with a higher growth for rural residents. In the first half of this year, the per capita total income of urban households was 12,076 yuan. Specifically, the per capita disposable income of urban population was 11,041 yuan.

[24] 当前,经济发展面临的国内外环境依然十分复杂,不稳定、不确定因素较多。

At present, the external and internal environment for China's economic development is still rather complicated with numerous instabilities and uncertainties.

[25] 这些会谈只是进程的开始,需要人们有决心和勇气来参与。但是我敦促双方将谈判进行下去。我想对他们说,这是你们结束你们国家破败局面的一个机会。

These talks are only the start of a process, so will require commitment and courage, but I urge both sides to remain at the negotiating table. And to them I say, this is your opportunity to put an end to the devastation of your country.

[26] 今天的厦门已经发展成一座高素质的创新创业之城,新经济新产业快速发展,贸易投资并驾齐驱,海运、陆运、空运通达五洲。

Xiamen today has become well known for its innovation and entrepreneurship, with burgeoning new economic forms and new industries, robust trade and investment and easy access to the world with air, land and sea links.

[27] 经济全球化遭遇更多不确定性,新兴市场国家和发展中国家发展的外部环境更趋复杂。世界和平与发展之路还很长,前行不会一路坦途。

Economic globalization is facing more uncertainties. Emerging market and developing countries find themselves in a more complex external environment. The long road to global peace and development will not be a smooth one.

[28] 金砖国家是世界和平的维护者、国际安全秩序的建设者。

We BRICS countries are committed to upholding global peace and contributing to the international security order.

[29] 我们要维护联合国宪章宗旨和原则以及国际关系基本准则,坚定维护多边主义,推动国际关系民主化,反对霸权主义和强权政治。

We should uphold the purposes and principles of the UN Charter and basic norms governing international relations, firmly support multilateralism, work for greater democracy in international relations, and oppose hegemonism and power politics.

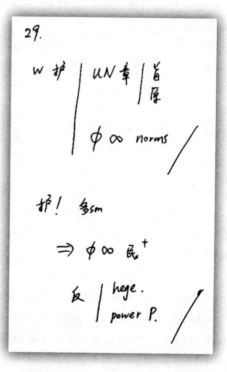

[30]新兴市场国家和发展中国家的发展,是要努力把世界经济的蛋糕做大。我们要合力引导好经济全球化走向,提供更多先进理念和公共产品。

The development of emerging market and developing countries is to make the pie of the global economy bigger. We should join hands to steer the course of economic globalization, and offer more vision and public goods.

[31]今年上半年,中国经济增长 6.9%,第三产业增加值占国内生产总值的 54.1%,新增城镇就业 735 万人。

In the first half of this year, China's economy grew by 6.9%, the value added from the service industries accounted for 54.1% of the GDP, and 7.35 million urban jobs were created.

[32]面向未来,中国将深入贯彻创新、协调、绿色、开放、共享的发展理念,不断适应、引领经济发展新常态。

Going forward, China will continue to put into practice the vision of innovative, coordinated, green, open and inclusive development. We will adapt to and steer the new normal of economic development.

[33] 中国在世界经济最困难的时刻,承担了拉动增长的重任。2009 年到 2011 年间,中国对世界经济增长的贡献率达到 50% 以上。

China shouldered the responsibility of driving economic growth in times of the world economic hardship. China had contributed up to 50% of world economic growth from 2009 to 2011.

[34] 世界各国相互联系日益紧密、相互依存日益加深,遍布全球的众多发展中国家、几十亿人口正在努力走向现代化,和平、发展、合作、共赢的时代潮流更加强劲。

Countries have become increasingly inter-connected and inter-dependent. Several billion people in a large number of developing countries are embracing modernization. The trend of the times, namely, peace, development, cooperation and mutual benefit, is gaining momentum.

[35] 人类只有一个地球,各国共处一个世界。共同发展是持续发展的重要基础。

Mankind has only one earth, and it is home to all countries. Common development is the very foundation of sustainable development.

[36] 互联网和移动宽带的出现令全球数十亿人得以获得世界各地的知识与信息、享受高保真通信，以及各种各样成本更低、更便捷的服务。

The advent of the internet and mobile broadband has empowered billions of people globally to have access to the world's knowledge and information, high-fidelity communications, and a wide range of lower-cost, more convenient services.

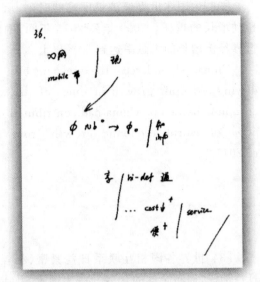

[37] 近期，人民币汇率走势出现一定幅度波动，有人认为是中国有意为之，这是不符合实际的，因为人民币汇率单向贬值对中国弊多利少。

The recent fluctuations in the RMB exchange rate have been seen by some as an intentional measure on the part of China. This is simply not true. Persistent depreciation of the RMB will only do more harm than good to our country.

[38] 新产业革命孕育着无限的希望，自然科学、社会科学、人文艺术等从来没有像今天这样可以深度交织。

The new industrial revolution holds out infinite promise. Today, natural sciences, social sciences and liberal arts are deeply entwined as never before.

[39]2004年6月8日——历史将永远铭记这一刻。奥运圣火带着人类对和平、友谊、文明、进步的追求,带着希腊人民对中国人民的友谊,来到中华大地。

June 8th to 9th, 2004, the history shall forever remember the date. The Olympic flame came down to China's divine land, with mankind's yearning for peace, friendship, civilization and progress and with the Greek people's friendship for the Chinese people.

[40]哈佛建校三百六十年来,培养出许多杰出的政治家、科学家、文学家和企业家,曾出过六位美国总统,三十多位诺贝尔奖获得者。

Since its founding some 360 years ago, Harvard has nurtured a great number of outstanding political leaders, scientists, writers and businessmen, including six of the American Presidents and over thirty Nobel Prize winners.

8.3.3 Note-taking Training—Sentences (E-C)

[1] What I'd like to do today is to make some opening comments, and then what I'm really looking forward to doing is taking questions, not only from students who are in the audience, but also we've received questions online.

我今天准备这样,先做一个开场白,我真正希望做的是回答在座的问题,不但回答在座的学生问题,同时还可以从网上得到一些问题。

[2] Shanghai is a city that has great meaning in the history of the relationship between the United States and China.

上海在美中关系的历史中是个具有意义的重大城市。

[3] It was here, 37 years ago, that the Shanghai Communique opened the door to a new chapter of engagement between our governments and among our people.

正是在这里,37 年前,《上海公报》打开了我们两国政府和两国人民接触交往的新的篇章。

[4] A different kind of connection was made nearly 40 years ago when the frost between our countries began to thaw through the simple game of table tennis.

40年前,我们两国间开启了又一种联系,两国关系开始通过乒乓球比赛解冻。

[5] The commerce affects our people's lives in so many ways. America imports from China many of the computer parts we use, the clothes we wear; and we export to China machinery that helps power your industry.

贸易在许多方面影响人民的生活,比如美国电脑中许多部件,还有美国人民穿的衣服都是从中国进口的,我们向中国出口中国工业要使用的机器。

[6] China has lifted hundreds of millions of people out of poverty, an accomplishment unparalleled in human history while playing a larger role in global events.

中国使得亿万人民脱贫,而这种成就是人类历史上史无前例的。而中国在全球问题中也发挥了更大的作用。

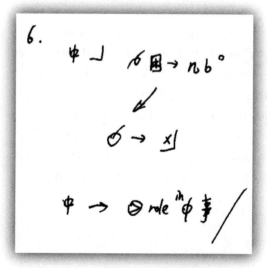

[7] Even after they were freed, African Americans persevered through conditions that were separate and not equal, before winning full and equal rights.

即使他们被解放以后,非洲裔美国人也经过一些分开的、不平等的条件,经过一段时间才争取到全面的平等权利。

[8] Obviously in the United States and many developed countries, per capita, per individual, they are already using much more energy than each individual here in China.

很显然,在美国以及在很多发达国家,人均能耗量都比中国的人均能耗量大。

[9] There are still a lot of conflicts in the world that can be dated back for centuries. If you look at the Middle East, there are wars and conflict that are rooted in arguments going back a thousand years.

现在世界上有很多冲突,这些冲突有数百年的历史,比如你看看中东的情况,这些战争和冲突来源于一千年以前的斗争。

[10] As Secretary-General of the United Nations, I hold high the banner of empowering women and girls, promoting their health and defending their rights.

我作为联合国秘书长,要大力增强妇女和女童的权能,维护她们的健康,捍卫她们的权利。

[11] Keep in mind: one reason for the success of the Millennium Development Goals was their limited number.

请记住:千年发展目标取得成功的原因之一是目标数量有限。

[12] We are all aware that some new challenges, especially those driven by the globalization of unhealthy lifestyles, can only be addressed through collaboration with multiple sectors, including some industries.

我们都知道,只有通过多部门合作,包括与工业界合作,才能应对一些新挑战,特别是那些不健康生活方式的全球化所带来的挑战。

[13] Public expectations for health care are rising and costs are soaring. Some new medicines and medical devices are unaffordable, even for the wealthiest countries in the world.

公众对于卫生保健的期望值越来越高,而卫生保健成本也在飙升。一些新药和医疗器械价格让人负担不起,即使对于世界上最富裕的国家也是如此。

[14] This is the kind of joined-up effort that makes the most effective use of our human and financial resources, which will always be limited, and has a dramatic and measurable impact.

正是这种携手使我们能够最有效地使用总是非常有限的人力和财政资源,并产生巨大的可衡量影响。

[15] The homicide rate in London—which includes murder and manslaughter—fell from 22 per million to 12 per million people during his time as mayor.

伦敦的凶杀犯罪率——包括谋杀和过失杀人——在他担任市长期间从每百万人中 22 起下降到每百万人中 12 起。

[16] Nepal is home to eight of the world's 14 highest mountains, and mountain climbing is a key source of employment and income for the poor nation.

世界最高的 14 座山峰中,尼泊尔就占了 8 座。登山是这个较为贫穷的国家的重要就业渠道和收入来源。

Chapter VIII Note-taking

[17] The rule targets immigrants who rely on public benefits, such as food aid or public housing, for more than a year. Their applications will be rejected if the government decides they are likely to rely on public assistance in future.

这项规定针对的是那些依赖食品券和公共住房等公共福利生活超过一年的移民。如果政府认为他们未来可能依赖公共援助,其申请将被拒绝。

[18] Immigrants who are already permanent residents in the US are unlikely to be affected by the rule change. It also does not apply to refugees and asylum applicants.

已经是美国永久居民的移民不太可能受到新规的影响。这项新规也不适用于难民和庇护申请人。

[19] President Trump has made immigration a central theme of his administration. This latest move is part of his government's efforts to curb legal immigration.

特朗普总统将移民问题作为政府的中心议题。这是其减少合法移民数量的最新举措。

[20] We have no illusions about how difficult and challenging this process is likely to be but we should all do everything possible to help the people of Syria achieve peace.

我们对这一进程的困难程度和挑战性非常清楚。但是我们应该尽一切可能帮助叙利亚人民实现和平。

[21] We will make all the preparations proceed forward to the highest standard, in the highest quality and with the highest level for the 2008 Olympic Games.

我们将以最高的标准、质量和水平做好 2008 年奥运会的各项筹备工作。

[22] The winner of this year's Nobel Peace Prize, Kenyan environmentalist, Wangari Maathai, is in New York to call attention to her message linking environment protection and peace.

今年的诺贝尔和平奖得主,肯尼亚的环境保护人士旺加里马塔伊在纽约宣传把环境与和平相联系的主张。

[23] Education is provided from primary school to university, and is compulsory between the ages of six to fifteen.

提供从小学到大学的教育,并且对 6~15 岁青少年实行义务教育。

[24] We have set a clear and focused goal: to work with all members of the UN to disrupt, dismantle, and defeat Al Qaeda and its extremist allies

我们制定了坚定不移的明确目标：同联合国所有成员共同努力，打击、摧垮并击溃"基地"组织（Al Qaeda）及其极端主义同伙。

[25] I have outlined a comprehensive agenda to seek the goal of a world without nuclear weapons.

我提出了一项综合议程，寻求实现一个没有核武器的世界的目标。

[26] To overcome an economic crisis that touches every corner of the world, we worked with the G20 nations to forge a coordinated international response of over \$2 trillion in stimulus to bring the global economy back from the brink.

为渡过一场波及全世界各个角落的经济危机，我们与G20成员国共同制定了相互协调的国际性举措，以超过2万亿美元的刺激计划挽救了濒临崩溃的全球经济。

[27] We mobilized resources that helped prevent the crisis from spreading further to developing countries.

我们调动资源,帮助阻止这场危机进一步波及发展中国家。

[28] We joined with other countries to launch a $20 billion global food security initiative that will lend a hand to those who need it most, and help them build their own capacity.

我们还与其他一些国家共同发起了一项200亿美元的全球粮食保障计划,向最需要救助的人伸出援手,并帮助他们进行能力建设。

[29] The civilization of different nations are all fruits of human wisdom and contribution to human progress; they call for mutual respect.

各民族的文明都是人类智慧的成果,对于人类进步作出了贡献,应该彼此尊重。

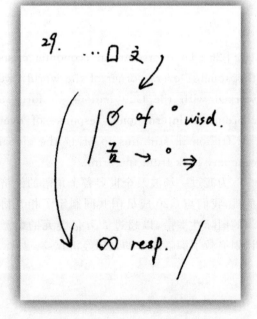

[30] The United Nations was founded on the belief that the nations of the world could solve their problems together.

联合国的建立以世界各国能够共同解决问题的信念为基础。

[31] That is the future America wants—a future of peace and prosperity that we can only reach if we recognize that all nations have rights, but all nations have responsibilities as well.

这就是美国渴望的未来,一个和平与繁荣的未来,我们只有在承认所有国家拥有权利但同时又承担责任的时候才能如愿以偿。

[32] We must stop the spread of nuclear weapons, and seek the goal of a world without them.

我们必须停止核武器的扩散,寻求一个没有核武器的世界。

[33] Democracy cannot be imposed on any nation from the outside. Each society must search for its own path, and no path is perfect.

民主不可能从外部强加给任何国家。每个社会必须寻求自身的道路,而没有一条路会尽善尽美。

[34] We have set aside $63 billion to carry forward the fight against HIV/AIDS, to end deaths from tuberculosis and malaria, to eradicate polio, and to strengthen public health systems.

我们已拨款630亿美元继续进行防治艾滋病病毒/艾滋病的工作,挽救结核病和疟疾患者的生命,根治小儿麻痹症,并增强公共医疗体制。

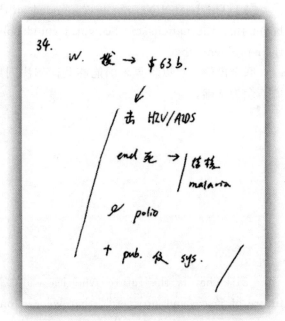

[35] The world is still recovering from the worst economic crisis since the Great Depression.

全世界经历了自大萧条以来最严重的一场经济危机,目前还在复苏之中。

[36] Those wealthy nations that did so much damage to the environment in the 20th century must accept the obligation to lead.

对于所有在20世纪给环境造成了如此严重破坏的富裕国家,必须尽自己的义务,率先采取行动。

[37] We will press ahead with deep cuts in emissions to reach the goals that we set for 2020, and eventually 2050.

我们将积极推行大幅度减排,实现我们到 2020 年要实现的目标,并最终实现 2050 年的既定目标。

[38] We will continue to promote renewable energy and efficiency, and share new technologies with countries around the world.

我们将继续提倡可再生能源和提升节能效率,并同世界各国分享新技术。

[39] We will seize every opportunity for progress to address the environment threat in a cooperative effort with the entire world.

我们将抓住一切寻求进展的机会,同全世界同心协力应对环境威胁。

[40] Australia is a land of exceptional beauty; it is the world's smallest continent and largest island, and a relatively young nation established in an ancient land.

澳大利亚是一个异常美丽的国家,它是世界上最小的洲,也是最大的岛,是最古老的土地上建立起来的较为年轻的国家。

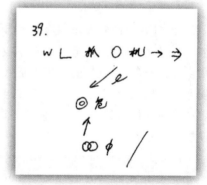

8.3.4 Note-taking Training—Passages (C-E)

[1]我曾经说过,有一天我的篮球职业生涯结束了,我希望那只是个逗号,不是句号。今天,这一天终于到来了,但我没有离开心爱的篮球,我的生活还在继续,我还是姚明,我还有很多事情要做,远远没有到画上句号的那一天。

I have once said, when I retire from my professional career, I hope that it is a comma, not a period. Today, that day has finally arrived, but I am not leaving the sport of basketball that I love. My life will continue. I am still Yao Ming and there are still many things that I wish to accomplish. The day of drawing a period is still far far away.

[2]教育要面向青年。青年是我们的未来。教育之所以重要,是因为它不仅要教授知识和技能,而且也帮助青年人成长为具有强烈责任感的公民。作为教科文组织的一名特使和一位母亲,我也愿意恪尽职守,实现教育的进展和进步。

Education is about the young people. Young people are the future. Education is important because it not only gave young people knowledge and skills but also help them become responsible citizens. As the UNESCO special envoy and the mother myself my commitment to education for all will never change.

[3] 我们要坚持党对人民军队的绝对领导，全面贯彻新时代党的强军思想，不断推进政治建军、改革强军、科技兴军、依法治军，加快形成中国特色、世界一流的武装力量体系，构建中国特色现代作战体系，推动人民军队切实担负起党和人民赋予的新时代使命任务。

We will stick to the absolute leadership of the CPC over the people's armed forces and fully implement the Party's thinking on strengthening the military for the new era. We will continue to enhance the political loyalty of the armed forces, strengthen them through reform and technology, and run them in accordance with law. We will act more quickly to put into place the system of world-class armed forces with Chinese characteristics. We will create a modern combat system with distinctive Chinese characteristics. Our armed forces must be up to shouldering the missions and tasks of the new era entrusted to them by the Party and the people.

[4] 中国的老龄化的确有自己的特点，就是未富先老，一般国家在人均 GDP 达到 10 000 美元以后才进入老龄化社会，而中国在 3000 美元的时候就进入老龄化社会了，所以这需要我们政府和全社会特别认真对待。

China's aging issue has its own characteristics, that is, China is getting old before getting rich. And normally countries become an aging society after their per capital GDP reaches 10,000 US dollars. In China, our per capital GDP is only 3,000 US dollars at the moment. However, China is already an aging society. I think this calls for the serious attention from the government and across the society.

[5]下阶段要坚持宏观经济政策取向不动摇，继续保持政策的连续性、稳定性，继续把稳定物价总水平放在宏观调控的首要位置，增强政策的针对性、灵活性、有效性，进一步处理好保持经济平稳较快发展、调整经济结构和管理通胀预期的关系，加大改革创新力度。

In the next phase, we should adhere firmly to the macro-control policies, maintain their continuity and stability, give first priority of work to the stabilization of overall price level and improve the relevance, flexibility and effectiveness of policies. We should also persist in balancing the relationship among a steady and comparatively rapid economic development, adjustment of economic structures and management of the inflation expectation; and promote reform and innovation.

[6]10年中，中国经济总量增长239%，货物进出口总额增长73%，成为世界第二大经济体，13亿多中国人民的生活水平实现大幅飞跃，中国为世界和地区经济发展作出的贡献也越来越大。

Over these ten years, China's economic aggregate has grown by 239% and its total volume of exports and imports in goods has risen by 73%. China has become the world's second largest economy, the lives of its 1.3 billion-plus people have been significantly improved, and China has made increasingly greater contribution to both regional and global economic development.

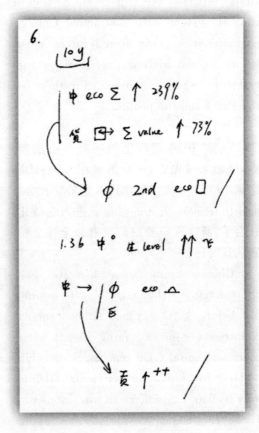

[7] 今年5月，中方成功主办"一带一路"国际合作高峰论坛，29个国家的元首和政府首脑，140多个国家、80多个国际组织的1600多名代表出席，标志着共建"一带一路"倡议已经进入从理念到行动、从规划到实施的新阶段。

Last May, China successfully hosted the Belt and Road Forum for International Cooperation, which was attended by 29 heads of state or government and over 1,600 representatives from more than 140 countries and 80-plus international organizations. This ushered in a new stage of translating the Belt and Road Initiative from vision to action and from planning to implementation.

[8] 我们看到，围绕智能手机的开发应用，衍生出庞大的产业集群，很重要的原因就是千千万万人在开放的平台上，提供了海量的技术解决方案和产业应用方案。

As we can see, the development of smart phone applications has spawned massive industrial clusters. An important reason is that tens of thousands of people upload their technical solutions and industrial application proposals onto open platforms, providing a sea of technical solution and industrial application plans.

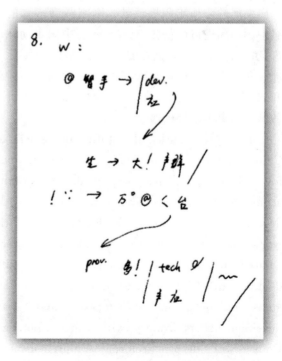

[9] 把更多的可能变为现实,关键是要营造良好的环境。要健全权利公平、机会公平、规则公平的制度安排,打造平衡普惠的发展模式,发展面向人人的教育,加强对弱势群体的扶持,实现惠及面更广、包容性更强的发展。

To turn possibilities into reality, an enabling environment is indispensable. It is imperative to enhance institutional arrangements for equal rights, equal opportunities and fair rules, follow a balanced and inclusive development approach, make education universal, and better support the vulnerable groups so as to achieve more inclusive development that benefits all.

[10] 今年是中国改革开放 40 周年。40 年来,中国在取得自身巨大发展成就的同时,也为东亚和世界发展进步作出积极贡献。刚刚圆满落幕的首届中国国际进口博览会,充分显示了中国主动开放市场、与各国共享发展机遇的真诚愿望和实际行动。我们将全面深化改革,实施新一轮高水平对外开放,在推动自身迈向高质量发展的同时,为世界各国提供更多发展机遇。

This year marks the 40th anniversary of China's reform and opening-up. Over the past four decades, China has made remarkable achievements and contributed its share to the development and progress in East Asia and the world beyond. The just-concluded inaugural China International Import Expo fully demonstrated China's sincere desire and voluntary steps to open up its market and share development opportunity with other countries. China will deepen reform comprehensively, advance a new round of high-standard opening-up, and move toward high-quality development. All this will only bring more opportunities to the world.

8.3.5 Note-taking Training—Passages (E - C)

[1] Now, like all of you, my responsibility is to act in the interest of my nation and my people, and I will never apologize for defending those interests. But it is my deeply held belief that in the year 2009—more than at any point in human history—the interests of nations and peoples are shared. The religious convictions that we hold in our hearts can forge new bonds among people, or they can tear us apart. The technology we harness can light the path to peace, or forever darken it. The energy we use can sustain our planet, or destroy it.

同各位一样,我的职责是采取符合本国和本国人民利益的行动,我绝不会为捍卫这些利益而道歉。但我深深感到,与人类历史上任何一个时期相比,在2009年各个国家及其人民之间都更具有共同的利益。我们心中怀有的宗教信念能够在人民之间缔结新的纽带,也能在我们之间制造隔阂。我们掌控的技术能够照亮通向和平的道路,也能永远将其笼罩在黑暗之中。我们使用的能源能够维持我们这个星球的生存,也能造成它的毁灭。

[2] The structure of world peace cannot be the work of one man, or one party, or one nation... It cannot be a peace of large nations—or of small nations. It must be a peace which rests on the cooperative effort of the whole world.

世界和平的大厦不可能是一个人、一个政党或一个国家的产物……不能只有大国的和平——或只有小国的和平。和平必须以全世界同心协力为基础。

[3] Today, let me put forward four pillars that I believe are fundamental to the future that we want for our children: non-proliferation and disarmament; the promotion of peace and security; the preservation of our planet; and a global economy that advances opportunity for all people.

今天，我谨在此提出四大要素，我认为这些要素对我们希望为后代所创造的未来至关重要：不扩散与裁军；促进和平与安全；保护我们的地球；以及为全体人民增进机会的全球经济。

[4] But if the governments of Iran and North Korea choose to ignore international standards; if they put the pursuit of nuclear weapons ahead of regional stability and the security and opportunity of their own people; if they are oblivious to the dangers of escalating nuclear arms races in both East Asia and the Middle East—then they must be held

accountable.

但是，如果伊朗和朝鲜政府决意无视国际准则；如果他们把谋求核武器置于地区安全稳定和本国人民的机遇之上；如果他们将东亚和中东地区核军备竞赛升级的危险置之不顾——那么他们必须对此承担责任。

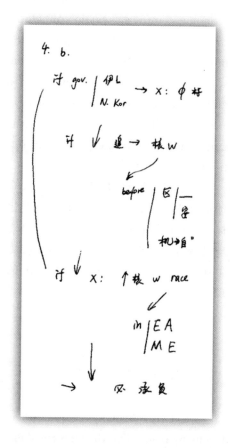

[5] We must remember that the greatest price of this conflict is not paid by us. It's not paid by politicians. It's paid by the Israeli girl in Sderot who closes her eyes in fear that a rocket will take her life in the middle of the night. It's paid for by the Palestinian boy in Gaza who has no clean water and no country to call his own. These are all god's children.

我们必须记住，为这场冲突付出最大代价的并不是我们，也不是政客们，而是住在斯德洛特（Sderot）的以色列女孩。她惊恐万分，闭上自己的眼睛，害怕会被半夜袭来的火箭弹夺走生命。付出代价的还有加沙（Gaza）地带的巴勒斯坦男孩，他喝不上干净的水，也没有自己的祖国。他们都是上帝的子民。

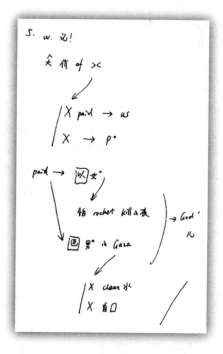

[6] We will integrate more economies into a system of global trade. We will support the millennium development goals, and approach next year's summit with a global plan to make them a reality. And we will set our sights on the eradication of extreme poverty in our time.

我们将帮助更多的经济体加入全球贸易体系。我们将支持千年发展目标,并将在明年的峰会上提出一项实现这些目标的全球计划。我们还将力争在我们这个时代根除极端贫困的现象。

[7] Far too many people in far too many places live through the daily crises that challenge our humanity—the despair of an empty stomach; the thirst brought on by dwindling water supplies; the injustice of a child dying from a treatable disease; or a mother losing her life as she gives birth.

在太多的地方,有太多的人每天都生活在挑战人性的艰辛之中——饥肠辘辘,顿生绝望;供水短缺,干渴难熬;疾病可治,但患病儿童却得不到救治;或者产妇在生育过程中死亡。

[8] The death of Osama bin Laden, announced by President Obama last night, is a watershed moment in our common global fight against terrorism. The crimes of Al Qaeda touched most continents, bringing tragedy and loss of life to thousands of men, women and children. The United Nations condemns in the strongest possible terms terrorism in all its forms, regardless of its purpose and wherever it is committed.

奥巴马总统昨晚宣布奥萨马·本·拉登死亡,此刻是全球共同打击恐怖主义斗争的分水岭!"基地"组织的罪行遍及所有大陆,制造了一场场悲剧,夺去了数以千计男女老少的生命。联合国最强烈措辞谴责一切形式的恐怖主义,无论出于什么目的,发生在何时何地。

[9] Unfortunately, tuberculosis and HIV/AIDS work very well together in a ferocious synergy, each one amplifying the consequences of the other. But we have made enormous progress against both diseases in just the past decade. We know what to do to prevent infections and save or prolong lives. The numbers of infections and deaths are still way too high, but they are going down as access to information, medicines, and care becomes more widely available.

不幸的是,肺结核和艾滋病十分融洽地结合在一起,产生了极大的协同作用,每种疾病都使另外一种疾病带来的后果得以扩大。但是仅仅在过去的十年中,我们与两种疾病的斗争取得了巨大进展。我们知道该怎么去做,来预防感染并且拯救或者延长生命。感染人数和死亡人数仍然过高,但是伴随着人们可以越来越广泛地获得信息、药品和医护,这两个数字正在下降。

[10] Some 110 to 190 million people encounter very significant difficulties in their daily lives. In fact, most people with disabilities face obstacles at every turn in their lives. Some of the biggest barriers include stigma and discrimination, lack of adequate health care and rehabilitation services, and inaccessible transport. Other barriers arise from the design of buildings, such as schools and workplaces, and of information and communication technologies.

约有1.1亿至1.9亿人在日常生活中遇有很大困难。事实上,患有残疾的大多数人都会在其生活的每一个转折点遇到障碍。其中一些最大障碍包括耻辱和被歧视,缺乏适当的卫生保健以及康复服务,还有难以使用交通工具。其他方面的障碍源自建筑物的设计,比如学校和工作场所,还源自信息和通信技术的设计。

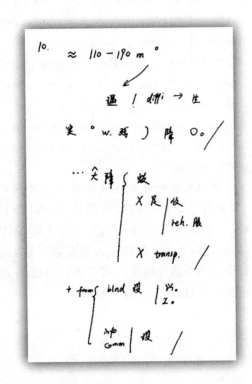

Exercises and Practice

8-3-1 Sight note-taking: read the following passages and transcribe them into CI notes.

Passage 1

尊敬的慕尼黑安全会议主席沃尔夫冈·伊申格尔先生,
女士们,先生们!

很高兴出席本届慕尼黑安全会议。作为全球性的安全政策论坛,慕尼黑安全会议为各国人士就世界和平与发展问题阐述主张、交流看法提供了重要平台。今年会议以"倡导国际合作,维护多边主义"为主题,紧扣时代脉搏,契合各方期待,具有重要现实意义。

当前,国际形势加速深刻演变,不确定性不稳定性凸显。单边主义、保护主义持续上升,国际多边秩序和全球治理体系遭到挑战。世界面临单边与多边、对抗与对话、封闭与开放的重大选择,处于何去何从的关键十字路口。习近平主席指出,多边主义是维护和平、促进发展的有效路径,世界比以往更加需要多边主义。中方一贯认为,联合国是多边主义的旗帜,以联合国为中心的国际多边架构是国际合作的主要平台。《联合国宪章》集中体现了国际社会关于多边主义的共识,为当代国际秩序奠定了基石。作为联合国创始会员国和安理会常任理事国,中国始终支持和践行多边主义,始终高举和平、发展、合作、共赢的旗帜,始终做世界和平的建设者、全球发展的贡献者、国际秩序的维护者。

从中国人民和世界人民共同和根本利益出发,习近平主席提出推动构建相互尊重、公平正义、合作共赢的新型国际关系,推动构建人类命运共同体,建设持久和平、普遍安全、共同繁荣、开放包容、清洁美丽的世界的重要理念。这一理念蕴含了中国对多边主义一以贯之的立场和主张。主权平等,这是国与国规范彼此关系最重要的准则。国家不分大小、强弱、贫富都一律平等,要尊重各国人民自主选择发展道路的权利,反对强加于人,反对干涉别国内政。对话协商,这是现代国际治理的重要方法。要坚持通过对话协商以和平方式解决争议问题,以对话解争端,以协商化分歧,反对动辄诉诸武力或以武力相威胁,反对霸权主义和强权政治。遵守法治,这是国际关系法治化的根本要求。要维护以《联合国宪章》宗旨和原则为核心的国际关系基本准则,确保国际法平等统一适用,不搞双重标准,不能合则用、不合则弃。合作共赢,这是实现共同发展的正确选择。要在互利互惠基础上寻求各国利益最大公约数,扩大各方共同利益的汇合点。

倡导和践行多边主义,不仅是中国的选择,也是世界绝大多数国家的共同选择。以联合国为中心的国际机构广泛开展政治、经济、安全、文化等领域对话合作,协力应对全球性问题和挑战,积极推动国际关系民主化,有力促进了世界和平稳定与发展繁荣。二十国集团、亚太经合组织、金砖国家、上海合作组织、亚欧会议等秉持多边主义核心原则,开展了富有成效的国际合作。欧盟、东盟、非盟、阿盟、拉共体等坚持推进区域合作,为维护各地区和平与发展作出贡献。实践证明,国际合作是时代潮流,多边主义是人间正道,构建人类命运共同体是大势所趋。

——节选自杨洁篪在第55届慕尼黑安全会议上的主旨演讲《倡导国际合作,维护多边主义,推动构建人类命运共同体》,2019年2月16日,慕尼黑

来源:外交部网站

(https://www.fmprc.gov.cn/web/ziliao_674904/zyjh_674906/t1638506.shtml)

Passage 2

My administration is committed to giving every American the opportunity to find a great job and have a rewarding career.

There's nothing like it. Whether you're a high school student or a late-career worker, there has never been a better time to learn a trade, hone a skill, and pursue your dreams.

Last quarter, the United States economy grew by 4.1 percent. We've created 3.7 million new jobs since the election. Unemployment recently fell to its lowest rate in almost 50 years. Unemployment for Americans with disabilities has reached the lowest level ever recorded. In the month of June alone, 600,000 workers entered or re-entered the workforce, pretty good numbers.

To continue this incredible momentum, we launched the Pledge to America's Workers. More than 100 companies, associations and others have pledged to train or retrain over 4 million American students.

We're encouraging companies across the country to join our historic initiative and pledge to invest in training Americans for the jobs of today and the careers of tomorrow.

In the last two weeks, I established the National Council for the American Worker, which will develop a national workforce strategy and sign the modernized and long-awaited Perkins Career and Technical Education Act, which will deliver jobs and training to more than 11 million students and workers. We're very proud of that.

When we invest in our workers, we are investing in our people, we are investing in our communities and we are investing in the American dream. And every single day, we are making new American dreams come true.

Thank you, and God bless America.

—American President Donald Trump's weekly speech, August 3, 2018

来源:搜狐网(sohu.com/a/246464369_100077706)

8-3-2 Read or listen to the following sentences or passages, take notes, and then interpret them into the target language. (Audio 8-3-2 CN, Audio 8-3-2 En)

1. 我们要坚持和平发展道路,奉行互利共赢的开放战略,继续同世界各国人民一道推动共建人类命运共同体。

2. 前进征程上,我们要坚持"和平统一、一国两制"的方针,保持香港、澳门长期繁荣稳定,推动海峡两岸关系和平发展,团结全体中华儿女,继续为实现祖国完全统一而奋斗。

3. 没有任何力量能够撼动我们伟大祖国的地位,没有任何力量能够阻挡中国人民和中华民族的前进步伐。

4. 我们要坚持建设开放型世界经济大方向。这是二十国集团应对国际金融危机的重要经验,也是推动世界经济增长的重要路径。

5. 70年来,中国人民奉行独立自主的和平外交政策,坚持和平发展道路,坚持在和平共处五项原则基础上发展同各国的友好合作,为推动构建人类命运共同体、推动人类和平与发展的崇高事业作出了重大贡献!

6. 今天,来自38个国家的领导人和联合国、国际货币基金组织负责人在这里举行了领导人圆桌峰会。

7. 我们积极评价共建"一带一路"合作取得的进展和意义。我们都认为,共建"一带一路"是通向共同繁荣的机遇之路。

8. 我们一致支持开放、廉洁、绿色发展,反对保护主义,努力建设风清气正、环境友好的新时代丝绸之路。

9. 我们的共同目标是,携手努力让各国互联互通更加有效,经济增长更加强劲,国际合作更加密切,人民生活更加美好。

10. 当前,世界经济出现向好势头,有关国际组织预计,今年世界经济有望增长3.5%。这是近年来最好的经济形势。同时,世界经济中的深层次问题尚未解决,仍然面临诸多不稳定不确定因素。

11. 当前,世界经济发展仍不平衡,技术进步对就业的挑战日益突出。世界经济论坛预计,到2020年,人工智能将取代全球逾500万个工作岗位。

12. 我们要坚持走开放发展、互利共赢之路,共同做大世界经济的蛋糕。作为世界主要经济体,我们应该也能够发挥领导作用,支持多边贸易体制,按照共同制定的规则办事,通过协商为应对共同挑战找到共赢的解决方案。

13. 我们要在数字经济和新工业革命领域加强合作,共同打造新技术、新产业、新模式、新产品。

14. 本轮中美战略与经济对话是在国际政治经济形势出现新变化、中美关系发展面临新机遇的重要时刻举行的。推动本轮对话取得积极成果,对我们两国都具有重要意义。

15. 毋庸置疑,中美国情不同,双方难免存在一些矛盾和分歧,关键是要尊重和照顾对方的核心利益和重大关切,妥善处理相互之间存在的一些敏感问题,不断增强互信基础。

16. 全球警察合作组织国际刑警组织周一罕见地向全球发出呼吁,通缉八名涉嫌谋杀或对女性实施暴力的男子。

17. 欧洲和全球每年都有许多女性因家暴丧生,人数令人震惊,人们对政府在此方面未能取得进展日益愤怒,这迫使各国政府开始采取行动,但活动人士警告称,这还远远不够。

18. 这份报告对迄今为止的残疾问题首次做出了全球评估,这是利用在这个复杂问题上所掌握的最新科学证据来完成的。最新估计数字现在使我们看到,有十多亿人存有某种形式的残疾情况。

19. 据路透社报道,官方统计数据显示,今年约有329人在新南威尔士州的公路上丧生,而2018年这一数据为354人。新南威尔士州交通部称,这款摄像头将用人工智能技术回顾监控录像,从而识别出违法使用手机的情况。

20. 我们要共同为世界经济增长发掘新动力。这个动力首先来自创新。研究表明,全球95%的工商业同互联网密切相关,世界经济正在向数字化转型。另一动力也来自更好解决发展问题,落实2030年可持续发展议程。这对发展中国家有利,也将为发达国家带来市场和投资机遇,大家都是赢家。

21. He spoke of the early days of the U.S.-China diplomatic relationship going back 40 years now. And he discussed many of the challenges that his generation of diplomats on both sides had to overcome.

22. Tonight, I cannot help but marvel at how far we have come together. These have been decades of unprecedented growth and progress for China.

23. China has lifted hundreds of millions of people out of poverty and has helped to drive global prosperity. The United States has welcomed China's growth and we have benefited from it.

24. Today, our economies are entwined and so are our futures. Relations are far broader and deeper than even Dr. Kissinger and his colleagues could have imagined all those years ago.

25. This change has brought with it our own new challenges. History teaches that often, the rise of new powers ushers in periods of conflict and uncertainty.

26. Deng Xiaoping once described China's process of reform and modernization as being like a person crossing a river by feeling his way over the stones. That is a good description of the way forward that we must chart together.

27. Over one year ago, President Obama and I met for the first time in London. We agree to work together to build a positive, cooperative and comprehensive China-US relationship for the 21st century, setting up the goal for the development of China-US

relations in the new era.

28. To our Chinese colleagues and partners, thank you for making this long journey—not only the journey you made by the airplane that brought you here, but the journey that we are making together to build a better future for our children and our grandchildren.

29. If there is one fundamental basis for confidence in this relationship today, the future of this relationship, it is in the reality that today, thousands and thousands of Americans are studying in China, and thousands and thousands of Chinese have the experience of learning more about the United States.

30. We've made a lot of progress the last two years. If you find it hard to appreciate how hard this is to do, or hard to appreciate the importance of the progress we have achieved, just think back to the breakdown in cooperation during the Great Depression that turned a severe financial crisis into a global catastrophe.

31. The record of cooperation we have built with China in this period of crisis was decisive in helping lift the world out of the fires of crisis and into a period now where we can say the world is growing again.

32. I remember, personally, vividly, the day of September 11, 2001. I was in New York on that dark day. The United Nations is committed to continue to lead this campaign with world leaders to fight against international terrorism.

33. Road crashes kill nearly 1.3 million people every year, and leave millions more injured or permanently disabled. Impaired driving, unsafe roads and other dangers shatter lives in a matter of seconds.

34. Tuberculosis and HIV/AIDS are killer diseases, together claiming more than 3.5 million lives each year, mainly in the developing world. They cause immense suffering, place a heavy burden on health care services, and carry enormous consequences for societies and economies.

35. As a result of these barriers, people with disabilities have poorer health, lower educational achievements, fewer economic opportunities, and higher rates of poverty than people without disabilities.

36. The links between HIV and disability are strong. HIV can lead to disability, and people with disabilities have also been shown to be at higher risk of becoming infected with HIV.

37. WHO stands ready to support any Member State requesting our guidance in the areas of policy development, capacity building, and technical assistance.

38. We would be pleased to work with countries wishing to improve their data, make health systems inclusive, strengthen rehabilitation services, and expand community-based rehabilitation.

39. We were also united in our resolve to protect our nation and to bring those who committed this vicious attack to justice. We quickly learned that the 9 • 11 attacks were carried out by Al Qaeda—an organization headed by Osama bin Laden, which had openly

declared war on the United States and was committed to killing innocents in our country and around the globe. And so we went to war against Al Qaeda to protect our citizens, our friends, and our allies.

40. I first went to China about 30 years ago to study Chinese. I went to Beijing. I studied for the summer at Beijing Daxue(Peking University). And at that time, that was an exceptional thing. It was a rare thing for an American to have the privilege of traveling and studying in China, and rare as well for Chinese to have the experience of studying in the United States. And of course, that is no longer a rare thing.

Additional Materials

1. Video 8 – 1: "Note-taking" from the European Union's interpreters' training course
中华人民共和国国务院总理李克强在第 13 届东亚峰会上的讲话,2018 年 11 月 15 日(全文)
2. Speech at the 13th East Asia Summit, Singapore, 15 November 2018, by H. E. Li Keqiang, Premier of the State Council of the People's Republic of China(Full text)
中文来源:新华网
http://www.xinhuanet.com/politics/leaders/2018-11/16/c_1123720563.htm
译文来源:中国日报网
https://www.chinadaily.com.cn/a/201811/16/ws5beela9ea310eff3032890d5.html
李显龙总理,各位同事:
Prime Minister Lee Hsien Loong, Colleagues,

很高兴与各位同事在"狮城"相聚,感谢新加坡政府为本次会议所做的周到安排。
It gives me great pleasure to join you in the Lion City. I wish to thank the Singapore government for its thoughtful arrangements for our summit.

新加坡作为亚洲最发达的国家之一,既有东方传统文化的深厚积淀,也吸纳了西方现代先进理念和技术,体现了东西方文明的交汇融合。新加坡的开放包容精神也是东亚峰会的重要特色。东亚峰会成立 13 年以来,已成为推动东亚地区对话合作的重要平台,为增进各方理解信任、促进地区发展繁荣发挥了重要作用。
Singapore, one of the most developed countries in Asia, stands as a fine example of mutual cultural convergence between the East and the West by retaining its rich traditional heritage of the East and embracing advanced Western ideas and technologies at the same time. The spirit of openness and inclusiveness that Singapore espouses is also an important feature of the East Asia Summit (EAS), which, over the past 13 years, has become a significant platform for dialogue and cooperation and played a substantial role in enhancing understanding and trust among participating countries and promoting development and

prosperity in the region.

当前,国际政治经济格局正经历深刻调整,世界形势中的不稳定不确定因素明显增多,全球经济增长内生动力仍然不足,保护主义、单边主义抬头,经济全球化遭遇波折,地区热点问题和恐怖主义等非传统安全威胁相互交织,谋和平、促发展的任务仍然艰巨。在这样的背景下,东亚仍然保持总体稳定局面,仍然是最具增长活力的地区,仍然被视为最具吸引力的投资热土,这既是地区国家自强不息、勇于进取的结果,也离不开各国互利合作、求同存异的努力。这些来之不易的成果值得倍加珍惜。我们要继续秉持和睦相处、合作共赢的理念,加强协商对话、推进开放发展,做东亚和平稳定的坚定维护者、经济繁荣的积极贡献者、区域合作的有力推动者。

The international political and economic landscape has been undergoing profound adjustments. Uncertainties and destabilizing factors have been on the increase, from weak global growth, rising unilateralism and protectionism, backlash against economic globalization, to regional hotspots coupled with terrorism and other non-traditional security threats. The pursuit of peace and development remains a daunting task. In such a global context, East Asia has kept overall stability and remained a most robustly growing region and a most attractive investment destination. This has been the result of both the perseverance and enterprise of countries in the region and their joint endeavors to promote mutually beneficial cooperation and seek common ground while shelving differences. Such hard-won accomplishments need to be cherished. With a renewed commitment to amicable co-existence and win-win cooperation, we will step up consultation and dialogue and pursue greater opening-up and progress in East Asia. Together, we will strive to be a vigorous facilitator of peace and stability in East Asia, leading contributor to economic prosperity, and powerful locomotive for regional cooperation.

近年来,东亚合作取得长足进展,东盟共同体建成,东盟与对话伙伴合作(10+1)、东盟与中日韩合作(10+3)、澜沧江-湄公河合作等机制不断取得丰硕成果,地区融合发展和相互贸易投资呈现显著上升势头。东亚峰会各方应抓住这一难得机遇,坚持"领导人引领的战略论坛"定位,坚持聚焦东亚、聚焦发展,坚持东盟中心地位,坚持经济发展和政治安全合作"双轮驱动",持续推进重点领域合作,为东亚合作注入新动能。中方愿在此提出几点建议:

East Asian cooperation has come a long way in recent years. We have seen ASEAN Communities being established, frameworks such ASEAN Plus One, ASEAN Plus Three and Lancang-Mekong cooperation producing fruitful results, and growing momentum of trade and investment and integrated development in the region. EAS participating countries need to seize such precious opportunities to advance cooperation in priority areas and inject fresh impetus to East Asian cooperation. We should maintain the nature of EAS as a "leaders-led strategic forum" focusing on East Asia and on development, uphold ASEAN centrality, and advance economic development and political and security cooperation in parallel as the two wheels driving EAS forward. In this connection, I wish to make the following points.

一是坚持多边主义。当今世界,各国利益相互交融,命运休戚与共,唯有践行多边主义,相互尊重、平等协商、遵守规则、携手合作,才能有效应对全球各种挑战,促进地区共同发展。我们能够战胜亚洲金融危机和国际金融危机,靠的就是大家同舟共济、守望相助,这种多边主义精神仍将是克服当前严峻复杂挑战的法宝。中国是国际秩序的维护者和多边主义的践行者,主张推动构建相互尊重、公平正义、合作共赢的新型国际关系,推动构建人类命运共同体。中国愿与各方一道,坚定维护以规则为基础的国际秩序,坚定不移发展同东亚各国友好合作,以规则守护安全、以合作促进发展,为地区和平繁荣作出应有努力。

First, we need to uphold multilateralism. In today's world where the interests and future of countries are interconnected, only by committing to multilateralism, mutual respect and consultations on an equal footing, playing by the rules and working with one another can we effectively tackle global challenges and promote common development in the region. It was the spirit of solidarity and mutual assistance that helped us overcome the Asian and international financial crises. This same spirit of multilateralism will again be vital to our efforts to prevail over the daunting challenges today. As an advocate for upholding the international order and multilateralism, China calls for the building of a new type of international relations featuring mutual respect, fairness, justice and win-win cooperation and a community with a shared future for mankind. China will work with other countries to safeguard the rules-based international order, unswervingly pursue friendship and cooperation with our East Asian neighbors, and promote security based on rules and development through cooperation. This way, we will do our part for peace and prosperity in the region.

二是维护自由贸易。自由贸易是现代经济体系的重要支柱,是国家发展繁荣的重要基石。随着全球产业链、供应链、价值链的深入发展,各国经济你中有我、我中有你,相互嵌入、彼此关联。任何自我封闭和树立壁垒的做法终将损人害己,唯有扩大市场开放和分工协作才能实现共赢。我们应着眼构建开放型世界经济,坚定支持以世贸组织为核心的多边贸易体制,不断推动贸易和投资自由化便利化,促进世界经济稳定增长。对现行世贸组织规则可以进行适当调整完善,但必须坚持自由贸易的大方向,必须充分照顾各方利益关切,必须有利于缩小南北差距。

Second, we need to promote free trade. Free trade is a vital pillar of the modern economy and bedrock for national development and prosperity. As the global industrial, supply and value chains continue to develop, countries around the world are seeing their economies mutually interlinked and integrated. In such an interdependent relationship, any attempt to close doors and raise barriers will only backfire. Greater market openness and collaboration through division of labor is the right way to achieve win-win results. We need to focus our efforts on building an open world economy, supporting the multilateral trading system centered around the WTO, advance trade and investment liberalization and facilitation and promote steady growth of the world economy. In making necessary adjustments to improve the existing WTO rules, parties should adhere to the general direction of free trade, and see to it that the adjustments will fully accommodate the interests and concerns of all players and help narrow the North-South gap.

三是加快区域经济一体化进程。战后70多年亚洲的繁荣发展,得益于经济全球化,得益于地区国家的开放合作。面向未来,东亚要保持世界经济主要引擎地位、实现更高水平发展,区域经济一体化是必由之路。当前,地区自贸安排进入加速推进期。东盟已建成经济共同体,中日韩也已分别与东盟建立自贸区,中国-东盟自贸区完成升级谈判,东亚经济共同体建设迈出积极步伐。"区域全面经济伙伴关系协定"是东亚地区最大的自贸协定,涵盖范围广、符合地区发展实际,目前谈判正处于关键时期。各方应展示政治决断,推动谈判尽快结束,早日惠及地区各国人民和企业。中方对"全面与进步跨太平洋伙伴关系协定"持开放态度,希望它生效后有利于促进东亚区域合作和包容发展。

Third, we need to accelerate regional economic integration. Over the past 70 years and more since the end of the World War II, Asia has achieved progress and prosperity thanks to economic globalization and opening-up and cooperation among countries in the region. For East Asia to keep its role as a main engine for global growth and realize a higher level of development, economic integration would be a natural choice. Regional free trade arrangements have picked up pace. ASEAN has established the AEC. China, Japan and the ROK have all established free trade areas with ASEAN. China and ASEAN have completed negotiations to upgrade their FTA. Positive steps have been taken in developing an East Asia Economic Community. The RCEP is the biggest free trade agreement in East Asia that meets the development needs of its extensive membership. At this crucial moment, what is needed is political resolve to conclude the negotiations as quickly as possible to deliver early benefits to people and businesses in the region. China holds an open attitude toward the CPTPP and hopes that when effective, it will be conducive to East Asian cooperation and inclusive development.

四是推动地区可持续发展合作。东亚地区有不少发展中国家,发展仍然是东亚国家的首要任务,改善民生需要持续关注和加大投入。今年以来,中方举办了环境资源管理、清洁能源、肿瘤防控、特殊食品等领域合作项目。各方应落实好《马尼拉行动计划》,继续推进能源与环保、教育、金融、公共卫生、灾害管理、东盟互联互通等六个重点领域合作,加强在粮食安全、减贫等领域的交流与合作。本次峰会中方参与共提新加坡倡议的《关于东盟智慧城市的声明》,推动地区国家创新合作。明年中方将继续举办新能源论坛、海事管理研讨会、清洁能源论坛和自然资源与信息共享研讨会,倡议开展地球科学领域联合研究,促进地区平衡普惠发展。

Fourth, we need to advance regional cooperation for sustainable development. Development remains the top priority of East Asian countries, many of whom are developing countries in need of sustained attention to and greater investment in people's wellbeing. This year, China has implemented cooperation projects in such areas as environment and resource management, clean energy, tumor prevention and control and special food. Continued efforts are needed to follow through on the Manila Plan of Action, advance cooperation in the six priority areas, namely, energy, education, finance, public health, environmental protection and disaster management, and ASEAN connectivity. Exchanges and cooperation on food security and poverty reduction need to be stepped up. The Statement on ASEAN Smart Cities co-sponsored by Singapore and China will facilitate innovation cooperation among countries in the region. China will host a new energy forum and a seminar on maritime management next year, and continue to hold the clean energy forum and the seminar on natural resources and information sharing. China further calls for joint studies on geosciences to promote balanced and inclusive development of the region.

五是开展政治安全对话合作。安全稳定的环境是地区繁荣发展的前提。各方应就发展战略和政策加强沟通，增进政治互信，减少疑虑误判。中方倡导共同、综合、合作、可持续的安全观，支持探讨符合地区实际的区域安全理念和架构，主张通过对话协商和平解决争端。中方愿与各方就反恐、气候变化、网络安全等领域开展非传统安全合作，支持俄罗斯提出的打击恐怖分子的声明，并于明年举办反恐联合演习，共同维护地区和平安宁。

Fifth, we need to conduct dialogue and cooperation in political and security areas. A safe and stable environment is a prerequisite for development and prosperity in the region. Parties need to increase communication on development strategies and policies to dispel misgivings, reduce misjudgment and enhance political trust. China advocates the vision on common, comprehensive, cooperative and sustainable security, supports discussions on regional security outlook and architecture that suits this region, and advocates peaceful settlement of disputes through dialogue and consultation. China will carry out non-traditional security cooperation with parties on counter-terrorism, climate change and cyber security. China supports the statement sponsored by Russia on fighting terrorism and will hold joint counter-terrorism exercises next year to promote peace and tranquility in the region.

各位同事，

Colleagues,

当前，朝鲜半岛形势出现重大积极变化。北南双方改善关系，朝美对话进程得到推进。各方应抓住机遇，加强对话协商，照顾彼此合理关切，将政治承诺转化为实际行动，向着实现半岛完全无核化和建立半岛和平机制的大方向努力，早日实现半岛长治久安。

Major positive changes have taken place on the Korean Peninsula with improved North-South relations and advancement in the dialogue process between the DPRK and the United States. Parties need to seize the opportunities to step up dialogue and consultation, accommodate each other's legitimate concerns, and convert political commitment into concrete actions in order to move toward the goal of complete denuclearization and a peace mechanism and achieve early, lasting peace on the Peninsula.

平静的南海是各方期盼所在,符合地区国家利益。中国是南海最大沿岸国,60%以上的海上货物贸易途经南海,中国坚定维护符合国际法的航行和飞越自由,比任何国家都更希望南海和平稳定。600多年前,中国航海家郑和七下西洋,开创了亚洲地区以德睦邻、和平共处的友好传统。今天,中国经济已经深度融入世界经济,中国与周边国家已形成密不可分的命运共同体,坚定奉行与邻为善、以邻为伴的周边外交方针,愿与地区国家妥善处理好南海问题,把南海建成和平之海、友谊之海、合作之海。中方致力于同东盟国家全面有效落实《南海各方行为宣言》,开展海上务实合作,积极推进"南海行为准则"磋商。

Tranquility in the South China Sea is the aspiration of all parties and serves the interests of countries in this region. China is the biggest littoral state with over 60 percent of its seaborne trade in goods passing through the South China Sea. China firmly supports the freedom of navigation and overflight pursuant to international law. China is probably more keen than any other country to see peace and stability in the South China Sea. In his seven voyages to Southeast Asia and onward over 600 years ago, the Chinese navigator Zheng He laid the foundations for a tradition of benevolence, neighborliness and peaceful coexistence among Asian countries. Today, the Chinese economy has deeply integrated into the world economy and China and its neighbors live in a closely-knit community with a shared future. China will steadfastly pursue a foreign policy of building friendships and partnerships with its neighbors. We are ready to properly manage the South China Sea issue with countries in this region to turn the South China Sea into a sea of peace, friendship and cooperation. China is committed to working with ASEAN countries to fully and effectively implement the DOC, carry out practical maritime cooperation and actively advance COC consultations.

中方致力于推进"准则"磋商的意愿是真诚的。在昨天结束的中国-东盟领导人会议上,各方同意2019年内完成单一磋商文本草案第一轮审读,中方和一些东盟国家也提出了通过中国和东盟国家共同努力争取未来3年完成"准则"磋商的愿景。相信中国和东盟国家一定能共同努力,达成符合地区实际、服务地区人民的"准则",为南海和平稳定和长治久安发挥重要作用,也希望域外国家能尊重和支持地区国家为此所作努力。

China is sincerely committed to take forward COC consultations. At the China-ASEAN Summit yesterday, all parties agreed to complete the first reading of the single draft negotiating text within 2019. And China and some ASEAN countries put forward a vision of concluding COC consultations in three years' time through the concerted efforts of China and ASEAN countries. By working together, we are confident that China and ASEAN countries will reach a COC that reflects the realities of our region, serves our peoples, and anchors peace, stability and enduring tranquility in the South China Sea. We also hope that non-regional states will respect and support these efforts by regional countries.

各位同事,

Colleagues,

今年是中国改革开放 40 周年。40 年来,中国在取得自身巨大发展成就的同时,也为东亚和世界发展进步作出积极贡献。刚刚圆满落幕的首届中国国际进口博览会,充分显示了中国主动开放市场、与各国共享发展机遇的真诚愿望和实际行动。我们将全面深化改革,实施新一轮高水平对外开放,在推动自身迈向高质量发展的同时,为世界各国提供更多发展机遇。

This year marks the 40th anniversary of China's reform and opening-up. Over the past four decades, China has made remarkable achievements and contributed its share to the development and progress in East Asia and the world beyond. The just-concluded inaugural China International Import Expo fully demonstrated China's sincere desire and voluntary steps to open up its market and share development opportunity with other countries. China will deepen reform comprehensively, advance a new round of high-standard opening-up, and move toward high-quality development. All this will only bring more opportunities to the world.

"滴水不成海,独木难成林。"中方愿与各国加强团结互信,深化对话合作,守护住地区繁荣稳定的好局面,共同开创东亚和平发展的美好未来!

As a Chinese saying goes, "A single drop of water cannot make an ocean, nor can a single tree form a forest." China will enhance solidarity and mutual trust and deepen dialogue and cooperation with all countries. Together, let us sustain the sound momentum of prosperity and stability in our region, and build an even brighter future of peace and development for East Asia.

谢谢大家。
Thank you.

Chapter IX Reproduction

Learning questions:
√ *What are the general principles for reproduction?*
√ *What strategies can be used in reproduction?*

So far in this book, we have covered the input and processing stages of CI, including listening, information processing, memory and note-taking. This chapter mainly focuses on the next stage in CI, the output stage—reproduction in the target language, also called the delivering stage or the expression stage. In this chapter, we will learn the general principles for reproduction in the target language, and some strategies used in it.

9.1 Principles for Reproduction in the Target Language

The main purpose of CI is to pass the message, or the content, of the spoken language from the source language to the target language to a given audience. Whether this purpose can be achieved depends heavily on the interpretation produced by the interpreters which happens at the reproduction stage. It is the stage where interpreters integrate all the information they have acquired from listening, processing, memorizing and note-taking, and deliver it to the audience in the target language in a clear and structured way.

Every interpreter has their own style of interpreting, but there are some general principles for reproduction.

1. Deliver the content, or the key information points of the source language

As we have discussed several times, CI is not word-for-word interpreting. Seleskovitch first put forward the idea of deverbalization in 1976. According to him, in CI, the source language should be stripped down to its language-independent sense. That means, interpreters should not pay attention to the language forms, but the meaning they carry. Therefore, interpreters should always focus on the meaning, and make what they have produced clear and easy to understand.

2. Make the target language clear and coherent

Even when speakers are speaking incoherently or unclearly, interpreters should try their best to reconstruct the coherence, and make the final interpretation logically clear and well-structured.

3. Never reproduce without understanding

Understanding is the foremost task in CI. It happens before memorizing and note-taking. Interpreters should always make sure that they understand correctly before interpreting. Otherwise, it may cause mistakes, misunderstanding, miscommunication, or even conflicts. For criteria for good interpreting, please refer back to Section 2.1.7.

4. Never fabricate

Fabricating means to invent false information in order to deceive people. Interpreters should never fabricate information in CI. It is unprofessional and it does not fit the interpreters' code of conduct. Never think that the audience does not understand the source language. There are always people who can. However, it is quite common for interpreters to miss out a word or a sentence. In these cases, do not fabricate. Simply ask the speakers to repeat or explain, or leave it out until further information comes.

9.2 Strategies Used in Reproduction in the Target Language

Generally speaking, there are two general strategies that can be used in reproduction in the target language: deverbalization and coherence reconstruction. Each involves some specific techniques.

9.2.1 Deverbalization (脱形抓意,得"意"忘"形")

As we have explained earlier, deverbalization means to deliver the sense of the source language to the audience in the target language. To achieve that, we have three techniques: explain, reworking grammatical structure of sentences and generalization and omission.

9.2.1.1 Explaining

Very often in CI, there are some expressions that the interpreters cannot find any equivalent expression due to cultural or other factors, such as culture-loaded words, metaphors, proverbs, ironies, etc. In these cases, we may need to use explanation in reproduction. Here are some examples.

[1]加大"破、立、降"力度。推进钢铁、煤炭行业市场化去产能。

We strengthened work to <u>cut ineffective supply, foster new growth drivers, and reduce costs</u> in the real economy. We made progress in using market mechanisms to cut capacity in the steel and coal industries.

[2]乡村振兴战略有力实施,粮食总产量保持在<u>1.3万亿斤</u>以上。

The rural revitalization strategy was implemented with vigor; grain output was kept above <u>650 million metric tons</u>.

[3]我们要乘着新时代的<u>浩荡东风</u>,加满油,把稳舵,鼓足劲。

We should ride on the mighty driving force of the new era with full steam, steady helmsmanship and strong morale.

[4]亚洲合作需要百尺竿头、更进一步。

We need to build on past success and make new progress in promoting cooperation in Asia.

[5]Last month, 20,000 migrant children were illegally brought into the United States—a dramatic increase. These children are used as human pawns by vicious coyotes and ruthless gangs.

上个月,2万名移民儿童被非法带入美国,人数急剧增长。这些孩子被恶毒的蛇头和残酷的帮派拿来利用。

In the first example,"破、立、降"is a concept that Chinese may understand, but if we literally interpret it as "cut, foster and reduce", people of other cultures may be confused. Here the interpret used simple explanation to make the concept more understandable. The second example also has a Chinese concept "斤" which people from other countries may not be able to comprehend. Here the interpreter switched "斤" to "吨", which is an internationally accepted measurement. Of course, this requires the interpreters to be familiar with the measurement system and to be fast in calculation.

In Examples [3]-[5],"东风""百尺竿头" and "vicious coyotes" are all not interpreted directly as "east wind""a hundred feet bamboo stick" or "土狼", which may make no sense or sound weird for the audience. Instead, the intepreters used explanation to make the reproduction more acceptable and understandable to the audience. More examples can be found in Section 5.2.2.2 of this book.

9.2.1.2 Reworking Grammatical Structure of Sentences

As we have explained in Section 2.1.6.2 of this book, Chinese is Parataxis(意合) while English is hypotaxis(形合). This means very often we cannot interpret the same sentence in similar sentence structures in the target language. So we need to rework on the grammatical structure by changing word or sentence order, changing voice, part of speech or negation, or breaking or connecting sentences. The following are some examples.

[1]三大攻坚战开局良好。防范化解重大风险,宏观杠杆率趋于稳定,金融运行总体平稳。

The three critical battles got off to a good start. We forestalled and defused major risks. The macro leverage ratio trended toward a stable level; the financial sector was generally stable.

[2]统筹城乡区域发展,良性互动格局加快形成。乡村振兴战略有力实施,粮食总产量保持在1.3万亿斤以上。

We pursued balanced development across rural and urban areas and regions and sped up the formation of a pattern of positive interplay. The rural revitalization strategy was implemented with vigor; grain output was kept above 650 million metric tons.

[3]我们要以更大的力度、更实的措施保障改善民生,加强和创新社会治理,坚决打赢脱贫攻坚战,促进社会公平正义,在幼有所育、学有所教、劳有所得、病有所医、老有所养、住有所居、

弱有所扶上不断取得新进展,让实现全体人民共同富裕在广大人民现实生活中更加充分地展示出来。

We will devote more energy and take more concrete measures in ensuring and improving people's living standards, strengthening and developing new approaches to social governance, resolutely winning the battle against poverty, promoting social fairness and justice, making steady progress in ensuring people's access to childcare, education, employment, medical services, elderly care, housing, and social assistance, so as to better demonstrate the realization of common prosperity for everyone in people's real life.

[4]维护国家主权和领土完整,实现祖国完全统一,是全体中华儿女的共同愿望,是中华民族根本利益所在。

It is the shared aspiration of all Chinese people and in the fundamental interests of the Chinese nation to safeguard China's sovereignty and territorial integrity and realize China's complete reunification.

[5] We met today in Washington, D. C. to launch a new phase in the relationship between the United States and the European Union—a phase of close friendship, of strong trade relations in which both of us will win, of working better together for global security and prosperity, and of fighting jointly against terrorism.

我们今天在华盛顿特区会见,以启动美国与欧盟之间关系的新阶段——一种为实现双方共赢的有力经贸合作,以更好地为全球安全与繁荣而共同努力、共同打击恐怖主义的密切关系。

In the above examples, Example [1] is a typical Chinese parataxis structure where there is no subject. In English, however, subject should be added. In Example [2], the Chinese sentences use active voice to express passive meaning. So in interpreting, they were switched to passive voice. Example 3 is a good example of changing the part of speech in interpreting. Example 4 is an example of changing the entire sentence structure. Example 5 is an example of changing the position of attributives in interpreting. These changes are all made to make the sentences more understandable to the target audience.

9.2.1.3 Generalization and Omission

Generalization and omission means that sometimes in CI, the source language may be heavily-loaded with information, too much that the interpreters simply cannot handle in a limited time. In this case, interpreters can choose to keep the essential message, and generalize the given information or leave out some redundant or unimportant information. This is especially true with SI, negociations, private talks or with impromptus speeches. The following are some examples:

[1]联合国反对所有大规模杀伤性武器,这包括放射性武器、生物武器、化学武器、氢弹、裂变式原子弹、中子弹、燃烧弹、毒理学武器等多种高致命性杀伤性武器。

The United Nations is against all kinds of weapons of mass destruction, including the most lethal ones such as radioactive, biological, chemical weapons, etc.

[2]……在幼有所育、学有所教、劳有所得、病有所医、老有所养、住有所居、弱有所扶上不

断取得新进展。

... making steady progress in <u>ensuring people's access to childcare, education, employment, medical services, elderly care, housing, and social assistance</u>.

[3]总而言之,我感谢所有的亲人和朋友多年来的陪伴,我会继续做好我自己,<u>不会离开大家。姚明和朋友们永远在一起</u>! 谢谢大家。

In short, I want to thank everyone who has accompanied me these years. And I will continue to do my best and <u>will continue to be with everyone</u>. Thank you.

The above examples all involve certain degree of generalization and omission. Example [1] omitted some of the names of the weapons, many of which are hard to interpret, and generalized them as "etc." Example [2] generalizes all the "有所" into "ensuring people's access to..." Example [3] omitted one sentence which expresses basically the same meaning as the previous one.

Generalization and omission are only used when too much information can be handled. They should not be done if they violate the original meaning or leave out important information.

9.2.2 *Coherence Reconstruction* (连贯重建)

Coherence refers to the quality of being logical and consistent. In CI, sometimes, the speakers may not be speaking in the most coherent way. Their speeches, especially the unprepared ones, could be semi-coherent or incoherent. They could be illogical, unclear or confusing. In such cases, we may need to reconstruct the coherence in reproduction to make it clearer and more understandable to the audience. Generally speaking, there are two techniques that we can use to reconstruct coherence: rearranging ideas and adding logical connectors.

9.2.2.1 **Rearranging Ideas**

By rearranging ideas in the source language, we can make the target language sounds more logical.

[1]推进西部开发、东北振兴、中部崛起、东部率先发展,<u>出台一批改革创新举措</u>。

<u>A full range of reforms and innovative measures were introduced to</u> advance development in the western region, revitalize the northeast, energize the central region, and support the eastern region in spearheading development.

[2]Part of the problem stems from the simple fact that <u>the determinants of health have become broader and much more complex</u> in a world where not only countries, but also policy spheres are closely interconnected.

部分问题来源于这样一个简单事实:当今世界,各国和各政策领域之间相互关联密切,<u>因而健康的决定因素也更为广泛、更为复杂</u>。

In the first example, there is no clear logical connection between the two parts of the sentence in the source language, Chinese. But in the target language, English, "a full range of..." was put in front to introduce purpose. This fits the target audience' way of understanding better because English is a hypotaxis language that put emphasis on logical connections.

The second example is also a good one to show the different thinking habit of the speakers of Chinese and English. English tends to put the result first before illustrating the reasons, while Chinese prefer to state the reasons first before coming to the result.

By rearranging the ideas, the final reproduction can be more acceptable to the audience.

9.2.2.2 Adding Logical Connectors

By adding logical connectors, the reproduction in the target language will sound more smooth, and more logically clear.

[1]我们隆重庆祝改革开放40周年,深刻总结改革开放的伟大成就和宝贵经验,郑重宣示在新时代将改革开放进行到底的坚定决心,激励全国各族人民接续奋斗,再创新的历史伟业。

We solemnly commemorated the 40th anniversary of reform and opening up, thoroughly reviewed its great achievements and the valuable experience gained in its pursuit, and pledged our resolve to see reform and opening up through in the new era, thus galvanizing the Chinese people of all ethnic groups to continue their hard work to make new historic achievements.

[2]我们要以更大的力度、更实的措施保障改善民生,加强和创新社会治理,坚决打赢脱贫攻坚战,促进社会公平正义,在幼有所育、学有所教、劳有所得、病有所医、老有所养、住有所居、弱有所扶上不断取得新进展,让实现全体人民共同富裕在广大人民现实生活中更加充分地展示出来。

We will devote more energy and take more concrete measures in ensuring and improving people's living standards, strengthening and developing new approaches to social governance, resolutely winning the battle against poverty, promoting social fairness and justice, making steady progress in ensuring people's access to childcare, education, employment, medical services, elderly care, housing, and social assistance, so as to better demonstrate the realization of common prosperity for everyone in people's real life.

[3]We need to make changes and they need to be made now: we need to defeat the Islamist extremism by turning people's mind away from this violence and make them understand that our values—pluralistic British values—are superior to anything offered by the preachers and supporters of hate. We need to work with allied democratic governments to reach international agreements that regulate cyberspace to prevent the spread of extremist and terrorism planning. The whole of our country needs to come together to take on this extremism. And we need to review Britain's counter-terrorism strategy to make sure the police and security services have all the powers they need.

我们现在就必须要做出改变:第一,要通过让人们不再关注暴力,崇尚多元化的英国价值观而不是那些灌输仇恨的价值观之时,我们才能战胜极端伊斯兰主义;第二,我们需要与盟国达成共识来监管互联网,防止恐怖分子借用互联网策划恐怖袭击;第三,整个英国应当团结起来共同对抗极端伊斯兰主义;第四,我们需要重新审视英国的反恐政策,从而让警察和安全部门拥有他们所需要的权力。

As shown in the above three examples, logical connectors such as "thus""so as to" and "第一""第二" can make the logic clearer. It is not required in all interpreting though. Without them, the reproduction may still work.

Exercises and Practice

9-1　Explain to your partner the general principles of CI reproduction.

9-2　Interpret the following sentences or passages by using the strategies we have learned. (Audio 9-2 CN, Audio 9-2 En)

1. 我们将为外国投资者建立"一条龙"服务中心,提供审批业务。

2. 所谓中国盗窃美国军事机密的问题可以说是天方夜谭。

3. "三资企业"对我国经济有着较大影响。

4. 污染防治得到加强,细颗粒物(PM2.5)浓度继续下降,生态文明建设成效显著。

5. 坚持在发展中保障和改善民生,改革发展成果更多更公平惠及人民群众。针对外部环境变化给就业带来的影响,及时出台稳就业举措。

6. As the saying goes, "Rome was not built in one day."

7. It gives me a great pleasure to join you for this important initiative as the UN marks its 70th anniversary.

8. Many air pollutants also cause global warming. Black carbon is one such example. Produced by diesel engines, burning trash and dirty cookstoves, it is extremely harmful when inhaled.

9. I thank those who are willing to speak out against terrorism every day. Your voices matter, and your courage in the face of adversity is a lesson to us all.

10. Supporting victims and their families is a moral imperative, based on promoting, protecting and respecting their human rights.

Additional Materials

1. "合作应对气候变化,建设全球生态文明"——习近平主席特别代表、国务委员兼外交部长王毅在联合国气候行动峰会上的发言,2019 年 9 月 23 日,联合国总部(全文)

"A Joint Response to Climate Change, A Better Environment for Our Planet"-Remarks by H. E. Wang Yi, Special Representative of President Xi Jinping, State Councilor and Minister of Foreign Affairs at the UN Climate Action Summit, UN Headquarters, 23 September 2019 (Full text)

中文来源:外交部网站
https://www.fmprc.gov.cn/web/ziliao_674904/zyjh_674906/t1700637.shtml

译文来源:外交部英文网站
https://www.fmprc.gov.cn/mfa_eng/wjdt_665385/zyjh_665391/t1700987.shtml

尊敬的古特雷斯秘书长，
尊敬的各位国家元首和政府首脑，
女士们，先生们：

Your Excellency Secretary-General Antonio Guterres,
Your Excellencies Heads of State and Government,
Ladies and Gentlemen,

中方高度赞赏和支持古特雷斯秘书长倡议举办这次峰会。
China highly commends and supports the Secretary-General's initiative for convening this Summit.

气候变化是各国面临的共同挑战。合力应对气候变化，保护我们赖以生存的地球家园，关系到人类未来的命运。
Climate change is a common challenge to all countries. To jointly tackle this challenge and protect the planet we all call home will be a journey critical to the future and destiny of humankind.

当前，全球气候治理进入关键阶段。国际社会应牢牢把握应对气候变化的正确方向，坚持信念不动摇，力度不降低。
As global climate governance enters a crucial stage, the international community must stick to the right approach, that is, making a joint response to climate change with unwavering commitment and unrelenting efforts. In tackling climate change, we must:

——应对气候变化，要有必胜的决心。我们要恪守承诺，落实好《巴黎协定》及其实施细则，推动本次峰会和《联合国气候变化框架公约》第25次缔约方会议取得积极成果，为2020年后应对气候变化多边进程注入新的动力。个别国家的退群改变不了国际社会的共同意志，也不可能逆转国际合作的历史潮流。
—First, be determined to win the fight. We must honor our commitments, follow through on the Paris Agreement and its implementation guidelines, and see to it that both this Summit and the COP25 produce positive outcomes that will inject fresh impetus into the post-2020 multilateral process. The withdrawal of certain parties will not shake the collective will of the international community, nor will it possibly reverse the historical trend of international cooperation.

——应对气候变化，要有行动的恒心。应对气候变化和实现发展不是非此即彼的选择题。我们要把应对气候变化与促进经济社会发展有机结合这篇大文章做好，在加快发展的进程中实现绿色低碳转型，提升应对气变的韧性。要调动全社会力量和资源，强化2020年前行动力度,不向2020年后转嫁责任。

——Second, be prepared to take sustained actions. A response to climate change does not have to be made at the expense of development. We must make sure that our climate actions are mutually reinforcing with our socio-economic endeavors, realize a transformation toward green and low-carbon development and enhance climate resilience in the process of accelerating development. We must mobilize stakeholders and resources across all sectors to scale up pre-2020 to avoid passing on the responsibilities to the post-2020 process.

——应对气候变化,要有合作的诚心。应对气候变化必须坚持多边主义,在"公约"(指《联合国气候变化框架公约》)和《巴黎协定》框架下讨论和解决问题。尤其要恪守"共同但有区别的责任"、公平和各自能力原则,尊重发展中国家的发展需要和特殊国情,帮助发展中国家提升应对能力。发达国家应承担率先减排义务,履行到2020年每年动员1000亿美元的承诺。

——Third, be committed to cooperation. The joint fight against climate change requires us to uphold multilateralism and explore solutions within the framework of the UNFCCC and the Paris Agreement. In particular, it is important that we follow the principles of "common but differentiated responsibilities", equity and respective capabilities, respect the need for development and the special conditions of developing countries, and help them build preparedness. Developed countries, on their part, need to take the lead in reducing emissions and honor their commitment of mobilizing US $ 100 billion a year in climate finance by 2020.

女士们,先生们!
Ladies and Gentlemen,

作为国际社会的负责任一员,中国言必信、行必果,在应对气候变化的征程中不断迈出新步伐。
As a responsible member of the international community, China honors its words and keeps taking actions on climate change.

中国践行创新、协调、绿色、开放、共享的发展理念,着力促进经济实现高质量发展,决心走绿色、低碳、可持续发展之路。2018年,中国单位GDP二氧化碳排放比2005年下降45.8%,超额完成了当年的目标,相当于减少二氧化碳排放约52.6亿吨。同年,非化石能源占一次能源消费比重达14.3%,森林蓄积量比2005年增加45.6亿立方米。2000年以来,全球新增绿化面积约四分之一来自中国。2018年,中国新能源汽车新增125万辆,这一数字在全球遥遥领先。中国已启动全国碳排放交易体系,积极推进全国碳排放权交易市场建设,为控制温室气体排放、加速产业结构升级提供助力。

Guided by a philosophy of innovative, coordinated, green, open and shared development, China is pursuing high-quality growth and following a path of green, low-carbon and sustainable development. In 2018, China's CO_2 emissions per unit of GDP dropped by 45.8 percent from the 2005 level, or a reduction of around 5.26 billion tons of

CO_2 emissions, exceeding the target set for the year; the share of non-fossil fuel in primary energy consumption reached 14.3 percent; forest stock increased by 4.56 billion cubic meters from 2005, as a result of new afforestation in China since 2000, which accounts for 25 percent of the global total; and a total of 1.25 million electric vehicles were sold in China, far more than in any other country. A national emission trading system has been introduced, and the development of a national emission trading market is well underway. Such efforts have proved helpful to controlling greenhouse gas emissions and upgrading the industrial structure.

中国将认真履行《联合国气候变化框架公约》和《巴黎协定》义务,如期实现提交给气变公约秘书处的自主贡献目标。

China will faithfully fulfill our obligations under the UNFCCC and the Paris Agreement, and realize as scheduled its nationally determined contribution targets submitted to the UNFCCC secretariat.

中国将坚持共建绿色"一带一路",实施"一带一路"应对气候变化南南合作计划,通过"一带一路"绿色发展国际联盟等平台,为应对气候变化国际合作汇聚更多力量。

We will continue to promote joint building of a green Belt and Road. We are implementing the Belt and Road South-South Cooperation Initiative on Climate Change, and mobilizing stronger support for international cooperation against climate change through the BRI International Green Development Coalition and other platforms.

女士们,先生们,

Ladies and Gentlemen,

"基于自然的解决方案"是此次峰会9大行动领域之一。应古特雷斯秘书长邀请,中国和新西兰担任该领域牵头国,会同相关国家和国际组织一道,推动该领域取得了丰硕成果。

Nature-Based Solutions (NBS) is one of the nine action tracks of this Summit. China is honored to co-lead this track with New Zealand at the invitation of the Secretary-General. Through collaborating with many other countries and international organizations in this area, we gained fruitful results in the following aspects.

一是为深入理解人与自然关系带来新视角。人与自然是生命共同体,我们需要尊重自然、顺应自然、保护自然。"基于自然的解决方案"倡导人与自然和谐共生,重视生态文明建设,将可持续利用自然资源纳入应对气候变化政策和行动框架,最大限度发挥自然的促进作用,增强应对气候变化的有效性。

First, a deeper insight into the relations between man and nature. Human beings and nature are inseparable. We need to respect, adapt to, and protect nature. NBS advocates the harmonious co-existence between man and nature, values ecological progress, and incorporates the sustainable use of natural resources into climate policies and action frameworks, thus leveraging the role of nature to the fullest extent possible in enhancing the effectiveness of climate actions.

二是为全球应对气候变化行动提出新举措。我们提出林业、农业、海洋、水资源、全生态系统等领域150多个行动倡议,并建立"基于自然的解决方案"之友机制推动后续落实,巩固相关领域国际合作势头,致力于发挥自然系统每年减少100~120亿吨二氧化碳的减缓潜力。

Second, new measures for the global fight against climate change. We have proposed over 150 initiatives in such areas as forestry, agriculture, ocean, water resources, and the systemic role of nature, and set up a Group of Friends for NBS mechanism for follow-ups to keep up the momentum of international cooperation in these areas. Our goal is to achieve nature's mitigation potential of cutting 10 to 12 gigatons of CO_2 per year.

三是为实现可持续发展目标提供新支持。绿水青山就是金山银山,改善生态环境就是发展生产力。我们汇编了森林碳汇、生物多样性保护、荒漠化防治等30余个示范案例,展现出"基于自然的解决方案"推动经济、社会、环境协调发展所产生的巨大综合效益。相信这些案例将给各国提供有益借鉴,以更好落实2030年可持续发展议程。

Third, fresh support for the Sustainable Development Goals. The Chinese often say that green is as precious as gold. In other words, a better environment can bring about greater productivity. We have collected over 30 best practices in forest carbon sink, bio-diversity protection, and desertification prevention and treatment to demonstrate how NBS can significantly promote coordinated economic, social and environmental development. I believe that those best practices will provide useful references for countries to better implement the 2030 Agenda for Sustainable Development.

女士们,先生们,

Ladies and Gentlemen,

应对气候变化,道阻且长,但行则将至。无论国际风云如何变幻,中国积极应对气候变化的行动不变,与各国深化气候合作的意愿不变,推动气候多边进程的努力不变。我相信,只要各国勠力同心,就一定能建成一个清洁美丽、共同繁荣、命运与共的美好世界!

Long and difficult as the journey of tackling climate change is, sustained actions will take us to the destination. No matter how the international landscape may evolve, there will be no change in China's efforts to fight climate change, its readiness to deepen climate cooperation with other countries, or its commitment to the multilateral process on climate change. I am convinced that by working together as one and in the same direction, we will build a clean and beautiful world where we enjoy shared prosperity and shared future.

谢谢大家。

Thank you.

2. 中华人民共和国国务院总理李克强在 2019 年中国北京世界园艺博览会闭幕式上的讲话,2019 年 10 月 9 日,北京。(全文)

Remarks by H. E. Li Keqiang, Premier of the State Council of the People's Republic of China at the Closing Ceremony of the International Horticultural Exhibition 2019 Beijing China, Beijing, 9 October 2019. (Full text)

中文来源:外交部网站
https://www.fmprc.gov.cn/web/ziliao_674904/zyjh_674906/t1706843.shtml
译文来源:外交部英文网站
https://www.fmprc.gov.cn/mfa_eng/wjdt_665385/zyjh_665391/t1706851.shtml

尊敬的各位政府首脑、副首脑和夫人,
尊敬的国际展览局秘书长和国际园艺生产者协会主席,
尊敬的各国使节,各位国际组织代表,
女士们,先生们,朋友们:

Your Excellencies Heads of Government, Deputy Heads of Government and Spouses,
Your Excellencies Secretary General of the Bureau International des Expositions and President of the International Association of Horticultural Producers,
Diplomatic Envoys and Representatives of International Organizations,
Ladies and Gentlemen,
Friends,

从芳菲春日到斑斓金秋,历时 5 个多月的 2019 年中国北京世界园艺博览会即将圆满落下帷幕。我谨代表中国政府和中国人民,对本届世园会的成功举办表示衷心祝贺!对支持和参与北京世园会的各国朋友表示诚挚感谢!对前来参加闭幕式的各位嘉宾表示热烈欢迎!

Spanning five-plus months from balmy spring to golden autumn, the International Horticultural Exhibition 2019 Beijing China is now drawing to a successful close. On behalf of the Chinese government and people, I wish to express warm congratulations on the success of the Expo and heartfelt appreciation to friends from across the world for their support and participation. My warm welcome goes to all the distinguished guests attending tonight's closing ceremony.

本次世园会以"绿色生活,美丽家园"为主题,精彩纷呈、成果丰硕。全球 110 个国家和国际组织、120 多个非官方参展方积极响应,是历史上参展方最多的一届世园会。

This Expo, under the theme of "Live Green, Live Better", has been a spectacular and fruitful event, attracting a record participation of 110 countries and international organizations, and over 120 non-official participants.

在 4 月 28 日举行的世园会开幕式上,中国国家主席习近平倡导共同建设美丽地球家园、构建人类命运共同体。这是一场文明互鉴的绿色盛会,100 余场国家日和荣誉日、3000 多场民族民间文化活动,促进了各国文明交流、民心相通和绿色合作。这是一场创新荟萃的科技盛会,世界园艺前沿技术成果悉数登台,展现了绿色科技应用的美好前景。这是一场走进自然的体验盛会,近千万中外访客走进世园会,用心感受环保与发展相互促进、人与自然和谐共处的美好。

At the opening ceremony on 28 April, President Xi Jinping called for a joint endeavor in building a better homeland and a community with a shared future for mankind. The Expo has celebrated the achievements of green development by different countries and cultures. The over 100 National Day and Honor Day events, and 3,000-odd ethnic and folk culture activities have boosted cultural exchanges, friendship and green cooperation among participating countries. The Expo has showcased the latest progress of innovation in science and technology. The cutting-edge horticultural technologies on full display herald a bright future of green technology application. The Expo has provided up-close experiences with Mother Nature. Here, nearly ten million visitors from China and abroad have seen with their own eyes how environmental protection and development advance in parallel, and humans and nature coexist in harmony.

女士们,先生们,朋友们!
Ladies and Gentlemen, Friends,

几天前,我们隆重庆祝了中华人民共和国成立 70 周年。70 年来,中国人民筚路蓝缕、砥砺奋进,经济社会发展取得举世瞩目的成就,生态文明建设实现历史性的进展。进入新世纪以来,全球绿化面积增加 5%,其中四分之一的贡献来自中国。

Just several days ago, we celebrated the 70th anniversary of the founding of the People's Republic. In the past seven decades, with the hard work and fortitude of the Chinese people, China has made historic progress in economic and social domains and in ecological conservation. Since the beginning of the new century, of the five percent increase in the global green leaf area, one quarter has come from China.

中国仍然是世界上最大的发展中国家,将继续坚持以经济建设为中心,把发展作为解决一切问题的基础和关键。中国面临发展经济、改善民生、加强生态环境保护的繁重任务,将坚持统筹兼顾,在改革开放中协同推动经济高质量发展和生态环境高水平保护,坚定走生产发展、生活富裕、生态良好的文明发展道路。

That said, China remains the biggest developing country in the world. We will continue to put economic development front and center, and promote development as the underpinning force for tackling all challenges. Facing the daunting tasks of growing the economy, improving people's lives and enhancing environmental protection, we will stick to a holistic approach to pursue both high-quality economic development and high-standard environmental protection through reform and opening-up. We will stay on the path of sustainable development featuring advanced production, higher living standards and healthy ecosystems.

我们将加快转变发展方式,持续推动绿色发展,优化经济结构,发挥创新引领发展第一动力作用,加快培育新动能,大力发展节能环保产业和循环经济,倡导绿色低碳消费,以更低的资源消耗推动经济社会持续健康发展。

We will consistently pursue green development by accelerating the shift of the growth model and improving our economic structure. Harnessing innovation, the primary driving force for development, we will foster new drivers of growth at a faster pace, and boost the development of energy-saving and environment-friendly industries and a circular economy. Green and low-carbon consumption will be encouraged, and we will aim for sustained and sound economic and social progress with less resource input.

我们将努力促进绿色惠民,坚决打好污染防治攻坚战,着力解决突出的环境问题,推进人居环境建设,抓好基础性、经常性、长远性工作,推进重要生态系统保护和修复工程,让人民群众享有美丽宜居的环境。

We will work to deliver a greener and better life to the people by resolutely tackling pollution and resolving acute environmental problems. We will improve the living environment, with a focus on addressing fundamental, recurrent and long-term challenges, push forward the protection and restoration of key ecosystems, and provide the people with a more beautiful and livable environment.

我们将不断加强绿色合作,支持和践行多边主义,坚持共同但有区别的责任原则、公平原则和各自能力原则,积极履行应对气候变化《巴黎协定》。加强生态文明领域交流合作,推动成果分享,力所能及地帮助发展中国家培育绿色经济、实现可持续发展。

We will further enhance green cooperation. We will continue to support and follow a multilateral approach, stick to the principles of common but differentiated responsibilities, equity and respective capabilities, and actively implement the Paris Agreement on climate change. We will bolster exchanges and cooperation on ecological conservation and promote the sharing of best practices to help other developing countries, to the best of our ability, to grow a green economy and realize sustainable development.

女士们,先生们,朋友们!
Ladies and Gentlemen, Friends,

刚才,我同各国领导人参观了世园会部分展区,可谓步步如画、处处皆景。希望这些美丽的景色越来越多地出现在中国乃至世界的各个地方。期待国际社会共同努力,为子孙后代建设一个美丽的地球家园。让我们携起手来,推动人与自然和谐发展,共创人类美好未来。

As I walked around the Park with other leaders earlier in the evening, I was deeply impressed by the picturesque sceneries. I cannot help but hope that such a charming sight can be seen in more places across China and the world. It behooves us all in the international community to build and leave to our children and grandchildren a beautiful planet to live in. Let us join hands to promote harmony between man and nature and bring a better future to the human race.

现在我宣布,2019年中国北京世界园艺博览会闭幕!
I now declare close the International Horticultural Exhibition 2019 Beijing China!

MODULE III   THEME-BASED CI TRAINING

Chapter X Consecutive Interpreting Materials for Different Themes

In this chapter, we will employ all the skills we have learned so far and train comprehensively. We will provide training materials on six most commonly seen CI themes: politics and diplomacy, economy and trade, education and cultural exchange, science and technology, sports and health, and environment and terrorism.

However, the training materials provided by this book are far from enough for CI training. Learners should read and listen extensively and train intensively, and polish their CI skills on a daily basis.

10.1 Politics and Diplomacy

1. 习近平主席在第十三届全国人民代表大会第一次会议上的讲话,2018年3月20日(有删减)

Speech delivered by Xi Jinping at the first session of the 13th NPC, March 20, 2018 (Reduced version)

中文来源:中国政府网

www.gov.cn/gongbao/content_5286355.htm

译文来源:中国日报网

https://www.chinadailyasia.com/articles/184/187/127/1521628772832.html

各位代表,这次大会选举我继续担任中华人民共和国主席,我对各位代表和全国各族人民给予我的信任,表示衷心的感谢!

担任中华人民共和国主席这一崇高职务,使命光荣,责任重大。我将一如既往,忠实履行宪法赋予的职责,忠于祖国,忠于人民,恪尽职守,竭尽全力,勤勉工作,赤诚奉献,做人民的勤务员,接受人民监督,决不辜负各位代表和全国各族人民的信任和重托!

Fellow deputies, I was elected at this session to continue to serve as the President of the People's Republic of China (PRC). I would like to express my heartfelt gratitude to the trust placed on me by all deputies and Chinese people of all ethnic groups.

It is a glorious mission and weighty responsibility to take on this great position of PRC President. I will, as always, faithfully fulfill my responsibilities empowered by the Constitution, be loyal to the motherland and the people, perform my duty scrupulously, do all my best, be diligent at work, and stay devoted and dedicated. I will continue to serve as a servant of the people, accept supervision by the people, and will absolutely

一切国家机关工作人员,无论身居多高的职位,都必须牢记我们的共和国是中华人民共和国,始终要把人民放在心中最高的位置,始终全心全意为人民服务,始终为人民利益和幸福而努力工作。

各位代表!人民是历史的创造者,人民是真正的英雄。波澜壮阔的中华民族发展史是中国人民书写的!博大精深的中华文明是中国人民创造的!历久弥新的中华民族精神是中国人民培育的!中华民族迎来了从站起来、富起来到强起来的伟大飞跃是中国人民奋斗出来的!

今天,中国人民比历史上任何时期都更接近、更有信心和能力实现中华民族伟大复兴。我相信,只要13亿多中国人民始终发扬这种伟大梦想精神,我们就一定能够实现中华民族伟大复兴!

各位代表!人民有信心,国家才有未来,国家才有力量。中国特色社会主义进入了新时代,勤劳勇敢的中国人民更加自信自尊自强。中国这个古老而又现代的东方大国朝气蓬勃、气象万千,中国特色社会主义道路、理论、制度、文化焕发出强大生机活力,奇迹正在中华大地上不断涌现。我们对未来充满信心。

我们要适应我国发展新的历史

not betray the great trust from all deputies and Chinese people of all ethnic groups.

No matter how high a position one holds, all personnel of state organs should keep firmly in mind that our republic is the People's Republic of China, always put the people in the most prominent place in their hearts, always serve the people wholeheartedly, and always work hard for the people's interests and happiness.

Fellow deputies, people are the creators of history; people are real heroes. The magnificent development history of the Chinese nation was written by the Chinese people! The extensive and profound Chinese civilization was created by the Chinese people! The spirit of the Chinese nation, which has been kept fresh and alive throughout history, was cultivated by the Chinese people! The endeavor of the Chinese people has led to a tremendous transformation of the Chinese nation: it has stood up, grown rich, and is becoming strong!

Today, we are closer, more confident, and more capable than ever before in making the goal of national rejuvenation a reality. I believe that as long as more than 1.3 billion Chinese people keep carrying forward this great spirit of pursuing dreams, we can and will realize the great rejuvenation of the Chinese nation.

Fellow deputies, only when people have faith, will the nation have a bright future and strength. Now socialism with Chinese characteristics has entered a new era, the hard-working, brave Chinese people have shown more confidence, self-respect and self-improvement. China, a nation in the East that is both ancient and modern, is full of vigor and undergoes great changes. The path, theory, system and culture of socialism with Chinese characteristics have radiated with great vitality, while miracles keep happening in our land. We have full confidence in our future.

We should adapt ourselves to the new historic

Chapter X Consecutive Interpreting Materials for Different Themes

方位,紧扣我国社会主要矛盾的变化,高举中国特色社会主义伟大旗帜,全面贯彻党的十九大和十九届二中、三中全会精神,坚持以马克思列宁主义、毛泽东思想、邓小平理论、"三个代表"重要思想、科学发展观、新时代中国特色社会主义思想为指导,坚持稳中求进工作总基调,坚持以人民为中心的发展思想,统揽伟大斗争、伟大工程、伟大事业、伟大梦想,统筹推进"五位一体"总体布局,协调推进"四个全面"战略布局,奋力开创新时代中国特色社会主义事业新局面!

我们的目标是,到本世纪中叶把我国建成富强民主文明和谐美丽的社会主义现代化强国。

我们要以更大的力度、更实的措施全面深化改革、扩大对外开放,贯彻新发展理念,推动经济高质量发展,建设现代化经济体系,不断增强我国经济实力、科技实力、综合国力,让社会主义市场经济的活力更加充分地展示出来。

我们要以更大的力度、更实的措施发展社会主义民主,坚持党的领导、人民当家作主、依法治国有机统一,建设社会主义法治国家,推进国家治理体系和治理能力现代化,巩固和发展最广泛的爱国统一战

juncture for the development of our country, act in response to the evolution of the principal contradiction in Chinese society, uphold the great banner of socialism with Chinese characteristics, fully implement the spirit of the 19th CPC National Congress and the second and third plenary sessions of the 19th CPC Central Committee. We should follow the guide of Marxism-Leninism, Mao Zedong Thought, Deng Xiaoping Theory, the Theory of Three Represents, the Scientific Outlook on Development, and the Thought on Socialism with Chinese Characteristics for a New Era. We should remain committed to the underlying principle of pursuing progress while ensuring stability, stick to the people-centered development vision, plan great struggle, great project, great cause, and great dream as a whole, ensure coordinated implementation of the five-sphere integrated plan, and the four-pronged comprehensive strategy, so as to break a new ground for the cause of socialism with Chinese characteristics for the new era.

Our goal is to build China into a great modern socialist country that is prosperous, strong, democratic, culturally advanced, harmonious, and beautiful by the middle of the century.

We will devote more energy and take more concrete measures in deepening reform in all areas, expanding opening up, applying a new vision of development, promoting high-quality economic development and developing a modernized economy to increase China's economic and technological strength, and composite national strength, so as to better demonstrate the vitality of the socialist market economy.

We will devote more energy and take more concrete measures in developing socialist democracy, upholding the unity of Party leadership, the running of the country by the people, and law-based governance, building a country of socialist rule of law, promoting the modernization of China's system

线,确保人民享有更加广泛、更加充分、更加真实的民主权利,让社会主义民主的优越性更加充分地展示出来。

我们要以更大的力度、更实的措施加快建设社会主义文化强国,培育和践行社会主义核心价值观,推动中华优秀传统文化创造性转化、创新性发展,让中华文明的影响力、凝聚力、感召力更加充分地展示出来。

我们要以更大的力度、更实的措施保障和改善民生,加强和创新社会治理,坚决打赢脱贫攻坚战,促进社会公平正义,在幼有所育、学有所教、劳有所得、病有所医、老有所养、住有所居、弱有所扶上不断取得新进展,让实现全体人民共同富裕在广大人民现实生活中更加充分地展示出来。

我们要以更大的力度、更实的措施推进生态文明建设,加快形成绿色生产方式和生活方式,着力解决突出环境问题,使我们的国家天更蓝、山更绿、水更清、环境更优美,让绿水青山就是金山银山的理念在祖国大地上更加充分地展示出来。

我们要坚持党对人民军队的绝对领导,全面贯彻新时代党的强军思想,不断推进政治建军、改革强军、科技兴军、依法治军,加快形成

and capacity for governance, consolidating and developing the broadest possible patriotic united front, to ensure that people enjoy the democratic rights in a broader, fuller and more genuine way, so as to better demonstrate the strength of socialist democracy.

We will devote more energy and take more concrete measures in developing a great socialist culture in China, cultivating and observing core socialist values, and promoting the creative evolution and innovative development of fine traditional Chinese culture, so as to better demonstrate the influence of the Chinese civilization, and its power to unite and ability to inspire.

We will devote more energy and take more concrete measures in ensuring and improving people's living standards, strengthening and developing new approaches to social governance, resolutely winning the battle against poverty, promoting social fairness and justice, making steady progress in ensuring people's access to childcare, education, employment, medical services, elderly care, housing, and social assistance, so as to better demonstrate the realization of common prosperity for everyone in people's real life.

We will devote more energy and take more concrete measures to advance the building of an ecological civilization, accelerate efforts to develop green production and ways of life, and work harder to tackle prominent environmental problems. We will make the skies of our country more blue, mountains more green, waters more clear and the environment more beautiful so that the concept that lucid waters and lush mountains are invaluable assets is better demonstrated on the great land of our country.

We will stick to the absolute leadership of the CPC over the people's armed forces and fully implement the Party's thinking on strengthening the military for the new era. We will continue to enhance

Chapter X Consecutive Interpreting Materials for Different Themes

中国特色、世界一流的武装力量体系,构建中国特色现代作战体系,推动人民军队切实担负起党和人民赋予的新时代使命任务。

我们要全面准确贯彻"一国两制"、"港人治港"、"澳人治澳"、高度自治的方针,严格依照宪法和基本法办事,支持特别行政区政府和行政长官依法施政、积极作为,支持香港、澳门融入国家发展大局,增强香港、澳门同胞的国家意识和爱国精神,维护香港、澳门长期繁荣稳定。我们要坚持一个中国原则,坚持"九二共识",推动两岸关系和平发展,扩大两岸经济文化交流合作,同台湾同胞分享大陆发展的机遇,增进台湾同胞福祉,推进祖国和平统一进程。

维护国家主权和领土完整,实现祖国完全统一,是全体中华儿女的共同愿望,是中华民族根本利益所在。在这个民族大义和历史潮流面前,一切分裂祖国的行径和伎俩都是注定要失败的,都会受到人民

the political loyalty of the armed forces, strengthen them through reform and technology, and run them in accordance with law. We will act more quickly to put into place the system of world-class armed forces with Chinese characteristics. We will create a modern combat system with distinctive Chinese characteristics. Our armed forces must be up to shouldering the missions and tasks of the new era entrusted to them by the Party and the people.

We will fully and faithfully implement the policies of "one country, two systems", "the people of Hong Kong governing Hong Kong", "the people of Macao governing Macao", and a high degree of autonomy for both regions. It is imperative to act in strict compliance with China's Constitution and the basic laws of the two special administrative regions. We will support the governments and chief executives of both regions in exercising law-based governance and pursuing endeavors. We will support Hong Kong and Macao in integrating their own development into the overall development of the country. We will foster greater patriotism and a stronger sense of national identity among the people in Hong Kong and Macao. We will maintain long lasting prosperity and stability in Hong Kong and Macao. We must uphold the onE - China principle, stick to the 1992 Consensus, promote peaceful development of cross-Straits relations and expand cross-Straits economic and cultural exchanges and cooperation. We are ready to share the development opportunities on the mainland with our Taiwan compatriots, improve the wellbeing of Taiwan compatriots and advance the process toward the peaceful reunification of China.

It is the shared aspiration of all Chinese people and in the fundamental interests of the Chinese nation to safeguard China's sovereignty and territorial integrity and realize China's complete reunification. In front of the great national interests and the tide of history, any actions and tricks to split

的谴责和历史的惩罚！中国人民有坚定的意志、充分的信心、足够的能力挫败一切分裂国家的活动！中国人民和中华民族有一个共同信念，这就是：我们伟大祖国的每一寸领土都绝对不能也绝对不可能从中国分割出去！

中国将继续积极参与全球治理体系变革和建设，为世界贡献更多中国智慧、中国方案、中国力量，推动建设持久和平、普遍安全、共同繁荣、开放包容、清洁美丽的世界，让人类命运共同体建设的阳光普照世界！

新时代属于每一个人，每一个人都是新时代的见证者、开创者、建设者。只要精诚团结、共同奋斗，就没有任何力量能够阻挡中国人民实现梦想的步伐！

我们要乘着新时代的浩荡东风，加满油，把稳舵，鼓足劲，让承载着13亿多中国人民伟大梦想的中华巨轮继续劈波斩浪、扬帆远航，胜利驶向充满希望的明天！谢谢大家。

China are doomed to fail. They are certain to meet with the people's condemnation and the punishment by the history. The Chinese people have the resolve, the confidence, and the ability to defeat secessionist attempts in any form! The Chinese people and the Chinese nation share a common belief that it is never allowed and it is absolutely impossible to separate any inch of territory of our great country from China!

China will continue to actively participate in the evolution and construction of the global governance system. China will contribute more Chinese wisdom, Chinese solutions and Chinese strength to the world, to push for building an open, inclusive, clean, and beautiful world that enjoys lasting peace, universal security, and common prosperity. Let the sunshine of a community with a shared future for humanity illuminate the world!

The new era belongs to everyone, and we are all its witnesses, creators and builders. No force can stop Chinese people's march toward realizing their dreams as long as we unite as one and strive together!

We should ride on the mighty driving force of the new era with full steam, steady helmsmanship and strong morale. The giant steamer of Chinese nation bearing the great dreams of the 1.3-billion-plus Chinese people hence will keep summoning difficulties and forging ahead, and setting sail for a long voyage into a future full of hopes successfully! Thank you.

2. 习近平主席在博鳌亚洲论坛2013年年会开幕式上的主旨演讲（有删减）
President Xi Jinping's keynote speech (reduced version) at the opening plenary of the Boao Forum for Asia Annual Conference 2013 on Sunday in South China's Hainan province

中文来源：中国政府网
www.gov.cn/ldhd/2013-04/07/content_2371801.htm
译文来源：中国日报网
https://www.chinadaily.com.cn/china/2013-04/07/content_16381450.htm

Chapter X Consecutive Interpreting Materials for Different Themes

尊敬的各位元首、政府首脑、议长、国际组织负责人、部长，博鳌亚洲论坛理事会各位成员，各位来宾，女士们，先生们，朋友们！

椰风暖人，海阔天高。在这美好的季节里，同大家相聚在美丽的海南岛，参加博鳌亚洲论坛2013年年会，我感到十分高兴。首先，我谨代表中国政府和人民，并以我个人的名义，向各位朋友的到来，表示诚挚的欢迎！对年会的召开，表示热烈的祝贺！

12年来，博鳌亚洲论坛日益成为具有全球影响的重要论坛。在中国文化中，每12年是一个生肖循环，照此说来，博鳌亚洲论坛正处在一个新的起点上，希望能更上一层楼。本届年会以"革新、责任、合作：亚洲寻求共同发展"为主题，很有现实意义。相信大家能够充分发表远见卓识，共商亚洲和世界发展大计，为促进本地区乃至全球和平、稳定、繁荣贡献智慧和力量。

当前，国际形势继续发生深刻复杂变化。世界各国相互联系日益紧密、相互依存日益加深，遍布全球的众多发展中国家、几十亿人口正在努力走向现代化，和平、发展、合作、共赢的时代潮流更加强劲。同时，天下仍很不太平，发展问题依然突出，世界经济进入深度调整期，整体复苏艰难曲折，国际金融领域仍然存在较多风险，各种形式的保护主义上升，各国调整经济结构面临

Your Excellencies, Heads of State and Government, Speakers of Parliament, Heads of International Organizations, Ministers, Members of the Board of Directors of the Boao Forum for Asia, Distinguished Guests, Ladies and Gentlemen, Dear Friends,

In this balmy season with clear sky and warm, coconut-scented breeze, I am so glad to meet all of you at the Annual Conference 2013 of the Boao Forum for Asia here in Hainan, a picturesque island embraced by the vast ocean. Let me begin by extending, on behalf of the Chinese government and people and also in my own name, a heartfelt welcome to you and warm congratulations on the opening of the Annual Conference of the Boao Forum.

In the past 12 years since its birth, the Boao Forum for Asia has become an important forum with growing global influence. In the Chinese culture, 12 years form a zodiac cycle. In this sense, the Boao Forum has reached a new starting point and I hope it will scale an even greater height. The theme of the current annual conference, namely, "Asia Seeking Development for All: Restructuring, Responsibility and Cooperation", is a highly relevant one. I hope you will engage in an in-depth discussion on promoting development in Asia and beyond and thus contributing, with your vision and commitment, to peace, stability and prosperity in Asia and the world at large.

The world today is experiencing profound and complex changes. Countries have become increasingly inter-connected and inter-dependent. Several billion people in a large number of developing countries are embracing modernization. The trend of the times, namely, peace, development, cooperation and mutual benefit, is gaining momentum. On the other hand, our world is far from peaceful. Development remains a major challenge; the global economy has entered a period of profound readjustment, and its recovery remains elusive. The

不少困难,全球治理机制有待进一步完善。实现各国共同发展,依然任重而道远。

亚洲是当今世界最具发展活力和潜力的地区之一,亚洲发展同其他各大洲发展息息相关。亚洲国家积极探索适合本国情况的发展道路,在实现自身发展的同时有力促进了世界发展。亚洲与世界其他地区共克时艰,合作应对国际金融危机,成为拉动世界经济复苏和增长的重要引擎,近年来对世界经济增长的贡献率已超过50%,给世界带来了信心。亚洲同世界其他地区的区域次区域合作展现出勃勃生机和美好前景。

当然,我们也清醒地看到,亚洲要谋求更大发展、更好推动本地区和世界其他地区共同发展,依然面临不少困难和挑战,还需要爬一道道的坡、过一道道的坎。

亚洲发展需要乘势而上、转型升级。对亚洲来说,发展仍然是头等大事,发展仍然是解决面临的突出矛盾和问题的关键,迫切需要转变经济发展方式、调整经济结构,提高经济发展质量和效益,在此基础上不断提高人民生活水平。

亚洲稳定需要共同呵护、破解难题。亚洲稳定面临着新的挑战,

international financial sector is fraught with risks, protectionism of various forms is on the rise, countries still face many difficulties in adjusting economic structure, and the global governance mechanisms call for improvement. Achieving common development for all countries remains an uphill battle.

Asia is one of the most dynamic and most promising regions in the world, and its development is closely connected with the development of other continents. The Asian countries have energetically explored development paths suited to their national conditions and greatly boosted global development through their own development. Working side by side with the rest of the world in time of difficulty to tackle the international financial crisis, Asia has emerged as an important engine driving world economic recovery and growth. In recent years, Asia has contributed to over 50 percent of global growth, instilling much needed confidence in the world. What is more, Asia's cooperation with other regions of the world at regional and sub-regional levels has great vitality and promising prospects.

But we should also be keenly aware that Asia still faces many difficulties and challenges in boosting both its own development and joint development with other regions. The road ahead remains a bumpy and twisting one.

Asia needs to transform and upgrade its development model in keeping with the trend of the times. Sustaining development is still of paramount importance to Asia, because only development holds the key to solving major problems and difficulties it faces. It is important that we should shift the growth model, adjust the economic structure, make development more cost effective and make life better for our people.

We need to make concerted efforts to resolve major difficulties to ensure stability in Asia. Stability

Chapter X Consecutive Interpreting Materials for Different Themes

热点问题此起彼伏,传统安全威胁和非传统安全威胁都有所表现,实现本地区长治久安需要地区国家增强互信、携手努力。

亚洲合作需要百尺竿头、更进一步。加强亚洲地区合作的机制和倡议很多,各方面想法和主张丰富多样,协调各方面利益诉求,形成能够保障互利共赢的机制需要更好增进理解、凝聚共识、充实内容、深化合作。

女士们、先生们、朋友们!
人类只有一个地球,各国共处一个世界。共同发展是持续发展的重要基础,符合各国人民长远利益和根本利益。我们生活在同一个地球村,应该牢固树立命运共同体意识,顺应时代潮流,把握正确方向,坚持同舟共济,推动亚洲和世界发展不断迈上新台阶。

女士们、先生们、朋友们!中国是亚洲和世界大家庭的重要成员。中国发展离不开亚洲和世界,亚洲和世界繁荣稳定也需要中国。

亲仁善邻,是中国自古以来的传统。亚洲和世界和平发展、合作共赢的事业没有终点,只有一个接一个的新起点。中国愿同五大洲的朋友们携手努力,共同创造亚洲和世界的美好未来,造福亚洲和世界

in Asia now faces new challenges, as hotspot issues keep emerging, and both traditional and non-traditional security threats exist. The Asian countries need to increase mutual trust and work together to ensure durable peace and stability in our region.

We need to build on past success and make new progress in promoting cooperation in Asia. There are many mechanisms and initiatives for enhancing cooperation in Asia, and a lot of ideas on boosting such cooperation are being explored by various parties. What we need to do is to enhance mutual understanding, build consensus, and enrich and deepen cooperation so as to strike a balance among the interests of various parties and build mechanisms that bring benefits to all.

Ladies and Gentlemen, Dear Friends,

Mankind has only one earth, and it is home to all countries. Common development, which is the very foundation of sustainable development, serves the long-term and fundamental interests of all the people in the world. As members of the same global village, we should foster a sense of community of common destiny, follow the trend of the times, keep to the right direction, stick together in time of difficulty and ensure that development in Asia and the rest of the world reaches new highs.

Ladies and Gentlemen, Dear Friends, China is an important member of the Asian family and the global family. China cannot develop itself in isolation from the rest of Asia and the world. On their part, the rest of Asia and the world cannot enjoy prosperity and stability without China.

Promoting good neighborliness is a time-honored tradition of China. To enhance peaceful development and win-win cooperation in Asia and the world is a race that has one starting point after another and knows no finishing line. We in China are ready to join hands with friends from across the world in a

人民!

最后,预祝年会取得圆满成功!谢谢大家!

concerted effort to create a bright future for both Asia and the world and bring benefit to the Asian people and the people around the world.

In conclusion, I wish the Boao Forum for Asia Annual Conference 2013 every success!

3. U. S. President Trump's speech (reduced version) on border issues
特朗普就边境安全问题的讲话(有删减)
(中文及译文全文:美国之音网<https://www.51voa.com/Voa_English_Learning/president-donald-j-trumps-address-nation-crisis-border-81204.html>)

My fellow Americans: Tonight, I am speaking to you because there is a growing humanitarian and security crisis at our southern border.

Every day, Customs and Border Patrol agents encounter thousands of illegal immigrants trying to enter our country. We are out of space to hold them, and we have no way to promptly return them back home to their country.

America proudly welcomes millions of lawful immigrants who enrich our society and contribute to our nation. But all Americans are hurt by uncontrolled, illegal migration. It strains public resources and drives down jobs and wages. Among those hardest hit are African Americans and Hispanic Americans.

Our southern border is a pipeline for vast quantities of illegal drugs, including meth, heroin, cocaine, and fentanyl. Every week, 300 of our citizens are killed by heroin alone, 90 percent of which floods across from our southern border. More Americans will die from drugs this year than were killed in the entire Vietnam War.

In the last two years, ICE officers made 266,000 arrests of aliens with criminal records, including those charged or convicted of 100,000 assaults,

我的美国同胞们,今晚我向你们讲话,因为在我们的南部边境正有一场越来越严重的人道和安全危机。

每一天,海关与边境巡逻人员遇到数以千计试图进入我国的非法移民。我们没有容纳他们的空间了。我们没有办法立即把他们送回本国。

美国自豪地欢迎数以百万计的合法移民,他们使我们的社会更加丰富,为我们的国家作出贡献。但是,不受控制的非法移民伤害了所有美国人。它给公共资源带来压力,压低就业和工资。受害最严重的包括非洲裔美国人和拉美裔美国人。

我们的南部边境是大量非法药物的输送渠道,包括冰毒、海洛因、可卡因和芬太尼。每个星期,仅仅海洛因就造成我们300名公民的死亡,90%的海洛因通过南部边境涌入。今年,死于毒品的美国人将超过整个越南战争期间被打死的美国人。

过去两年来,移民与海关执法局人员逮捕了266 000有刑事犯罪记录的外国人,包括那些被指控或

30,000 sex crimes, and 4,000 violent killings. Over the years, thousands of Americans have been brutally killed by those who illegally entered our country, and thousands more lives will be lost if we don't act right now.

This is a humanitarian crisis—a crisis of the heart and a crisis of the soul.

Last month, 20 000 migrant children were illegally brought into the United States—a dramatic increase. These children are used as human pawns by vicious coyotes and ruthless gangs. One in three women are sexually assaulted on the dangerous trek up through Mexico. Women and children are the biggest victims, by far, of our broken system.

This is the tragic reality of illegal immigration on our southern border. This is the cycle of human suffering that I am determined to end.

My administration has presented Congress with a detailed proposal to secure the border and stop the criminal gangs, drug smugglers, and human traffickers. It's a tremendous problem. Our proposal was developed by law enforcement professionals and border agents at the Department of Homeland Security. These are the resources they have requested to properly perform their mission and keep America safe. In fact, safer than ever before.

The proposal from Homeland Security includes cutting-edge technology for detecting drugs, weapons, illegal contraband, and many other things. We have requested more agents, immigration judges, and bed space to process the sharp rise in unlawful migration fueled by our very strong economy. Our plan also contains an urgent request for humanitarian assistance and medical support.

Furthermore, we have asked Congress to close border security loopholes so that illegal immigrant children can be safely and humanely returned back home.

判定犯有10 000项攻击罪、30 000项性犯罪和4000项暴力杀人罪的人。多年来,数以千计的美国人被那些非法进入我国的人所残杀,如果我们不立刻采取行动,还会有数以千计的人失去生命。

这是一场人道危机,一场触及人心的危机,一场触及灵魂的危机。

上个月,20 000名移民儿童被非法带入美国,人数急剧增长。这些孩子被恶毒的蛇头和残酷的帮派拿来利用。三分之一的妇女在通过墨西哥的危险旅途中受到性侵。妇女和儿童是我们失灵的系统最大的受害者,远超过任何人。

这是我们南部边界非法移民的悲惨现实。我决心要制止这种人类痛苦的循环。

我的政府已向国会提出了详细的建议,以确保边境安全并制止犯罪帮派、毒品走私者和人口拐卖者。这是一个严重的问题。我们的建议是由国土安全部的专业执法人员和边境人员制定的。这些是他们要求得到的资源,以恰当履行使命并保护美国安全。事实上,是让美国比所有时候更安全。

国土安全部的建议包括使用先进技术,用来侦测毒品、武器、非法违禁物和其他很多物品。我们要求能有更多的执法人员、移民法官和床位,以受理急剧上升的非法移民,我们非常强劲的经济助长了这种上升。我们的方案还包括得到紧急人道协助和医疗支持。

此外,我们已要求国会堵住边境安全的漏洞,以便安全和人道地把非法移民儿童送回他们的国家。

Finally, as part of an overall approach to border security, law enforcement professionals have requested $5.7 billion for a physical barrier. At the request of Democrats, it will be a steel barrier rather than a concrete wall. This barrier is absolutely critical to border security. It's also what our professionals at the border want and need. This is just common sense.

　The border wall would very quickly pay for itself. The cost of illegal drugs exceeds $500 billion a year—vastly more than the $5.7 billion we have requested from Congress. The wall will also be paid for, indirectly, by the great new trade deal we have made with Mexico.

　The federal government remains shut down for one reason and one reason only: because Democrats will not fund border security.

　My administration is doing everything in our power to help those impacted by the situation. But the only solution is for Democrats to pass a spending bill that defends our borders and re-opens the government.

　Some have suggested a barrier is immoral. Then why do wealthy politicians build walls, fences, and gates around their homes? They don't build walls because they hate the people on the outside, but because they love the people on the inside. The only thing that is immoral is the politicians to do nothing and continue to allow more innocent people to be so horribly victimized.

　Over the last several years, I've met with dozens of families whose loved ones were stolen by illegal immigration. I've held the hands of the weeping mothers and embraced the grief-stricken fathers. So sad. So terrible. I will never forget the pain in their eyes, the tremble in their voices, and the sadness gripping their souls.

　How much more American blood must we shed before Congress does its job?

最后，作为边境安全整体措施的一部分，专业执法人员要求拨款57亿美元，修建实体屏障。在民主党人的要求下，这将是一道钢铁屏障，而不是水泥墙。这道屏障对边界安全绝对至关重要。这也是我们的专业执法人员所希望和需要的。这完全是常识。

　边界墙很快将收回成本。每年，非法药物的代价就超过5000亿美元，远远超过我们要求国会提供的57亿美元。这道墙将永远由我们与墨西哥达成的新的、很棒的贸易协议来间接支付。

　联邦政府仍处在关闭状态，一个原因，而且唯一的原因就是民主党人不为边境安全拨款。

　我的政府正在尽我们的一切能力来帮助那些受到这一局面影响的人。但是危机的解决办法是民主党人通过一项议案，保护我们的边境并让政府重新开门。

　有些人认为竖起一道屏障是不道德的。那为什么有钱的政界人士在他们家周围修建围墙、围栏和大门？他们建墙不是因为他们恨外面的人，而是因为他们爱里面的人。唯一不道德的事情就是政界人士无所作为，持续让更多无辜的民众受到可怕的伤害。

　在过去几年中，我和数十个家庭见过面，他们亲爱的家人的生命被非法移民夺走了。我握过满脸泪痕的母亲的手，拥抱过伤心欲绝的父亲。太悲伤了。太可怕了。我永远不会忘记他们痛苦的眼神、颤抖的声音和悲痛的灵魂。

　我们还要让多少美国人流血，国会才会做自己的本职工作？

To every member of Congress: Pass a bill that ends this crisis.

To every citizen: Call Congress and tell them to finally, after all of these decades, secure our border.

This is a choice between right and wrong, justice and injustice. This is about whether we fulfill our sacred duty to the American citizens we serve.

When I took the Oath of Office, I swore to protect our country. And that is what I will always do, so help me God.

Thank you and goodnight.

我想对国会每位成员说,请通过结束这场危机的法案。

我想对每位公民说,给国会打电话,告诉他们在过去了这几十年之后,让我们终于能有边境安全。

这事关是与非、正义与非正义的抉择。这事关我们能否对我们所服务的美国公民履行自己的神圣使命。

当我宣誓就职时,我誓言保护我们的国家。我将一直这样做。愿神助我。

谢谢你们,晚安。

10.2 Economy and Trade

1. 习近平主席在 G20 领导人汉堡峰会上关于世界经济形势的讲话,2017 年 7 月 8 日(全文)

President Xi Jinping's speech at Hamburg Summit on the world economic situation July 8, 2017 (Full text)

中文来源:外交部网站

https://www.fmprc.gov.cn/web/ziliao_674904/zyjh_674906/t1476375.shtml

译文来源:

http://www.China.org.cn/world/2017-07/08/content_41176936.htm

尊敬的默克尔总理,各位同事:

汉堡被誉为"世界桥城"。很高兴同大家在这里相聚,共商架设合作之桥、促进共同繁荣大计。首先,我谨对默克尔总理及德方的热情周到接待,表示衷心感谢。

当前,世界经济出现向好势头,有关国际组织预计,今年世界经济有望增长 3.5%。这是近年来最好的经济形势。有这样的局面,同二十国集团的努力分不开。同时,世界经济中的深层次问题尚未解决,

Chancellor Merkel, Dear colleagues,

It is a great pleasure to be with you in Hamburg, the City of Bridges, to discuss ways of building a bridge of cooperation to advance our shared prosperity. First of all, I express heartfelt appreciation to you, Chancellor Merkel, and the German government for your warm hospitality.

The global economy is showing signs of moving in the right direction. The related international organizations forecast that it will grow by 3.5 percent this year, the best performance that we have seen in several years. This would not be possible without the efforts of the G20. On the other hand,

仍然面临诸多不稳定不确定因素。

面对挑战,杭州峰会提出了二十国集团方案:建设创新、活力、联动、包容的世界经济。汉堡峰会把"塑造联动世界"作为主题,同杭州峰会一脉相承。我们要共同努力,把这些理念化为行动。这里,我愿谈几点意见。

第一,我们要坚持建设开放型世界经济大方向。这是二十国集团应对国际金融危机的重要经验,也是推动世界经济增长的重要路径。国际组织当前调高世界经济增长预期,一个重要原因就是预计国际贸易增长2.4%、全球投资增加5%。我们要坚持走开放发展、互利共赢之路,共同做大世界经济的蛋糕。作为世界主要经济体,我们应该也能够发挥领导作用,支持多边贸易体制,按照共同制定的规则办事,通过协商为应对共同挑战找到共赢的解决方案。

第二,我们要共同为世界经济增长发掘新动力。这个动力首先来自创新。研究表明,全球95%的工商业同互联网密切相关,世界经济正在向数字化转型。我们要在数字经济和新工业革命领域加强合作,共同打造新技术、新产业、新模式、新产品。这个动力也来自更好解决发展问题,落实2030年可持续发展议程。这对发展中国家有利,也将为发达国家带来市场和投资机遇,

the global economy is still plagued by deep-seated problems and faces many uncertainties and destabilizing factors.

Facing such challenges, the G20 agreed in Hangzhou last year on the path forward: building an innovative, invigorated, interconnected and inclusive world economy. This year, building on the theme of the Hangzhou Summit, the Hamburg Summit has made "Shaping an Interconnected World" its theme. What we need to do now is to work together to translate our vision into action. With this in mind, I wish to state the following:

Firstly, we should stay committed to building an open global economy. This commitment of the G20 to build open economies saw us through the global financial crisis, and this commitment is vital to reenergizing the global economy. Various international organizations have revised upward forecast for this year's global growth, mainly because of a projected 2.4 percent growth for global trade and 5 percent growth for global investment. We must remain committed to openness and mutual benefit for all so as to increase the size of the global economic "pie". As the world's major economies, we should and must lead the way, support the multilateral trading system, observe the jointly established rules and, through consultation, seek all-win solutions to common challenges we face.

Secondly, we should foster new sources of growth for the global economy. Innovation, more than anything else, is such a new source of growth. Research shows that 95 percent of the world's businesses are now closely linked with the Internet, and the global economy is transitioning toward a digital economy. This means we should boost cooperation in digital economy and the new industrial revolution and jointly develop new technologies, new industries, new business models and new products. Another source of growth derives from making

大家都是赢家。杭州峰会就创新和发展达成重要共识,有关合作势头在德国年得以延续,下一步要不断走深、走实。

第三,我们要携手使世界经济增长更加包容。当前,世界经济发展仍不平衡,技术进步对就业的挑战日益突出。世界经济论坛预计,到2020年,人工智能将取代全球逾500万个工作岗位。二十国集团的一项重要使命,就是本着杭州峰会确定的包容增长理念,处理好公平和效率、资本和劳动、技术和就业的矛盾。要继续把经济政策和社会政策有机结合起来,解决产业升级、知识和技能错配带来的挑战,使收入分配更加公平合理。二十国集团应该更加重视在教育培训、就业创业、分配机制上交流合作。这些工作做好了,也有利于经济全球化健康发展。

第四,我们要继续完善全球经济治理。国际金融危机爆发以来,二十国集团在加强宏观政策协调、改革国际金融机构、完善国际金融监管、打击避税等方面取得积极成果,为稳定金融市场、促进经济复苏

greater efforts to address the issue of development and implement the 2030 Agenda for Sustainable Development, and such efforts will both benefit developing countries and generate business and investment opportunities for developed countries. In other words, this will be a win-win game for all. At the Hangzhou Summit last year, we reached important consensus on innovation and development. This momentum of cooperation created has been sustained this year under the German chairmanship of G20. Going forward, we should see that more substantial and concrete outcomes are delivered.

Thirdly, we should work together to achieve more inclusive global growth. Currently, global economic growth is not balanced, and technological advances work against job creation. According to the projection of the World Economic Forum, artificial intelligence will take away more than 5 million jobs in the world by 2020. The G20 has an important mission, which is to reaffirm the vision of pursuing inclusive growth agreed upon at the Hangzhou Summit last year, and strike a balance between fairness and efficiency, between capital and labor, and between technology and employment. To achieve this goal, we must ensure synergy between economic and social policies, address the mismatch between industrial upgrading and knowledge and skills, and ensure more equitable income distribution. The G20 needs to place more importance on cooperation in education, training, employment, business start-up and wealth distribution-related mechanisms, as progress on these fronts will make economic globalization work better.

Fourthly, we should continue improving global economic governance. In the wake of the global financial crisis, the G20 has done a lot to improve macroeconomic policy coordination, reform international financial institutions, tighten international financial regulation and combat tax

作出了重要贡献。下一步,我们要在上述领域继续努力,特别是要加强宏观政策沟通,防范金融市场风险,发展普惠金融、绿色金融,推动金融业更好服务实体经济发展。

不久前,中国成功举办"一带一路"国际合作高峰论坛。与会各方本着共商、共建、共享精神,在促进政策沟通、设施联通、贸易畅通、资金融通、民心相通上取得丰硕成果,努力打造治理新理念、合作新平台、发展新动力。这同二十国集团的宗旨高度契合。

德国谚语说,一个人的努力是加法,一个团队的努力是乘法。让我们携手合作,推动联动增长,促进共同繁荣,不断向着构建人类命运共同体的目标迈进!

谢谢大家。

avoidance, thus ensuring financial market stability and recovery. We should build on these achievements. In particular, we should strengthen coordination of macroeconomic policies, forestall risks in financial markets and develop financial inclusion and green finance to make the financial sector truly drive the development of the real economy.

China recently hosted a successful Belt and Road Forum for International Cooperation. Acting in the spirit of extensive consultation, joint contribution and shared benefits, the forum participants achieved fruitful outcomes in terms of boosting the connectivity of policies, infrastructure, trade, finance and people. Guided by a new vision of governance, we built a new platform of cooperation to tap into new sources of growth. The commitment of the Belt and Road Forum is highly compatible with the goal of the G20.

A German saying goes to the effect that, "Those who work alone, add; those who work together, multiply." In this spirit, let us work together to promote interconnected growth for shared prosperity and build toward a global community with a shared future.

Thank you.

2. 习近平主席在第八轮中美战略与经济对话和第七轮中美人文交流高层磋商联合开幕式上的讲话,2016年6月6日(有删减)

President Xi Jinping's speech (reduced version) at the opening ceremony of the eighth round of the China-US Strategic and Economic Dialogue(SED), June 6, 2016

中文来源:外交部网站

https://www.fmprc.gov.cn/web/ziliao_674904/zyjh_674906/t1369845.shtml

译文来源:中国驻美大使馆网站

http://www.China-embassy.org/eng/zgyw/t1370191.htm

克里国务卿,雅各布·卢财长,各位来宾,女士们,先生们,朋友们:

Secretary of State John Kerry, Secretary of the Treasury Jacob Lew, Distinguished Guests, Ladies and Gentlemen, Friends,

Chapter X Consecutive Interpreting Materials for Different Themes

今天,第八轮中美战略与经济对话和第七轮中美人文交流高层磋商在北京举行。首先,我对对话和磋商的开幕,表示衷心的祝贺!对远道而来的美国朋友,表示热烈的欢迎!

3年前的这个时节,我同奥巴马总统在安纳伯格庄园举行会晤,双方同意加强战略沟通,拓展务实合作,妥善管控分歧,努力构建中美新型大国关系。

一分耕耘,一分收获。3年耕耘,我们有了不少收获。在双方努力下,中美两国在双边、地区、全球层面众多领域开展合作,推动两国关系发展取得新成果。两国贸易额和双向投资达到历史新高,人文和地方交流更加密切,网络、执法等领域合作和两军交往取得新进展。两国发表了3个气候变化联合声明,同国际社会一道推动达成具有历史意义的《巴黎协定》。两国在朝鲜半岛核、伊朗核、阿富汗、叙利亚等热点问题上也保持了有效沟通和协调。这些合作给中美双方带来了实实在在的利益,也有力促进了亚太地区及世界和平、稳定、发展。

3年的成果来之不易,也给了我们很多启示,最根本的一条就是双方要坚持不冲突不对抗、相互尊重、合作共赢的原则,坚定不移推进中美新型大国关系建设。这个选择

Today, the eighth round of the China-US Strategic and Economic Dialogue (SED) and the seventh round of the China-US High-level Consultation on People-to-People Exchange (CPE) are held here in Beijing. Let me begin by extending hearty congratulations on the opening of the SED and the CPE and a big welcome to American friends who have traveled all the way to China.

Almost around this time three years ago, President Obama and I met at the Annenberg Estate where agreement was reached for the two sides to step up strategic communication, expand practical cooperation, properly manage differences and work vigorously to build a new model of major-country relationship between China and the United States.

Hard work pays off, and our efforts over the past three years have come to fruition. Thanks to our concerted efforts, our two countries have cooperated at the bilateral, regional and global levels in a wide range of areas, registering new progress in our relations. We witnessed record highs in trade and two-way investment, enjoyed closer people-to-people and sub-national exchanges, and made new headway in cooperation in cyberspace, law enforcement and military-to-military exchanges. We issued three joint statements on climate change, and worked together with other countries for the conclusion of the historic Paris Agreement. We maintained effective communication and coordination on hotspot issues like the Korean nuclear issue, the Iranian nuclear issue, and Afghanistan and Syria. Such cooperation has brought tangible benefits to both countries and given a strong boost to peace, stability and development of the Asia-Pacific and beyond.

What we achieved over the past three years has not come by easily, and could well serve as guide for the growth of China-US relations in the time to come. Most important, I believe, is that the two sides need to stay committed to the principles of non-

符合中美两国人民根本利益,也是各国人民普遍愿望。无论国际风云如何变幻,我们都应该坚持这个大方向,毫不动摇为之努力。

现在,我们正处在一个快速发展变化的世界里。世界多极化、经济全球化、社会信息化深入推进,各种挑战层出不穷,各国利益紧密相连。零和博弈、冲突对抗早已不合时宜,同舟共济、合作共赢成为时代要求。作为世界上最大的发展中国家、最大的发达国家和前两大经济体,中美两国更应该从两国人民和各国人民根本利益出发,勇于担当,朝着构建中美新型大国关系的方向奋力前行。

我们要增强两国互信。中国人历来讲究"信"。2000多年前,孔子就说:"人而无信,不知其可也。"信任是人与人关系的基础、国与国交往的前提。我们要防止浮云遮眼,避免战略误判,就要通过经常性沟通,积累战略互信。这个问题解决好了,中美合作基础就会更加坚实,动力就会更加强劲。

我们要积极拓展两国互利合作。建交37年来,中美合作内涵和

confrontation, non-conflict, mutual respect and win-win cooperation, and work steadily toward this new model of major-country relations, for this is a choice that meets the fundamental interests of both the Chinese and American people as well as the wish of all people in the world. Whatever changes in the international landscape, we need to stay on track and work unswervingly toward this overarching goal.

We now live in a world of rapid development and changes. The move toward multi-polarity, the increasing trend of globalization, and the quick application of information technologies have all been accompanied by growing challenges of various sorts, and have brought countries even closer than ever before. It is a time when ideas of zero-sum game and conflicts and confrontation must give way to common development and win-win cooperation. It thus falls upon China and the US, the largest developing and developed country respectively, and the two largest economies in the world, to act in the fundamental interests of our people and people of the world, and move steadily forward along the path of building this new model of major-country relationship.

China and the US need to increase mutual trust. For the Chinese, trust is always something to be cherished. In the word of Confucius, who lived over 2,000 years ago, a man without trust can hardly accomplish anything. Trust stands as the basis of relationship among people, and provides a prerequisite for state-to-state exchanges. For China and the US, we need to maintain frequent communication and build up strategic mutual trust in order to avoid strategic misjudgment and prevent temporary problems from affecting our overall relations. With sufficient mutual trust, China-US cooperation will stand on a more solid basis and enjoy even more robust growth.

China and the US need to expand mutually-beneficial cooperation. Over the past 37 years since

外延不断扩大,两国人民从中受益。要秉持共赢理念,不断提高合作水平。当前,要着力加强宏观经济政策协调,同有关各方一道推动二十国集团领导人杭州峰会取得积极成果,向国际社会传递信心,为世界经济注入动力。要全力争取早日达成互利共赢的中美投资协定,打造经贸合作新亮点。要深化两国在气候变化、发展、网络、反恐、防扩散、两军、执法等领域交流合作,加强双方在重大国际和地区以及全球性问题上的沟通和协调,给两国人民带来更多实际利益,为世界和平、稳定、繁荣提供更多公共产品。

我们要妥善管控分歧和敏感问题。中美两国各具特色,历史、文化、社会制度、民众诉求等不尽相同,双方存在一些分歧是难以避免的。世界是多样的,没有分歧就没有世界。一个家庭里还经常有这样那样的分歧。有了分歧并不可怕,关键是不要把分歧当成采取对抗态度的理由。有些分歧是可以通过努力解决的,双方应该加把劲,把它们解决掉。有些分歧可能一时解决不了,双方应该多从对方的具体处境着想,以务实和建设性的态度加以管控。只要双方遵循相互尊重、平等相待原则,坚持求同存异、聚同化异,就没有过不去的坎,中美两国关

the establishment of diplomatic ties, China-US cooperation has grown steadily in both width and depth, bringing real benefits to our people. We need to embrace a win-win perspective and move our cooperation to a higher level. It is imperative that we increase macro-economic policy coordination and work together with other parties concerned to ensure that the G20 Hangzhou Summit delivers positive outcomes to boost confidence and invigorate global growth. It is important that we do our best to conclude a mutually-beneficial bilateral investment treaty at the earliest possible date to foster a new highlight in business and trade cooperation. And it is important that we deepen exchange and cooperation in climate change, development, cyber issues, counter-terrorism, non-proliferation, military-to-military relations and law enforcement, and step up communication and coordination on major international and regional issues as well as issues of global significance. This way, we could bring more real benefits to our people and provide more public goods for greater peace, stability and prosperity of the world.

China and the US need to properly manage differences and sensitive issues. China and the US, each with its own uniqueness, are different in terms of history, culture, social system and people's aspiration. Differing views between us are hardly avoidable. In fact, in this world of diversity, differences among countries are just natural. Even family members do not always see eye to eye. One should not be afraid of differences. What is most important is to refrain from taking the differences as excuses for confrontation. There are differences that could be addressed by redoubling our efforts. For those differences that cannot be settled for the time being, we need to manage them in a pragmatic and constructive fashion by putting ourselves in each other's shoes. As long as we observe the principles of

系就能避免受到大的干扰。

mutual respect and equality, shelve differences to seek consensus, and try to resolve them through expanding common ground, we will be able to overcome difficulties and obstacles, and prevent major disruptions in bilateral relations.

最后,祝本轮中美战略与经济对话和人文交流高层磋商取得圆满成功!

To conclude, I wish this round of the China-US SED and CPE a complete success.

谢谢大家。

Thank you.

3. 携手迈向中瑞务实合作的新未来——在瑞士经济金融界人士午餐会上的演讲(有删减)
Work Hand-in-Hand to Create a New Future of China-Switzerland Pragmatic Cooperation—Speech at Luncheon Hosted by the Swiss Economic and Financial Community (Reduced version)

中华人民共和国国务院总理李克强　2013年5月24日,苏黎世
H. E. Li Keqiang, Premier of the State Council of the People's Republic of China, Zurich, 24 May 2013

中文来源:外交部网站

https://www.fmprc.gov.cn/web/ziliao_674904/zyjh_674906/t1369845.shtml

译文来源:外交部英文网站

https://www.fmprc.gov.cn/mfa_eng/wjdt_665385/zyjh_665391/t1055953.shtml

尊敬的施奈德-阿曼联邦委员、约尔丹行长,女士们、先生们、朋友们:

很高兴在苏黎世同瑞士经济金融界的朋友们见面。瑞士是欧洲大陆的一颗明珠,也是全球金融强国之一,吸引着众多跨国公司和国际组织在此落户。这次是我担任总理后的首次出访,把瑞士作为访问欧洲国家的首站,是因为中瑞关系十分紧密、非常友好。

瑞士拥有现代化的工业和农业,支撑了发达的金融业和服务业。在不久的将来,瑞士生产的精密仪

Your Excellency Federal Councilor Schneider-Ammann, Your Excellency President Jordan, Ladies and Gentlemen, Dear Friends,

I am delighted to meet you, friends of the Swiss economic and financial community, in the city of Zurich. Switzerland is a shining pearl on the European continent and one of the world's strongest financial powers. It is home to a large number of multinational companies and international organizations. This is my first overseas trip after becoming the premier of China. I have chosen Switzerland as my first stop in Europe, because we have very close and friendly relations with Switzerland.

Switzerland's modern industries and agricultural sectors have provided the foundation for the development of advanced financial and service

Chapter Ⅹ Consecutive Interpreting Materials for Different Themes

器、工业制成品和农产品出口中国将享受十分优惠的关税待遇，中国产品出口瑞士也将享受同等待遇，原因是中瑞已经谈成了自贸协定。

中瑞自贸协定的成果十分丰富。这是一个高水平、内容广泛的协定，不仅涵盖货物贸易、服务贸易，而且包涵了环境保护、劳工就业、知识产权、市场竞争等新时期的新议题。双方同意给予对方绝大多数产品零关税或低关税待遇，并推进包括金融业在内的服务贸易自由化和便利化进程。这既有利于降低交易成本、促进企业在竞争中发展，更有利于发挥市场在资源配置中的基础作用，有利于经济全球化进程。

中瑞建设自贸区的意义不仅仅在于中瑞两国。这是中国同欧洲大陆国家的第一个自贸区，是中国同世界经济 20 强国家的第一个自贸区，是一件具有里程碑意义的大事。首先，这对深化中瑞经贸合作是重大利好，将使各项制度和政策更加透明，使各具优势的"中国制造"和"瑞士制造"更容易进入对方市场，给两国企业和消费者都带来好处。第二，这对发展中欧关系是重大利好，瑞士与欧盟各成员国和欧元区经济联系密切，是中国企业与欧洲企业合作的重要纽带。第三，这对全球贸易和投资自由化便利化是重大利好，中瑞经济总量分别居世界第二位和第十九位，贸易总量分别

industries. Swiss-made precision instruments, industrial goods and agricultural products will soon enjoy very low tariff rate when exporting to China, and the same preferential treatment will be provided for Chinese products entering Switzerland. That is because China and Switzerland have reached a deal on the FTA agreement.

China-Switzerland FTA is a fruitful agreement with high quality and rich content. It not only covers trade in goods and services, but also includes new trade issues such as environmental protection, labor and employment, intellectual property and market competition. The two sides have agreed to provide low—or even zero-tariff treatment to the vast majority of each other's products, and advance liberalization and facilitation of trade in services, including the financial sector. This will help reduce the cost of transactions, promote the development of companies through competition, better leverage the fundamental role of the market in resources allocation, and generate momentum for economic globalization.

The significance of the building of a China-Switzerland FTA goes beyond the two countries. It is China's first FTA with a country from the European continent and with one of the world's top 20 economies. It is a milestone achievement. First, it is good news for China-Switzerland business cooperation. It will make our rules and policies more transparent, and help "made in China" and "made in Switzerland" products, each competitive in their own ways, gain access to the other side's market more easily, and bring benefits to the companies and consumers of both countries. Second, it is good news for China-Europe relations. Switzerland is closely linked with the EU member states and the euro zone economies, and it is an important bond connecting Chinese and European enterprises. Third, it is good news for global trade and investment liberalization

居世界的第二位和欧洲的第二位，达成自贸协定对各国会产生重要的示范甚至引领作用。

中瑞达成自贸协定，充分表明中国将进一步扩大对外开放，把加快实施自贸区战略作为对外开放的关键举措。迄今为止，中国已经与19个国家和地区签署了11个自由贸易协议，与其他一些国家商谈自贸区也在进行当中，我们将坚定地推进这些谈判。中国将更加积极主动地扩大对外开放，与自贸区伙伴共同获取新时期的"开放红利"，共同释放更多的"改革红利"，共同分享更大的"发展红利"。中国服务业发展相对滞后，服务贸易规模仅相当于货物贸易规模的约1/8，这制约了中国经济的转型升级。我们不仅需要高质量的产品，也需要优质的服务。中国将进一步扩大物流、金融、商务、医疗、教育等服务贸易领域开放，促进服务业加快发展。

女士们，先生们！

瑞士是重要的国际金融中心，拥有完备而具活力的金融体系，孕育了众多久负盛名的金融企业，被称为银行密度最高的国家。今天我们所在的苏黎世就是一个国际金融中心城市。我此次访期间将与贵国领导人宣布建立中瑞金融对话机制，加强双方金融合作和在国际金融领域的合作。这里，我就金融经

and facilitation. China and Switzerland are respectively the world's second and nineteenth largest economies, and the second largest trading nation in the world and Europe. The FTA agreement reached between China and Switzerland can serve as a model and guide for other countries.

The conclusion of the FTA agreement with Switzerland fully shows that China stands ready to open wider to the outside world and takes the accelerated implementation of the FTA strategy as an important step in its opening-up. Up to date, China has signed 11 FTA agreements with 19 countries and regions, and FTA negotiations with some other countries are also well underway. We will make unremitting efforts to advance these negotiations. China will be more active in opening to the outside world, and work with its FTA partners to reap the "dividends of opening-up" in the new era, unleash more "reform dividends" and share greater "development dividends". China's service sector is relatively underdeveloped, and the size of trade in services is only equivalent to about 1/8 of that of trade in goods. This has proven to be a constraint on the transformation and upgrading of the Chinese economy. We need not only high-quality products but also better services. We will promote further opening in such service sectors as logistics, finance, business, medical services and education, and accelerate the development of the service industry.

Ladies and Gentlemen,

Switzerland is an important international financial center with a well-established and dynamic financial sector. It is home to numerous renowned financial firms and known as the country with the highest density of banks. The city that hosts today's event, Zurich, is an international financial center. During my visit this time, I will announce with the Swiss leaders the establishment of a financial dialogue mechanism to enhance cooperation on bilateral and international financial issues. Now, I wish

Chapter X Consecutive Interpreting Materials for Different Themes

济问题谈几点看法，与大家交流。

第一，我们坚持深化中国金融改革开放。改革开放以来，中国金融业伴随现代化建设而快速成长，但实现持续发展依然任重道远。以开放促改革发展、促转型创新，实现中国经济持续健康发展，也会给世界经济增长及金融业发展提供机遇。

第二，我们主张稳定国际金融经济政策。新的形势下，国际社会应当继续把推动世界经济强劲、可持续、平衡增长作为共同目标，坚持实施稳增长、促就业的宏观经济政策，推进财政金融改革，防范全球性通货膨胀风险，维护国际金融市场稳定。主要经济体实施量化宽松货币政策时，也应考虑对其他国家产生的负面溢出效应，同时妥善解决政府债务问题，尽快修复金融部门，为全球金融稳定、市场复苏和经济增长创造条件。

第三，我们期望改革和完善国际金融体系。中国是国际政治经济秩序的维护者和建设者，愿意承担作为发展中国家和新兴经济体应当承担的责任。中方主张，优先考虑和积极推进国际货币基金组织和世

to share with you some of my observations on economic and financial issues.

First, we are committed to deepening reform and opening-up of China's financial sector. Since the beginning of reform and opening-up, China's financial sector has enjoyed rapid growth together with the modernization of the country. However, to sustain this momentum of growth remains a long and arduous task. We will promote reform, development, economic transformation and innovation in the course of opening-up to achieve the sustainable and healthy growth of the Chinese economy. This will also create opportunities for the economic growth and development of the financial industry of the world.

Second, we believe countries should ensure the stability of their financial and economic policies. In the new situation, members of the international community should continue to commit to the common goal of ensuring strong, sustainable and balanced growth of the world economy, pursue macroeconomic policies that help stabilize growth and generate jobs, advance fiscal and financial reforms, guard against the risk of global inflation, and maintain the stability of international financial markets. When introducing the monetary policy of quantitative easing, major economies should also take into account its negative spillover effects on other countries, and at the same time, properly resolve the issue of government debt, repair their financial sector as quickly as possible, and create conditions for achieving global financial stability, market recovery and economic growth.

Third, we hope the international financial system will be reformed and improved. China is committed to upholding and building the international political and economic order, and stands ready to fulfill its due obligations as a developing country and an emerging economy. China believes that we need to give priority

界银行改革,更多地发挥国际货币基金组织在解决欧债问题中的作用。我们认为,现行合理有效的国际经济机制和规则应当维护,同时应当推进改革,加强国际金融监管,鼓励开展金融区域合作,提高发展中国家的话语权和代表性。中方愿继续与国际社会一道,凝聚智慧与共识,共同改革和完善国际金融体系。

女士们,先生们!

中瑞虽然分处亚洲和欧洲两端,但广袤的亚欧大陆把两国连接在一起。喜马拉雅山和阿尔卑斯山雄踞亚欧地理的制高点,召唤着人们知难而进、攀登全球经济合作的制高点。中瑞关系之所以历久弥新,成为不同制度和文化国家之间友好交往的典范,主要得益于一种敢为天下先、争当"第一"的品质。我们应当传承并弘扬这种开拓进取精神,促进中瑞关系始终站在历史、时代和世界的潮头,不断追求卓越!

谢谢大家。

to and actively advance the reform of the International Monetary Fund (IMF) and the World Bank, and make fuller use of the role of the IMF in resolving the European debt issue. We believe that the existing sound and effective international economic system and rules must be upheld. In the meantime, efforts should be made to push forward reform, strengthen international financial supervision and regulation, encourage regional financial cooperation, and enhance the voice and representation of developing countries. We will continue to work with the international community to pool our wisdom and build consensus, and jointly reform and strengthen the international financial system.

Ladies and Gentlemen,

Although China and Switzerland are situated respectively in Asia and Europe, the vast Eurasian continent has brought us together. The Himalayas and the Alps, where the highest peaks of Asia and Europe are, inspire us to meet difficulties head on and scale new height of global economic cooperation. China and Switzerland both have the courage and determination to always be the first in the world, and that is exactly why our bilateral relations have grown from one generation to another and become a model of friendly exchanges between countries with different social systems and culture. We should preserve and promote this enterprising spirit, and ensure China-Switzerland relations will always stay ahead of history, ahead of the times and at the forefront of the world and continue to strive for excellence.

Thank you.

4. Joint U. S.-EU Statement following President Juncker's visit to the White House, Washington, July 25, 2018(Full text)

欧盟委员会主席容克在华盛顿同美国总统特朗普会谈后美欧发表联合声明,华盛顿,2018

Chapter Ⅹ Consecutive Interpreting Materials for Different Themes

年 7 月 25 日(全文)
英文来源:欧盟官网
https://ec.europa.eu/commission/presscorner/detail/en/STATEMENT_18_4687
译文来源:搜狐网
https://www.sohu.com/a/243527224_117959

We met today in Washington, D.C. to launch a new phase in the relationship between the United States and the European Union—a phase of close friendship, of strong trade relations in which both of us will win, of working better together for global security and prosperity, and of fighting jointly against terrorism.	我们今天在华盛顿特区会见,以启动美国与欧盟之间关系的新阶段——一种为实现双方共赢的有力经贸合作,以更好地为全球安全与繁荣而共同努力、共同打击恐怖主义的密切关系。
The United States and the European Union together count more than 830 million citizens and more than 50 percent of global GDP. If we team up, we can make our planet a better, more secure, and more prosperous place.	美国与欧盟总计共有8.3亿多公民,占据全球50%以上GDP。如果我们合作,可以让我们的星球成为一个更美好、更安全、更繁荣的地方。
Already today, the United States and the European Union have a $1 trillion bilateral trade relationship—the largest economic relationship in the world. We want to further strengthen this trade relationship to the benefit of all American and European citizens.	美国与欧盟今天就已经拥有一万亿美元的双边贸易关系——这是全球最大的经贸伙伴关系。我们想进一步加强这份贸易伙伴关系,以使得全部美国与欧洲公民获益。
This is why we agreed today, first of all, to work together toward zero tariffs, zero non-tariff barriers, and zero subsidies on non-auto industrial goods. We will also work to reduce barriers and increase trade in services, chemicals, pharmaceuticals, medical products, as well as soybeans.	这就是为什么我们今天同意首先要共同致力于零关税、消除非关税壁垒、消除对非汽车工业产品的补贴。我们也同样会努力在服务贸易、化工、医药产品以及大豆等领域减少贸易壁垒并增加贸易量。
This will open markets for farmers and workers, increase investment, and lead to greater prosperity in both the United States and the European Union. It will also make trade fairer and more reciprocal.	这将会为农民以及工人打开市场、增加投资并使得美国与欧盟更加繁荣。这也会使得贸易更加公平、更加互惠。
Secondly, we agreed today to strengthen our strategic cooperation with respect to energy. The European Union wants to import more liquefied natural gas (LNG) from the United States to	其次,我们今天同意加强我们的能源战略性合作。欧盟想从美国进口更多液化天然气(LNG)来使得其能源供给更加多样化。

321

diversify its energy supply.

Thirdly, we agreed today to launch a close dialogue on standards in order to ease trade, reduce bureaucratic obstacles, and slash costs.

Fourthly, we agreed today to join forces to protect American and European companies better from unfair global trade practices. We will therefore work closely together with like-minded partners to reform the WTO and to address unfair trading practices, including intellectual property theft, forced technology transfer, industrial subsidies, distortions created by state owned enterprises, and overcapacity.

We decided to set up immediately an Executive Working Group of our closest advisors to carry this joint agenda forward. In addition, it will identify short-term measures to facilitate commercial exchanges and assess existing tariff measures. While we are working on this, we will not go against the spirit of this agreement, unless either party terminates the negotiations.

We also want to resolve the steel and aluminum tariff issues and retaliatory tariffs.

第三,我们今天同意围绕标准展开紧密对话,以此来放宽交易,减少官僚障碍以及降低成本。

第四,我们今天同意共同致力于保护美国与欧盟的公司,以更好地保护他们免受不公平的全球贸易行为的侵害。为此,我们会与有着类似想法的伙伴紧密合作,推动WTO改革,去解决不公平贸易行为,包括知识产权窃取行为、强制性技术转让行为、工业补贴、国有企业造成的扭曲以及产能过剩问题。

我们决定立即成立由我们最密切的咨询顾问组成的行政工作小组,推进此项联合议程。此外,它还会制定短期措施,以便利商业交易并评估现有关税措施。在我们致力于此的同时,我们不会违背这份协议的精神,除非任一方终止协商。

此外,我们也想解决钢铁与铝的关税问题以及报复性关税问题。

10.3　Education and Cultural Exchange

1. Peng Liyuan's speech on education at the United Nations conference, Sept. 26, 2015. (Full text)
彭丽媛在联合国大会上的讲话,2015年9月26日(全文)
英文及译文来源:搜狐网
https://www.sohu.com/a/33808081_221914

Director-General Bokova, ladies and gentlemen,

It gives me a great pleasure to join you for this important initiative as the UN marks its 70th anniversary.

Education is very close in my heart. My father

尊敬的博科娃总干事,女士们先生们:

我非常高兴在联合国成立70周年之际出席这次教育第一倡议高级别会议。

我非常关注教育。我的父亲生

grew up in a very small village in China. In those days, not many villagers could read. So my father opened a night school to teach them how to read. With his help, many people learned to write their own names; with his help many people learned to read newspapers for the first time; with his help, many women were able to teach their children how to read.

As his daughter, I know what education means to the people, especially those without it. After generations of hard work, China has come a long way in education. I myself am a beneficiary of that progress. Otherwise I would never become a soprano and a professor of musical.

I am following my father's footsteps by teaching at China's Conservatory of Music to help continue China's success story. I want to thank Director-General Bokova and UNESCO for naming me the Special Envoy for Women and Girls Education. I am truly honored to work with the UN and do something about Global Education. I have visited many schools around the world. I've seen first-hand on how much we can do for education.

Education is about women and the girls. It is important for girls to go to school because they will become their children's first teacher someday. But women still account for over half of the world's poor in population and 60% of adults who can't read.

Education is crucial in the addressing such inequalities. In China, Spring Bud Education Program has helped over 3 million girls go back to school. Many of them have finished university education and they are doing well at work.

Education is about equality. In poor countries and regions the number of school dropouts is

长在中国的一个小山村,那个时候,许多农民都不识字。当时我的父亲开办了一所夜校,教大家认字。在他的帮助下,许多人第一次写出了自己的名字,第一次看懂了报纸和书刊,许多女性也能教自己的孩子认字了。

在父亲的教育下,我自幼就清楚地认识到,教育对每个人,尤其是对得不到教育的人来说是多么的重要。经过几代人的努力,中国的教育事业取得了显著成就。我自己就是中国教育发展的受益者。否则我也永远不能成为一名女高音歌唱家和音乐教师。

我现在也追随父亲的脚步投身教育工作,在中国音乐学院任教,为推动中国教育事业的发展尽绵薄之力。我想感谢博科娃总干事和联合国教科文组织授予我"促进女童和妇女教育特使"称号,我非常荣幸能够与联合国共同努力,为全球教育贡献一己之力。我走访了世界很多国家的学校,我也亲眼看到了在教育方面我们可以做出更多的努力。

教育要关注女性和女童。女童要上学,这是很重要的一点,因为她们长大之后会成为自己孩子的启蒙老师。但是,全球贫困者中,女性过半,不识字的成年人中,女性占到了60%。

教育是改变女性不公平待遇的重要途径。中国的"春蕾计划"帮助了300多万女童重返学校。其中很多人已经从高校毕业,并成为了社会的有用之才和优秀分子。

教育要倡导公平公正。在很多贫困国家和地区,辍学比例很高。

astonishing. We call for more educational resources to these places.

Education is about the young people. Young people are the future. Education is important because it not only gave young people knowledge and skills but also help them become responsible citizens. As the UNESCO special envoy and the mother myself my commitment to education for all will never change.

Many years ago my father made a small difference in his village. Together we can make a big difference in the world. I was once asked about my Chinese dream. I said I hope all children especially girls can have access to good education. This is my Chinese dream. I believe one day education first will no longer be a dream, it will be a reality enjoyed by every young woman on this planet.

Thank you very much.

我们呼吁,加大对这些地区的教育投入。

教育要面向青年。青年是我们的未来。教育之所以重要,是因为它不仅要教授知识和技能,而且也帮助青年人成长为具有强烈责任感的公民。作为教科文组织的一名特使和一位母亲,我也愿意恪尽职守,实现教育的进展和进步。

多年前,我的父亲通过他的努力,改变了他的小山村。今天,只要大家携手努力,就能改变世界。有人问过什么是我的中国梦,我说,我希望所有的孩子,特别是女孩,都能接受良好的教育,这就是我的中国梦。我相信,总有一天,教育第一的梦想将不会是一个梦想,将会成为全世界年轻女性共享的美好现实。

谢谢大家。

2. 深化文明交流互鉴 共建亚洲命运共同体——习近平在亚洲文明对话大会开幕式上的主旨演讲,2019 年 5 月 15 日,北京(全文)
Deepening Exchanges and Mutual Learning Among Civilizations for an Asian Community with a Shared Future—Keynote speech by Xi Jinping, President of the People's Republic of China at the opening ceremony of the Conference on Dialogue of Asian Civilizations, Beijing, 15 May 2019(Full text)

中文来源:外交部网站

https://www.fmprc.gov.cn/web/ziliao_674904/zyjh_674906/t1663571.shtml

译文来源:外交部英文网站

https://www.fmprc.gov.cn/mfa_eng/wjdt_665385/zyjh_665391/t1663857.shtml

尊敬的各位国家元首、政府首脑、国际组织负责人,尊敬的各位嘉宾,女士们,先生们,朋友们:

在这个草木生长的美好季节,来自亚洲 47 个国家和五大洲的各方嘉宾,为深化文明交流互鉴共聚一堂,共襄盛举。首先,我谨代表中国政府和中国人民,并以我个人的

Your Excellencies Heads of State and Government, Your Excellencies Heads of International Organizations, Distinguished Guests, Ladies and Gentlemen, Friends,

In this lovely season of thriving green, I am delighted to join you, distinguished guests from 47 Asian countries and five continents, in a dialogue on deepening exchanges and mutual learning among civilizations. On behalf of the Chinese government

Chapter X Consecutive Interpreting Materials for Different Themes

名义,对亚洲文明对话大会的召开,表示诚挚的祝贺!对各位嘉宾的到来,表示热烈的欢迎!

当前,世界多极化、经济全球化、文化多样化、社会信息化深入发展,人类社会充满希望。同时,国际形势的不稳定性不确定性更加突出,人类面临的全球性挑战更加严峻,需要世界各国齐心协力、共同应对。

应对共同挑战、迈向美好未来,既需要经济科技力量,也需要文化文明力量。亚洲文明对话大会,为促进亚洲及世界各国文明开展平等对话、交流互鉴、相互启迪提供了一个新的平台。

女士们、先生们、朋友们!

亚洲是人类最早的定居地之一,也是人类文明的重要发祥地。亚洲地大物博、山河秀美,在世界三分之一的陆地上居住着全球三分之二的人口,47 个国家、1000 多个民族星罗棋布。从公元前数千年起,生活在底格里斯河-幼发拉底河、印度河-恒河、黄河-长江等流域的人们,开始耕耘灌溉、铸器造皿、建设家园。一代又一代亚洲先民历经岁月洗礼,把生产生活实践镌刻成悠久历史、积淀成深厚文明。广袤富饶的平原,碧波荡漾的水乡,辽阔壮美的草原,浩瀚无垠的沙漠,奔腾不息的江海,巍峨挺拔的山脉,承载和滋润了多彩的亚洲文明。

and people and in my own name, I extend sincere congratulations on the opening of the Conference on Dialogue of Asian Civilizations and a very warm welcome to all of you!

The world today is moving toward greater multi-polarity, economic globalization and cultural diversity, and is becoming increasingly information-oriented. All this points to promising prospects for the future. Meanwhile, instability and uncertainties are mounting and the global challenges faced by humanity are becoming ever more daunting, calling for joint responses from countries around the world.

To meet our common challenges and create a better future for all, we look to culture and civilization to play their role, which is as important as the role played by economy, science and technology. The Conference on Dialogue of Asian Civilizations is convened just for this purpose, as it creates a new platform for civilizations in Asia and beyond to engage in dialogue and exchanges on an equal footing to facilitate mutual learning.

Ladies and Gentlemen, Friends,

Asia is home to one of the earliest human settlements and an important cradle of human civilizations. This vast and beautiful continent covers a third of the earth's land mass and has two-thirds of the world's population. It has more than 1,000 ethnic groups living in 47 countries. For several thousand years before the Common Era, our forefathers living along the Tigris and the Euphrates, the Indus and the Ganges, the Yellow River and the Yangtze, tilled and irrigated the land, made tools and utensils, and built homes to live in. Generation after generation, our ancestors in Asia, with their tireless endeavors, created a time-honored history and profound and rich civilizations. Our vast and fertile plains, beautiful river basins, large steppes, immense deserts, mighty rivers and oceans, and lofty mountains have nourished and enriched diverse

在数千年发展历程中,亚洲人民创造了辉煌的文明成果。《诗经》《论语》《塔木德》《一千零一夜》《梨俱吠陀》《源氏物语》等名篇经典,楔形文字、地图、玻璃、阿拉伯数字、造纸术、印刷术等发明创造,长城、麦加大清真寺、泰姬陵、吴哥窟等恢宏建筑……都是人类文明的宝贵财富。各种文明在这片土地上交相辉映,谱写了亚洲文明发展史诗。

亚洲先人们早就开始了文明交流互鉴。丝绸之路、茶叶之路、香料之路等古老商路,助推丝绸、茶叶、陶瓷、香料、绘画雕塑等风靡亚洲各国,记录着亚洲先人们交往交流、互通有无的文明对话。现在,"一带一路""两廊一圈""欧亚经济联盟"等拓展了文明交流互鉴的途径,各国在科技、教育、文化、卫生、民间交往等领域的合作蓬勃开展,亚洲文明也在自身内部及同世界文明的交流互鉴中发展壮大。

璀璨的亚洲文明,为世界文明发展史书写了浓墨重彩的篇章,人类文明因亚洲而更加绚烂多姿。从宗教到哲学、从道德到法律、从文学到绘画、从戏剧到音乐、从城市到乡村,亚洲形成了覆盖广泛的世俗礼

and colorful civilizations across Asia.

In building our civilizations over the course of several millennia, we the people of Asia have made splendid achievements. I think of literary classics such as The Book of Songs, The Analects of Confucius, The Talmud, One Thousand and One Nights, The Rigvedaand Genji Monogatari; of inventions such as the cuneiform script, maps, glass, Arabic numerals, paper making and printing techniques; and of majestic structures like the Great Wall, the Great Mosque of Mecca, Taj Mahal and Angkor Wat. They are all invaluable assets of human civilization. Through interactions on this continent, Asian civilizations have enriched each other and written an epic of development.

Our forefathers in Asia have long engaged in inter-civilizational exchanges and mutual learning. The ancient trade routes, notably the Silk Road, the Tea Road and the Spice Road, brought silk, tea, porcelain, spices, paintings and sculpture to all corners of Asia, and witnessed inter-civilizational dialogue in the form of trade and cultural interflow. Today, the Belt and Road Initiative, together with the Two Corridors and One Belt, the Eurasian Economic Union and other initiatives, have greatly expanded inter-civilizational exchanges and mutual learning. Cooperation among nations in science, technology, education, culture, health and people-to-people exchanges are thriving like never before. Thanks to exchanges and mutual learning among themselves and with other civilizations in the world, Asian civilizations have grown from strength to strength.

The great Asian civilizations have a special place in the annals of world civilizations, and they have added to the diversity of human civilizations. Think of what Asia stands to offer in terms of religion, philosophy, ethic code, law, literature, painting, drama, music, and even the building of towns and

仪,写下了传承千年的不朽巨著、留下了精湛深邃的艺术瑰宝、形成了种类多样的制度成果,为世界提供了丰富的文明选择。

回顾历史、展望世界,我们应该增强文明自信,在先辈们铸就的光辉成就的基础上,坚持同世界其他文明交流互鉴,努力续写亚洲文明新辉煌。

女士们、先生们、朋友们!

亚洲各国山水相连、人文相亲,有着相似的历史境遇、相同的梦想追求。面向未来,我们应该把握大势、顺应潮流,努力把亚洲人民对美好生活的向往变成现实。

——亚洲人民期待一个和平安宁的亚洲。维护和平是每个国家都应该肩负起来的责任。没有和平,冲突不断甚至战火纷飞,经济增长、民生改善、社会稳定、人民往来等都会沦为空谈。亚洲各国人民希望远离恐惧,实现安居乐业、普遍安全,希望各国互尊互信、和睦相处,广泛开展跨国界、跨时空、跨文明的交往活动,共同维护比金子还珍贵的和平时光。

——亚洲人民期待一个共同繁荣的亚洲。经济发展是文明存续的有力支撑,繁荣富强是国家进步的重要基石。亚洲一些民众特别是妇女儿童正忍受着贫困、饥饿、疾病的折磨,这样的局面必须改变。亚洲

villages. They speak volumes for Asia's proud achievements: extensive systems of social customs, immortal classics that have endured for millennia, the fine pool of exquisite art, and diverse institutions, among others. All these offer rich choices for civilizations the world over to draw on.

As we review our past and look beyond Asia, we should have greater confidence in our civilizations. We may build on the rich heritage of our forefathers, stay engaged with other civilizations and increase mutual learning. By doing so, we will add new glory to Asian civilizations.

Ladies and Gentlemen, Friends,

We Asian countries are closely connected and share a natural bond of affinity. We went through similar historical trials and hold the same dream for the future. Going forward, we need to see where the world is going, ride on the trend of the times and turn our people's longing for a better life into reality.

—We Asian people hope to see peace and stability across Asia. Upholding peace is the responsibility of every country. When peace is interrupted by conflict or war, economic growth, decent lives, social stability and people-to-people exchanges will all be out of the question. We the people of Asian countries wish to live and work in content and security free from fear. We hope that all countries will respect and trust each other, live in harmony, and interact with each other in a manner that transcends national boundaries, time and space, as well as the difference between civilizations. We should work together and jointly safeguard peace, something that is even more precious than gold.

—We Asian people hope to see common prosperity in Asia. Economic growth sustains a civilization, and prosperity underpins the progress of a nation. In some parts of Asia, people, women and children in particular, are still suffering from poverty, hunger and disease. This must change. We

各国人民希望远离贫困、富足安康,希望各国合力推进开放、包容、普惠、平衡、共赢的经济全球化,共同消除一些国家民众依然面临的贫穷落后,共同为孩子们创造衣食无忧的生活,让幸福和欢乐走进每一个家庭。

——亚洲人民期待一个开放融通的亚洲。亚洲近几十年快速发展,一条十分重要的经验就是敞开大门,主动融入世界经济发展潮流。如果各国重新回到一个个自我封闭的孤岛,人类文明就将因老死不相往来而丧失生机活力。亚洲各国人民希望远离封闭、融会通达,希望各国秉持开放精神,推进政策沟通、设施联通、贸易畅通、资金融通、民心相通,共同构建亚洲命运共同体、人类命运共同体。

女士们、先生们、朋友们!

文明因多样而交流,因交流而互鉴,因互鉴而发展。我们要加强世界上不同国家、不同民族、不同文化的交流互鉴,夯实共建亚洲命运共同体、人类命运共同体的人文基础。为此,我愿提出4点主张。

第一,坚持相互尊重、平等相待。每一种文明都扎根于自己的生存土壤,凝聚着一个国家、一个民族的非凡智慧和精神追求,都有自己存在的价值。人类只有肤色语言之别,文明只有姹紫嫣红之别,但绝无高低优劣之分。认为自己的人种和文明高人一等,执意改造甚至取代

Asian people long for decent lives free of poverty. We hope that countries will work together to promote economic globalization and make it more open, inclusive, balanced and beneficial to all. Doing so will enable us to eradicate poverty and backwardness that still plague people in some countries. It will make life carefree for our children and bring happiness to all families.

—We Asian people hope to see an open and better-connected Asia. Asia's rapid development over the past decades shows that it is important to open one's door to the outside world and ride on the trend of global economic development. If countries choose to close their doors and hide behind them, human civilizations would be cut off from each other and lose all vitality. We Asian people hope that all countries will reject self-exclusion, embrace integration, uphold openness and promote policy, infrastructure, trade, financial and people-to-people connectivity. This way, we can jointly foster a community with a shared future for both us Asians and all humanity.

Ladies and Gentlemen, Friends,

Diversity spurs interaction among civilizations, which in turn promotes mutual learning and their further development. We need to promote exchanges and mutual learning among countries, nations and cultures around the world, and strengthen popular support for jointly building a community with a shared future for both Asia and humanity as a whole. To that end, I believe it is imperative that we act in the following ways:

First, we need to respect each other and treat each other as equals. All civilizations are rooted in their unique cultural environment. Each embodies the wisdom and vision of a country or nation, and each is valuable for being uniquely its own. Civilizations only vary from each other, just as human beings are different only in terms of skin color and the language used. No civilization is superior

Chapter X Consecutive Interpreting Materials for Different Themes

其他文明,在认识上是愚蠢的,在做法上是灾难性的!如果人类文明变得只有一个色调、一个模式了,那这个世界就太单调了,也太无趣了!我们应该秉持平等和尊重,摒弃傲慢和偏见,加深对自身文明和其他文明差异性的认知,推动不同文明交流对话、和谐共生。

我访问过世界上许多地方,最吸引我的就是韵味不同的文明,如中亚的古城撒马尔罕、埃及的卢克索神庙、新加坡的圣淘沙、泰国的曼谷玉佛寺、希腊的雅典卫城等。中国愿同各国开展亚洲文化遗产保护行动,为更好传承文明提供必要支撑。

第二,坚持美人之美、美美与共。每一种文明都是美的结晶,都彰显着创造之美。一切美好的事物都是相通的。人们对美好事物的向往,是任何力量都无法阻挡的!各种文明本没有冲突,只是要有欣赏所有文明之美的眼睛。我们既要让本国文明充满勃勃生机,又要为他国文明发展创造条件,让世界文明百花园群芳竞艳。

文明之美集中体现在哲学、社会科学等经典著作和文学、音乐、影视剧等文艺作品之中。现在,大量外国优秀文化产品进入中国,许多中国优秀文化产品走向世界。中国

over others. The thought that one's own race and civilization are superior and the inclination to remold or replace other civilizations are just stupid. To act them out will only bring catastrophic consequences. If human civilizations are reduced to only one single color or one single model, the world would become a stereotype and too dull a place to live in. What we need is to respect each other as equals and say no to hubris and prejudice. We need to deepen understanding of the difference between one's own civilization and others', and work to promote interaction, dialogue and harmony among civilizations.

In the many places I have visited around the world, what fascinates me the most is civilizations in their rich diversity. I cannot but think of the Central Asian city of Samarkand, the Luxor Temple in Egypt, Sentosa in Singapore, Wat Phra Kaew in Bangkok, and the Acropolis in Athens, to mention just a few. China is ready to work with other countries to protect Asian cultural heritage and better preserve and sustain our civilizations.

Second, we need to uphold the beauty of each civilization and the diversity of civilizations in the world. Each civilization is the crystallization of human creation, and each is beautiful in its own way. The aspiration for all that is beautiful is a common pursuit of humanity that nothing can hold back. Civilizations don't have to clash with each other; what is needed are eyes to see the beauty in all civilizations. We should keep our own civilizations dynamic and create conditions for other civilizations to flourish. Together we can make the garden of world civilizations colorful and vibrant.

The beauty of a civilization finds concrete expression in the classic works of philosophy and social sciences and works of literature, music, film and TV drama. Now, a large number of outstanding cultural works from other countries are brought into China, and a lot of fine

愿同有关国家一道,实施亚洲经典著作互译计划和亚洲影视交流合作计划,帮助人们加深对彼此文化的理解和欣赏,为展示和传播文明之美打造交流互鉴平台。

第三,坚持开放包容、互学互鉴。一切生命有机体都需要新陈代谢,否则生命就会停止。文明也是一样,如果长期自我封闭,必将走向衰落。交流互鉴是文明发展的本质要求。只有同其他文明交流互鉴、取长补短,才能保持旺盛生命活力。文明交流互鉴应该是对等的、平等的,应该是多元的、多向的,而不应该是强制的、强迫的,不应该是单一的、单向的。我们应该以海纳百川的宽广胸怀打破文化交往的壁垒,以兼收并蓄的态度汲取其他文明的养分,促进亚洲文明在交流互鉴中共同前进。

人是文明交流互鉴最好的载体。深化人文交流互鉴是消除隔阂和误解、促进民心相知相通的重要途径。这些年来,中国同各国一道,在教育、文化、体育、卫生等领域搭建了众多合作平台,开辟了广泛合作渠道。中国愿同各国加强青少年、民间团体、地方、媒体等各界交流,打造智库交流合作网络,创新合作模式,推动各种形式的合作走深走实,为推动文明交流互鉴创造条件。

Chinese cultural products are introduced to other countries. China is happy to launch initiatives with relevant countries to translate Asian classics both from and into Chinese and promote film and TV exchanges and cooperation in Asia. This will help people in Asia better understand and appreciate each other's cultures and build a platform of exchange and mutual learning for the best of Asian civilizations to spread and be known to more in the world.

Third, we need to stay open and inclusive and draw on each other's strengths. All living organisms in the human body must renew themselves through metabolism; otherwise, life would come to an end. The same is true for civilizations. Long-term self-isolation will cause a civilization to decline, while exchanges and mutual learning will sustain its development. A civilization can flourish only through exchanges and mutual learning with other civilizations. Such exchanges and mutual learning should be reciprocal, equal-footed, diversified and multi-dimensional; they should not be coercive, imposed, one-dimensional or one-way. We need to be broad-minded and strive to remove all barriers to cultural exchanges. We need to be inclusive and always seek nourishment from other civilizations to promote the common development of Asian civilizations through exchanges and mutual learning.

People are the best bridge for exchanges and mutual learning among civilizations. Closer people-to-people exchanges and mutual learning, for that matter, is a sure way to eliminate estrangement and misunderstanding and promote mutual understanding among nations. Over the years, China has, in collaboration with other countries, established many platforms and channels for cooperation in education, culture, sports, health and other fields. China will work with other countries to step up exchanges among the youth, non-governmental organizations, subnational entities and media organizations, create a

Chapter Ⅹ Consecutive Interpreting Materials for Different Themes

第四,坚持与时俱进、创新发展。文明永续发展,既需要薪火相传、代代守护,更需要顺时应势、推陈出新。世界文明历史揭示了一个规律:任何一种文明都要与时偕行,不断吸纳时代精华。我们应该用创新增添文明发展动力、激活文明进步的源头活水,不断创造出跨越时空、富有永恒魅力的文明成果。

激发人们创新创造活力,最直接的方法莫过于走入不同文明,发现别人的优长,启发自己的思维。2018年,中国国内居民出境超过1.6亿人次,入境游客超过1.4亿人次,这是促进中外文明交流互鉴的重要力量。中国愿同各国实施亚洲旅游促进计划,为促进亚洲经济发展、增进亚洲人民友谊贡献更大力量。

女士们、先生们、朋友们!

中华文明是亚洲文明的重要组成部分。自古以来,中华文明在继承创新中不断发展,在应时处变中不断升华,积淀着中华民族最深沉的精神追求,是中华民族生生不息、发展壮大的丰厚滋养。中国的造纸术、火药、印刷术、指南针、天文历

network of exchanges and cooperation between think tanks, explore new models of cooperation, and deliver more solid outcomes in diverse forms. Such efforts will boost exchanges and mutual learning among civilizations.

Fourth, we need to advance with the times and explore new ground in development. For a civilization to endure, efforts must be made to keep it alive and build on its heritage from one generation to the next. More importantly, a civilization needs to adapt itself to the changing times and break new ground. The history of world civilizations tells us that every civilization needs to advance with the times and take in the best of its age in order to develop itself. We need to come up with new ideas to add impetus and inspiration to the development of our civilizations. With these efforts, we will deliver achievements for our civilizations to transcend time and space and have a lasting appeal.

To spur people's innovation and creativity, the best way is to come into contact with different civilizations, see the strengths of others and draw upon them. Last year, Chinese tourists made over 160 million overseas trips and more than 140 million foreign tourists visited China. These visits played an important role in promoting exchanges and mutual learning between China and the rest of the world. In this connection, China will work with other countries to implement a plan to promote tourism in Asia. This will further boost economic development in Asia and deepen friendship among the Asian people.

Ladies and Gentlemen, Friends,

Being an inseparable part of Asian civilizations, Chinese civilization has, since its early days, evolved and grown by drawing on its past achievement, exploring new ground and adapting to changes. It represents the profound pursuit of the Chinese nation and provides a rich source of strength for its lasting development. Chinese inventions such as paper

法、哲学思想、民本理念等在世界上影响深远,有力推动了人类文明发展进程。

中华文明是在同其他文明不断交流互鉴中形成的开放体系。从历史上的佛教东传、"伊儒会通",到近代以来的"西学东渐"、新文化运动、马克思主义和社会主义思想传入中国,再到改革开放以来全方位对外开放,中华文明始终在兼收并蓄中历久弥新。亲仁善邻、协和万邦是中华文明一贯的处世之道,惠民利民、安民富民是中华文明鲜明的价值导向,革故鼎新、与时俱进是中华文明永恒的精神气质,道法自然、天人合一是中华文明内在的生存理念。

今日之中国,不仅是中国之中国,而且是亚洲之中国、世界之中国。未来之中国,必将以更加开放的姿态拥抱世界、以更有活力的文明成就贡献世界。

女士们、先生们、朋友们!

这次亚洲文明对话大会议题广泛、内容丰富,希望大家集思广益、畅所欲言,提出真知灼见,共同创造亚洲文明和世界文明的美好未来!

最后,预祝亚洲文明对话大会圆满成功!

谢谢大家。

making, gunpowder, printing and the compass as well as China's astronomical knowledge, calendar system, philosophy and the people-centered doctrine have all had a global impact and propelled the development of human civilizations.

Chinese civilization, as an inclusive and integrated whole, has become what it is today through constant interactions with other civilizations. It has been enriched by the introduction of Buddhism and the confluence of Islam and Confucianism in the old days, and by the introduction of Western learning, the launch of the New Culture Movement and the introduction of Marxism and socialism in modern times. All-round opening-up of the country, starting with the reform and opening-up program, has added to its vitality today. For Chinese civilization, amity and good neighborliness is the principle guiding our interactions with other countries; and to deliver prosperity and security to the people is the overarching goal, to keep pace with the times through reform and innovation the abiding commitment, and to achieve harmony between man and nature the underlying philosophy.

China today is more than the country itself; it is very much a part of Asia and the world. In the time to come, China will open its arms wider to embrace the world and contribute the dynamic achievements of Chinese civilization to a better world in the future.

Ladies and Gentlemen, Friends,

The Conference on Dialogue of Asian Civilizations has a wide-ranging agenda, and I look forward to your keen perspectives and insights. By putting our heads together, we will create an even better tomorrow for civilizations in Asia and beyond!

To conclude, I wish this conference every success!

Thank you.

10.4 Science and Technology

1. 李克强总理在国家科学技术奖励大会上的讲话,2017 年 1 月 9 日(全文)
Premier Li Keqiang's speech at the National Science & Technology Awards Conference, Jan 9,2017(Full text)

中文来源:新华网
http://www.xinhuanet.com/politics/2017-01/09/c_1120275574.htm
译文来源:中国科学院网
http://english.cas.cn/newsroom/archive/news_archive/nu 2017/201701/t20170112_173336.shtml

同志们,朋友们:

今天,我们隆重召开国家科学技术奖励大会,表彰为我国科技事业和现代化建设作出突出贡献的科技工作者。刚才,习近平总书记等党和国家领导同志,向获得国家最高科学技术奖的赵忠贤院士、屠呦呦研究员和其他获奖代表颁了奖。在此,我代表党中央、国务院,向全体获奖人员表示热烈祝贺!向全国广大科技工作者致以崇高敬意和诚挚问候!向参与和支持中国科技事业的外国专家表示衷心感谢!

刚刚过去的一年,面对复杂严峻的国内外环境,在以习近平同志为核心的党中央坚强领导下,我国经济社会发展取得了显著成就,科技战线大事喜事多、创新成果多。党中央、国务院召开全国科技创新大会,明确提出要建设世界科技强国。创新驱动发展战略深入实施,

Comrades, Friends,

Today, we are gathered for the important occasion of the National Science and Technology Award Conference to honor professionals in science and technology who have made outstanding contribution to advances in their own fields and to the modernization of China overall. Just now, General Secretary Xi Jinping and other Party and state leaders presented the Highest National Award of Science and Technology to academician Zhao Zhongxian and researcher Tu Youyou and conferred other awards to their winners. Here, on behalf of the CPC Central Committee and the State Council, I wish to extend warm congratulations to all the award-winners, and convey cordial greetings and high regard to all the science and technology professionals in China. My deep appreciation also goes to foreign experts who have participated in and supported the development of science and technology in China.

Last year, thanks to the strong leadership of the CPC Central Committee with Comrade Xi Jinping as the core, China made notable strides in economic and social development despite complex and grim internal and external environment. Major milestones were recorded in fields of science and technology and numerous outcomes in innovation were achieved. The CPC Central Committee and State Council

《国家创新驱动发展战略纲要》颁布施行,面向2030年的科技创新重大项目部署启动,科技体制改革和管理方式创新加快推进,以增加知识价值为导向的分配政策制定实施,有效调动了广大科技人员的积极性。一批具有标志性意义的重大科技成果涌现,不少达到国际先进水平。神舟十一号载人飞船与天宫二号空间试验室成功交会对接,航天员实现中期驻留,世界最大单口径射电望远镜建成使用,世界首颗量子科学实验卫星"墨子号"发射升空,使用中国自主研发芯片的超级计算机"神威·太湖之光"再次刷新世界纪录。科技创新成果加速转化,大众创业、万众创新蓬勃兴起,创新作为引领发展的第一动力作用更加显现。中国创新令世界瞩目、让人民自豪。中华大地在创新中展现出勃勃生机与活力。

当前,世界新一轮科技革命和产业变革孕育兴起,抢占未来制高点的国际竞争日趋激烈。我国经济结构深度调整、新旧动能接续转换,已到了只有依靠创新驱动才能持续发展的新阶段,比以往任何时候都更加需要强大的科技创新力量。必

convened the National Science, Technology and Innovation Conference, issuing a clarion call to build China into a science and technology giant. Vigorous efforts were made to implement the innovation-driven development strategy, such as the promulgation of the Outline of the National Strategy on Innovation-driven Development and the launch of programs for major science, technology and innovation projects toward 2030. Reform of science and technology institutions and innovation in management were accelerated, and a distribution policy that puts premium on the value of knowledge was introduced, which effectively incentivized science researchers. Significant breakthroughs were made in science and technology, many of which reached an internationally advanced level. Let me list a few. The Shenzhou-11 manned spacecraft successfully docked with Tiangong-2 space lab and astronauts managed a medium-term stay in space. The world's largest single aperture spherical telescope went into operation. The world's first quantum science experimental satellite "Mozi" was launched. The supercomputer "Sunway TaihuLight" powered by a home-made chip held the current world record. Outcomes of science, technology and innovation are now commercialized at a faster pace. The initiative of mass entrepreneurship and innovation gained a strong momentum. Innovation as the primary driving force is exerting a notably positive impact on growth. "Innovated in China" won international recognition, made the Chinese people proud and unleashed enormous energy that invigorated the whole nation.

A new round of technological revolution and industrial transformation is in the making, further sharpening international competition to stay ahead of the curve. China has entered a new phase of economic development featuring deep structural adjustments and renewal of driving forces. Only through innovation can China sustain the strong

Chapter Ⅹ Consecutive Interpreting Materials for Different Themes

须认真学习贯彻习近平总书记系列重要讲话精神,把创新摆在国家发展全局的核心位置,以新发展理念为引领,以供给侧结构性改革为主线,深入实施创新驱动发展战略,加快培育壮大新动能、改造提升传统动能,推动经济保持中高速增长、迈向中高端水平。

我们要全面提高科技创新能力,筑牢国家核心竞争力的基石。瞄准世界科技前沿,紧扣经济社会需求,在战略必争领域前瞻部署、超前研究,推进国家科技重大项目、重大工程和重大基础设施建设,夯实科技创新的基础支撑。要大力加强基础研究和原始创新,充分发挥科研院所和高校的主力军作用,建立长期稳定的支持机制,鼓励从事基础研究和原始创新的科研人员潜心研究,可以十年不鸣,争取一鸣惊人。要建立以企业为主体、以市场为导向的技术创新机制,引导社会各方面力量投入创新领域。推动开放式科技创新,深化国际科技合作,利用互联网等新平台新模式,加强产学研协同,集聚优化创新要素,提高科技创新和成果转化效率。

momentum of development. More than ever the powerful force of science, technology and innovation is called for. We must conscientiously study and act on the thinking laid out in the important speeches of General Secretary Xi Jinping, put innovation at the center of development and follow the new vision on development. Specifically, we will focus on supply-side structural reform, deepen the implementation of innovation-driven development, and transform traditional drivers of growth while fostering new ones, with a view to maintaining a medium-high rate of growth and reaching a medium-high level of development.

We will build up the capability of scientific and technological innovation across the board to lay a solid foundation for our country's core competitiveness. We should closely follow frontier trends in science and technology, and make early and visionary planning for research and application in focal areas in light of the needs of our economy and society. National scientific and technological programs and projects and key infrastructure must be implemented and built to support innovations in science and technology. We must strengthen basic research and original innovation, give full play to the central role of scientific research institutes and universities, and develop long-term and stable supporting mechanisms for researchers engaged in these areas to delve deep into their areas of endeavor. It is by no means easy for them to work quietly and thanklessly for long years. Yet their efforts will be adequately rewarded once the breakthrough comes. To encourage social input in innovation, a mechanism needs to be put in place to encourage companies to play a leading role based on market rules. We should also encourage greater openness in scientific and technological innovation by enhancing international cooperation and leveraging the internet and other new platforms and models to develop

我们要深化科技体制改革,充分调动科技人员积极性。人才是科技创新最关键的因素。必须充分尊重科技人才,保障科技人才权益,最大限度激发科技人才的创造活力。要深入推进科技领域简政放权、放管结合、优化服务改革,推行科研管理清单制度,实施更加方便简约有效的规则,赋予科研院所和高校更大的科研自主权,赋予创新领军人才更大的人财物支配权。要加大成果处置、收益分配、股权激励、人才流动、兼职兼薪等政策落实力度,使创新者得到应有荣誉和回报,增强科技人员的持久创造动力。

我们要推动大众创业、万众创新,着力激发全社会创新潜能。人民群众是历史的创造者,也是推动创新的根本力量。我们有1.7亿多受过高等教育或拥有专业技能的人才,蕴藏着巨大的创新潜能,这是我国发展用之不竭的最大"富矿"。要不拘一格用好各方面创新人才,集众智、汇众力,提高社会创新效率。既要支持专业人才在创新上不断突破,也要激发普通民众的创造潜力;

synergy among industries, universities and research institutes. We should pool and upgrade factors of innovation and raise the efficiency of commercialization of innovation and research outcomes.

We will deepen institutional reform for scientific and technological development and fully motivate professionals working in these fields. Talents hold the key to innovation. We must give full respect to scientists, engineers and technicians, guarantee their rights and interests, and tap their potential to the full. The government must further streamline science and technology administration, delegate powers and provide better services. A checklist-based management approach should be taken to strengthen and simplify rules, whereby greater autonomy will be given to institutes and universities in their research activities, and greater say to leading professionals of innovation in allocating research personnel, funding and resources. The government will vigorously implement policies regarding the usage of research outcomes, distribution of research yields, equity incentives, mobility of talents and permission for researchers to take part-time roles and be remunerated for that. All these will help to duly recognize and reward innovators, thus providing long-term motivation for scientific and technological research and innovation.

We will encourage mass entrepreneurship, and bring out the society's potential for innovation. Our people are makers of history and also the fundamental driving force for innovation. We have over 170 million people with higher education or professional skills, who are endowed with great potential for innovation and form the biggest treasure house for our country's development. We must enable all talents to apply their potential, pool their talents and strength, and raise the efficiency of the innovation. We should help both professionals to

既要支持本土人才勇攀高峰,也要吸引海归人才、外国人才来华创业创新。我们要以海纳百川、求贤若渴的气度,为各类创新人才施展才华提供更大空间、更广阔的舞台。

我们要全面提高创新供给能力,推动科技创新成果向各行业各领域覆盖融合,加快新旧动能转换。新动能既来自新兴产业成长,也来自于传统产业的改造提升。在科技创新的推动下,我国新兴产业快速成长,数字经济、分享经济、平台经济等新业态方兴未艾,对这些产业要审慎监管,使之健康发展。同时,要促进新技术、新业态、新模式加快与一二三产业融合发展,推动实体经济升级,使传统产业焕发新的生机与活力。要实施普惠性创新政策,落实和完善研发费用加计扣除、固定资产加速折旧等措施,支持企业与高校、科研院所、创客合作建立协同创新平台,推广"小核心、大协作"的"双创"模式,促进源头创新、成果转化、市场开发齐头并进,重点围绕提升产业竞争力、满足多层次消费需求和助力破解医疗、环保等领域民生难题,大力研发新品、多出优品、打造精品,着力提升"中国制造"的品质和"中国创造"的影响力。

make new innovations and the common people to explore their creativity. We should both support domestically-educated talents to scale the heights of their professions, and encourage overseas talents and foreign professionals to pursue start-ups and innovation in China. The Chinese government welcomes talents with an open mind and open arms. We will provide greater space and broader platforms for all innovators to fulfill their potential.

We will comprehensively improve our supply capacity for innovation and facilitate the application and integration of scientific achievements into all sectors and fields to speed up the shift to new growth drivers, which are derived both from the emerging industries and the upgrading of traditional sectors. Driven by scientific innovations, the emerging industries in China are thriving, spearheaded by new forms of business, like the digital economy, sharing economy and platform economy. Proper regulation must be exercised to ensure healthy development of these new sectors. Meanwhile, the new technologies, new forms of business and new models must be integrated into the first, second and tertiary industries at a faster pace, to infuse traditional industries with new vitality. We need to introduce extensive policy incentives to encourage innovation. Such measures as additional deduction of R&D spending in taxable income and accelerated depreciation of fixed assets should be better implemented. Greater support should be given to companies in setting up collaborative innovation platforms with universities, research institutes and makers. We should popularize the innovation approach based on core-group innovation enabled by wider circles of collaboration. We need to strive for parallel progress of innovation at the source, commercialization of R&D results and market development, and aim to develop more new, high-quality products that boost the competitiveness of

我们要加强知识产权保护，打造良好创新生态环境。保护知识产权就是保护和激励创新。要开展知识产权综合管理改革试点，构建知识产权创造、保护、运用体系，严厉打击侵权假冒行为，使创新者的合法权益得到切实有力的保护，使知识产权更多转化为现实生产力。要努力营造支持创新、追求卓越的社会氛围，让尊重劳动、尊重知识、尊重人才、尊重创造蔚然成风，让人人皆可创新、处处是创新之地，促进科学创新精神与企业家精神、工匠精神相结合，形成推动创新发展的强大动力。

同志们，朋友们，科技改变世界，创新决定未来。让我们更加紧密地团结在以习近平同志为核心的党中央周围，倍加珍惜荣誉，切实担当使命，奋力创造辉煌，推动科技事业更好更快发展，以优异成绩迎接党的十九大胜利召开，为实现"两个一百年"奋斗目标和中华民族伟大复兴的中国梦、建设富强民主文明和谐的社会主义现代化国家，作出新的更大贡献。

our industries, meet the diverse consumer demand and help tackle thorny issues such as in medical care and environmental protection, with a view to raising the quality of Chinese manufacturing and influence of products "Created in China".

We need to enhance protection of intellectual property rights and foster an innovation-friendly environment. Protecting intellectual property is protecting and incentivizing innovation. We will pilot integrated management of IPR, establish a system for IPR creation, protection and application, and crack down on IPR infringement and counterfeiting to safeguard the legal rights and interests of innovators and turn more intellectual property into real productivity. We need to foster a social environment that embraces innovation and excellence, and respects hard work, knowledge, talent and creativity. We should enable each and every one to innovate wherever possible, and celebrate the spirit of innovation together with entrepreneurship and workmanship to generate strong impetus for innovative development.

Comrades, Friends, As science and technology change the world, innovation shapes the future. Let us rally more closely around the CPC Central Committee with Comrade Xi Jinping as the core, cherish the honor the country has conferred, conscientiously fulfill our mission and strive for greater achievements. Attaining better and faster progress of our scientific and technological endeavors would be the best way for you to greet the opening of the 19th CPC National Congress. By joining hands, we will make fresh and greater contribution to the realization of the "Two Centenary Goals" and the Chinese dream of the great national renewal and to the building of a prosperous, strong, democratic, culturally advanced, harmonious and modern socialist country.

Chapter Ⅹ Consecutive Interpreting Materials for Different Themes

2. Address by Vice Foreign Minister Li Baodong at the Opening Ceremony of the International Workshop on Information and Cyber Security, Beijing, June 5, 2014. (Full text)
外交部副部长李保东在信息与网络安全问题国际研讨会开幕式上的讲话,北京,2014 年 6 月 5 日(全文)
中文来源:外交部网站 https://www.fmprc.gov.cn/web/ziliao_674904/zyjh_674906/t1162436.shtml
译文来源:外交部英文网站 https://www.fmprc.gov.cn/mfa_eng/wjdt_665385/zyjh_665391/t1162458.shtml

各位来宾,女士们,先生们:

首先,请允许我代表中国外交部,欢迎各位参加中国外交部军控司与联合国亚太裁军中心联合举办的信息与网络安全问题国际研讨会。信息和网络安全问题是当前国际议程中的热点问题,具有很强的战略性、前沿性和综合性。我希望与会代表能充分利用本次会议,围绕共同关心的全球网络安全问题,加强政策交流,分享做法和经验,共谋应对之策。

借此机会,我还要感谢联合国方面为举办本次会议所做出的积极贡献。中国一贯高度重视与联合国的合作,支持联合国在国际事务中发挥重要作用。本次会议是中方首次与联合国共同举办网络安全领域的国际研讨会,相信会议将有助于国际社会在网络安全领域凝聚共识。

各位来宾!
信息和通信技术的快速发展,深刻影响着人类经济和社会生活的方方面面,为人类文明发展与进步提供了全新的数字机遇,同时带来了前所未有的挑战。网络犯罪和网

Distinguished Guests, Ladies and Gentlemen,

To begin with, on behalf of China's Ministry of Foreign Affairs (MFA), I would like to welcome you to this workshop co-hosted by the Department of Arms Control and Disarmament of the MFA and the UN Regional Center for Peace and Disarmament in Asia and the Pacific. Information and cyber security are hotly-debated issues on the international agenda. They are strategic and cutting-edge issues that touch upon many areas. I hope delegates will make full use of this workshop to share policies, practices and experience on global cyber security, an issue of shared interest, and explore solutions to it.

I also want to thank the UN for its efforts to make this workshop possible. China always values its cooperation with the UN and supports the UN in playing an important role in international affairs. This is the first time for China to co-host with the UN an international workshop on cyber security. I believe it will help to build international consensus on cyber security.

Distinguished Guests,
The fast growth of the information and communication technology (ICT) has exerted profound impacts on all aspects of social and economic life of mankind, and offered brand new digital opportunities for the advancement of human civilization. But at the

络恐怖主义呈蔓延之势,个别国家大规模网络数据监控活动严重侵犯别国主权和公民隐私,网络攻击事件和军事化倾向损害国际安全与互信,全球范围内互联网发展不平衡的状况亟待改善。

网络空间是一个新空间,需要我们倍加珍惜。维护网络空间的安全、稳定与繁荣,是国际社会的共同责任。为此,应把握好以下四点重要原则:

第一,和平原则。网络空间互联互通,各国在网络空间利益交融、休戚与共,形成"你中有我,我中有你"的命运共同体。人类不需要一个新的战场,一个和平安宁的网络空间符合所有国家的利益。为此,应摈弃"零和"思维和冷战时期的意识形态,树立互信、互利、平等、协作的新安全观,在充分尊重别国安全的基础上,致力于在共同安全中实现自身安全,切实防止网络军事化和网络军备竞赛。

第二,主权原则。网络的发展没有改变以《联合国宪章》为核心的国际关系基本准则,国家主权原则在网络空间同样适用。网络空间的主权原则至少包括以下要素:

国家对其领土内的信息通信基础设施和信息通信活动拥有管辖权;各国政府有权制定符合本国国情的互联网公共政策;任何国家不得利用网络干涉他国内政或损害他国利益。明确网络空间的主权原

same time, it has also brought unprecedented challenges. Cybercrime and terrorism have been on the rise. The massive-scale surveillance activities by an individual country have severely infringed on other countries' sovereignty and their citizen's privacy. Cyber-attacks and militarized tendency in cyber space can diminish international security and mutual trust, and the imbalanced development of the Internet worldwide needs to be corrected in a timely way.

Cyber space is a new frontier that deserves our special care. The international community has a shared responsibility to maintain security, stability and prosperity in cyber space. To this end, we need to uphold the following principles:

First, the principle of peace. Cyber space is one of connectivity. Countries are bound by intertwined interests, have high stakes in each other and form a community of common destiny in cyber space. Mankind does not need a new battlefield. A peaceful and tranquil cyber space is in the interest of all countries. That is why we should discard the zero-sum mentality and Cold War ideology, and foster a new concept of security featuring mutual trust, mutual benefit, equality and coordination. We should seek our own security through common security and on the basis of full respect for other countries' security, and ward off militarized tendency and arms race in cyber space.

Second, the principle of sovereignty. Development of cyber space has not changed the basic norms governing international relations that are anchored in the UN Charter. The principle of state sovereignty applies also to cyber space.

The sovereignty principle in cyber space includes at least the following factors: states own jurisdiction over the ICT infrastructure and activities within their territories; national governments are entitled to making public policies for the Internet based on their national conditions; no country shall use the Internet

则,既能体现各国政府依法管理网络空间的责任与权利,也有助于推动各国构建政府、企业和社会团体之间良性互动的平台,为信息技术的发展以及国际交流与合作营造一个健康的生态环境。

第三,共治原则。网络属于每个人,也属于所有人,需要大家共同建设,共同治理。互联网治理是全球治理的重要组成部分。国际社会应共同努力,构建一个公正合理的互联网全球治理体系。在此过程中,应切实落实信息社会世界峰会两阶段会议的重要成果,遵循多边、民主、透明的原则,努力实现互联网资源共享、责任共担、合作共治。

第四,普惠原则。网络为世界经济增长和实现千年发展目标提供了强劲动力,在未来全球发展议程中也占据着极为重要的位置。我们应倡导互利共赢理念,鼓励开展双边、区域及国际发展合作,特别应加大对发展中国家的援助,帮助他们跨越"数字鸿沟"。应努力推动互联网的普遍接入,确保人人从网络发展机遇中获益,共享发展成果,实现信息社会世界峰会确定的建设以人为本、面向发展、包容性的信息社会目标。

to interfere in other countries' internal affairs or undermine other countries' interests. Upholding the principle of sovereignty in cyber space not only reflects governments' responsibilities and rights to administer cyber space in accordance with law, but also enables countries to build platforms for sound interactions among governments, businesses and social groups. This will in turn foster a healthy environment for the growth of information technology and international exchange and cooperation.

Third, the principle of co-governance. As the Internet is open to everyone, it needs to be built and managed by all. The governance of the Internet is an important part of global governance. The international community should work together to build a global Internet governance system that is fair and equitable. In this process, the important outcomes of the two phases of the World Summit on Information Society (WSIS) should be earnestly implemented. And the principles of multilateralism, democracy and transparency should be upheld, so that the Internet will be a place of open resources and shared responsibilities and is governed through cooperation.

Fourth, the principle of universal benefit. The Internet is a strong driving force for world economic growth and achievement of the Millennium Development Goals and takes an important place in the future global development agenda. We need to advocate the concept of mutual benefit and encourage bilateral, regional and international development cooperation. In particular, we need to increase assistance to developing countries and help them bridge the "digital divide". Efforts should be made to promote universal access to the Internet, enable everyone to benefit from the opportunities brought by the Internet's development and share in its achievements, and ensure that we meet the goal of

各位来宾!

上述目标的实现,离不开国际社会的共同努力。中方认为,相关国际努力应从以下几点做起。

一是要坚持对话与合作。在当前网络空间事端频发的背景下,各方应在相互尊重和信任的基础上,以建设性态度开展对话,合作解决分歧。个别国家在网络问题上奉行双重标准,以一己私利划线,炮制只适用于别国的"规则",我们对此表示严重关切。个别国家对自己损害别国主权和公民隐私的行径不进行应有的反思,反而把自己装扮成受害者,对他国进行无端指责与抹黑。这种虚伪、霸道的行径必须予以纠正。

二是要制定各国普遍接受的国际规范。当前形势下,尽快建立相关国际规则框架,规范各方行为,是厘清网络空间秩序、增强各方信心、实现共同安全的重要步骤。在继续研究现有国际法如何适用网络空间的同时,应当积极探索适合网络空间特点的新的国际规范,包括负责任国家行为准则。可采取先易后难的方式,循序渐进加以推进。中俄等国于2011年向联合国大会提交了"信息安全国际行为准则",我们愿与各方为完善准则继续做出努力。

building a people-centered, inclusive and development-oriented information society set at the WSIS.

Distinguished Guests,

To meet this goal would be impossible without the joint efforts of the international community. China believes that relevant international efforts should be focused on the following areas.

First, we need to be committed to dialogue and cooperation. Amidst the frequent occurrence of incidents in cyber space, parties concerned should take a constructive approach, engage in dialogue onthe basis of mutual respect and trust, and resolve differences through cooperation. An individual country has exercised double standards on the cyber issue, drawn lines out of its selfish interests and concocted "regulations" only applicable to other countries. We express strong concerns over this. Instead of reflecting on its behaviors that undermine the sovereignty of other countries and privacy of citizens, it has painted itself as a victim and made groundless accusations against or defamed other countries. This kind of hypocritical and hegemonic behaviors must be corrected.

Second, we need to formulate international norms accepted by all countries. Under current circumstances, to establish a relevant international framework of norms to regulate behaviors of various parties is an important step towards keeping cyber space in order, boosting confidence of various parties and achieving common security. We should continue to study how to apply existing international laws to cyber space and at the same time actively explore new international norms that accord with features of cyber space, including Norms of Responsible Behaviors by States. We may take a gradual approach and address easier issues first before moving to difficult ones. China, Russia and some other countries submitted to the UN General Assembly the International Code of Conduct for

三是要保证各方共同参与。建立各国政府和其他利益攸关方的新型合作关系，使大家能够平等参与讨论，发挥各自应有作用，共同营造全球网络安全文化。要确保相关国际进程的包容与开放，加强发展中国家在其中的代表性，照顾发展中国家的合理关切。

各位来宾！

21世纪是网络和信息化的世纪。作为拥有6.18亿网民的网络大国，中国高度重视网络安全和信息化工作，致力于不断提高自身网络安全水平。今年2月，中国成立了中央网络安全和信息化领导小组，形成了网络安全工作统筹领导、有效推进的新局面。在领导小组首次会议上，习近平主席提出了建设网络强国的宏伟目标。这一构想是中国人民追求实现"中国梦"的重要组成部分。正如习主席所说，"中国梦"是追求和平的梦、追求幸福的梦、奉献世界的梦。中国始终是网络空间的建设者、维护者和贡献者，致力于与国际社会携手共建和平、安全、开放、合作的网络空间。我们愿为创造更加繁荣美好的网络空间做出更大贡献。

最后，我预祝会议取得圆满成功。

谢谢大家！

Information Security in 2011 and we are ready to work with othersides for its improvement.

Third, we need to ensure participation of all parties. The establishment of a new-type cooperative relationship between governments and other stakeholders will facilitate equal-footed participation in discussions and enable them to play their respective roles and jointly foster global awareness of cyber security. We need to ensure the inclusiveness and openness of relevant international processes, strengthen the representation of developing countries and accommodate their legitimate concerns.

Distinguished Guests,

The 21st century is an era of the Internet and IT application. As a major cyber state with 618 million Internet users, China attaches great importance to cyber security and IT application and is committed to improving its level of cyber security. In February, China established the central leading group on internet security and informatization, making possible unified leadership and effective enforcement in the work of cyber security. At the first meeting of the leading group, President Xi Jinping put forward the ambitious goal of turning China into a strong cyber state, which is an important part of the Chinese people's efforts to realize the Chinese dream. As President Xi said, the Chinese dream is about the pursuit of peace and happiness and devotion to the world. China has always been contributing its part to building and maintaining cyber space and committed to working with the rest of the international community to create a peaceful, secure, open and cooperative cyber space. We are ready to make greater contribution to building a more prosperous and enabling cyber space.

Finally, I wish this workshop a complete success.

Thank you.

3. CNN News: head of tech companies met with President Obama, Dec 2013 (Full report)
CNN 新闻:奥巴马总统会见科技行业的精英首脑,2013 年 12 月(全文)
英文及译文来源:可可英语网
http://m.kekenet.com/broadcast/201312/270427.shtml

Apple, Google, Microsoft, Twitter – What do they all have in common?

Their bosses were all at the White House yesterday.

President Obama met with the heads of more than a dozen tech industry leaders.

Part of the meeting was about the industry possibly helping the government with its I.T. problems, like the highly problematic rollout of the Obamacare website.

They also talked about spying.

Technology executives recently asked the government to change its spying practices.

Details about secret surveillance programs were leaked by Edward Snowden, a former National Security Agency workers.

He's in Russia now and asking Brazil about asylum there.

In the U.S., the programs that Snowden revealed are facing a new challenge.

Six months after Edward Snowden revealed it to the world, a federal judge ruled the NSA program that sweeps up Americans phone call records is likely unconstitutional.

The judge wrote, "I cannot imagine a more indiscriminate and arbitrary invasion than this systematic and high-tech collection and retention of personal data on virtually every citizen."

Snowden described it as a vindication of his hacking, saying, "I acted on my belief that the NSA mass surveillance program would not withstand a constitutional challenge."

Today, a secret program authorized by a secret court was, when exposed to the light of day, found to violate Americans' rights.

苹果、谷歌、微软、推特,它们有什么共同点?

昨天他们的老板们都现身白宫。

奥巴马总统会见了十几位科技行业的精英首脑。

会议的一部分内容是关于这个行业如何运用 IT 帮助政府,比如奥巴马医改网站引发的诸多问题。

他们也谈到了间谍活动。

技术高管们最近要求政府改变其间谍监控行为。

秘密监视项目细节已经被前国家安全局工作人员爱德华·斯诺登泄露。

他现在在俄罗斯,并且正在询问巴西避难事宜。

而在美国,斯诺登揭露的项目正面临着新的挑战。"

爱德华·斯诺登将监控项目展示给世界六个月后,一位联邦法官裁定美国国家安全局程序清理电话记录的行为可能违宪。

法官记录道,"我无法想象比这更糟糕的情境,随意入侵系统并且采用高科技方法收集和保留几乎所有公民的个人资料。"

而斯诺登为自己的黑客行为澄清,"我认为国家安全局监测项目将无法承受一部宪法的挑战。"

现如今,一个秘密政府授权的一个秘密项目终于暴露在众目睽睽之下,美国人民发现自己的权利受

Chapter X　Consecutive Interpreting Materials for Different Themes

Snowden remains hold up in Russia, avoiding charges in the U.S. of espionage.	斯诺登仍然身在俄罗斯,避免到亵渎。斯诺登仍然身在俄罗斯,避免美国间谍的指控。
But a senior NSA official floated un unlikely solution on CBS *60 Minutes* to get Snowden back here:give him amnesty.	但国家安全局的一位高级官员在哥伦比亚广播公司《60分钟》节目中提出收回斯诺登可能解决方案:给他特赦。
An idea that White House quickly dismissed.	然而该提议迅速被白宫拒绝。
He should be returned to the United States as soon as possible where he will be accorded all due process and protections in our system, so that's our position and it hasn't changed.	他应该尽快回到美国,在那里他将在我们的体系中被给予所有正当程序并受到保护,这就是我们的立场并且没有改变。
Still, the court's decision is a body blow for the administration.	不过,法院的判决是政府的打击。
Well, it is just an absolutely scathing rejection of the NSA program that the government has defended so strongly.	嗯,这仅仅是政府如此强烈维护国家安全局计划绝对严厉的拒绝。
And if it's worth noting that the judge was a George W. Bush—appointee, someone who would work for Republicans in Congress.	而值得注意的是那位法官是乔治·布什所任命的人,他将为共和党人在国会工作。
Jim Sciutto, CNN, Washington.	CNN新闻,吉姆·斯科特,华盛顿报道。

10.5　Sports and Health

1."明谢"姚明新闻发布会致辞,2011年07月20日,上海(全文)
Yao Ming's goodbye and thank-you speech at the press conference, July 20, 2011, Shanghai(Full text)
中文及译文来源:新浪体育
http://sports.sina.com.cn/k/2011-07-20/16255667464.shtml

各位领导,各位来宾,新闻界的朋友们:	Esteemed Director Li Yuyi, distinguished guests, friends in the media:
大家好,感谢大家的光临。	Good afternoon! Thank you for coming.
今天对我来说是一个重要的日子,无论是对我以往的篮球职业生涯,还是未来的个人发展,都具有特殊的意义。	Today is an important day for me. It is a day of special significance for both my past professional career and future endeavors.

— 345 —

去年年底,我的左脚第三次应力性骨折,我不得不离开赛场。半年多以来,和许多关心我的朋友一样,我也是在漫长的期待当中度过的。这段时间里,内心十分纠结,反复思考。为此,今天我要宣布一个个人决定:作为篮球运动员,我将结束自己的运动生涯,正式退役。

此时此刻,回顾过去,展望未来,我的内心充满感激。

我首先要感谢篮球。这项伟大的运动为无数人带来了快乐,当然也包括我自己。四岁我有了第一个篮球,九岁进入徐汇区少体校,十四岁进入上海青年队,十六岁背上父亲当年的号码,代表上海队比赛。篮球使我延续了家庭的传承,每每看到父母欣慰的眼神,我都无比自豪;也非常幸运能和上海大鲨鱼队的队友们一起为上海赢得了一次CBA总冠军。从那时起,篮球把我和身后这座城市联系在了一起;同样在CBA夺冠的2002年,我进入NBA,篮球引领我步入了一个更宽广的舞台,使我可以尽情地展现自己;更要感谢能有机会为中国国家队战十年,那是无数青年人的梦想;同时因为篮球,与心爱的人结缘,建立了美满的家庭,获得了一生的幸福。所有这些,都是我无比热爱的篮球运动带给我的,我要感谢篮球。

我还要感谢生活。无论我所热爱的篮球,还是别的什么东西,都是生活的一部分。我觉得生活就像一

At the end of last year, I once again had a stress fracture in my left foot and had to sit out of basketball. Since then, like many friends who cared about me, I waited and hoped that I could return. It was also a frustrating period, many thoughts crossed my mind. Today, I am ready to announce to everyone my decision: I will end my athletic career and formally retire from the game of basketball.

At this moment, looking towards the future and looking back through the past, my heart is full of gratitude.

First and foremost, I want to thank the game of basketball. This great sport has brought joy to untold numbers of people, including myself. When I was four years old, I got my first basketball. At nine, I entered a youth sports school in Xuhui district (in Shanghai). I joined the Shanghai Junior Team at 14. And when I was 16 years old, I put on my dad's former number, and joined the Shanghai Sharks senior team in competition. Basketball has allowed me to follow in my family's footsteps. Whenever I see the joy and satisfaction in my parents' eyes, I feel a strong sense of pride. I was also fortunate to win a CBA Championship with my teammates for the city of Shanghai in 2002. From that moment on, basketball has connected me with this great city. During that same year, I entered the NBA. Basketball has led me to a bigger and broader stage to showcase my abilities. It's a dream for many to play for the National Team. So in fulfilling my dream, I am especially grateful of the opportunity to play for my country for so many years. And because of basketball, I have found the love of my life Ye Li, and a lifetime of happiness. Basketball has given me so much and for this, I want to thank the game of basketball.

I also want to thank life. No matter if it's my beloved basketball or other endeavors. It is all just a part of life. I believe life is like a guide. If you follow

个向导,你虔诚地追随他,他就会为你打开一扇又一扇的门,而门外的世界各不相同,无比精彩。今天我退役了,一扇门已经关上,而另一扇门却正在徐徐开启,而门外有崭新的生活正在等着我去认真品读。

我虽然离开了赛场,但我不会离开篮球。上海东方大鲨鱼篮球队,将是我篮球生涯的延续,我正在学习用我的方式管理俱乐部,以这种方式继续为家乡带来荣誉,为球迷带来快乐,为中国篮球继续作贡献。

我将继续投身社会公益事业,"姚基金"是我个人的基金会,已经成立三年了,接下来我会以此为依托,影响更多的人参与慈善事业,帮助更多的人。同时,我希望结识更多的朋友,一起做些共同喜欢的事情。相信在和各行各业的有识之士的交往中,我会学到更多的东西。丰富多彩的生活引领着我从上海走向了全国,从中国走向了世界。我要感谢生活,今后,唯有认真对待他,才是对生活最好的回报。

最后,我要感谢我的亲人,感谢所有的朋友。我这里有一份长长的名单,但由于时间的原因,不能一一提及。只能选读其中的代表,还望朋友们多多谅解。我首先感谢的是我的家人,父亲、母亲是我人生的启蒙者,叶莉是我最好的倾听者,而可爱的姚沁蕾则是我们新的希望。

我还要感谢我的教练们,是他们教育培养了我,见证了我每一步的成长,其中有我的启蒙教练李章明指导,我在上海大鲨鱼队的教练李秋平指导、王群指导、王重光指

him faithfully, he will open doors to wonderful worlds for you. Today, I am retired from basketball, and one of those doors is closed. But elsewhere, another door is opening and outside that door is a new world waiting for me to experience and explore.

Even though I am leaving the basketball court, I will not leave the game. The Shanghai Sharks team is how my professional life will continue. I am continuing to learn about managing and running the team and will do my best to bring honor and glory to my hometown and to Chinese basketball.

I will continue my philanthropic work. The Yao Foundation has been established for three years now. I will work with the foundation to influence more people to join philanthropic activities to help others. I wish to meet and work with new and old friends on projects of mutual interest. I believe that through meeting and working with people from different fields and professions, I can gain new knowledge and new understandings. Life has guided me from Shanghai to China, from China to the world. I want to thank life and continue to repay my good fortune by embracing and treasuring every moment.

Finally, I want to thank the many special people in my life, my family and my friends. I have a long list of people. But due to time, I can only mention a few here. I am missing a lot of names, but I hope my friends will understand. First, I want to thank my family. My parents were my first teachers in life. My wife, Ye Li is my best friend and best listener. Our lovely daughter, Amy, is our new hope for the future.

I also want to thank my coaches. They educated and guided me and have watched over me every step of way. I want to thank my first coach Li Zhangming, coaches Li Qiuping, Wang Qun, and Wang Chongguang from the Shanghai Sharks, coach

导，我在国家青年队的主教练马连保指导，以及我在国家队的历任主教练王非指导、蒋兴权指导以及哈里斯和尤纳斯，还有我在火箭队的历任主教练汤姆贾诺维奇、范甘迪、阿德尔曼，教练 Tom Tip。我要感谢各位领导，特别是国家体育总局、上海市、中国篮协、上海市体育局以及上海文广集团和原上海东方篮球俱乐部的各级领导，他们的关心、关注、支持和鼓励，使我不断进步，取得了今天的成绩。我要感谢 NBA 和休斯敦火箭队的管理层，他们的理解和支持帮助我克服了语言和文化的障碍，使我可以在世界最高水平的联赛当中站稳脚跟。

接下来我要感谢我的队友和对手们，首先是刘炜，我们并肩成长，一起打拼，这段共同的经历是我最珍视的人生片段，还有大郅和奥尼尔，他们是我追赶的目标与前进的动力，没有他们，我就不是今天的我；还有范斌，他是我国家队的良师益友，还有沈巍、贾效忠、章文琪、李楠、巴特尔、易建联、弗朗西斯、莫布里、麦蒂、巴蒂尔、穆托姆博、海耶斯、斯科拉、布鲁克斯和洛里以及所有和我一起在徐汇区业余体校、上海青年队、上海大鲨鱼、休斯敦火箭队、国青男篮、国家男篮一起奋斗过的队友们，还有在 CBA 和 NBA 同场比赛过的对手们，一起挥汗如雨的日子永远令人难忘。

Ma Lianbao with the Chinese National Junior team, head coaches Wang Fei, Jiang Xingquan, Del Harris, and Jonas Kazlauskas from the Chinese National Team, and head coaches Rudy Tomjanovich, Jeff Van Gundy, and Rick Adelman with the Houston Rockets. I also wish to thank officials and organizations that have helped me, especially officials from National Sports Administration, city of Shanghai, China Basketball Association, Shanghai Sports Administration, the Shanghai Media Group, and Shanghai Oriental Basketball Club (Shanghai Sharks). It is through their care, interest, support, and encouragement that allowed me to develop and reach where I am today. I want to thank the NBA and the Houston Rockets. Their understanding and support helped me overcome the language and cultural barrier to play in the highest level basketball games in the world.

Next, I want to thank all of my teammates and opponents. First is Liu Wei. We grew up together, played and battled together, and those experiences are some of my most precious memories in life. I also want to thank Wang Zhizhi and Shaquille O'Neal. They were the benchmark players that I was chasing after. They motivated me and pushed me forward, and without them, I would not be the player I am today. I want to thank Fan Bin, my friend and mentor on the National team; Shen Wei, Jia Xiaozhong, Zhang Wenqi, Li Nan, Mengke Bateer, Yi Jianlian, Steve Francis, Cuttino Mobley, Tracy McGrady, Shane Battier, Dikembe Mutombo, Chuck Hayes, Luis Scola, Aaron Brooks, Kyle Lowry, as well as all of my former teammates from the Xuhui District Youth Sports School, the Shanghai Sharks Junior team, the Shanghai Sharks, the National Junior Team, the Chinese National Team, and the Houston Rockets, and of course all my opponents in CBA and NBA who I played against. The time we spent sweating and competing will forever be etched

Chapter Ⅹ Consecutive Interpreting Materials for Different Themes

当然,要感谢的还有我的管理团队——"姚之队",感谢章明基、陆浩、约翰·海逊格、比尔·达菲、比尔·桑德斯、李璐、伊朗纳和张弛,以及现在还在台前幕后忙碌的成员们!多年来,你们帮我做了很多事情,我不会忘记。

借此机会,我还要特别感谢常年关注我的新闻界的朋友们,感谢我的赞助商和合作伙伴,和你们的交往使我受益匪浅。还有各位球迷朋友,不论是"黑"还是"蜜",无论是国内的还是国外的,感谢所有关注我的朋友。大家的关心使我得到了信心和勇气,大家的批评使我修正了缺点和不足。今天提到的和没提到的,你们每一个人,都在我的心里。总而言之,我感谢所有的亲人和朋友多年来的陪伴,我会继续做好我自己,不会离开大家。姚明和朋友们永远在一起!谢谢大家。

最后要感谢这个伟大、进步的时代,使我有机会去实现自我的价值和梦想。

我曾经说过,有一天我的篮球职业生涯结束了,我希望那只是个逗号,不是句号。今天,这一天终于到来了,但我没有离开心爱的篮球,我的生活还在继续,我还是姚明,我还有很多事情要做,远远没有到画上句号的那一天。

祝朋友们健康快乐,祝福我的家乡上海、第二故乡休斯敦,祝福我的祖国,愿我所热爱的篮球运动,拥有更加美好的未来。

谢谢大家。

in my memory.

I also want to thank my management team, "Team Yao". I want to thank Erik Zhang, Lu Hao, John Huizinga, Bill Duffy, Bill Sanders, Huang Xiaopeng, Li Lu, Ilana, and Larry Zhang, as well as everyone who has worked behind the scenes. I will never forget everything you have done for me over the years.

I'd also like to take this opportunity to thank my friends in the media, my sponsors, and partners. I am honored to have worked with all of you. Finally, I want to sincerely thank all of the fans. Those who liked me or those who didn't, those who are in China, or those abroad, I want to thank everyone who has watched me over the years. It is through everyone's support that has allowed me to play with confidence and courage; and through everyone's criticism that has helped me improve in areas that I was lacking. For those I have mentioned, and for those I have not, you are all in my heart. In short, I want to thank everyone who has accompanied me these years. And I will continue to do my best and will continue to be with everyone. Thank you.

Finally, I want to thank this enlightened time of progress that we live in: giving me the opportunities to realize my dreams, and find my self-worth.

I have once said, when I retire from my professional career, I hope that it is a comma, not a period. Today, that day has finally arrived, but I am not leaving the sport of basketball that I love. My life will continue. I am still Yao Ming and there are still many things that I wish to accomplish. The day of drawing a period is still far far away.

I wish everyone health and happiness, I wish the best blessings for my mother land, my home Shanghai, and my second home Houston. And I wish that my beloved sport of basketball will continue to have a bright and prosperous future.

Thank you.

2. Keynote address at the World Health Summit, by Dr. Margaret Chan, Director-General of the World Health Organization, Berlin, 11 October 2015 (Full text)

世界卫生组织总干事陈冯富珍博士在世界卫生峰会上的主旨讲话,柏林,2015 年 10 月 11 日(全文)

英文来源:世界卫生组织官网

https://www.who.int/dg/speeches/detail/keynote-address-at-the-world-health-summit

译文来源:可可英语网

http://www.kekenet.com/kouyi/201601/420927.shtml

Excellencies, honourable ministers, distinguished participants, ladies and gentlemen,	诸位阁下,各位尊敬的部长,尊敬的与会者,女士们、先生们:
The world has changed dramatically since the start of this century, when the Millennium Development Goals became the focus of international efforts to reduce human misery.	本世纪初,千年发展目标成为减少人类苦难的国际努力的焦点。自那之后,全世界已经发生巨大变化。
At that time, human misery was thought to have a discrete set of principal causes, like poverty, hunger, poor water and sanitation, several infectious diseases, and lack of essential care during pregnancy, childbirth, and childhood.	当时,人们认为,人类苦难有一系列不相关联的主要原因,例如贫困、饥饿、缺乏饮用水和卫生设施、多种传染病以及在妊娠、分娩和儿童期缺乏基本诊疗服务。
The results of that focus, and all the energy, resources, and innovations it unleashed, exceeded the wildest dreams of many. It demonstrated the power of international solidarity and brought out the best in human nature.	当时的关注及其带来的所有能源、资源和创新所产生的结果已经超出许多人最狂野的想象。它显示了国际团结的力量和人性最美好的一面。
Maternal and child mortality fell at the fastest rate in history, with some of the sharpest drops recorded in sub-Saharan Africa. Each day, 17,000 fewer children die than in 1990. AIDS reached a tipping point in 2014 when the number of people newly receiving antiretroviral therapy surpassed the number of new infections.	孕产妇和儿童死亡率以历史上最快的速度下降,其中一些最大降幅出现在撒哈拉以南非洲。与 1990 年相比,儿童死亡人数每天减少 1.7 万名。2014 年,艾滋病达到一个转折点:新接受抗逆转录病毒治疗的人数超过了新发感染数。
Since the start of the century, an estimated 37 million lives were saved by effective diagnosis and treatment of tuberculosis. Over the same period, deaths from malaria declined by 60%. An estimated 6.2 million lives, mainly in young African children,	据估计,自本世纪初以来,有效诊断并治疗结核病已经挽救了 3700 万人的生命。同时,疟疾死亡降低了 60%,约 620 万人获救,其中主要是非洲幼童。

were saved.

Drug donations by the pharmaceutical industry allowed WHO to reach more than 800 million people each year with preventive therapy for river blindness, lymphatic filariasis, schistosomiasis, and other neglected topical diseases. These are ancient, debilitating diseases that anchor more than a billion people in poverty. By reaching so many millions, we are paving the way for a mass exodus from poverty.

I would like to thank the German government, Chancellor Merkel, and other G7 leaders for putting these diseases on the global agenda. If we believe in poverty reduction, we must address these neglected diseases. I also thank the private sector for providing preventive medicines at no cost. This is how public-private partnerships work at their best.

Last month, the United Nations General Assembly finalized a new agenda for sustainable development. The number of goals has grown from 8 to 17, including one for health. The related targets increased 8-fold, from 21 to 169.

The factors that now govern the well-being of the human condition, and the planet that sustains it, are no longer so discrete. The new agenda will try to shape a very different world.

This is a world that is seeing not the best in human nature, but the worst: international terrorism, senseless mass shootings, bombings in markets and places of worship, ancient and priceless archaeological sites reduced to rubble, and the seemingly endless armed conflicts that have contributed to the worst refugee crisis since the end of the second World War.

Ladies and gentlemen,

Since the start of this century, newer threats to health have gained prominence. Like the other problems that cloud humanity's prospects for a sustainable future, these newer threats to health are much bigger and more complex than the problems

制药企业捐赠的药品使世卫组织能够每年为8亿多人提供针对河盲症、淋巴丝虫病、血吸虫病和其它被忽视热带病的预防性治疗。这些令人衰弱的古老疾病主要影响10亿贫困人口。通过为上亿人提供药物，我们正在为大量人口摆脱贫困铺平道路。

我要感谢德国政府、默克尔总理和其它七国集团领导人将这些疾病纳入全球议程。如果我们相信减贫，我们就必须处理这些被忽视的疾病。我还要感谢私营部门免费提供预防用药。这正是最有利于公私伙伴关系发挥作用的方式。

上个月，联合国大会确定了可持续发展新议程。目标数量从8个增加到17个，其中包括一个卫生目标。相关具体目标约增加7倍，从21个到169个。

现在，决定人类福祉和星球状况的因素再也不是不相关联。新议程将努力塑造一个非常不同的世界。

在这个世界上，我们看到的不是人性中最美好的一面，而是最糟糕的：国际恐怖主义、毫无人性的大规模枪击事件、集贸市场和礼拜场所的爆炸、古老而珍贵的考古遗址沦为瓦砾堆以及已经造成二战结束以来最严重难民危机的似乎永无终止的武装冲突。

女士们、先生们，

自本世纪初以来，新的卫生威胁愈发突出。和其它为人类可持续未来前景罩上阴影的问题一样，卫生面临的这些更新的威胁比15年前主导卫生议程的那些问题更大也

that dominated the health agenda 15 years ago.

All around the world, health is being shaped by the same powerful forces, like population ageing, rapid urbanization, and the globalized marketing of unhealthy products.

Under the pressure of these forces, chronic noncommunicable diseases have overtaken infectious diseases as the world's biggest killers. This shift in the disease burden has profound implications. It challenges the very way socioeconomic progress is defined.

Beginning in the 19th century, improvements in hygiene and living conditions were followed by vast improvements in health status and life-expectancy. These environmental improvements aided the control of infectious diseases, totally vanquishing many major killers from modern societies.

Today, the tables are turned. Instead of diseases vanishing as living conditions improve, socioeconomic progress is actually creating the conditions that favour the rise of noncommunicable diseases. Economic growth, modernization, and urbanization have opened wide the entry point for the spread of unhealthy lifestyles.

The world is ill-prepared to cope with NCDs. Few health systems were built to manage chronic if not life-long conditions. Even fewer doctors were trained to prevent them. And even fewer governments can afford to treat them.

In some countries, the costs of treating diabetes alone absorb from 25% to 50% of the entire health budget. As a recent Lancet Oncology Commission concluded, the costs of cancer therapy are becoming unaffordable, even for the wealthiest countries in the world. Many newly approved cancer drugs cost more than $120,000 per person per year.

The climate is changing. WHO's recent estimate

更复杂。

在全世界，卫生都受到同样强大力量的影响，包括人口老龄化、快速城市化和不健康产品的全球营销。

在这些力量的压力下，慢性非传染性疾病已经超过传染病成为全世界第一大死因。疾病负担方面的这一变化具有深远影响。它直接挑战人类对于社会经济进步的定义。

自19世纪以来，卫生和生活条件的改善使人类健康状况大幅度改善，预期寿命大幅度延长。这些环境方面的改善有助于控制传染病，使许多主要死因从现代社会消失。

今天，形势发生了逆转。疾病没有随着生活条件改善而消失，相反，社会经济进步正在创造助长非传染性疾病增加的条件。经济增长、现代化和城市化为不健康生活方式的传播大开其门。

全世界都没有做好应对非传染性疾病的准备。没有哪些国家的卫生系统是为了管理慢性乃至终身疾病而建立起来的。受过预防慢性病培训的医生数量更少。能够负担得起慢性病治疗的政府数量还要少。

在一些国家，单是治疗糖尿病的支出就占去整个卫生预算的25%至50%。正如最近《柳叶刀》肿瘤学委员会得出的结论，癌症治疗的费用将超出各国负担能力，即使世界上最富裕的国家也是如此。许多新批准的抗癌药费用超过每人每年12万美元。

气候正在发生变化。世卫组织

that air pollution kills around 7 million people each year has finally given health a place in debates about the consequences of climate change. Worldwide, this past July was the hottest since at least 1880, when records began. This year's thousands of deaths associated with heat waves in India and Pakistan provide further headline evidence of the health effects of extreme weather events.

Antimicrobial resistance has become a major health and medical crisis. If current trends continue, this will mean the end of modern medicine as we know it. WHO warmly welcomes the G7 health ministers declaration and the commitment it makes to address this crisis in all its multiple dimensions.

No one working in public health should underestimate the challenges that lie ahead. These newer threats to health do not neatly fit the biomedical model that has historically guided public health responses. Their root causes lie outside the traditional domain of public health.

The health sector acting alone cannot protect children from the marketing of unhealthy foods and beverages, persuade countries to reduce their greenhouse gas emissions, or get industrialized food producers to reduce their massive use of antibiotics.

The newer threats to health also lie beyond the traditional domain of sovereign nations accustomed to governing what happens in their territories. In a world of radically increased interdependence, all are transboundary threats.

The globalized marketing of unhealthy products respects no borders. By definition, a changing climate affects the entire planet.

As sharply illustrated by malaria, tuberculosis, and bacteria carrying the NDM-1 enzyme, drug-resistant pathogens are notorious globe-trotters. They travel well in infected air passengers and through global trade in food. In addition, the growth

最近估计,空气污染每年造成约700万人死亡。这终于使卫生问题在有关气候变化后果的辩论中获得一席之地。刚过去的7月是自1880年有记录以来最热的。今年有数千人在印度和巴基斯坦热浪中死亡,消息占据了头条,也是极端天气事件造成健康影响的进一步证据。

抗微生物药物耐药性也已成为主要卫生和医药危机。如果目前的趋势继续下去,这将意味着我们所知的现代医药的终结。世卫组织热情欢迎七国集团卫生部长做出的有关全面应对此危机的宣言和承诺。

公共卫生领域的每一个人都不应低估未来的挑战。卫生面临的这些更新威胁不能完全适用历史上一直指导着公共卫生应对工作的生物医药模式。其根源在公共卫生传统领域之外。

卫生部门单打独斗不能保护儿童不受不健康食品饮料营销的影响,不能说服各国减少温室气体排放,也不能让工业化食品生产商减少抗生素的大规模使用。

卫生面临的更新威胁也在习惯于在本国领土范围内进行治理的主权国家的传统领域之外。在一个相互依存急剧上升的世界,所有威胁都是跨国威胁。

不健康产品的全球化营销不受边界限制。根据定义,正在变化的气候也影响整个星球。

正如疟疾、结核病和携带Ⅰ型新德里金属β-内酰胺酶(NDM-1)的细菌所突出表明的那样,耐药病原体是恶名昭彰的全球旅行者。它们在被感染航空乘客体内并通过全

of medical tourism has accelerated the international spread of hospital-acquired infections that are frequently resistant to multiple drugs.

We face other challenges. The poverty map has changed. Today, 70% of the world's poor live in middle-income countries. This is a game-changing statistic. Growth in GDP has long been the yardstick for measuring national progress.

If the economy is doing well, where is the incentive to invest in equitable health care? The world does not need any more rich countries full of poor people.

Our world is profoundly interconnected and this, too, has consequences. The refugee crisis in Europe shattered the notion that wars in faraway lands will stay remote. The Ebola outbreak shattered the notion that a disease of poor African nations will have no consequences elsewhere.

Ladies and gentlemen,

In the most dramatic and tragic way possible, the Ebola outbreak focused international attention on the need to invest in health systems, especially in fragile and vulnerable states.

WHO welcomes the G7 commitment to act on lessons learned from Ebola. I welcome, in particular, the emphasis it places on strengthening health systems as a first line of defence against the infectious disease threat.

As noted, the goal is to build resilient and sustainable health systems that offer quality, comprehensive care and aim to progressively achieve universal health coverage.

The attention given to health systems is a most welcome focus that was not present when the Millennium Development Goals were agreed 15 years ago.

球食品贸易旅行。此外，医疗旅游的增长也加快了医院获得性感染的国际传播，而这类感染往往对多种药物耐药。

我们还面临其它挑战。贫困地图已然发生变化。今天，全世界70％贫困人口生活在中等收入国家。这一统计数据改变了游戏规则。国民生产总值（GDP）的增长长期以来一直是衡量国家进步的标准。

如果经济状况很好，投资于公平卫生保健的动力何在？全世界再也不需要任何满是贫困人口的富裕国家。

我们的世界深刻地相互关联，而这，也有其后果。欧洲的难民危机打碎了遥远之地的战争将永远遥远的观念。埃博拉疫情打碎了某个贫困非洲国家的疾病不会对其它地方产生后果的观念。

女士们、先生们，

埃博拉疫情以最具戏剧性和悲剧性的方式使国际社会注意到需要投资于卫生系统，特别是在脆弱和弱势国家。

世卫组织欢迎七国集团有关在埃博拉疫情教训基础上采取行动的承诺。特别是，我欢迎七国集团强调加强卫生系统使之成为针对传染病威胁的第一道防线。

如前所述，目标是建设有恢复力的可持续卫生系统，提供高质量的全面诊疗服务并逐步实现全民健康覆盖。

对卫生系统的关注最令人高兴，这种关注在15年前商定千年发展目标时并不存在。

Chapter Ⅹ　Consecutive Interpreting Materials for Different Themes

The global health initiatives that brought such spectacular results did so largely through the delivery of commodities, like bednets, vaccines, and cocktails of medicine. Confronted with weak health systems, the initiatives often built their own parallel systems for procurement, delivery, financial management, and reporting.

Fortunately, many development partners now recognize that virtually all health targets on the new development agenda need a well-functioning and inclusive health system to achieve sustainable results.

Last month, 267 prominent economists from 44 countries published a declaration in the Lancet. That declaration called on global leaders to prioritize a pro-poor pathway to universal health coverage as an essential pillar of sustainable development.

The economic arguments for doing so are compelling. UHC transforms livelihoods as well as lives, and works as a poverty-reduction strategy. The economic benefits of investing in UHC are estimated to be more than ten times greater than the costs.

The evidence is now overwhelming that providing quality health services free at the point of delivery helps end poverty, boosts growth, and saves lives. UHC cushions shocks on communities when crises occur, whether these arise from a changing climate or a runaway virus.

Under normal conditions, UHC builds cohesive and stable societies and underpins economic productivity. These are valued assets for every country in the world.

Thank you.

在很大程度上，各项全球卫生倡议能够带来如此令人惊叹的结果是因为它们提供了商品，例如蚊帐、疫苗和药物鸡尾酒。面对薄弱的卫生系统，这些倡议常常建立起自己的采购、供货、财务管理和报告系统。

幸运的是，许多发展伙伴现在已经认识到新发展议程上几乎所有具体卫生目标都需要具有包容性且运转良好的卫生系统才能实现可持续的结果。

上个月，来自44个国家的267位杰出经济学家在《柳叶刀》上发表宣言，呼吁全球领导者将以有利于穷人的方式实现全民健康覆盖并使之成为可持续发展的必要支柱确定为重点。

这样做的经济理由是有说服力的。全民健康覆盖会改变民生和生命，并且有助于减贫。投资于全民健康覆盖的经济效益预计将十余倍于其成本。

有关在服务提供点免费提供高质量卫生服务有助于终结贫困、促进增长并挽救生命的证据令人信服。危机发生时，全民健康覆盖可以缓冲社区面临的冲击，不论危机来自气候变化还是病毒失控。

正常情况下，全民健康覆盖使社会更有凝聚力、更稳定，且支撑经济生产率。这是世界上所有国家的宝贵资产。

谢谢大家。

3. "团结合作战胜疫情，共同构建人类卫生健康共同体"，中华人民共和国主席习近平在第73届世界卫生大会视频会议开幕式上的致辞，北京，2020年5月18日(全文)

"Fighting COVID‐19 Through Solidarity and Cooperation, Building a Global Community of Health for All", Statement by H. E. Xi Jinping, President of the People's Republic of China, At Virtual Event of Opening of the 73rd World Health Assembly, Beijing, 18 May 2020 (Full Text)

中文来源：外交部网站
https://www.fmprc.gov.cn/web/ziliao_674904/zyjh_674906/t1780241.shtml
译文来源：外交部英文网站
https://www.fmprc.gov.cn/mfa_eng/wjdt_665385/zyjh_665391/t1780221.shtml

大会主席先生，世界卫生组织总干事先生，各位代表：

首先，我认为，在人类抗击新冠肺炎疫情的关键时刻举行这次世卫大会，具有十分重要的意义！

人类正在经历第二次世界大战结束以来最严重的全球公共卫生突发事件。新冠肺炎疫情突如其来，现在已波及210多个国家和地区，影响70多亿人口，夺走了30余万人的宝贵生命。在此，我谨向不幸罹难者表示哀悼！向他们的家属表示慰问！

人类文明史也是一部同疾病和灾难的斗争史。病毒没有国界，疫病不分种族。面对来势汹汹的新冠肺炎疫情，国际社会没有退缩，各国人民勇敢前行、守望相助、风雨同舟，展现了人间大爱，汇聚起同疫情斗争的磅礴之力。

经过艰苦卓绝努力，付出巨大代价，中国有力扭转了疫情局势，维护了人民生命安全和身体健康。中方始终本着公开、透明、负责任的态度，及时向世卫组织及相关国家通报疫情信息，第一时间发布病毒基

President of the World Health Assembly, Director General of the World Health Organization, Dear Delegates,

To begin with, I wish to say that it is of significant importance for this World Health Assembly to be held at such a critical moment as the human race battles this novel coronavirus.

What we are facing is the most serious global public health emergency since the end of World War II. Catching the world by surprise, COVID-19 has hit over 210 countries and regions, affected more than seven billion people around the world and claimed over 300,000 precious lives. I mourn for every life lost and express condolences to the bereaved families.

The history of human civilization is one of fighting diseases and tiding over disasters. The virus does not respect borders. Nor is race or nationality relevant in the face of the disease. Confronted by the ravages of COVID-19, the international community has not flinched. The people of all countries have tackled the virus head on. Around the world, people have looked out for each other and pulled together as one. With love and compassion, we have forged extraordinary synergy in the fight against COVID-19.

In China, after making painstaking efforts and enormous sacrifice, we have turned the tide on the virus and protected the life and health of our people. All along, we have acted with openness, transparency and responsibility. We have provided information to WHO and relevant countries in a most

Chapter X Consecutive Interpreting Materials for Different Themes

因序列等信息，毫无保留同各方分享防控和救治经验，尽己所能为有需要的国家提供了大量支持和帮助。

主席先生！

现在，疫情还在蔓延，防控仍需努力。我愿提出以下建议。

第一，全力搞好疫情防控。这是当务之急。我们要坚持以民为本、生命至上，科学调配医疗力量和重要物资，在防护、隔离、检测、救治、追踪等重要领域采取有力举措，尽快遏制疫情在全球蔓延态势，尽力阻止疫情跨境传播。要加强信息分享，交流有益经验和做法，开展检测方法、临床救治、疫苗药物研发国际合作，并继续支持各国科学家们开展病毒源头和传播途径的全球科学研究。

第二，发挥世卫组织领导作用。在谭德塞总干事带领下，世卫组织为领导和推进国际抗疫合作作出了重大贡献，国际社会对此高度赞赏。当前，国际抗疫正处于关键阶段，支持世卫组织就是支持国际抗疫合作、支持挽救生命。中国呼吁国际社会加大对世卫组织政治支持和资金投入，调动全球资源，打赢疫情阻击战。

第三，加大对非洲国家支持。发展中国家特别是非洲国家公共卫

timely fashion. We have released the genome sequence at the earliest possible time. We have shared control and treatment experience with the world without reservation. We have done everything in our power to support and assist countries in need.

Mr. President,

Even as we meet, the virus is still raging, and more must be done to bring it under control. To this end, I want to make the following proposals:

First, we must do everything we can for COVID-19 control and treatment. This is a most urgent task. We must always put the people first, for nothing in the world is more precious than people's lives. We need to deploy medical expertise and critical supplies to places where they are needed the most. We need to take strong steps in such key areas as prevention, quarantine, detection, treatment and tracing. We need to move as fast as we can to curb the global spread of the virus and do our best to stem cross-border transmission. We need to step up information sharing, exchange experience and best practice, and pursue international cooperation on testing methods, clinical treatment, and vaccine and medicine research and development. We also need to continue supporting global research by scientists on the source and transmission routes of the virus.

Second, the World Health Organization should lead the global response. Under the leadership of Dr. Tedros, WHO has made a major contribution in leading and advancing the global response to COVID-19. Its good work is applauded by the international community. At this crucial juncture, to support WHO is to support international cooperation and the battle for saving lives as well. China calls on the international community to increase political and financial support for WHO so as to mobilize resources worldwide to defeat the virus.

Third, we must provide greater support for Africa. Developing countries, African countries in

生体系薄弱,帮助他们筑牢防线是国际抗疫斗争重中之重。我们应该向非洲国家提供更多物资、技术、人力支持。中国已向50多个非洲国家和非盟交付了大量医疗援助物资,专门派出了5个医疗专家组。在过去70年中,中国派往非洲的医疗队为两亿多人次非洲人民提供了医疗服务。目前,常驻非洲的46支中国医疗队正在投入当地的抗疫行动。

第四,加强全球公共卫生治理。人类终将战胜疫情,但重大公共卫生突发事件对人类来说不会是最后一次。要针对这次疫情暴露出来的短板和不足,完善公共卫生安全治理体系,提高突发公共卫生事件应急响应速度,建立全球和地区防疫物资储备中心。中国支持在全球疫情得到控制之后,全面评估全球应对疫情工作,总结经验,弥补不足。这项工作需要科学专业的态度,需要世卫组织主导,坚持客观公正原则。

第五,恢复经济社会发展。有条件的国家要在做好常态化疫情防控的前提下,遵照世卫组织专业建议,有序开展复工复产复学。要加强国际宏观经济政策协调,维护全球产业链供应链稳定畅通,尽力恢复世界经济。

particular, have weaker public health systems. Helping them build capacity must be our top priority in COVID-19 response. The world needs to provide more material, technological and personnel support for African countries. China has sent a tremendous amount of medical supplies and assistance to over 50 African countries and the African Union. Five Chinese medical expert teams have also been sent to the African continent. In total, in the past seven decades, over 200 million people in Africa have received care and treatment from Chinese medical teams. At present, 46 resident Chinese medical teams are in Africa helping with COVID-19 containment efforts locally.

Fourth, we must strengthen global governance in the area of public health. We human beings will eventually prevail over the coronavirus. Yet this may not be the last time a major health emergency comes knocking at our door. In view of the weaknesses and deficiencies exposed by COVID-19, we need to improve the governance system for public health security. We need to respond more quickly to public health emergencies and establish global and regional reserve centers of anti-epidemic supplies. China supports the idea of a comprehensive review of the global response to COVID-19 after it is brought under control to sum up experience and address deficiencies. This work should be based on science and professionalism, led by WHO and conducted in an objective and impartial manner.

Fifth, we must restore economic and social development. While working on an ongoing basis to contain the virus, countries where conditions permit may reopen businesses and schools in an orderly fashion in observance of WHO's professional recommendations. In the meantime, international macroeconomic policy coordination should be stepped up and the global industrial and supply chains be kept stable and unclogged if we are to restore growth to

第六,加强国际合作。人类是命运共同体,团结合作是战胜疫情最有力的武器。这是国际社会抗击艾滋病、埃博拉、禽流感、甲型H1N1流感等重大疫情取得的重要经验,是各国人民合作抗疫的人间正道。

主席先生!

中国始终秉持构建人类命运共同体理念,既对本国人民生命安全和身体健康负责,也对全球公共卫生事业尽责。为推进全球抗疫合作,我宣布:

——中国将在两年内提供20亿美元国际援助,用于支持受疫情影响的国家特别是发展中国家抗疫斗争以及经济社会恢复发展。

——中国将同联合国合作,在华设立全球人道主义应急仓库和枢纽,努力确保抗疫物资供应链,并建立运输和清关绿色通道。

——中国将建立30个中非对口医院合作机制,加快建设非洲疾控中心总部,助力非洲提升疾病防控能力。

——中国新冠疫苗研发完成并投入使用后,将作为全球公共产品,为实现疫苗在发展中国家的可及性和可担负性作出中国贡献。

——中国将同二十国集团成员

the world economy.

Sixth, we must strengthen international cooperation. Mankind is a community with a shared future. Solidarity and cooperation is our most powerful weapon for defeating the virus. This is the key lesson the world has learned from fighting HIV/AIDS, Ebola, avian influenza, influenza A (H1N1) and other major epidemics. And solidarity and cooperation is a sure way through which we, the people of the world, can defeat this novel coronavirus.

Mr. President,

China stands for the vision of building a community with a shared future for mankind. China takes it as its responsibility to ensure not just the life and health of its own citizens, but also global public health. For the sake of boosting international cooperation against COVID-19, I would like to announce the following:

—China will provide US $2 billion over two years to help with COVID-19 response and with economic and social development in affected countries, especially developing countries.

—China will work with the UN to set up a global humanitarian response depot and hub in China, ensure the operation of anti-epidemic supply chains and foster "green corridors" for fast-track transportation and customs clearance.

—China will establish a cooperation mechanism for its hospitals to pair up with 30 African hospitals and accelerate the building of the Africa CDC headquarters to help the continent ramp up its disease preparedness and control capacity.

—COVID-19 vaccine development and deployment in China, when available, will be made a global public good. This will be China's contribution to ensuring vaccine accessibility and affordability in developing countries.

—China will work with other G20 members to

一道落实"暂缓最贫困国家债务偿付倡议",并愿同国际社会一道,加大对疫情特别重、压力特别大的国家的支持力度,帮助其克服当前困难。

我呼吁,让我们携起手来,共同佑护各国人民生命和健康,共同佑护人类共同的地球家园,共同构建人类卫生健康共同体!

谢谢大家。

implement the Debt Service Suspension Initiative for the poorest countries. China is also ready to work with the international community to bolster support for the hardest-hit countries under the greatest strain of debt service, so that they could tide over the current difficulties.

To conclude, I call on all of us to come together and work as one. Let's make concerted efforts to protect the life and health of people in all countries. Let's work together to safeguard planet Earth, our common home. Let's work together to build a global community of health for all!

I thank you.

10.6 Environment and Terrorism

1. 习近平主席2015年在巴黎气候变化大会开幕式上的讲话,巴黎,2015年11月30日(全文)

President Xi Jinping's speech at the opening ceremony of the Paris Conference on Climate Change, Nov. 30, 2015, Paris

中文来源:外交部网站
https://www.fmprc.gov.cn/web/ziliao_674904/zyjh_674906/t1319983.shtml
译文来源:外交部英文网站
https://www.gov.cn/mfa_eng/wjdt_665385/zyjh_665391/t1321560.shtml

尊敬的奥朗德总统,尊敬的各位同事,女士们,先生们,朋友们:

今天,我们齐聚巴黎,出席联合国气候变化巴黎大会开幕式。这表明,恐怖主义阻挡不了全人类应对气候变化、追求美好未来的进程。借此机会,我愿向法国人民致以诚挚的慰问,同时对奥朗德总统和法国政府为这次大会召开所作的精心筹备表示感谢。

《联合国气候变化框架公约》生

President Hollande, Dear Colleagues, Ladies and Gentlemen, Dear Friends,

Today, we are gathering here in Paris for the opening ceremony of the United Nations Conference on Climate Change. Our presence shows that terrorism cannot hold back mankind's efforts to address climate change and pursue a better future. Let me take this opportunity to express my sincere sympathy to the French people and my gratitude to President Hollande and the French government for their meticulous preparations for this conference.

Thanks to joint efforts of all parties since the

Chapter Ⅹ Consecutive Interpreting Materials for Different Themes

效20多年来,在各方共同努力下,全球应对气候变化工作取得积极进展,但仍面临许多困难和挑战。巴黎大会正是为了加强公约实施,达成一个全面、均衡、有力度、有约束力的气候变化协议,提出公平、合理、有效的全球应对气候变化解决方案,探索人类可持续的发展路径和治理模式。法国作家雨果说:"最大的决心会产生最高的智慧。"我相信,只要各方展现诚意、坚定信心、齐心协力,巴黎大会一定能够取得令人满意的成果,不辜负国际社会的热切期盼。

尊敬的各位同事,女士们、先生们!

一份成功的国际协议既要解决当下矛盾,更要引领未来。巴黎协议应该着眼于强化2020年后全球应对气候变化行动,也要为推动全球更好实现可持续发展注入动力。

巴黎协议应该有利于实现公约目标,引领绿色发展。协议应该遵循公约原则和规定,推进公约全面有效实施。既要有效控制大气温室气体浓度上升,又要建立利益导向和激励机制,推动各国走向绿色循环低碳发展,实现经济发展和应对气候变化双赢。

United Nations Framework Convention on Climate Change entered into force over 20 years ago, global actions on climate change have made progress although there are still numerous difficulties and challenges. This Paris Conference is hence convened to strengthen implementation of the UNFCCC and bring about a comprehensive, balanced, ambitious and binding agreement on climate change. The conference is also expected to come up with equitable, reasonable and effective global solutions to climate change and explore pathways and governance models for mankind to achieve sustainable development. The French writer Victor Hugo once observed in Les Miserables that "supreme resources spring from extreme resolutions". (Les resources supremes sortent des resolutions extremes.) I believe that with all parties making joint efforts with sincerity and confidence, the Paris Conference will yield satisfying results and meet the high expectations of the international community.

Dear Colleagues, Ladies and Gentlemen,

A successful international agreement should not just address immediate challenges but more importantly, it should also present a vision for the future. The Paris agreement should focus on strengthening post-2020 global actions on climate change and boost global efforts to pursue sustainable development.

The Paris agreement should help meet the goals of the UNFCCC and chart the course for green development. The agreement should follow the principles and rules set out in the UNFCCC and contribute to its full and effective implementation. The agreement should put effective control on the increase of atmospheric concentration of greenhouse gases and set up incentive mechanisms to encourage countries to purse green, circular and low-carbon development featuring both economic growth and an

— 361 —

巴黎协议应该有利于凝聚全球力量，鼓励广泛参与。协议应该在制度安排上促使各国同舟共济、共同努力。除各国政府，还应该调动企业、非政府组织等全社会资源参与国际合作进程，提高公众意识，形成合力。

巴黎协议应该有利于加大投入，强化行动保障。获取资金技术支持、提高应对能力是发展中国家实施应对气候变化行动的前提。发达国家应该落实到2020年每年动员1000亿美元的承诺，2020年后向发展中国家提供更加强有力的资金支持。此外，还应该向发展中国家转让气候友好型技术，帮助其发展绿色经济。

巴黎协议应该有利于照顾各国国情，讲求务实有效。应该尊重各国特别是发展中国家在国内政策、能力建设、经济结构方面的差异，不搞一刀切。应对气候变化不应该妨碍发展中国家消除贫困、提高人民生活水平的合理需求。要照顾发展中国家的特殊困难。

尊敬的各位同事，女士们、先生们！

巴黎协议不是终点，而是新的起点。作为全球治理的一个重要领域，应对气候变化的全球努力是一面镜子，给我们思考和探索未来全球治理模式、推动建设人类命运共

effective response to climate change.

The Paris agreement should help galvanize global efforts and encourage broad participation. The agreement should provide institutional arrangements that propel countries to make concerted efforts. Besides governments, it should also mobilize businesses, non-governmental organizations and all players in society to participate in international cooperation on climate change, thus raising public awareness of pooling resources on climate change.

The Paris agreement should help increase input of resources to ensure actions on climate change. To obtain financial and technical support for capacity building is essential for developing countries to address climate change. Developed countries should honor their commitment of mobilizing US＄100 billion each year before 2020 and provide stronger financial support to developing countries afterwards. It is also important that climate-friendly technologies should be transferred to developing countries to help them build green economy.

The Paris agreement should accommodate the national conditions of various countries and lay emphasis on practical results. It is imperative to respect differences among countries, especially developing countries, in domestic policies, capacity building and economic structure. A one-size-fits-all approach must be avoided. Addressing climate change should not deny the legitimate needs of developing countries to reduce poverty and improve their people's living Standards. Special needs of the developing countries must be well attended to.

Dear colleagues, Ladies and Gentlemen,

The Paris Conference is not the finishing line but a new starting point. As an important part of global governance, the global efforts on climate change can be taken as a mirror for us to reflect on what models to have for future global governance and how to build

Chapter X Consecutive Interpreting Materials for Different Themes

同体带来宝贵启示。

我们应该创造一个各尽所能、合作共赢的未来。对气候变化等全球性问题,如果抱着功利主义的思维,希望多占点便宜、少承担点责任,最终将是损人不利己。巴黎大会应该摈弃"零和博弈"狭隘思维,推动各国尤其是发达国家多一点共享、多一点担当,实现互惠共赢。

我们应该创造一个奉行法治、公平正义的未来。要提高国际法在全球治理中的地位和作用,确保国际规则有效遵守和实施,坚持民主、平等、正义,建设国际法治。发达国家和发展中国家的历史责任、发展阶段、应对能力都不同,共同但有区别的责任原则不仅没有过时,而且应该得到遵守。

我们应该创造一个包容互鉴、共同发展的未来。面对全球性挑战,各国应该加强对话,交流学习最佳实践,取长补短,在相互借鉴中实现共同发展,惠及全体人民。同时,要倡导和而不同,允许各国寻找最适合本国国情的应对之策。

尊敬的各位同事,女士们、先生们!

中国一直是全球应对气候变化事业的积极参与者,有诚意、有决心为巴黎大会成功作出自己的贡献。

a community of shared future for mankind. Much valuable inspiration may thus be drawn.

We should create a future of win-win cooperation, with each country making contribution to the best of its ability. For global issues like climate change, a take-more-give-less approach based on expediency is in nobody's interest. The Paris Conference should reject the narrow-minded mentality of "zero sum game" and call on all countries, the developed countries in particular, to assume more shared responsibilities for win-win outcomes.

We should create a future of the rule of law, fairness and justice. It is imperative to enhance the standing and role of international law in global governance, ensure effective observance and implementation of international rules, uphold democracy, equity and justice, and build international rule of law. Given the difference between developed and developing countries in historical responsibility, developing stage and coping capability, the principle of common but differentiated responsibilities, instead of being obsolete, must continue to be adhered to.

We should create a future of inclusiveness, mutual learning and common development. Facing global challenges, countries need to increase dialogue and exchange best practices. We should draw on each other's strengths to achieve common development through mutual learning, and deliver benefits to all our people. At the same time, we should be prepared to accept harmony without uniformity, allowing individual countries to seek their own solutions that best suit their respective national conditions.

Dear colleagues, Ladies and Gentlemen,

China has been actively engaged in the global campaign on climate change. China is both sincere and determined to contribute its share to the success of the Paris Conference.

过去几十年来,中国经济快速发展,人民生活发生了深刻变化,但也承担了资源环境方面的代价。鉴往知来,中国正在大力推进生态文明建设,推动绿色循环低碳发展。中国把应对气候变化融入国家经济社会发展中长期规划,坚持减缓和适应气候变化并重,通过法律、行政、技术、市场等多种手段,全力推进各项工作。中国可再生能源装机容量占全球总量的24%,新增装机占全球增量的42%。中国是世界节能和利用新能源、可再生能源第一大国。

"万物各得其和以生,各得其养以成。"中华文明历来强调天人合一、尊重自然。面向未来,中国将把生态文明建设作为"十三五"规划重要内容,落实创新、协调、绿色、开放、共享的发展理念,通过科技创新和体制机制创新,实施优化产业结构、构建低碳能源体系、发展绿色建筑和低碳交通、建立全国碳排放交易市场等一系列政策措施,形成人和自然和谐发展现代化建设新格局。中国在"国家自主贡献"中提出将于2030年左右使二氧化碳排放达到峰值并争取尽早实现,2030年单位国内生产总值二氧化碳排放比2005年下降60%~65%,非化石能源占一次能源消费比例达到20%左右,森林蓄积量比2005年增加45亿立方米左右。虽然需要付出艰苦的努力,但我们有信心和决心实现我们的承诺。

In the past few decades, China has seen rapid economic growth and significant improvement in people's lives. However, this has taken a toll on the environment and resources. Having learned the lesson, China is vigorously making ecological endeavors to promote green, circular and low-carbon growth. We have integrated our climate change efforts into China's medium—and long-term program of economic and social development. We attach equal importance to mitigation and adaption, and try to make progress on all fronts by resorting to legal and administrative means, technologies and market forces. China's installed capacity of renewable energy accounts for 24% of the world's total, with the newly installed capacity accounting for 42% of the global total. China tops the world in terms of energy conservation and utilization of new and renewable energies.

"All things live in harmony and grow with nourishments." Chinese culture values harmony between man and nature and respects nature. Going forward, ecological endeavors will feature prominently in China's 13th Five-Year Plan. China will work hard to implement the vision of innovative, coordinated, green, open and inclusive development. China will, on the basis of technological and institutional innovation, adopt new policy measures to improve industrial mix, build low-carbon energy system, develop green building and low-carbon transportation, and build a nation-wide carbon emission trading market so as to foster a new pattern of modernization featuring harmony between man and nature. In its Intended Nationally Determined Contributions, China pledges to peak CO_2 emissions by around 2030 and strive to achieve it as soon as possible, and by 2030, reduce CO_2 per unit of GDP by 60%-65% over the 2005 level, raise the share of non-fossil fuels in primary energy consumption to about 20% and increase forest stock by around 4.5

Chapter X Consecutive Interpreting Materials for Different Themes

中国坚持正确义利观,积极参与气候变化国际合作。多年来,中国政府认真落实气候变化领域南南合作政策承诺,支持发展中国家特别是最不发达国家、内陆发展中国家、小岛屿发展中国家应对气候变化挑战。为加大支持力度,中国在今年9月宣布设立200亿元人民币的中国气候变化南南合作基金。中国将于明年启动在发展中国家开展10个低碳示范区、100个减缓和适应气候变化项目及1000个应对气候变化培训名额的合作项目,继续推进清洁能源、防灾减灾、生态保护、气候适应型农业、低碳智慧型城市建设等领域的国际合作,并帮助他们提高融资能力。

尊敬的各位同事,女士们、先生们!

应对气候变化是人类共同的事业,世界的目光正聚焦于巴黎。让我们携手努力,为推动建立公平有效的全球应对气候变化机制、实现更高水平全球可持续发展、构建合作共赢的国际关系作出贡献!

谢谢大家。

billion cubic meters over 2005. This requires strenuous efforts, but we have confidence and resolve to fulfill our commitments.

China upholds the values of friendship, justice and shared interests, and takes an active part in international cooperation on climate change. Over the years, the Chinese government has earnestly fulfilled its policy commitments of South-South cooperation regarding climate change to support developing countries, especially the least developed countries, landlocked developing countries and small island developing states, in confronting the challenge of climate change. In a show of greater support, China announced in September the establishment of an RMB 20 billion South-South Climate Cooperation Fund. Next year, China will launch cooperation projects to set up 10 pilot low-carbon industrial parks and start 100 mitigation and adaptation programs in other developing countries and provide them with 1,000 training opportunities on climate change. China will continue to promote international cooperation in such areas as clean energy, disaster prevention and mitigation, ecological protection, climate-smart agriculture, and low-carbon and smart cities. China will also help other developing countries to increase their financing capacity.

Dear Colleagues, Ladies and Gentlemen,

Tackling climate change is a shared mission for mankind. All eyes are now on Paris. Let us join hands to contribute to the establishment of an equitable and effective global mechanism on climate change, work for global sustainable development at a higher level and bring about new international relations featuring win-win cooperation.

Thank you.

2. Secretary António Guterres' message on World Environment Day, June 5, 2019 (Full text)

古特雷斯秘书长2019年世界环境日致辞,2019年6月5日(全文)

英文来源:联合国英文官网

https://www.un.org/sg/en/content/sg/statement/2019-06-05/secretary-generals-message-world-environment-day-scroll-down-for-french-version-well-video-texts

译文来源:联合国中文官网

https://www.un.org/sg/zh/content/sg/statement/2019-06-05/secretary-generals-message-world-environment-day-scroll-down-for-french-version-well-video-texts

The theme for this year's World Environment Day is air pollution. All around the world—from megacities to small villages—people are breathing dirty air. An estimated nine out of ten people worldwide are exposed to air pollutants that exceed World Health Organization air quality guidelines. This is lowering life expectancy and damaging economies across the planet.

To improve air quality, we must know our enemy. Deaths and illnesses from air pollution are caused by tiny particles that penetrate our defenses every time we fill our lungs. These particles come from many sources: the burning of fossil fuels for power and transport; the chemicals and mining industries; the open burning of waste; the burning of forests and fields; and the use of dirty indoor cooking and heating fuels, which are major problems in the developing world.

This polluted air kills some 7 million people each year, causes long term health problems, such as asthma, and reduces children's cognitive development. According to the World Bank, air pollution costs societies more than $5 trillion every year.

Many air pollutants also cause global warming. Black carbon is one such example. Produced by diesel engines, burning trash and dirty cookstoves, it is extremely harmful when inhaled. Reducing emissions of such pollutants will not only improve public health, it could alleviate global warming by up to 0.5

今年世界环境日的主题是空气污染。在世界各地,无论是大城市还是小村庄,人们都呼吸着肮脏的空气。据估计,世界上90%的人所吸入的空气污染物都超过世界卫生组织的空气质量标准。这种情况缩短了预期寿命,损害了各国经济。

要改善空气质量,就必须了解我们的敌人是谁。空气污染之所以导致疾病、造成死亡,是因为人们每次把空气吸入肺中,都会有微粒穿透其防御系统。这些微粒有多种来源,包括:为发电和运输而燃烧化石燃料;生产和使用化学品、从事采矿业;露天焚烧废物;森林和田野烧荒;将重污染燃料用于室内烹饪和取暖(此问题主要存在于发展中国家)。

受污染的空气每年造成大约700万人死亡,引起哮喘等长期性健康问题,还损害儿童认知力的发展。世界银行的数据显示,空气污染每年给社会造成逾5万亿美元的损失。

多种空气污染物还导致全球变暖。黑炭就是一个例子。它产生于使用柴油机、燃烧垃圾、使用重污染炉灶。吸入黑炭后危害极大。减少这种污染物的排放不仅能改善公众健康,未来几十年内还可能使全球

Chapter Ⅹ Consecutive Interpreting Materials for Different Themes

degrees Celsius over the next few decades.

Tackling air pollution therefore presents a double opportunity, as there are many successful initiatives that both clear the air and reduce greenhouse gas emissions, such as phasing out coal-fired power plants and promoting less polluting industry, transport and domestic fuels. With investments in renewable energy sources outstripping those in fossil fuels every year, the rise of clean energy is helping globally. Cleaner transport is also growing around the world.

It is in such initiatives, designed to improve air quality and fight climate change, that hope lies. I urge everyone attending the Climate Action Summit that I am convening in September to draw motivation from such examples. There is no reason why the international community cannot act. Precedent exists in the *Montreal Protocol*. Scientists identified a grave threat to public and planetary health, and governments and businesses acted to successfully protect the ozone layer.

Today, we face an equally urgent crisis. It is time to act decisively. My message to governments is clear: tax pollution; end fossil fuel subsidies; and stop building new coal plants. We need a green economy not a grey economy.

On World Environment Day, I ask each of us to act so we can breathe more easily. From pressuring politicians and businesses to changing our own habits, we can reduce pollution and beat climate change.

变暖幅度减低0.5摄氏度。

因此,通过解决空气污染问题,有机会一举两得,因为许多成功的举措既能净化空气又能减少温室气体排放,例如逐步淘汰燃煤发电厂,促进将轻污染燃料用于工业、运输、住宅等等。随着每年对可再生能源的投资超过对化石燃料的投资,清洁能源的兴起在全球范围内起到了帮助作用。世界各地的清洁型运输也在增长。

这些改善空气质量、应对气候变化的举措让我们看到了希望。我将于9月召集举行气候行动峰会,特此敦促所有与会者从上述例子中汲取动力。没有理由表明国际社会不能采取行动。《蒙特利尔议定书》已树立了先例。科学家们确定了对人类健康和地球健康的一个严重威胁,各国政府和企业为妥善保护臭氧层采取了行动。

今天,我们面临同样紧迫的危机,果断采取行动的时刻已然到来。我向各国政府传达的明确信息是:针对污染行为征税;停止补贴化石燃料;停止新建燃煤发电厂。我们需要的是绿色经济,而不是灰色经济。

值此世界环境日,我呼吁人人都行动起来,使大家能更轻松地呼吸。我们定能减少污染、战胜气候变化,办法是给政界和企业施加压力,同时改变自己的习惯。

3. PM Teresa May's statement following London terror attack, June 4, 2017
英国首相特蕾莎·梅就伦敦恐袭事件发表声明
英文来源:
http://time.com/4804640/london - attack - theresa - may - speech - transcript - full/
译文来源:知乎

Last night, our country fell victim to a brutal terrorist attack once again. As a result, I have just chaired a meeting of the Government's emergency committee, and I want to update you with the latest information about the attack.	昨晚,我们国家又经历了一起野蛮的恐怖袭击。我刚刚主持了政府的一次紧急应对会议,现在我想向我的国民们传达这次恐怖袭击的最新消息。
Shortly before 10 past 10 yesterday evening, the Metropolitan Police received reports that a white van had struck pedestrians on London Bridge. It continued to drive from London Bridge to Borough Market, where three terrorists left the van and attacked innocent and unarmed civilians with blades and knives.	昨夜十点十分左右,伦敦警察厅接到了一份报告:一辆白色面包车在伦敦塔桥上撞向了数名行人。该辆面包车接着从伦敦塔桥开往了博罗市场。三名恐怖分子从面包车上下来后接着用刀具攻击了无辜的平民。
All three were wearing what appeared to be explosive vests, but the police have established that this clothing was fake and worn only to spread panic and fear.	三名恐怖分子都穿戴了自杀式炸弹背心,但警察经过调查后认为这些背心上的炸弹只是模型,只是用来造成恐慌的。
As so often in such serious situations, the police responded with great courage and great speed. Armed offices from the Metropolitan Police and the City of London Police arrived at Borough Market within moments and shot and killed the three suspects.	在这样紧急的情况下,我们的警察再一次快速勇敢地做出了反应。伦敦警察厅的武装警察和伦敦市警察(两者管辖范围不同)在短时间内就到达了博罗市场,并击毙了恐怖分子。
The terrorists were confronted and shot by armed officers within eight minutes of the police receiving the first emergency call.	三名恐怖分子在警察接到报警电话后八分钟内就被击毙。
Seven people have died as a result of the attack, in addition to the three suspects shot dead by the police. Forty-eight people are being treated in several hospitals across London. Many have life-threatening conditions.	在袭击中,除了被击毙的三名恐怖分子,有七人死亡。有四十八人正在医院接受治疗。其中很多人有生命危险。
On behalf of the people of London and on behalf of the whole country, I want to thank and pay tribute to the professionalism and bravery of the police and the emergency services, and the courage of members of the public who defended themselves and others from the attackers. And our thoughts and prayers are with the victims and with their friends, families	我代表所有伦敦市民以及全国人民感谢警察部门和应急反应部门在这起事件中展现出来的勇气和职业精神。感谢在袭击中勇敢地保护了自己和他人的普通市民。也感谢我们大家对受害者及其家人的祝福和祈祷。

and loved ones.

This is, as we all know, the third terrorist attack Britain has experienced in the last three months. In March a similar attack took place just around the corner on Westminster Bridge.

Two weeks ago the Manchester Arena was attacked by a suicide bomber and now London has been struck once more.

And at the same time the security and intelligence agencies and police have disrupted five credible plots since the Westminster attack in March.

In terms of their planning and execution, the recent attacks are not connected but we believe we are experiencing a new trend in the threat we face.

As terrorism breeds terrorism and perpetrators are inspired to attack, not only on the basis of carefully constructed plots after years of planning and training, and not even as lone attackers radicalized online, but by copying one another and often using the crudest of means of attack.

We cannot and must not pretend that things can continue as they are. Things need to change and they need to change in four important ways.

First, while the recent attacks are not connected by common networks, they are connected in one important sense. They are bound together by the single evil ideology of Islamist extremism that preaches hatred, sows division and promotes sectarianism.

It is an ideology that claims our Western values of freedom, democracy and human rights are incompatible with the religion of Islam. It is an ideology that is a perversion of Islam and a perversion of the truth.

Defeating this ideology is one of the great challenges of our time, but it cannot be defeated by military intervention alone. It will not be defeated by the maintenance of a permanent defensive counter-

这是近三个月来英国遭受的第三起恐怖袭击。在3月份的时候，西敏大桥发生了一次类似的事件。

两周前曼彻斯特竞技场遭受了自杀式炸弹袭击，而今天伦敦又再一次受到了袭击。

除此之外，3月份以来英国的情报部门已经破获了五起恐怖袭击未遂案件。

从计划和执行的形式来看，这些近期的恐怖袭击没有什么直接的联系，但我们认为我们面临着一种新的势头。

恐怖主义有惊人的传播效率。袭击者们不再花费数年小心谨慎地筹划恐怖袭击，甚至不再被网络蛊惑，而是互相模仿，进行没有技术含量的袭击。

我们不能再假装什么事都没发生了。我们要做出改变，我列出以下四点。

第一点，尽管最近的几次袭击没有直接关联，但它们在意识形态上拥有相似之处，那就是邪恶的极端伊斯兰主义。它教导人们仇恨，推动分裂和宗派主义。

极端伊斯兰主义认为我们西方的自由民主和人权观念与伊斯兰教不兼容。它背离了伊斯兰教的原意，也背离了真相。

战胜极端伊斯兰主义是我们这个时代的一大挑战。军事干预不是解决这个挑战的办法，防御性的反恐政策也不能解决这个问题。

terrorism operation, however skillful its leaders and practitioners.

It will only be defeated when we turn people's minds away from this violence and make them understand that our values—pluralistic British values—are superior to anything offered by the preachers and supporters of hate.

Second, we cannot allow this ideology the safe space it needs to breed. Yet that is precisely what the internet, and the big companies that provide internet-based services provide.

We need to work with allied democratic governments to reach international agreements that regulate cyberspace to prevent the spread of extremist and terrorism planning. And we need to do everything we can at home to reduce the risks of extremism online.

Third, while we need to deprive the extremists of their safe spaces online, we must not forget about the safe spaces that continue to exist in the real world. Yes, that means taking military action to destroy ISIS in Iraq and Syria. But it also means taking action here at home.

While we have made significant progress in recent years, there is—to be frank—far too much tolerance of extremism in our country. So we need to become far more robust in identifying it and stamping it out across the public sector and across society. That will require some difficult, and often embarrassing, conversations.

But the whole of our country needs to come together to take on this extremism, and we need to live our lives not in a series of separated, segregated communities, but as one truly United Kingdom.

Fourth, we have a robust counter-terrorism strategy, that has proved successful over many years. But as the nature of the threat we face becomes more complex, more fragmented, more

只有当人民不再关注暴力，崇尚多元化的英国价值观而不是那些灌输仇恨的价值观之时，我们才能战胜极端伊斯兰主义。

第二点，我们不能让极端伊斯兰主义在一个安全的环境里成长。然而这正是互联网和互联网提供商给予恐怖分子的东西。

我们需要与盟国达成共识来监管互联网，防止恐怖分子借用互联网策划恐怖袭击。在国内，我们也要尽一切手段减少网上的恐怖主义。

第三点，当我们在网络空间打击恐怖分子的时候，我们也不能忘了现实世界里存在的恐怖分子。是的，这意味着我们要采取军事手段打击在伊拉克和叙利亚的ISIS势力，这也意味着我们会在国内进行新的反恐行动。

虽然近些年在反恐上我们有很多进展，但直白地说，我们国内对恐怖主义太宽容了。我们要更加坚决地找出那些隐藏在国内的恐怖分子。这将会在社会激起一些艰难和尴尬的对话。

整个英国应当团结起来共同对抗极端伊斯兰主义。我们不应该再在许多封闭的小团体中生活，而应当联合起来在一个真正的联合王国中生活。

第四点，我们有一个强有力的反恐政策，它在过去几年非常成功。但随着我们所面临的威胁愈发复杂、分散和隐蔽，以及日益增长的网

Chapter Ⅹ Consecutive Interpreting Materials for Different Themes

hidden, especially online, the strategy needs to keep up.

So in light of what we are learning about the changing threat, we need to review Britain's counter-terrorism strategy to make sure the police and security services have all the powers they need.

And if we need to increase the length of custodial sentences for terrorist-related offences—even apparently less serious offences—that is what we will do.

Since the emergence of the threat from Islamist-inspired terrorism, our country has made significant progress in disrupting plots and protecting the public. But it is time to say "Enough is enough".

Everybody needs to go about their lives as they normally would. Our society should continue to function in accordance with our values. But when it comes to taking on extremism and terrorism, things need to change.

As a mark of respect, two political parties have suspended our national campaigns for today. But violence can never be allowed to disrupt the democratic process, so those campaigns will resume in full tomorrow and the General Election will go ahead as planned on Thursday.

As a country, our response must be as it has always been when we have been confronted by violence. We must come together, we must pull together, and united we will take on and defeat our enemies.

络恐怖问题,我们的反恐政策需要做出改变。

鉴于我们所面临的威胁,我们需要重新审视英国的反恐政策,从而让警察和安全部门拥有他们所需要的权力。

如果我们需要延长与恐怖主义相关罪犯的刑期,即使是小罪我们也会这样做的。

自从伊斯兰恐怖主义抬头后,我们的国家在反恐和保护国民方面取得了突出的进展。但现在是我们说我们已经忍无可忍的时候了。

每个人都应该过正常的生活。我们社会应该继续秉承我们的价值观。但在关系到恐怖主义和极端主义的事情上,我们应当作出改变。

出于(对死者的)尊重,两大党在今天会暂停竞选活动。但暴力永远不会妨碍我们的民主程序,竞选活动会在明天恢复,大选仍然会像计划一样在周四举行。

我们国家应当像过去面临暴力挑战时一样,团结起来共同击败我们的敌人。

4. Secretary António Guterres' message on the International Day of Remembrance and Tribute to the victims of terrorism, 21 August 2018(Full text)
古特雷斯秘书长纪念和悼念恐怖主义受害者国际日致辞,2018 年 8 月 21 日(全文)
英文来源:联合国英文官网

https://www.un.org/sg/en/content/sg/statement/2018-08-21/secretary-generals-message-first-international-day-remembrance-and

译文来源:联合国中文官网

https://www.un.org/sg/zh/content/sg/statement/2018-08-21/secretary-generals-message-

first-international-day-remembrance-and

Terrorism is one of the most challenging issues of our time and a serious threat to international peace and security. From Tajikistan to the United Kingdom, from Baghdad to Barcelona, these ruthless attacks have shaken us all to the core. No country can consider itself immune, with almost every nationality in the world falling victim to terrorist attacks.

The United Nations itself is regularly targeted. Twenty-two people lost their lives in the attack on the headquarters of the United Nations mission in Iraq, which took place 15 years ago this week. Some of our peacekeeping missions are under constant threat.

But after terrorist attacks, we rarely hear about those who were killed and injured; the ordinary women, men, girls and boys, who were going about their daily business when their lives ended or were changed forever. We rarely hear about their surviving families, friends and communities, who must learn to live with the burden of terrorism for their entire lives.

Today, the International day of Remembrance of, and Tribute to, the victims of terrorism, reminds us to stop and listen to the victims and survivors of terrorism, to raise up their voices and recognize the impact terrorism has on their lives.

We can all learn from their experiences. Communities around the world are demonstrating their resilience in response to terrorist attacks. They are countering terrorism and violent extremism in their everyday lives, in their schools, markets and places of worship.

Supporting victims and their families is a moral imperative, based on promoting, protecting and

恐怖主义是我们时代最具挑战性的问题之一,也是对国际和平与安全的严重威胁。从塔吉克斯坦到英国,从巴格达到巴塞罗那,这些残忍无情的袭击使我们所有人无比震惊。没有一个国家可以认为自己不受影响,世界上几乎每个民族都成为恐怖主义袭击的受害者。

联合国自身也经常成为袭击目标。15年前的本周,22人在对联合国伊拉克特派团总部发动的袭击中丧生。我们的一些维持和平特派团经常性地受到威胁。

但在恐怖袭击之后,我们很少听到伤亡者的消息;普通的女子、男子、女孩和男孩,他们当时正在做着他们日常要做的事,然后他们的生命就画上了句号或永远改变了。我们很少听到他们仍然活着的家人、朋友和社区的消息,他们必须学会在余生中承受恐怖主义的重负。

今天,纪念和悼念恐怖主义受害者国际日提醒我们停下来,倾听恐怖主义受害者和幸存者的声音,提高他们发声的调门,并认识到恐怖主义对他们的生活造成的影响。

我们都可以从他们的经历中学到些东西。世界各地的社区正在展示他们对恐怖袭击的应变能力。他们正在日常生活中,在学校、市场和礼拜场所,回击恐怖主义和暴力极端主义。

在促进、保护和尊重受害者及其家人人权的基础上,支持受害者

respecting their human rights. Caring for victims and survivors and amplifying their voices helps to challenge the narrative of hatred and division that terrorism aims to spread. We need to provide victims with long-term assistance, including financial, legal, medical and psychosocial support.

When we lift up the victims and survivors of terrorism, listen to their voices, respect their rights and provide them with support and justice, we are honouring our common bonds, and reducing the lasting damage done by terrorists to individuals, families and communities.

I thank those who are willing to speak out against terrorism every day. Your voices matter, and your courage in the face of adversity is a lesson to us all.

Today and every day, the United Nations stands in solidarity with you.

及其家人是一项道义责任。关心受害者和幸存者并放大他们的声音，有助于挑战恐怖主义旨在传播的仇恨和分裂说辞。我们需要向受害者提供长期援助，包括提供财务、法律、医疗和心理支持。

当我们提升恐怖主义受害者和幸存者的可见度，倾听他们的声音，尊重他们的权利，并使他们获得支持和享有正义时，我们正在履行我们的共同契约，正在减轻恐怖主义分子对个人、家庭和社区造成的持久伤害。

我感谢那些愿意每天大声反对恐怖主义的人。你们的声音很重要，你们面对逆境的勇气值得我们所有人学习。

今天，联合国声援你们，联合国每一天都声援你们。

APPENDIX

Appendix Ⅰ Interpreter's Code of Professional Ethics by International Association of Conference Interpreters(AIIC)

国际会议口译工作者协会关于职业道德准则的规定

AIIC:国际会议口译工作者协会是国际会议口译人员的国际组织,以其入会资格严苛著名,其会员身份是国际公认的合格会议口译人员的标志。以下是《职业道德准则》的英文内容。

· *Purpose and Scope*

Article 1

a. This Code of Professional Ethics (hereinafter called the "Code") lays down the standards of integrity, professionalism and confidentiality which all members of the Association shall be bound to respect in their work as conference interpreters.

b. Candidates shall also undertake to adhere to the provisions of this Code.

c. The Council, acting in accordance with the Regulation on Disciplinary Procedure, shall impose penalties for any breach of the profession as defined in this Code.

· *Code of Honor*

Article 2

a. Members of the Association shall be bound by the strictest secrecy, which must be observed towards all persons and with regard to all information disclosed in the course of the practice of the profession at any gathering not open to the public.

b. Members shall refrain from deriving any personal gain whatsoever from confidential information they may have acquired in the exercise of their duties as conference interpreters.

Article 3

a. Members of the Association shall not accept any assignment for which they are not qualified. Acceptance of an assignment shall imply a moral undertaking on the member's part to work with all due professionalism.

b. Any member of the Association recruiting other conference interpreters, be they members of the Association or not, shall give the same undertaking.

c. Members of the Association shall not accept more than one assignment for the same period of time.

Article 4

a. Members of the Association shall not accept any job or situation which might detract from the dignity of the profession.

b. They shall refrain from any act which might bring the profession into disrepute.

Article 5

For any professional purpose, members may publicize the fact that they are conference interpreters and members of the Association, either as individuals or as part of any grouping or region to which they belong.

Article 6

a. It shall be the duty of members of the Association to afford their colleagues moral assistance and collegiality.

b. Members shall refrain from any utterance or action prejudicial to the interests of the Association or its members. Any complaint arising out of the conduct of any other member or any disagreement regarding any decision taken by the Association shall be pursued and settled within the Association itself.

c. Any problem pertaining to the profession with arises between two or more members of the Association, including candidates, may be referred to the Council for arbitration.

• *Working Conditions*

Article 7

With a view to ensuring the best quality interpretation, members of the Association:

a. shall endeavor always to secure satisfactory conditions of sound, visibility and comfort, having particular regard to the Professional Standards as adopted by the Association as well as any technical standards drawn up or approved by it;

b. shall not, as a general rule, when interpreting simultaneously in a booth, work either alone or without the availability of a colleague to relieve them should the need arise;

c. shall try to ensue that teams of conference interpreters are formed in such a way as to avoid the systematic use of relay;

d. shall not agree to undertake either simultaneous interpretation without a booth or whispered interpretation unless the circumstances are exceptional and the quality of interpretation work is not thereby impaired;

e. shall require a direct view of the speaker and the conference room. They will thus refuse to accept the use of television monitors instead of this direct view, except in the case of video conferences;

f. shall require that working documents and texts to be read out at the conference be sent to them in advance;

g. shall request a briefing session whenever appropriate;

h. shall not perform any other duties except that of conference interpreter at conferences for which they have been taken on as interpreters.

Article 8

Members of the Association shall neither accept nor, a fortiori, offer for themselves or for other conference interpreters recruited through them, be they members of the Association or not, any working conditions contrary to those laid down in this Code or in the Professional Standards.

Appendix II Practical Phrases

1. Frequently used titles

阁下 Your/His/Her Excellency
陛下 Your/His/Her Majesty
殿下 Your/His/Her (Royal) Highness
国家主席 President (of PRC)
国务委员 State Councilor
人大常委会委员长 NPC Chairman
部长 Minister
局长 Director/Head of the Bureau
校长(大学) President of... University
校长(中小学) Principal/Headmaster of... Middle School
系主任(大学学院下属) Dean/Chairman of... Department
中科院院长 President of the Chinese Academy of Sciences
会长(学/协会) President
厂长 Director
院长(医院) President
董事长 President/Chairman of the Board
秘书长 Secretary-General
护士长 Head nurse
审判长 Chief Judge
社长(报社) Director
县/区/乡/镇/村长 County/District/Township/Town/Village Chief/Head
总书记 General Secretary
总检察长 Procurator-General
总会计师 Chief Accountant
总干事 Director-General
总代理 General Agent
总工程师 Chief Engineer
总导演 Head/Chief Director
总建筑师 Chief Architect
总编辑 Chief Editor; Editor-in-Chief
总指挥 Commander-in-Chief
总出纳 Chief/General Cashier
总领事 Consul-General
总裁判 Chief Referee
总监 Director; Chief Inspector
总经理 General Manager; Managing Director; Executive Manager
总厨 Head Cook; Chef
首席执行官 Chief Executive Officer(CEO)
首席运营官 Chief Operating Officer(COO)
首席财务官 Chief Financial Officer (CFO)
首席战略官 Chief Strategy Officer (CSO)
首席信息官 Chief Information Officer (CIO)
首席技术官 Chief Technology Officer (CTO)
首席仲裁员 Chief Arbitrator
首席谈判代表 Chief Negotiator
首席顾问 Chief Advisor
首席代表 Chief Representative
首席记者 Chief Correspondent
副总统 Vice President
副主席 Vice Chairman
副总理 Vice Premier
副部长 Vice Minster
副省长 Vice Governor
副市长 Vice Mayor
副领事 Vice Consul

副校长(大学) Vice President
副校长(中小学) Vice/Assistant Principal
副秘书长 Deputy Secretary-General
副书记 Deputy secretary
副院长 Deputy Dean
副总经理 Deputy/Assistant Manager
副教授 Associate Professor
副主编 Associate Managing Editor
副研究员 Associate Research fellow
副编审 Associate Senior Editor
副审判长 Associate Judge
副译审 Associate Senior Translator
助理教授 Assistant Professor
助理研究员 Assistant Research Fellow
助理教练 Assistant Coach
助理工程师 Assistant Engineer
助理农艺师 Assistant Agronomist
高级工程师 Senior Engineer
高级讲师 Senior lecturer
特派记者 Accredited Correspondent
特派员/专员 Commissioner
特约编辑 Contributing Editor
代理市长 Acting Mayor
代理主任 Acting Director
代理总理 Acting Premier
常务理事 Managing Director
常务副校长 Managing Vice President
执行主任 Executive Director
执行主席 Executive Chairman

执行秘书 Executive Secretary
名誉校长 Honorary President/Principal
名誉主席/会长 Honorary Chairman/President
客座教授 Visiting Professor
院士 Academician
高级记者 senior reporter
高级讲师 senior lecturer
劳动模范 model worker
优秀员工 outstanding employee
标兵 pacemaker
三好学生 "triple-A" outstanding student; outstanding student

以下机构的负责人可以用"Director","Head"或"Chief"来表示：
国务院 the State Council
司(部属)/厅(省属) department
署(省属) office
局 bureau
所 institute
处 division
科 section
股 section
室/办公室 office
特首(香港/澳门特别行政区行政长官) Chief Executive of the Hong Kong/Macao Special Administrative Region (SAR)

2. Frequently used expressions in foreign affairs

(Source:范文网 http://fanwen.jianlimoban.net/846206/)

Ministry of Foreign Affairs 外交部
Protocol Department 礼宾司
Information Department 新闻司
diplomatic mission 外交代表机构
embassy 大使馆
legation 公使馆
consulate-general 总领事馆
consulate 领事馆
office of the chargé d'affaires 代办处
military attaché's office 武官处
commercial counselor's office 商务处
press section, information service 新闻处

liaison office 联络处
diplomat 外交家，外交官
diplomatic rank 外交官衔
diplomatic representative 外交代表
members of the administrative and technical staff 行政技术人员
ambassador 大使
ambassador extraordinary and plenipotentiary 特命全权大使
nuncio 教廷大使
internuncio 教廷公使
counselor with the rank of minister, minister-counselor 公使衔参赞
chargé d' affaires 代办
counselor 参赞
first secretary 一等秘书
second secretary 二等秘书
third secretary 三等秘书
attaché 随员
commercial secretary 商务参赞
cultural secretary 文化参赞
commercial attaché 商务专员
cultural attaché 文化专员
military attaché 武官
naval attaché 海军武官
air attaché 空军武官
consul-general 总领事
consul 领事
doyen of the diplomatic corps, dean of the diplomatic corps 外交使团团长
roving ambassador 巡回大使
ambassador-at-large 无任所大使
special envoy 特使
accredited to... 向……派遣的
foreign affairs 外交
memorandum, aide-memoire 备忘录
persona non-grat 不受欢迎的人
de jure recognition 法律承认
communique 公报

announcement 公告，通告
letter of credence, credentials 国书
mutual recognition 互相承认
establishment of diplomatic relations 建立外交关系
letter of introduction 介绍书
during one's absence 离任期间
identification card 身份证
statement 声明
de facto recognition 事实上承认
persona grata 受欢迎的人
diplomatic practice 外交惯例
diplomatic immunities 外交豁免
diplomatic privileges 外交特权
diplomatic channels 外交途径
diplomatic courier 外交信使
diplomatic bag, diplomatic pouch 外交邮袋
letter of appointment 委任书
certificate of appointment 委任证书
exequatur 许可证书
declaration, manifesto 宣扬
letter of recall 召回公文
note 照会
verbal note 普通照会
circular note 通知照会
formal note 正式照会
normalization 正常化
be appointed ambassador to... 被任命为驻……大使
to express regret 表示遗憾
to sever diplomatic relations 断绝外交关系
to resume charge of the office, to return to one's post 返任
to proceed to take up one's post 赴任
to present one's credentials 递交国书
to exchange ambassadors 互派大使
to resume diplomatic relations 恢复外交关系

to establish diplomatic relations at ambassadorial level 建立大使级外交关系
to establish consular relations 建立领事关系
to assume one's post 就任
to take exception to; to object to 提出异议
to upgrade diplomatic relations 外交关系升格
to make representations to, to take up a (the) matter with 向……交涉
to lodge a protest with 向……提出抗议
to request the consent of... 征求……的同意
to suspend diplomatic relations 中断外交关系
tea party 茶会
an atmosphere of cordiality and friendship 诚挚友好的气氛
reciprocal banquet 答谢宴会
delegation 代表团
head of the delegation, leader of the delegation 团长
deputy head of the delegation, deputy leader of the delegation 副团长
member of the delegation 代表团成员
memorial speech 悼词
to develop the relations of friendship and cooperation 发展友好合作关系
prosperity and strength 繁荣富强
visit 访问
friendly visit, goodwill visit 友好访问
informal visit 非正式访问
official visit 正式访问
private visit 私人访问
state visit 国事访问
obituary 讣告
questions of common interest; question of common concern 共同关心的问题

state banquet 国宴
message of greeting, message of congratulation 贺电
speech of welcome 欢迎词
welcoming banquet 欢迎宴会
cocktail party 鸡尾酒会
good health and a long life 健康长寿
profound condolence 深切哀悼
cordial hospitality 盛情接待
the two sides, the two parties 双方
luncheon 午宴
message of condolence 唁电
reception 招待会
toast 祝酒词
memorial meeting 追悼会
to convey one's sympathy 表示慰问
to meet with 会见
to review the guard of honor 检阅仪仗队
to exchange views 交换意见
to receive 接见
to be shocked to learn of 惊悉
be of the opinion, to hold, to consider, to maintain 认为
to propose a toast to... 提议为……干杯
on the happy occasion of 欣逢
on learning with great joy 欣悉
to give a banquet in honour of... 宴请……
on invitation, upon invitation 应邀
at the invitation of... 应……邀请
in the company of..., accompanied by... 在……陪同下
to express one's sincere congratulations and best wishes 致以衷心的祝贺和最好的愿望
to wish prosperity to a country and well-being to its people 祝（某国）国家繁荣、人民幸福
to take note of... 注意到……

3. Frequently used expressions in Chinese politics

(Source:小 E 英语学习网 http://www.en8848.com.cn/fanyi/notes/kyflch/128947.html
新东方网 http://kyfy.xdf.cn/201911/10995389.html)

日益昌盛 become increasingly prosperous
快速发展 develop rapidly
隆重集会 gather ceremoniously
热爱和平 love peace
追求进步 pursue progress
履行权利和义务 perform the responsibilities and obligations
回顾奋斗历程 review the course of struggle
展望伟大征程 look into the great journey
充满信心和力量 be filled with confidence and strength
必胜 be bound to win
主张各国政府采取行动 urge governments of all countries to take action
和平共处 coexist peacefully
对内开放和对外开放 open up both externally and internally
经历两个不同时期 experience two different periods
战胜无数的困难 overcome numerous difficulties
赢得一个又一个胜利 win one victory after another
完全意识到 be fully aware that
迈出重要的一步 make an important step
采取各种措施 adopt various measures
得出结论,告一段落 draw (arrive at, come to reach) a conclusion
实现民族独立 realize national independence
追求真理 seek the truth
建立社会主义制度 establish a socialist system
根除(防止,消除)腐败 root out (prevent, eliminate) corruption
响应号召 respond to the call
进入新时期 enter a new period
实行新政策 practice new policies
展现生机和活力 display one's vigor and vitality
增强综合国力和国际竞争力 enhance comprehensive (overall) national strength and international competitiveness
进入世界先进行列 edge into the advanced ranks in the world
解决温饱问题 solve the problem of food and clothing
吸收各国文明的先进成果 absorb what is advanced in other civilizations
与日俱增 increase every day
实现夙愿 fulfill the long-cherished wishes
必将实现 be bound to come true
锻造一支人民军队 forge a people's army
建立巩固的国防 build a strong national defense
进行和谈 hold peace talks
修改法律 amend the laws
在……中起(至关)重要的作用 play a major (crucial, an important) role in
对……作出重要(巨大)贡献 make important (great, major) contributions to
遵循规则 follow the principles
把理论和实际结合起来 integrate theory with practice...
把……作为指导 take... as the guide
缓和紧张状况 ease the tension
高举伟大旗帜 hold high the great banner

解决新问题 resolve new problems
观察当今世界 observe the present-day world
开拓前进 open up new ways forward
增强凝聚力 enhance the rally power
结束暴力，开始和平谈判 end the violence and resume peace talks
进行战略性调整 make strategic readjustment
开始生效 go into effect / enter into force
就……接受妥协 accept a compromise on
接受……的采访 be interviewed by
把……看成社会公敌 look upon... as a threat to society
把……捐给慈善机构 donate... to charities
维护世界和平 maintain world peace
摆脱贫穷落后 get rid of poverty and backwardness
实现发展繁荣 bring about development and prosperity
反对各种形式的恐怖主义 be opposed to all forms of terrorism
宣布……召开 announce the opening of
对……具有深远的影响 have a far-reaching impact on
面对……明显的缺陷 face up to the obvious defects of
保护妇女权利不受侵犯 guarantee (protect) women's rights against infringement
中华人民共和国成立70周年 the 70th anniversary of the founding of the People's Republic of China(PRC)
中国特色社会主义道路 path of socialism with Chinese characteristics
民族独立 national independence
全国各族人民 Chinese people of all ethnic groups
同心同德 concerted efforts
艰苦奋斗 arduous struggle
主体地位 principal status
和平发展道路 path of peaceful development
开放战略 strategy of opening-up
和平统一 peaceful reunification
人类命运共同体 a community with a shared future for humanity
共和国勋章 the Medal of the Republic
国家最高荣誉 the highest state honor
友谊勋章 the Friendship Medal
国家荣誉称号 national titles of honor
共和国史册 the history of the PRC
英雄模范 heroes and role models
人民英雄纪念碑 the Monument to the People's Heroes
烈士纪念日 Martyrs' Day
历史性成就 historic accomplishments
革命先辈 revolutionary forefathers
世界和平 world peace
重大贡献 great contributions
理想信念 ideals and convictions
社会主义革命 socialist revolution
捍卫国家主权 safeguard China's sovereignty
阅兵 military parade
联合军乐团 military band
空中护旗梯队 airborne flag-guarding echelons
徒步方队 foot formations
装备方队 armament formations
空中梯队 air echelons
中国人民解放军 Chinese People's Liberation Army (PLA)

4. Frequently used expressions in economics and trade

(Source: 小 E 英语学习网 http://www.en8848.com.cn/fanyi/notes/kyflch/128946.html)

给……带来机遇和挑战 present (bring) both opportunities and challenges to
给……带来积极影响 bring a more positive impact on……
给予财政资助 support financially
有巨大潜力 have huge potential for
开发/青睐中国市场 tap /favor the Chinese market
申请专利 apply for a patent
阻碍……的经济发展 handicap (hamper) the economic development
增加农业投入 invest more in agriculture
有望达到（上升到）be expected to reach (rise to, be up to)
造成很大压力 pose a big pressure on
占领市场10% occupy (take, account for) 10 percent of the market
缩小……间的距离 narrow the gap between
加快经济发展和结构调整 speed up economic development and restructuring
夺回失去的市场 take back lost market
减轻……的负担 reduce (lighten) the burden of (on)
采取反垄断措施 take anti-monopoly measures to
加快努力 speed up efforts to
在……建立分公司 set up branches in
促进改革 promote reform
面对可能的压力和竞争 face possible pressure and competition
充分利用 make full use of
把……列为基本国策 list... as fundamental national policies
发挥自身优势 give full play to one's advantages
开拓市场 exploit markets
扩大消费市场 expand consumption market
改善投资环境 improve the environment for investment
加强风险防范 prepare oneself against possible risks
扩大贫富差距 widen the gap between the rich and the poor
为……提供巨大商机 present huge business opportunities
快速稳定增长 grow fast and steadily
让……处于同一起跑线 put... on the same platform and at the same starting point
赶超先进 surpass the advanced
遵循市场经济的规律 follow the law of market economy
根据市场作出调整 gear ourselves to the market orientation
牟取暴利 seek excessive profits
做好充分准备 make good preparations for
对……造成/构成威胁 form/pose a threat to...
和……合作 cooperate with
和……进一步合作 further cooperation with
提高公务员工资 raise the salaries of civil servants
计算出准确的工资水平 figure out an exact salary level
和……有合作关系 have cooperative ties with
优胜劣汰 select the superior and eliminate the inferior
从国外引进先进技术和管理经验 introduce

from abroad the advanced technology and management expertise
保证下岗职工的基本生活 guarantee the basic needs of laid-off workers
取缔非法收入 ban unlawful incomes (ban illegal earnings)
深化改革 deepen the reform
控制通货膨胀 control inflation (keep inflation under control)
让位于竞争需要 give way to the need for competition
向……投资巨额资金 invest huge amounts of money into
损失惨重 suffer great losses
制造假象 create smoke screens to do
陷入困境 land oneself in deep trouble
吸引外商投资 attract foreign investment
抓住机遇 seize opportunities
适应……的发展 adapt oneself to the development of
被指控接受贿赂 be accused of accepting bribes
和……达成（签订）协议 reach (sign) an agreement with
促进地区间的合作 promote regional cooperation

退还大量钱款 give back an amount of money
举报非法行为 disclose any illegal activities
筹集足够的资金 raise enough funds
采取不同的办法 adopt various methods
承担风险 bear (take) risk
创收外汇 earn foreign exchange (currency)
活跃市场 enliven the market
造成损失 cause a loss to
十分重视 attach importance to
制定……法律 make a law of (to)
大力发展 strive to develop
提高居民生活水平 improve residents' standard of living
提高管理水平 raise the management level
加强管理 reinforce the management
完善服务 perfect services
刺激国内需求 stimulate domestic demand
打破垄断 break the monopoly
加快竞争步伐 accelerate the competition
为当地人带来多种经济的和社会效益的 bring multiple economic and social benefits to the local people
优先发展公共运输 give priority to the development of public transportation
调整产业结构 adjust the industrial structure

5. Frequently used expressions in cultural exchanges

(Source: 小E英语学习网 http://www.en8848.com.cn/fanyi/notes/kyflch/128945.html)

消除愚昧 eliminate ignorance
扫除文盲 eliminate (wipe out) illiteracy
营造良好的文化环境 create a healthy cultural environment
促进文化市场健康发展 facilitate the sound development of the markets for cultural products
开展对外文化交流 conduct cultural exchange with other countries
博采各国文化之长 draw on strong point of the cultures of other countries
开展群众性文化活动 carry out mass activities on culture
保护文化遗产 protect cultural heritage
继承优秀历史文化传统 carry on the fine cultural traditions handed

from history carry on the fine historical and cultural traditions
繁荣文学艺术 enable literature and art to flourish promote flourishing literature and art
举行每年一次的学术会议 hold an annual academic meeting
尊重知识,尊重人才 respect knowledge and respect competent people
向世界展示中国文化建设的成就 introduce China's achievements of cultural advancement to the world
加强文化基础设施建设 build more cultural establishments
提倡文明的生活方式 advocate civilized lifestyle (way of life)
不注重历史 neglect history
推动人类文明进步 push forward human civilization
对……持欢迎态度 take a welcoming attitude to
与各国人民交往 communicate with people of all countries
和……持相同观点 share views similar to
促进儿童身心健康发展 promote the healthy development of children both physically and mentally
改进教学 improve teaching and learning
保护文化遗产 protect cultural relics
触及现行法律的盲区 touch a blank area of the existing law
增强自我保护意识 strengthen one's awareness of protecting one's right
列为世界自然文化遗产 list... as a world natural heritage site
以全新的面貌进入新世纪 enter the new century with a brand-new colorful look
普及科学知识,传播科学思想,倡导科学精神 popularize scientific and technological knowledge, spread scientific thought and advocate the scientific spirit
提高公务员的综合素质 improve the overall quality of civil servants
通过资格考试 pass qualification examinations
举办文化节/展览会 hold (conduct, give) cultural festivals /an exhibition
普及九年制义务教育 make nine-year compulsory education universal
精心编写教材 compile the textbooks with great care
承担应有的义务 undertake the due obligations
促进相互了解 enhance (further) mutual understanding
相互促进 help each other forward
互派访问学者 exchange visiting scholars
交换意见 exchange views (ideas, opinions)
反映中国的灿烂文化 reflect the rich culture of China
容纳三千名旅客 accommodate 3000 travellers
发挥……的聪明才智 develop one's own talents and wisdom
充分发挥知识分子的积极性和创造性 give full play to the initiative and creativity of intellectuals
开设课程 offer courses
重视实用性 place stress on practicality
制止盗版软件 control the pirated software
提供受教育机会 offer a chance of education
有力地推动教育的发展 give a big push to the development of education
承前启后,继往开来 build on the past and prepare for the future; inherit the past and usher in the future

物质文明,精神文明一起抓 pay equal attention to the material progress and cultural progress

形成文明、健康、崇尚科学的社会风尚 form civilized, healthy and science-upholding social practice

6. Frequently used expressions in conferences

(Source:詹成. 会议口译常用语手册. 北京:外语教学与研究出版社,2015)

作开幕致辞 give an opening address
荣誉主席 honorary president
各国政要 dignitary
贵宾 honorable guests
尊敬的各位来宾 respectable guests
工信部部长 Minister of the Ministry of Industry and Information Technology
省长 Governor
阁下 Your Excellency
论坛 symposium
座谈会 seminar
在此 hereby
圆满成功 complete success
宣布……开幕 declare... open

本人非常高兴/荣幸
I am very overwhelmed with joy to
I am delighted to
I am proud to
I feel extremely honored to
I count it a great privilege to
I take great pleasure in
I give me great pleasure to
I am very pleased and honored to
I find it a pleasure and honor to

我/们衷心感谢/非常感谢
I owe a great debt of gratitude to
I wish to thank
I deeply appreciate...
We are extremely grateful to

My special thanks go to

我/们诚挚希望
It is our earnest hope that
I sincerely hope that

良好祝愿 warm greetings
请允许我再次致以诚挚的欢迎 Please let me once again express/extend/convey my sincere welcome
友谊和热情 friendship and hospitality
盛情好客的 gracious
热情邀请 cordial invitation
周到的安排 meticulous arrangements
光临 attendance
美好的回忆 fond and happy memories
非常需要 It is highly desirable that
知名度和影响力不断扩大 bring out a growing reputation and influence
经济和社会效益越来越好 greater economic and social benefits

筹备阶段 the planning stage
得到……的大力支持 obtain support from
我们将探讨 we plan to explore
尊敬的各位领导、各位来宾 Distinguished officials and guests
各位领导、各位嘉宾,女士们、先生们 Your excellencies, distinguished guests, ladies and gentlemen
会议代表及与会人员

Delegates and attendees

感谢大家光临 Thank you for your presence

首先,请允许我介绍出席今天活动的主要领导和嘉宾,他们是:

First of all, let me introduce the major officials and guests present at today's ceremony. They are:

让我们以热烈的掌声对各位领导和嘉宾朋友的到来表示热烈欢迎。

Please join me in a round of applause to welcome all our distinguished officials and guests.

我们今天的议程非常紧凑。

We are running on a rather tight schedule today.

因为时间的缘故,我们得开始了。

For the sake of time, we ought to begin now.

我谨代表组委会,向大家表示衷心的谢意,感谢你们让这次会议如此成功。

On behalf of the organizing committee, I wish to express our sincere appreciation to all of you who have made this conference such a great success.

今天的会议为各界探讨 ABC 省经济发展和商业进步提供了一个很好的平台。

Today's conference is an important occasion for all sectors to share insights for the economic development and commercial advancement in ABC Province.

今天对于 ABC 来说,是一个值得纪念的日子。

For ABC, this is indeed a memorable day.

我谨向各位致以 ABC 市政府和人民的良好祝愿。

I would like to bring to you the warm greetings from the government and people of ABC.

今天,我们高兴地迎来 ABC 世界历史会会议的隆重召开。

Today, we are very delighted to gather here for the grand opening of ABC World Council Meetings.

我们非常荣幸地邀请到剑桥大学的 ABC 教授。

We are especially honored today to have with us Professor ABC from Cambridge University.

非常感谢大家前来与我们共同庆祝这个特殊的时刻。

I deeply appreciate your coming here to celebrate this unique moment with us.

希望本次重要会议将创造机会,让我们讨论和增进在 ABC 及相关领域研究和开发的合作努力。

It is much hoped that this important conference will create the opportunity to discuss and promote all the collaborative efforts in research and development of ABC and related fields.

我谨此向东道主表示祝贺,他们开展了出色的工作,精心策划,设计出如此全面的会议安排。

I would like to congratulate out host on the wonderful work they have done in putting things together to make this well-rounded program for the conference.

我们一行感受到了盛情款待,由衷感谢你们为推进两国间更加紧密关系所付出的努力。

The warm hospitality accorded to our party has made us feel highly appreciative of your efforts to forge closer ties between our two countries.

下面,举行合作签约仪式。

Now we will hold the Signing Ceremony.

请各方交换合约文本,让我们以热烈的掌声对签约各方表示热烈祝贺,祝大家合作愉快。
Please exchange your agreement copies. Now let's congratulate the signing parties with a warm round of applause an wish them a smooth and successful cooperation.

我们诚挚地希望各位在本次国际会议期间心情愉快,不虚此行。
It is our earnest hope that this international conference will prove most pleasant and rewarding to all of you.

祝愿第二届 ABC 国际研讨会取得圆满成功,愿本次会议给各位与会者留下美好回忆。
May the 2nd International Symposium of ABC be a great success and may all the participants look upon this event with fond and happy memories.

祝大家回程顺利平安。
I wish everybody a good journey home, wherever you live.

祝大家在这里度过一段美好时光。
We wish you a pleasant stay here.

祝大家身体健康,家庭幸福,事业成功,万事如意!
I wish all of you good health, happiness and success in your career.

为此 to this end

来自世界各地 from different parts of the world

人类共同繁荣和进步 common prosperity and progress of mankind

我希望 It is my wish that

我相信 I am confident that

提供重要的启示 shed substantial light on

我热切期待 I look forward with great excitement and anticipation to

我们期待……论坛将成为本市有史以来举办过的最成功和富有成果的会议。
We trust the... forum will be one of the most successful and fruitful conferences that have ever been held in this city.

希望本次会议…… It is much hoped that this conference...

合作努力 collaborative efforts

主题报告 keynote presentation

知名学者 eminent scholars

我们可以了解 we can get some insights as to...

听众提问 questions from the floor

简单陈述自己的观点 state his or her position briefly

邀请到 have sb. with us

宣布会议开始 call the session to order

我想简单说明会议的形式 I would just like to go over the format briefly

如果一切顺利 If all goes well

携手打造 jointly organized

自创办以来 since its inauguration

并不是经常有机会 There haven't been many opportunities to...

难得的机会 an invaluable opportunity

畅叙友情 renew or forge friendship

探讨 share insights for

表达看法 lend some brief thoughts

很高兴担任今天下午会议的主席。
It is a pleasure for me to be in the chair for the afternoon session.

很遗憾地向大家报告 I am very sorry to report to you...

由于一些紧急事务 due to some emergent issues

我们开始吧。
I think it's about time to start.

我们已经延迟了 20 分钟开始。
We are 20 minutes late in getting started.

下面开今天论坛的第二部分。

We will now proceed with the second part of our seminar　会务通知 housekeeping announcement.

服务台 information desk

Appendix Ⅲ　Names and Abbreviations

1. Country(region) names and abbreviations

(注:部分国家名为简称)
AF:Afghanistan 阿富汗
AX:Aland Islands 奥兰群岛
AL:Albania 阿尔巴尼亚
DZ:Algeria 阿尔及利亚
AS:American Samoa 美属萨摩亚
AD:Andorra 安道尔
AO:Angola 安哥拉
AI:Anguilla 安圭拉
AG:Antigua and Barbuda
安提瓜和巴布达
AR:Argentina 阿根廷
AM:Armenia 亚美尼亚
AW:Aruba 阿鲁巴
AU:Australia 澳大利亚
AT:Austria 奥地利
AZ:Azerbaijan 阿塞拜疆
BS:Bahamas 巴哈马
BH:Bahrain 巴林
BB:Barbados 巴巴多斯
BD:Bangladesh 孟加拉国
BY:Belarus 白俄罗斯
BE:Belgium 比利时
BZ:Belize 伯利兹
BJ:Benin 贝宁
BM:Bermuda 百慕大
BT:Bhutan 不丹
BW:Botswana 博茨瓦纳
BO:Bolivia 玻利维亚
BA:Bosnia and Herzegovina 波斯尼亚和黑
塞哥维那(波黑)
BV:Bouvet Island 布维岛
BR:Brazil 巴西
BN:Brunei 文莱
BG:Bulgaria 保加利亚
BF:Burkina Faso 布基纳法索
BI:Burundi 布隆迪
KH:Cambodia 柬埔寨
CM:Cameroon 喀麦隆
CA:Canada 加拿大
CV:Cape Verde 佛得角
KY:Cayman Islands 开曼群岛
CF:The Central African Republic 中非
TD:Chad 乍得
CL:Chile 智利
CN:China 中国
CX:Christmas Island 圣诞岛
CC:Cocos (Keeling) Islands 可可斯(基林)
群岛
CO:Colombia 哥伦比亚
KM:Comoros 科摩罗
CG:Congo 刚果(布)
CD:Congo(Kinshasa)刚果(金)
CK:Cook Islands 库克群岛
CR:Costa Rica 哥斯达黎加
CI:Côte d'Ivoire 科特迪瓦
HR:Croatia 克罗地亚
CU:Cuba 古巴
CY:Cyprus 塞浦路斯

CZ:Czech 捷克
DK:Denmark 丹麦
DJ:Djibouti 吉布提
DM:Dominica 多米尼克
DO:Dominican Republic 多米尼加
EC:Ecuador 厄瓜多尔
EG:Egypt 埃及
SV:El Salvador 萨尔瓦多
GQ:Equatorial Guinea 赤道几内亚
ER:Eritrea 厄立特里亚
EE:Estonia 爱沙尼亚
ET:Ethiopia 埃塞俄比亚
FO:Faroe Islands 法罗群岛
FJ:Fiji 斐济
FI:Finland 芬兰
FR:France 法国
GF:French Guiana 法属圭亚那
PF:French Polynesia 法属玻利尼西亚
GA:Gabon 加蓬
GM:Gambia 冈比亚
GE:Georgia 格鲁吉亚
DE:Germany 德国
GH:Ghana 加纳
GI:Gibraltar 直布罗陀
GR:Greece 希腊
GL:Greenland 格陵兰岛
GD:Grenada 格林纳达
GP:Guadeloupe 瓜德罗普岛
GU:Guam 关岛
GT:Guatemala 危地马拉
GN:Guinea 几内亚
GW:Guinea-Bissau 几内亚比绍
GY:Guyana 圭亚那
HT:Haiti 海地
HN:Honduras 洪都拉斯
HU:Hungary 匈牙利
IS:Iceland 冰岛
IN:India 印度
ID:Indonesia 印度尼西亚

IR:Iran 伊朗
IQ:Iraq 伊拉克
IE:Ireland 爱尔兰
IL:Israel 以色列
IT:Italy 意大利
JM:Jamaica 牙买加
JP:Japan 日本
JO:Jordan 约旦
KZ:Kazakhstan 哈萨克斯坦
KE:Kenya 肯尼亚
KI:Kiribati 基里巴斯
KR:Republic of Korea 韩国
KP:Democratic People's Republic of Korea 朝鲜
KW:Kuwait 科威特
KG:Kyrgyzstan 吉尔吉斯斯坦
LA:Laos 老挝
LV:Latvia 拉脱维亚
LB:Lebanon 黎巴嫩
LI:Liechtenstein 列支敦士登
LR:Liberia 利比里亚
LY:Libya 利比亚
LS:Lesotho 莱索托
LT:Lithuania 立陶宛
LU:Luxembourg 卢森堡
MK:North Macedonia 北马其顿
MG:Madagascar 马达加斯加
MW:Malawi 马拉维
MY:Malaysia 马来西亚
MV:Maldives 马尔代夫
ML:Mali 马里
MT:Malta 马耳他
MH:Marshall Islands 马绍尔群岛
MQ:Martinique 马提尼克岛
MR:Mauritania 毛里塔尼亚
MU:Mauritius 毛里求斯
YT:Mayotte 马约特
MX:Mexico 墨西哥
FM:Micronesia 密克罗尼西亚联邦

MC: Monaco 摩纳哥	LC: Saint Lucia 圣卢西亚
MD: Moldova 摩尔多瓦	VC: Saint Vincent and the Grenadines 圣文森特和格林纳丁斯
MA: Morocco 摩洛哥	
MN: Mongolia 蒙古	WS: Samoa 萨摩亚
ME: Montenegro 黑山	SM: San Marino 圣马力诺
MS: Montserrat 蒙特塞拉特	ST: Sao Tome and Principe 圣多美和普林西比
MZ: Mozambique 莫桑比克	
MM: Myanmar 缅甸	SA: Saudi Arabia 沙特阿拉伯
NA: Namibia 纳米比亚	SN: Senegal 塞内加尔
NR: Nauru 瑙鲁	SC: Seychelles 塞舌尔
NP: Nepal 尼泊尔	SL: Sierra Leone 塞拉利昂
NL: Netherlands 荷兰	SG: Singapore 新加坡
NC: New Caledonia 新喀里多尼亚	RS: Serbia 塞尔维亚
NZ: New Zealand 新西兰	SI: Slovenia 斯洛文尼亚
NI: Nicaragua 尼加拉瓜	SK: Slovakia 斯洛伐克
NE: Niger 尼日尔	SB: Solomon Islands 所罗门群岛
NG: Nigeria 尼日利亚	SO: Somalia 索马里
NU: Niue 纽埃	ZA: South Africa 南非
NF: Norfolk Island 诺福克岛	SS: South Sudan 南苏丹
NO: Norway 挪威	ES: Spain 西班牙
OM: Oman 阿曼	LK: Sri Lanka 斯里兰卡
PK: Pakistan 巴基斯坦	SD: Sudan 苏丹
PW: Palau 帕劳	SR: Suriname 苏里南
PS: Palestine 巴勒斯坦	SZ: Eswatini 斯威士兰
PA: Panama 巴拿马	SE: Sweden 瑞典
PG: Papua New Guinea 巴布亚新几内亚	CH: Switzerland 瑞士
PY: Paraguay 巴拉圭	SY: Syria 叙利亚
PE: Peru 秘鲁	TJ: Tajikistan 塔吉克斯坦
PH: Philippines 菲律宾	TZ: Tanzania 坦桑尼亚
PN: Pitcairn Islands 皮特凯恩群岛	TH: Thailand 泰国
PL: Poland 波兰	TL: Timor-Leste 东帝汶
PT: Portugal 葡萄牙	TG: Togo 多哥
PR: Puerto Rico 波多黎各	TK: Tokelau 托克劳
QA: Qatar 卡塔尔	TO: Tonga 汤加
RE: Reunion Island 留尼汪岛	TT: Trinidad and Tobago 特立尼达和多巴哥
RO: Romania 罗马尼亚	
RU: Russia 俄罗斯	TN: Tunisia 突尼斯
RW: Rwanda 卢旺达	TR: Turkey 土耳其
KN: Saint Kitts and Nevis 圣基茨和尼维斯	TM: Turkmenistan 土库曼斯坦

TV: Tuvalu 图瓦卢
UG: Uganda 乌干达
UA: Ukraine 乌克兰
AE: United Arab Emirates 阿联酋
UK: United Kingdom 英国
US: United States of America 美国
UY: Uruguay 乌拉圭
UZ: Uzbekistan 乌兹别克斯坦
VU: Vanuatu 瓦努阿图

VA: The Vatican City State 梵蒂冈城国
VE: Venezuela 委内瑞拉
VN: Vietnam 越南
WF: Wallis and Futuna Islands 瓦里斯和富图纳群岛
EH: Western Sahara 西撒哈拉
YE: Yemen 也门
ZM: Zambia 赞比亚
ZW: Zimbabwe 津巴布韦

2. Names of U.S. states and their capital cities

美国州名	州名英文	州名英文缩写	首府	首府英文
亚拉巴马州	Alabama	AL	蒙哥马利	Montgomery
阿拉斯加州	Alaska	AK	朱诺	Juneau
亚利桑那州	Arizona	AZ	菲尼克斯	Phoenix
阿肯色州	Arkansas	AR	小石城	Little Rock
加利福尼亚州	California	CA	萨克拉门托	Sacramento
科罗拉多州	Colorado	CO	丹佛	Denver
康涅狄格州	Connecticut	CT	哈特福德	Hartford
特拉华州	Delaware	DE	多佛	Dover
佛罗里达州	Florida	FL	塔拉哈西	Tallahassee
佐治亚州	Georgia	GA	亚特兰大	Atlanta
夏威夷州	Hawaii	HI	檀香山，火奴鲁鲁	Honolulu
爱达荷州	Idaho	ID	博伊西	Boise
伊利诺伊州	Illinois	IL	斯普林菲尔德	Springfield
印第安纳州	Indiana	IN	印第安那波里斯	Indianapolis
爱荷华州	Iowa	IA	得梅因	Des Moines
堪萨斯州	Kansas	KS	托皮卡	Topeka
肯塔基州	Kentucky	KY	法兰克福	Frankfort
路易斯安那州	Louisiana	LA	巴吞鲁日	Baton Rouge
缅因州	Maine	ME	奥古斯塔	Augusta
马里兰州	Maryland	MD	安纳波利斯	Annapolis

Continued Table

美国州名	州名英文	州名英文缩写	首府	首府英文
马萨诸塞州	Massachusetts	MA	波士顿	Boston
密歇根州	Michigan	MI	兰辛	Lansing
明尼苏达州	Minnesota	MN	圣保罗	St. Paul
密西西比州	Mississippi	MS	杰克逊	Jackson
密苏里州	Missouri	MO	杰斐逊城	Jefferson City
蒙大拿州	Montana	MT	海伦娜	Helena
内布拉斯加州	Nebraska	NE	林肯	Lincoln
内华达州	Nevada	NV	卡森城	Carson City
新罕布什尔州	New Hampshire	NH	康科德	Concord
新泽西州	New Jersey	NJ	特伦顿	Trenton
新墨西哥州	New Mexico	NM	圣菲	Santa Fe
纽约州	New York	NY	奥尔巴尼	Albany
北卡罗来纳州	North Carolina	NC	罗利	Raleigh
北达科他州	North Dakota	ND	俾斯麦	Bismarck
俄亥俄州	Ohio	OH	哥伦布	Columbus
俄克拉荷马州	Oklahoma	OK	俄克拉荷马城	Oklahoma City
俄勒冈州	Oregon	OR	塞伦市	Salem
宾夕法尼亚州	Pennsylvania	PA	哈里斯堡	Harrisburg
罗得岛州	Rhode island	RI	普洛威顿斯	Providence
南卡罗来纳州	South Carolina	SC	哥伦比亚	Columbia
南达科他州	South Dakota	SD	皮尔	Pierre
田纳西州	Tennessee	TN	纳什维尔	Nashville
得克萨斯州	Texas	TX	奥斯汀	Austin
犹他州	Utah	UT	盐湖城	Salt Lake City
佛蒙特州	Vermont	VT	蒙彼利埃	Montpelier
弗吉尼亚州	Virginia	VA	里士满	Richmond
华盛顿州	Washington	WA	奥林匹亚	Olympia
西弗吉尼亚州	West Virginia	WV	查尔斯顿	Charleston
威斯康星州	Wisconsin	WI	麦迪逊	Madison
怀俄明州	Wyoming	WY	夏延	Cheyenne

3. Name and Acronyms of International Organizations

联合国日内瓦办事处（UNOG）
联合国维也纳办事处（UNOV）
联合国开发计划署（UNDP）
联合国环境规划署（UNEP）
联合国贸易和发展会议（UNCTAD）
联合国人口基金（UNFPA）
联合国儿童基金会（UNICEF）
联合国难民事务高级专员公署（UNHCR）
世界粮食计划署（WFP）
联合国人居署（UN-Habitat）
联合国妇女署（UN Women）
联合国艾滋病规划署（UNAIDS）
联合国训练研究所（UNITAR）
国际劳工组织（ILO）
联合国粮食及农业组织（FAO）
联合国教育、科学及文化组织（UNESCO）
世界卫生组织（WHO）
国际货币基金组织（IMF）
世界银行集团（WBG）
国际民用航空组织（ICAO）
万国邮政联盟（UPU）
国际电信联盟（ITU）
世界气象组织（WMO）
国际海事组织（IMO）
世界知识产权组织（WIPO）
国际农业发展基金会（IFAD）
联合国工业发展组织（UNIDO）
国际原子能机构（IAEA）

世界旅游组织（UNWTO）
世界贸易组织（WTO）
国际贸易中心（ITC）
联合国亚洲及太平洋经济社会委员会（ESCAP）
联合国可持续农业机械化中心（CSAM）
联合国国际贸易法委员会（UNCITRAL）
联合国科技促进发展委员会（UNCSTD）
联合国毒品和犯罪问题办公室（UNODC）
禁止化学武器组织（OPCW）
海牙国际法院（ICJ）
联合国国际法委员会（ILC）
亚洲基础设施投资银行（AIIB）
经合组织（OECD）
亚太经合组织（APEC）
国际清算银行（BIS）
非洲开发银行（ADB）
泛美开发银行（IADB）
亚洲开发银行（ADB）
亚欧基金（ASEF）
中国-东盟中心（ASEAN-China Centre）
中日韩三国合作秘书处（TCS）
西非开发银行（BOAD）
国际山地综合发展中心（ICIMOD）
国际移民组织（IOM）
亚太邮政联盟（APPU）
红十字会与红新月会国际联合会（IFRC）

Appendix IV　Useful Websites

中国翻译网 http://www.chinatranslation.org
口译网 http://www.kouyi.org
我爱口译网 http://www.52kouyi.com
可可英语网 http://www.kekenet.com

英文巴士网 http://www.en84.com
普特英语网 http://www.putclub.com
旺旺英语网 http://www.wwenglish.com
大耳朵英语网 http://www.ebigenglish.com
英文博客网 http://www.dioenglish.com/
小E英语学习网 http://www.en8848.com.cn/
中国日报 http://www.chinadaily.com.cn
在线英语听力室 http://www.tingroom.com/
CATTI考试资料与资讯 http://www.gocatti.com/
北京外国语大学高级翻译学院 http://gsti.bfsu.edu.cn/
上海外国语大学高级翻译学院 http://giit.shisu.edu.cn/
西安外国语大学高级翻译学院 http://www.xwfanyi.com/
广州外语外贸大学 http://www1.gdufs.edu.cn/sits/gfxy/
口译能力自我评价问卷 https://www.wjx.cn/jq/28215205.aspx
百家讲坛（讲稿）http://m.baijiajiangtan.org/biji/
百度文库 https://wenku.baidu.com/
原创力文档（文库）https://max.book118.com/
豆丁（文库）https://www.docin.com/
外交部网站（重要讲话）https://www.fmprc.gov.cn/web/ziliao_674904/zyjh_674906/default.shtml
外交部英文网站（speeches）https://www.fmprc.gov.cn/mfa_eng/wjdt_665385/zyjh_665391/default.shtml

KEYS

Note that keys to all discussion questions are omitted.
注:所有讨论问题答案省略。

Chapter Ⅱ

2-1-3

1. listening comprehension, memorizing, code-switching, delivering
2.

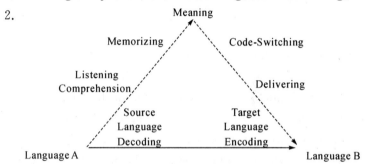

2-1-4

1. We should respect and learn from each other and draw upon others' strong points to offset one's own deficiencies for achieving common progress.

2. We should take a firm hold of the overall interests of Sino-US relations and settle our differences properly so as to reach the goal of promoting mutual understanding, broadening common ground, developing cooperation and building a future together.

3. We must increase investment and establish a stable medical security system.

4. We need to truly give talents full play to their leading role, provide them with a stage, trust them fully and give them full freedom.

5. It was a keen disappointment when I had to postpone the visit which I had intended to pay to China in May. I was delighted when, as a result of the effort of your company, it proved possible to reinstate the visit so quickly.

Chapter Ⅲ

3-1-1

1. F 2. T 3. T 4. F 5. F

3-1-3

1. A:今天真热。
　　B:咱们去游泳吧。
　　A:好主意!

2. 谨防小偷!

3. This product is for people of all ages.

4. Thank you for coming today. I hope you have enjoyed yourself. /I hope you have enjoyed yourself today.

5. You've had a long trip. How was your flight/trip?

6. She loves helping others without asking anything in return. /She always does good deeds and helps others here.

Chapter IV

4-1-1

1. E   2. B   3. A   4. D

4-1-2

1. C   2. B   3. A

Chapter V

5-1-1

1. Poor as he was, he was above selling his country at any price.

2. Because the work was so hard, we were very grateful to him.

3. As the weather was fine, we decided to hold the reception in the open air.

4. China is a country with 5,000 years of civilization. Therefore, it is important to approach China from a historical and cultural perspective.

5. This is only my personal view, which might be wrong. Thank you very much!

5-1-2

1. There is a bewildering variety of measurement equipment now available for the noise control engineers.

2. It's raining. We need to go home now.

3. Eating more fruits is good for your health.

4. The whole family is visiting the zoo this Saturday.

5. Science covers a wide range of subjects.

5-1-3

1. You must be a very bad learner, or you have a very bad teacher.

2. I used to be a day-dreamer.

3. Since he lost his job, he's been a loner.

4. Litmus paper can be an indicator of the presence or not of acid in a solution.

5. The greatest shocker was that things dragged on and on, far beyond the two weeks I had anticipated.

5-1-4

1. Care should be taken to see whether the letter is properly addressed.

2. Voices were heard calling for help.

3. Air resistance must be given careful consideration when the aircraft is to be manufactured.

4. It is well known that the compass was invented in China long ago.

5. The enemy's plot was exposed (by us).

5-1-5

1. The tall young man with a black bag in hand who is walking towards us is my classmate from college.

2. After visiting the Terra-cotta Army Pit and the Dayan Pagoda(the Big Wild Goose Pagoda), the delegates returned to the hotel.

3. I don't think he is reliable.

4. I will not leave if you don't, and I'll leave if you do.

5. 他既不是歌唱家,也不是舞蹈家。

5-2-1

The ancient Egyptians were masters of preserving dead people's bodies by making mummies of them. In short, mummification consisted of removing the internal organs, applying natural preservatives inside and out, and then wrapping the body in layers of bandages. And the process was remarkably effective. Indeed, mummies several thousand years old have been discovered nearly intact. Their skin, hair, teeth, fingernails and toenails, and facial features are still evident. Their diseases in life, such as smallpox, arthritis, and nutritional deficiencies, are still diagnosable. Even their fatal afflictions are still apparent: a middle-aged king died from a blow on the head; a child king died from polio. (This is not the only version of revision. It is only for reference.)

5-2-2

1. It is each individual's responsibility to beautify the environment.

2. He is having luck in love affair recently.

3. The assessment of technologies must stand the test of time. And in the assessment process, there are three barriers to overcome: quality, human biases, and utilitarianism.

4. The following work also went smoothly. It can be said that we were "working for the cause with one heart, advancing with one mind and leaping forward in one strike".

5. Among the 23 winners of China's renowned "the medal of 'two bombs and one satellite'", 21 were scholars returned from overseas.

Chapter VI

6-1-2

1.

2000 万	900 亿	25.6 万
60 亿	2.1 万	1020 亿
7 万亿	6.9 亿	500 万

2.

60,000	800 million	93 billion
6.7 billion	50 million	700 billion
4 trillion	110 thousand	5.01 million

6 – 1 – 3

1. 8.112 3   0.823
2. two and four fifths   thirty-four over ninety-one
3. the eighty-seventh   the third
4. 35 is five times as large as 7.
5. The total value increased six-fold/six times.
6. The value decrease by five times.
7. 数值增加到原来的六倍。
8. 总数下降到原来的三分之一。

6 – 2 – 3

1.
2910 万	210 亿	2091 亿
71.9 亿	4.5 万	1 亿 200 万
1.3 万亿	2 亿 8910 万	3 亿

2.
30 thousand	8.4 亿	29.88 万
1.85 billion	30 million	5 million
36 trillion	3 thousand	9.01 million

6 – 2 – 4

1. The main economic indicators were kept within an appropriate range. Gross domestic product (GDP) grew by 6.6 percent, exceeding 90 trillion yuan. Economic growth matched electricity consumption, freight transport, and other indicators. Consumer prices rose by 2.1 percent. In the balance of payments, a basic equilibrium was maintained.

2. A further 13.61 million new urban jobs were added, and the surveyed unemployment rate remained stable at a comparatively low level of around 5 percent. As a big developing country with a population close to 1.4 billion, we have attained relatively full employment.

3. Precision poverty alleviation made significant progress, with the rural poor population reduced by 13.86 million, including 2.8 million people assisted through relocation from inhospitable areas.

4. Other projected targets include: a CPI increase of around 3 percent, basic equilibrium in the balance of payments, and stable, better-structured imports and exports, a macro leverage ratio that is basically stable, and effective prevention and control of financial and fiscal risks, a reduction of over 10 million in the rural poor population, personal income growth that is basically in step with economic growth, a further improvement in the environment, a drop of around 3 percent in energy consumption per unit of GDP, and continued reductions in the discharge of major pollutants.

5. The rural revitalization strategy was implemented with vigor; grain output was kept above 650 million metric tons. Solid progress was made in the pursuit of new urbanization, and close to 14 million people originally from rural areas gained permanent urban residency.

6. 2001年建设项目竣工面积2亿2500万平方米,新开工面积2亿9200万平方米。

7. 以上海为例,在2001年前9个月中,二手房交易量达到119 096套。

8. 总成交面积为10.12亿平方米,成交额达到129亿美元。

9. 今年经济社会发展的主要预期目标是:国内生产总值增长6%～6.5%;城镇新增就业1100万人以上,城镇调查失业率5.5%左右,城镇登记失业率4.5%以内。

10. 货物进出口总额超过30万亿元,实际使用外资1383亿美元,稳居发展中国家首位。

Chapter Ⅶ

7-2-4

1. Last week China released economic data for 2013, which shows GDP grew by 7.7 per cent, a mid-to-high growth rate in global terms. More than 13 million new urban jobs were created, more than in any previous year.

2. Australian enterprises have been increasingly active in the development of central and western China. This year is going to be vital to world economic recovery. It will also be an important year for upgrading China-Australia economic ties. Both nations should work together to seize new opportunities and fully tap co-operation potential to create real benefits for their people.

3. The past 40 years eloquently prove that China's development provides a successful experience and offers a bright prospect for other developing countries as they strive for modernization. China's development has effectively served the cause of world peace and development and represents a great contribution of the Chinese nation to the progress of human civilization.

4. Mutual respect and trust is required in developing state-to-state relations. We need to observe the purposes and principles of the UN Charter and respect the sovereignty, independence and territorial integrity of each country and the political system and development path chosen by them.

5. China will continue to deepen its friendship and cooperation with other countries on the basis of the Five Principles of Peaceful Co-existence, pursue peaceful settlement to disputes with relevant countries over territorial sovereignty and maritime rights and interests. China will stay committed to opening-up for win-win outcomes and share development opportunities with other countries. China will work with all other parties to make good use of the platform of Belt and Road cooperation to secure a sustained driver for our common development.

6. 我们看到,获得并利用更好的信息可以触发一系列事件,最终使卫生结果得到改善。这一点在尼日尔表现得最为突出。作为世界上最穷的国家之一,获得高质量数据对于该国将儿童死亡率令人吃惊地降低43%发挥了关键作用。

7. 我们绝对可以肯定,如果这一和平进程失败的话,还将有成千上万无辜的叙利亚人成为战争的牺牲品。叙利亚政府则对本次危机负有特别重要的责任,并且可以尽一切所能结束危机。我呼吁双方致力于达成彼此同意的解决办法,并为此停止可能破坏谈判的行动。

8. 每年在解放奥斯威辛集中营的纪念日,我们都缅怀大屠杀受难者。我们回顾千百万无辜人的痛苦,并强调反犹太主义和任何仇恨的危险。

9. 我作为联合国秘书长,要大力增强妇女和女童的权能,维护她们的健康,捍卫她们的权利。残割女性生殖器零容忍国际日为我们提供了机会,来正视这个长期问题,希望找到结束这一做法的希望。

10. 我很高兴代表奥巴马总统和美国人民向世界各地在1月31日庆祝阴历新年的众多人民表示最良好的祝愿。在节日到来之际,我们应该利用这个机会思考把我们联系在一起的共同人性——不仅在美国,而且在全世界。

Chapter Ⅷ

8-2-1

☐ every word
☑ key points
☑ names
☐ repetitive information
☑ figures
☑ logical connectors
☑ list of items
☑ terminologies
☐ complete sentence
☑ meaning units
☐ unnecessary details

8-2-4

1. 中国已成为 | 澳大利亚最大的留学生来源国、
　　　　　　　| 第二大海外游客来源国,
　　　　　　　| 也是增长最快的旅客市场。

一些有战略眼光的澳大利亚企业
　　已经敏锐捕捉到了商机。

澳新银行
　　在去年11月
　　　　正式登陆上海自贸区。

2. Everywhere we look,
　　there is work to be done.
The state of the economy calls for action,
　　bold and swift,
and we will act
　　—not only to create new jobs,
　　but to lay a new foundation for growth.
We will build | the roads and bridges,
　　　　　　　| the electric grids
　　　　　　　| and digital lines

            | that feed our commerce
            | and bind us together.

3. The time has come
      | to reaffirm our enduring spirit;
      | to choose our better history;
      | to carry forward that precious gift,
            that noble idea,
                passed on from generation to generation:
the God-given promise
    that | all are equal,
         | all are free
         | and all deserve a chance to pursue their full measure of happiness.

4. 今年 | 是新中国成立70周年,
      | 是全面建成小康社会、
      | 实现第一个百年奋斗目标的关键之年。

做好政府工作,
    | 要在以习近平同志为核心的党中央坚强领导下,
    | 以习近平新时代中国特色社会主义思想为指导,
    | 全面贯彻党的十九大和十九届二中、三中全会精神。

8-3-2 参考译文及笔记

1. We will stay on the path of peaceful development, and pursue a mutually beneficial strategy of opening up, and we will continue to work with people from all countries to push for jointly building a community with a shared future for humanity.

2. On our journey forward, we must uphold the principles of "peaceful reunification" and "one country, two systems," maintain lasting prosperity and stability in Hong Kong and Macao, promote the peaceful development of cross-Strait relations, unite all Chinese sons and daughters, and continue to strive for the motherland's complete reunification.

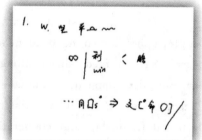

3. No force can ever shake the status of China, or stop the Chinese people and nation from marching forward.

4. We should stay committed to building an open global economy. This commitment of the G20 to build open economies saw us through the global financial crisis, and this commitment is vital to reenergizing the global economy.

5. Over the past 70 years, the Chinese people, upholding an independent foreign policy of peace, have forged ahead along the path of peaceful development. Guided by the Five Principles of Peaceful Coexistence, we have deepened friendship and cooperation with other countries and made an important contribution to building a community with a shared future for mankind and advancing the noble cause of peace and development for humanity!

6. The Leaders' Roundtable held today was attended by leaders from 38 countries as well as the United Nations (UN) and the International Monetary Fund.

7. We spoke positively of the progress and value of Belt and Road cooperation. We shared the view that Belt and Road cooperation has created opportunities for common prosperity.

8. We are committed to supporting open, clean and green development and rejecting protectionism, and are working hard to develop a clean and green Silk Road for the new era.

9. Our common goal is, to realize more effective connectivity between countries, promote stronger economic growth and closer international cooperation, and deliver better lives to our peoples.

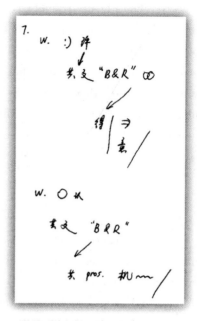

10. The global economy is showing signs of moving in the right direction. The related international organizations forecast that it will grow by 3.5 percent this year, the best performance that we have seen in several years. On the other hand, the global economy is still plagued by deep-seated problems and faces many uncertainties and destabilizing factors.

11. Currently, global economic growth is not balanced, and technological advances work against job creation. According to the projection of the World Economic Forum, artificial intelligence will take away more than 5 million jobs in the world by 2020.

12. We must remain committed to openness and mutual benefit for all so as to increase the size of the global economic "pie". As the world's major economies, we should and must lead the way, support the multilateral trading system, observe the jointly established rules and, through consultation, seek all-win solutions to common challenges we face.

13. We should boost cooperation in digital economy and the new industrial revolution and jointly develop new technologies, new industries, new business models and new products.

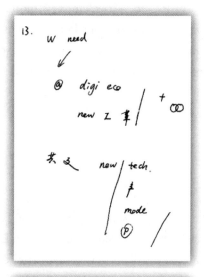

14. This round of the China-US Strategic and Economic Dialogues takes places at an important moment when new developments are unfolding in the international political and economic landscape and when China and the United States face new opportunities to further the bilateral relationship. It is of great significance for both of our two countries to achieve positive outcomes at this round of dialogue.

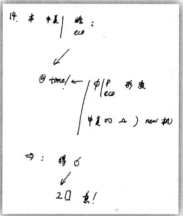

15. Admittedly, China and the United States differ in national conditions, and it is only natural that the two sides may disagree on some issues. What is important is to respect and accommodate each other's core interests and major concerns, appropriately handle the sensitive issues and strengthen the foundation of mutual trust.

16. In a rare move, global police cooperation organization Interpol launched an international appeal on Monday to find eight men suspected of murdering or committing violence against women.

17. Growing anger over the failures in Europe and globally to make progress ending the horrendous annual death toll of women from domestic violence has pressured governments to begin to take action, though activists warned that far more needs to be done.

18. The report provides the foremost global assessment of disability to date, and it does so using the latest scientific evidence on this complex subject. The new estimates now tell us that more than one billion people experience some form of disability.

19. Some 329 people have died this year on New South Wales' roads, Reuters news agency reported, compared with 354 people for all of 2018, according to official statistics. The cameras will use artificial intelligence to review images and detect illegal use of cell phones, according to Transport for NSW.

20. We should foster new sources of growth for the global economy. Innovation, more than anything else, is such a new source of growth. Research shows that 95 percent of the world's businesses are now closely linked with the Internet, and the global economy is transitioning toward a digital economy. Another source of growth derives from making greater efforts to address the issue of development and implement the 2030 Agenda for Sustainable Development, and such efforts will both benefit developing countries and generate business and investment opportunities for developed countries. In other words, this will be a win-win game for all.

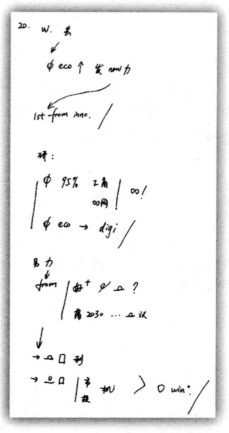

21. 他讲述了40年前美中早期外交关系的情况，谈到当年他那一代双方的外交家必须克服的很多困难。

22. 今晚，我不禁对双方交往的长足进展感到惊叹。几十年来，中国取得了前所未有的发展和进步。

23. 中国使亿万人民摆脱了贫困，并为推动全球繁荣作出了贡献。美国欢迎中国的发展并从中受益。

24. 今天，我们两国的经济以及我们的未来已密不可分，两国关系的广度与深度就连基辛格博士及其同事们在当年也难以想象。

25. 这一变化带来了我们这一代面临的新挑战。历史告诉我们，新的大国的兴起往往会带来一些冲突和不确定的时期。

26. 邓小平曾用"摸着石头过河"来形容中国的改革和现代化进程。用这句话来描述我们必须共同规划的前进道路也十分恰当。

27. 一年多以前,我同奥巴马总统在伦敦首次会晤,我们一致同意,共同努力建设 21 世纪积极合作全面的中美关系,为新时期中美关系的发展确立了目标。

28. 各位中国同事和伙伴,谢谢你们进行这次长途旅行——不仅是乘飞机前来与会,而且是和我们一道踏上为我们的子孙后代创造更美好未来的旅途。

29. 如果今天这个关系及其未来有一个最基本的信任基础,那就是这样一个现实:今天,成千上万的美国人正在中国学习,同时成千上万的中国人也有机会深入地了解美国。

30. 过去两年里我们已经取得了很大进展。如果你觉得难以理解这样做有多难,或者难以理解已经取得的进展有多重要,只需要回想一下大萧条时期,当时由于合作终止,一场严重的金融危机变成了一次全球性的灾难。

31. 在最近这场危机中,我们与中国的合作发挥了决定性作用,帮助世界摆脱了灾难,使之进入一个我们现在称为恢复经济增长的时期。

32. 我个人对 2011 年 9 月 11 日那天记忆犹新。在那个黑暗的日子，我正在纽约。联合国致力于继续领导这个运动，与世界各国领导人一同打击国际恐怖主义。

33. 道路交通事故每年造成近 130 万人死亡，数百万人受伤或终身残疾。酒后驾驶、不安全的道路和其他危险可在瞬间毁灭生命。

34. 肺结核及艾滋病都属于致命性疾病，加在一起每年使 350 多万人失去生命，这主要发生在发展中国家。这两种疾病会给人带来极大的痛苦，使卫生保健服务背上深重的负担，并且会造成巨大的社会和经济后果。

35. 由于存有这些障碍,与没有残疾的人相对而言,残疾人的健康状况较差,学业成就较低,参与经济活动的机会较少以及贫困发生率较高。

36. 艾滋病毒与残疾问题密切相关。艾滋病毒问题可造成残疾,残疾人也被证明面临着更高的感染艾滋病毒的风险。

37. 世卫组织做好了准备,向任何要求我们在政策制定、能力建设和技术支持方面提供指导的会员国提供支持。

38. 我们很愿意与那些希望改进数据,使卫生系统具备包容性,强化康复服务以及扩大社区康复的国家开展合作。

KEYS

39. 我们有着共同的决心,即矢志保卫我们的国家,并把那些发动了这场邪恶袭击的人绳之以法。我们很快查明,发动"9·11"袭击的是基地组织,该组织以奥萨马·本·拉登为首,他们早已公开对美国宣战,并在我们国家和全球其他地方杀害无辜人民。为了保护我们的公民、我们的朋友以及我们的盟友,我们展开了针对基地组织的战争。

40. 我第一次去中国大约是在 30 年前,去学习汉语。我去了北京。我在北大(北京大学)学了一个暑期。当时,这是很特殊的事情。很少有美国人能有幸访问中国、研究中国,也很少有中国人能到美国学习。当然,现在这已不稀奇了。

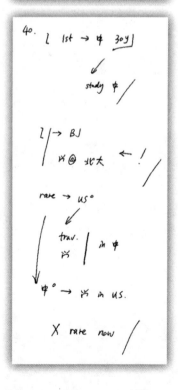

Chapter IX

9-2

1. We will set up a "one-station" service center for foreign investors to obtain approval.

2. The alleged Chinese theft of U.S. military technology is only a fiction.

3. The foreign-funded, joint adventure and wholly foreign-owned or funded enterprises have a comparatively large impact on our economy.

4. Pollution prevention and control was strengthened, and PM2.5 concentrations continued to fall. Marked achievements were made in ecological conservation.

5. We continued to ensure and improve living standards in the course of pursuing development and enabled the people to share more fully and fairly in the benefits of reform and development. We took prompt steps to ease the impact of changes in the external environment on employment.

6. 俗话说,"冰冻三尺非一日之寒"。

7. 我非常高兴在联合国成立70周年之际出席这次教育第一倡议高级别会议。

8. 多种空气污染物还导致全球变暖。黑炭就是一个例子。它产生于使用柴油机、燃烧垃圾、使用重污染炉灶。吸入黑炭后危害极大。

9. 我感谢那些愿意每天大声反对恐怖主义的人。你们的声音很重要,你们面对逆境的勇气值得我们所有人学习。

10. 在促进、保护和尊重受害者及其家人人权的基础上,支持受害者及其家人是一项道义责任。

BIBLIOGRAPHIES

[1] 梅德明. 口译技能教程[M]. 上海:上海外语教育出版社,2009.

[2] 王斌华. 口译:理论技巧实践[M]. 武汉:武汉大学出版社,2006.

[3] 卢信朝. 英汉口译技能教程:交替传译[M]. 北京:北京语言大学出版社,2015.

[4] 王斌华,伍志伟. 汉英口译:转换技能进阶[M]. 北京:外语教学与研究出版社,2010.

[5] 冯伟年. 实用英语口译教程[M]. 2版. 北京:清华大学出版社,2016.

[6] 高契,孙荧. 学术英语口语[M]. 西安:西北工业大学出版社,2020.

[7] 钟述孔. 实用口译手册[M]. 北京:中国对外翻译出版公司,1984.

[8] 梅德明. 中级口译教程[M]. 上海:上海外语教育出版社,1998.

[9] 鲍刚. 口译理论概述[M]. 北京:中国对外翻译出版公司,2005.

[10] 江晓梅. 英汉口译笔记入门[M]. 武汉:武汉大学出版社,2015.

[11] 吴钟明. 英语口译笔记法实战指导[M]. 武汉:武汉大学出版社,2008.

[12] 徐东风,陆乃圣,毛忠明. 英语口译实战技巧与训练[M]. 大连:大连理工大学出版社,2005.

[13] SETTON R, DAWRANT A. Conference interpreting:a complete course[M]. Philadelphia: John Benjamins Publishing Company, 2016.

[14] SETTON R, DAWRANT A. Conference interpreting:a trainer's guide[M]. Philadelphia: John Benjamins Publishing Company, 2016.

[15] JIN Y. Consecutive interpreting, in the routledge handbook of Chinese translation [M]. Abingdon:Taylor & Francis Group,2017.

[16] SCHNEIDER W. Effects of the knowledge base on memory development//Memory development from early childhood through emerging adulthood[M]. Cham:Springer International Publishing,2015:231-253.

[17] 李海波. 口译中影响记忆因素与记忆方法[J]. 文教资料,2011(12):55-56.

[18] 仲伟合. 英汉同声传译技巧与训练[J]. 中国翻译,2001(9):39-43.

[19] BAKER M. Interpreters and translators in the war zone narrated and narrators[J]. Translator,2010,16 (2):197-222.

[20] BAXTER R N. A simplified multi-model approach to preparatory training in consecutive interpreting[J]. The Interpreter and Translator Trainer,2012,6 (1):21-43.

[21] KOHN K. KALINA S. The strategic dimension of interpreting[J]. Meta,1996,41 (1):118-131.

[22] CHERRY K. How human memory works[EB/OL]. (2019-08-23)[2019-11-22]. https://www.verywellmind.com/what-is-memory-2795006.

[23] YOUNG S. Passive listening or active listening[EB/OL]. (2012-07-25)[2019-10-29]. https://blogs.transparent.com/language-news/2012/07/25/passive-listening-or-active-listening/.

[24] GILLESPIE C. Difference between active listening & passive listening[EB/OL].

(2019 - 02 - 08)[2019 - 10 - 29]. https://www.theclassroom.com/difference-between-active-listening-passive-listening-10014817.html.

[25] YU Z. Consecutive interpreting[EB/OL]. [2019 -12 -05]. http://www.icourse163.org/course/GDUFS-1002493010.

[26] LUO Y G. Introduction to interpreting[EB/OL]. (2016 - 02 - 24)[2019 - 06 - 12]. https://wenku.baidu.com/view/e7d37d0e6f1aff00bfd51e93.html.